OVER **50** YEARS OF
·····································
AMERICAN
·····································
COMIC
·····································
BOOKS

RON GOULART

**MALLARD
PRESS**

AN IMPRINT OF BDD Promotional Company, Inc.

ISBN 0-7924-5450-2

Library of Congress Catalog Card Number:

90-63456

First published in the United States 1991 by The Mallard Press.

All rights reserved.

Mallard Press and its accompanying design and logo are trademarks of BDD Promotional Book Company, Inc.

AP/WideWorld Photos: 86, 212; **Joe Buday Collection**: 245, 247, 250, 251; **Cinecom Pictures**: 207; **Don Glut Collection**: 4, 5, 54, 66, 74, 75, 76, 78, 79, 81, 82, 85, 89, 92, 94, 101, 103, 104, 108, 110, 111, 112, 113, 116, 118, 123, 126, 128, 129, 133, 134, 135, 137, 140, 141, 156, 162, 172, 178, 179, 180, 181, 184, 185, 186, 187, 188, 189, 198, 200, 208, 210, 211, 213, 216, 217, 218, 219, 221, 222, 223, 226, 227, 228, 234, 242, 243, 244, 248, 252, 255, 256, 258, 259, 261, 265; **Jim Harmon Collection**: 4, 5, 60, 62, 66, 67, 68, 70, 74, 82, 87, 110, 136, 165, 171, 243, 244; **David J. Hogan Collection**: 69, 72, 77, 88, 142, 148, 149, 153, 157, 160, 167, 174, 175, 176, 180, 181, 182, 188, 190, 199, 206, 215, 216, 217, 225, 229, 230, 231, 232, 233, 240, 249, 250, 253, 254, 258, 260, 261, 262, 263, 264, 266, 269, 270, 271, 272, 273, 274, 275, 276, 278, 279, 280, 281, 282, 283, 284, 285, 286, 287, 288, 289, 290, 292, 293, 294, 295, 298, 299, 300, 301, 302, 304, 305, 306, 307, 308, 310, 314, 315, 316, 317; **Todd Marsh Collection**: 265, 274, 299, 307; **Scott Shaw! Collection**: 144, 159, 185, 219, 220; **Universal Pictures**: 69.

All other comic book images: **Ron Goulart Collection.**

Special Photography: **Sam Griffith.**

Thanks to:
Joe Buday
Jim Harmon
Scott Shaw!
Maggie Thompson

Special thanks to Don Glut

CONTENTS

The diversity of comic books over the 50-plus years of their history has been remarkable. Readers have enjoyed coy, pin-up girl tease . . .

©1964 by Super

. . . rousing science-fiction adventure . . .

©1957 by National Periodical Publications, Inc.

. . . and colorful jungle action.

©1967 by National Periodical Publications, Inc.

As the 1990s began, comic book-industry sources were predicting annual retail sales of $400,000,000 and up. The average price of a new comic book was $1.45, and a report in the *Comics Buyer's Guide,* the weekly tabloid for comic book fans and collectors, estimated that to buy one copy of every new issue being published in 1990 would cost a dedicated reader about $1,115 per month. In 1934, the first year that modern-format comic books were available on newsstands, selling at ten cents a copy, a reader could have purchased the industry's entire annual output for less than one dollar. In the course of the color-fully illustrated history that follows, we'll trace the growth of the comic book industry from that humble start in the 1930s to the multi-million-dollar business it has become.

The comic book format that was developed in the thirties still prevails today. To millions of readers over the years, the colorful pamphlet with slick covers and a pulp-paper interior has been a convenient and inexpensive form of entertainment. For more than 50 years, then, the comic book has remained a popular and appealing storytelling medium.

This book's coverage includes the leading types of comics that have excited readers of all ages over the past half-century. Superheroes, cowboys, spacemen, teenagers, jungle women, gangsters, young lovers, monsters—all of these and many more have played out their adventures in comic books' four-color pages.

Starting with the books and magazines that were the antecedents of comic books in the early years of this century, we'll trace the development of the medium from its first great surge of popularity in the Depression years, through the boom-time "Golden Age" of the 1940s, and to the industry's near-collapse a decade later. We'll look at the great superhero revival of the late 1950s and early '60s, and at the increasing sophistication that came to comic books in the 1970s. We'll conclude by looking at the ambitious, sometimes controversial comic books of recent vintage—many of which are printed on high-quality paper and in unexpected formats. A special appendix describes the comic book-fan movement, and its impact on the comic book industry.

Throughout the book, illuminating sidebars discuss notable comic book artists, writers, and publishers; popular characters; and unusual types of comic books.

Along the way, hundreds of vivid, full-color covers (including many rare collectors' items), interior pages, and individual panels help tell the story of the vibrant, uniquely American art form known to countless millions of fans as the comic book.

Comic book fans have been whisked to remarkable adventures on other worlds . . .

©1961 by Vista Publications, Inc.

. . . and have thrilled to the exploits of superheroes such as the Sandman . . .

©1939 by National Periodical Publications, Inc.

. . . and have met still more pretty girls. It's a mixture of fantasy and fun that readers found irresistible.

©1968 by National Periodical Publications, Inc.

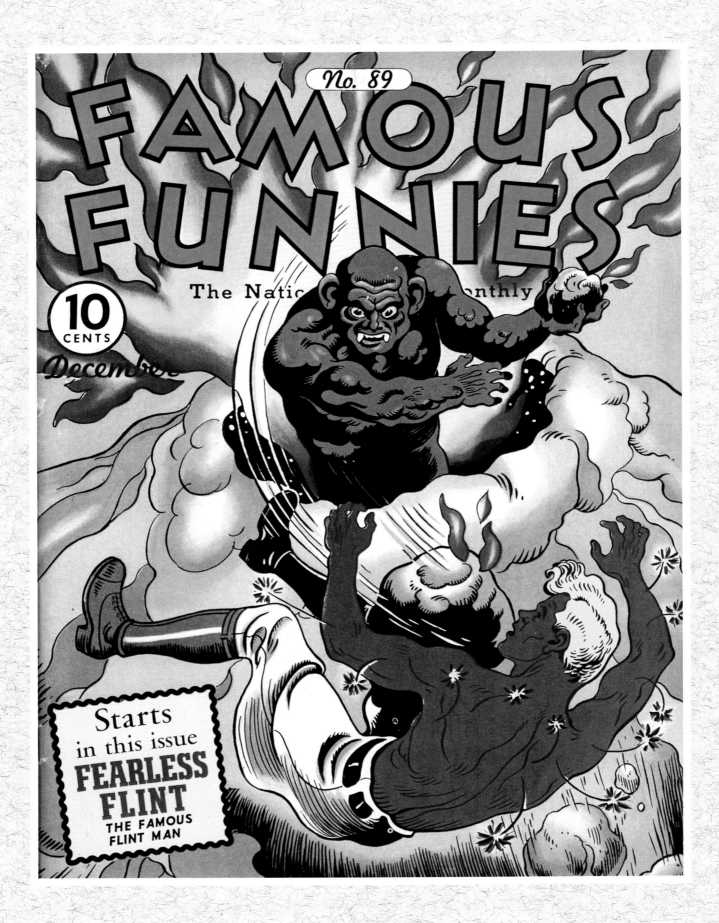

CHAPTER ONE

HOW IT BEGAN

The story of comic books really begins with newspaper comics. Long a popular part of America's newspapers, comic strips amused readers with simple, often farcical humor and drawings. By the tail end of the 19th century, newspaper funnies were going strong—at least on Sundays. Comic books of various sizes and shapes, all of them reprinting newspaper strips, showed up soon thereafter. The first decade of the 20th century saw an assortment of comic books; among the earliest titles were *The Yellow Kid, The Katzenjammer Kids*, and *Buster Brown*. Comics featuring these characters were successful, but the character most frequently seen in comic books during the years between the turn of the century and the advent of World War I was Carl Schultze's Foxy Grandpa. From 1901 to 1916 more than two dozen books reprinted "Bunny" Schultze's rather inane page about a clever old coot who was forever outfoxing his two prankish nephews. The feature began in 1900 in the New York *Herald,* a newspaper that had a hand in the earliest reprint publications.

Famous Funnies was the first of the modern-format comic books, and its success sparked what became a multi-million-dollar industry. This 1941 cover featuring Fearless Flint is by H. G. Peter, the first artist to draw Wonder Woman.

©1941 by Famous Funnies, Inc.

The newspaper-strip adventures of Rudolph Dirks's incorrigibly bratty Katzenjammer Kids were among the earliest to be reprinted in "comic book" form.

© Rudolph Dirks

The books, some of which were hardcovers, were colorful and ranged from twenty-four to fifty-two pages. They measured as large as 10 inches by 15 inches and as small as 6½ by 7¾.

Nearly as successful as Foxy Grandpa in these first fifteen years of the new century was Buster Brown. A creation of Richard F. Outcault, he was a sort of devilish Katzenjammer Kid inhabiting the body and outfit of a sissified Little Lord Fauntleroy. Between 1903 and 1917 Buster appeared in nearly two dozen reprint comic books of various shapes, sizes, and colors. Winsor McCay's *Little Nemo*, now considered the best strip to come out of these early years, made it into only two comic books during the same period. One was an 11 by 16½-inch color reprint of Sunday pages issued in 1906 and another, measuring 10 by 14, in 1909. McCay's dreamlike masterpiece was not reprinted again until 1945.

As noted above, the newspapers themselves were among the earliest publishers of comic books. Late in 1902 William Randolph Hearst's New York *Journal* introduced five titles, described as being "the best comic-books that have ever been published." Each book had cardboard covers, reprinted Sunday pages in color, and sold for 50 cents. The titles, available from Hearst newspaper dealers across the country, included Rudolph Dirks's *The Katzenjammer Kids* and F.B. Opper's *Happy Hooligan*. A book of Jimmy Swinnerton's kid strip *Jimmy* was released in 1905. That same year the *Herald* reprinted

Winsor McCay's *Little Sammy Sneeze*.

Much of the color went out of comic books in the second decade of the century, when the black and white format became the industry standard. The daily comic strip, with Bud Fisher's pioneering *Mutt & Jeff* as the role model, was becoming increasingly popular. Fisher's strip made its debut in 1907 and enjoyed considerable popularity into the 1940s. By about 1920, just about every newspaper in America would be running a full page of black and white strips six days a week. Ball Publications, in collaboration with Fisher, published its initial *Mutt and Jeff Cartoons* book in 1910. Selling for 50 cents, the book measured approximately 5 by 15 inches and reprinted only one daily strip on each page. In his kidding preface Fisher, one of the first cartoonists to benefit greatly from character merchandising, admitted that the only excuse for publishing the book was "to get the money." Get it he did, since sales figures on the first book prompted Ball to publish four more over the next six years.

The lanky, chinless Mutt—mean-minded and henpecked—had begun his strip life as a compulsive race track addict. Mutt's companion, the diminutive and dapper Jeff, always played the wise fool. Their funny-paper escapades were like daily doses of vaudeville comedy.

The largest and most successful publisher of comic books during the first three decades of the century was a now forgotten company, Cupples

& Leon. Based in Manhattan, the firm published more than one hundred different issues of a variety of comic book titles between 1906 and 1934. The company issued the majority of its output in the 1920s. Like almost all of its competitors in the then uncrowded comic book field, Cupples & Leon reprinted newspaper comics, and offered no original material. Among the earliest Cupples & Leon titles were *Buster Brown* and *Little Nemo*.

Victor Cupples and Arthur Leon founded their company in 1902. "The idea that enabled it to establish itself as a publishing house," as historian John Tebbel has pointed out, "was the partners' discovery that there was a market for bound collections of comic strips." In 1916 Cupples & Leon introduced a line of black and white comic books when they assumed the reprinting of *Mutt & Jeff*. These forty-eight-page books were 9½ inches square and had flexible cardboard covers printed in black and red. Each page offered a single daily strip, cut in half and run in two tiers. The price was 25 cents.

C & L added reprints of Sidney Smith's *The Gumps* in 1918 and George McManus's *Bringing Up Father* in 1919. This series of two-bit books proved extremely popular with readers. The American News Co. sold them on newsstands and also aboard railroad trains, a popular market during the period. According to Tebbel, "One of the largest contracts ever negotiated in publishing up to that time was the contract Cupples & Leon

Bud Fisher's Mutt & Jeff was an enormously popular newspaper strip that was reprinted in comic books for decades. These panels are from a 1910 Ball Publications comic. Bringing Up Father, George McManus's popular comic strip about marital disharmony, was a longtime reprint success in books published by Cupples & Leon.

©1987 by Estate of Aedita S. de Beaumont Bringing Up Father; ©1931 by Int'l Feature Service, Inc.

signed in 1921, when American News bought $405,000 worth of these comic books."

The most popular Cupples & Leon title was *Bringing Up Father*, which appeared in twenty-six different 25-cent issues and two 75-cent Big Book editions. Next in popularity was *Mutt & Jeff*, with sixteen paperbacks and three hardcovers. Also popular were reprint collections of *Little Orphan Annie*, *The Gumps*, and *Tillie the Toiler*. The *Annie* books, reprinting the melodramatic adventures of Harold Gray's reactionary, red-headed moppet, were ninety-two-page hardcovers with dust jackets. The books measured 7¼ by 8½ inches and sold for 60 cents each. Other strips packaged this way included *Smitty* and *Reg'lar Fellers*.

Toward the end of the company's involvement with the funnies C & L reprinted three of the strips that would become staples of the modern-format, full color comic books during the 1930s—*Joe Palooka*, *Tailspin Tommy*, and *Dick Tracy*. In 1934, after publishing final issues of *Little Orphan Annie* and *Bringing Up Father*, Cupples & Leon bid farewell to comics. It's ironic to note that the company's address at the time was 470 Fourth Avenue in New York City, not far from where another key player in comic book history, Major Malcolm Wheeler-Nicholson, would eventually set up shop.

In addition to comic books, Cupples & Leon pioneered the publishing of children's fiction in inexpensive hardcover formats.

Harold Gray's Orphan Annie, as optimistic as ever, was featured in issue #6 of the Cupples & Leon hardcover series.

©1931 by the Chicago Tribune

The company began a relationship with the enterprising Edward Stratemeyer in 1906 to launch a line of 50-cent novels. Stratemeyer, a writer and entrepreneur, was what would today be called a packager. He created characters and formats, then farmed the actual writing out to others. He had a hand in the creation of the Rover Boys, Tom Swift, and a pair of series that are still going strong today: Nancy Drew and the Hardy Boys. Of more than thirty major children's-book series published by Cupples & Leon before World War II, at least fifteen were turned out by Stratemeyer and his crew. A married couple, Howard and Lilian Garis, took care of many of the rest.

The Stratemeyer Syndicate's first series for C & L featured the Motor Boys—*The Motor Boys in Mexico*, *The Motor Boys Afloat*, et al—and credited the series to Clarence Young, a pen name. Stratemeyer produced many other series for C & L, including books about Baseball Joe, Dave Dashaway, the Boy Hunters, the Radio Girls, the Four Little Blossoms, and Bomba the Jungle Boy. Early on, Cupples & Leon touted the Motor Boys as "the biggest and best selling series for boys ever published." Eventually, the firm was selling more than a million copies of its various fiction titles each year.

Other publishers flirted with comic books from 1910 to 1930. The Saalfield Company, successful with low-priced kids' books since 1900, issued several titles in 1917. Among them were *Hawkshaw the Detective* and Rudolph Dirks's *Hans und Fritz*.

Measuring roughly 10 by 13, the books contained thirty-two pages of black and white Sunday-strip reprints, four panels to a page.

Charlie Chaplin became a comic book character in 1917, when the M. A. Donohue Company of Chicago started a series of large black and white books reprinting the *Charlie Chaplin's Comic Capers* newspaper strip drawn by E. C. Segar. Clare Briggs's *Ain't It A Grand and Glorious Feeling?* was reprinted in 1922 and Harry Tuthill's *Home, Sweet Home* (which later became *The Bungle Family*) appeared in 1925.

Edgar Rice Burroughs's famous jungle man made both his comic strip and his comic book debut in 1929. The daily strip adaptation of *Tarzan of the Apes*, drawn by Hal Foster, started in January. Later that year Grosset & Dunlap issued *The Illustrated Tarzan Book*, which reprinted the first seventy-eight strips. Although the cover of the 50-cent book said No. 1, there never was a second one. When the book was reissued in the Depression year of 1934, the price was cut to 25 cents.

Mickey Mouse, cinema star since the late 1920s, first appeared in comic books in 1931. These, published by the David McKay Co. of Philadelphia, reprinted the *Mickey Mouse* newspaper strips that were drawn by Floyd Gottfredson. The books appeared annually through 1934; three of them offered dailies in black and white and the other reprinted Sunday strips in color.

A pair of books that reprinted E. C. Segar's *Thimble Theatre*

A typical day with the Bungles, from their 1925 comic book.

©1925 by the M.C. Donahue Co.

Hawkshaw the Detective: An early comic book reprinting Gus
Mager's Holmesian spoof.

©1917 by Saalfield Publishing Co.

strip were published by the
Sonnet Publishing Co. of
Manhattan in 1931 and 1932. The
books were priced at 25 cents
each and appeared in a format
similar to the one established by
Cupples & Leon. In 1935 David
McKay published two reprint
books of Segar's strip, naming
them after its star, Popeye. That
same year McKay issued a comic
book reprinting Carl Anderson's
pantomime strip *Henry*. Both

these strips were syndicated by
Hearst's King Features. As we'll
see, when King went into the full
color, modern-format comic book
business in 1936, it was in
partnership with McKay.

In a sense, the type of comic
books we've been considering
thus far are still with us. Books
that reprint a newspaper strip in
either paperback or hardcover
format have continued to thrive
to this day. The best-selling trade

paperback collections of *Peanuts*,
Garfield, and *Calvin and Hobbes*
are obvious examples.

About the only thing that
came close to resembling a
contemporary comic book in the
years from 1900 to 1930 was an
experimental magazine called
Comic Monthly. It first hit the
newsstands in January 1922,
with each issue devoted to a
different comic strip. The
magazine sold for a dime, gave

Do You Like to Laugh?

Millions of People Follow the World Famous Funny Folks.

COMIC MONTHLY

Every Month Gives them the Best for 10c.

COMIC MONTHLY

out every month

10c on all newsstands

Send $1 for a Year's Subscription and you will get a circus of fun in your home every month.

Great for Children and Greater for Grown-ups

The covers of the first three issues of *Comic Monthly* are featured in this advertisement for what turned out to be a forerunner to modern comics.

©1922 by King Features Syndicate, Inc.

the reader twenty-four pages with a black and white daily on each page, and measured 8½ by 10 inches. It had a soft paper cover printed in red and black and was published by the Embee Distributing Co. of New York City. As comics historian Charles Wooley has pointed out, the format owed a great deal to that of Cupples & Leon's line of 25-cent comic books. But because of the 10-cent price, the cheaper paper and, most importantly, that it appeared on a regular monthly schedule, *Comic Monthly* was much closer to the comic books that would emerge in the 1930s.

The first title in the twelve-issue *Comic Monthly* series was Cliff Sterrett's *Polly & Her Pals*. Next came Rube Goldberg's *Mike & Ike*, followed by C. M. Payne's *S'Matter, Pop?* Subsequent reprints included *Barney Google*, *Tillie the Toiler*, *Little Jimmy*, and *Toots & Casper*.

As mentioned above, the Embee Distributing Co. was involved in early comic book publishing. The *Em* in the company name stood for cartoonist George McManus, creator of *Bringing Up Father*. His strip had been one of Cupples & Leon's best-selling titles since 1919, which probably accounts for the similarity in appearance between the two lines. The *bee* in Embee was Ruldolph Block, Jr. His father had joined the Hearst organization in 1896 and became comics editor of the *Journal* and *American*. A man not much admired by most of the cartoonists who had to work with him, Block, Sr. had been involved with the development of many of

Barney Google heads for the wire on the cover of the eleventh issue of *Comic Monthly*, the first regularly issued comic book.

©1922 by King Features Syndicate, Inc.

DEADWOOD GULCH

Panel 1: HOWDY, FOLKS! I'M PISTOL JACK!! EVER'TIME A SHERIFF GITS BUMPED OFF I HAVE T' FILL HIS BOOTS TILL DEADWOOD KIN GIT ANOTHER ---

Panel 2: I'M RATTLESNAKE PETE! TH' GUY THAT BUMPS 'EM OFF! I KIN RUN FASTER --DIVE DEEPER--AN' COME UP DRIER THAN ANY MAN IN DEADWOOD!

Panel 3: AN' THAT KID OVER THAR WUZ FOUND BY JACK AN' ME WHEN HE WUZ A BABY --HE WUZ HANGIN' ON A CACTUS AN' A-YELLIN' LIKE A CALF IN A THUNDER STORM --- G'OOK!

Panel 4: I'M SORRY I HIT YUH, PAPA PETE --- I WUZ SEEIN' HOW CLOSE I COULD COME TO YER HEAD WITHOUT HITTIN' IT-- AN'--AN' I **MISSED** !

Classic "bigfoot" cartoon style, as exemplified by Charles "Boody" Rogers's *Deadwood Gulch.*

©1931 by Dell Publishing

the major Hearst comic strips from *The Katzenjammer Kids* onward. Block, Jr. served as editor of *Comic Monthly*; not surprisingly, most of the strips reprinted in the magazine were from the Hearst syndicates. Obviously ahead of its time, the magazine survived for just one year before folding.

Early in 1929 George Delacorte, founder of the Dell Publishing Company, also tried his hand at inventing the modern comic book. What he actually produced, though, looked more like a tabloid funny paper section. Delacorte had concluded that the best part of the Sunday newspaper was the comic section and set out to produce one of his own. *The Funnies* was a twenty-four-page tabloid with a third of its pages in color. It came out each week and sold for 10 cents. In its pages could be found such original features as *Frosty Ayre* by Joe Archibald, *My Big Brudder* by Tack Knight, *Deadwood Gulch* by Boody Rogers, and *Clancy the Cop* by Vic E. Pazmino (VEP).

The Funnies struggled along for thirty-six issues before expiring. The editor of the brave but doomed venture was Harry Steeger, who went on to become a major publisher of pulp fiction magazines in the 1930s and 1940s—*The Spider, Dime Detective*, and others—and never had anything to do with another comic book. Dell briefly tried the black and white format as well, adopting the Cupples & Leon style. In 1930 they issued VEP's *Clancy the Cop.* The following year came Rogers's *Deadwood Gulch*, plus a second *Clancy.*

Although drawn in comic strip form, the material was original.

Just before the publication of the earliest modern-style comic books, a particularly novel method of recycling newspaper comic strips appeared when the Whitman Publishing Company of Racine, Wisconsin, introduced its first Big Little Book (BLB) in 1932. Sold mainly in 5-and-10-cent stores, these plump, board-covered books usually measured 3½ by 4½ inches and contained between three hundred and four hundred pages. They were miniature, illustrated novels in which each page of text was followed by a drawing. The text was based on the narrative of the comic strip sequence being adapted; the pictures were actual panels from the strip. Unfortunately, the artwork had to be butchered—dialogue balloons were whited out and the drawings were tinkered with to make them fit the standard BLB page size.

The Adventures of Dick Tracy was the very first BLB title, followed in 1933 by *Buck Rogers, 25th Century A.D.*; *Little Orphan Annie*; *Chester Gump at Silver Creek Ranch*; *Tarzan of the Apes*; and *Reg'lar Fellers*. Whitman also introduced a few originals, including one about cowboys and adaptations of *Robinson Crusoe* and *Treasure Island*.

Big Little Books continued to be published throughout the thirties and forties, although the name was changed to Better Little Books in 1938. Nearly three hundred different titles were issued during the first five years. Although these 10-cent BLBs used many of the same characters that were starting to appear in comic books—Dick Tracy, Mickey Mouse, Tarzan, the Lone Ranger, Buck Rogers, Wash Tubbs, Gene Autry, Little Orphan Annie, Flash Gordon— they were able to co-exist peacefully with their four-color competition. This was chiefly because Big Little Books and the several knockoff imitators that sprang up—including Saalfield's Little Big Book line—sold exclusively in the five-and-dime market, in chain and variety stores. The new comic books, on the other hand, were sold chiefly through newsstands.

According to John Tebbel, the average initial print run for a BLB title was between 250,000 and 350,000 copies. Lawrence Lowery, a leading authority on the genre, says authors of the original-material titles were "generally paid a $250 advance on royalties to write a manuscript. The royalties were one-quarter cent per book, and the amount was usually split between the author and the artist." The average hardcover mystery novel in the 1930s, by the way, didn't pay a much larger advance.

To illustrate its original titles, Whitman built up an interesting stable of artists that included Fred Harman, Henry E. Vallely, Ken Ernst, Bud Sagendorf, and Erwin L. Hess.

Whitman also experimented with black and white hardcover reprint books in 1934, publishing four issues of a *Famous Comics* series. These contained sixty-four pages and measured 7 by 8 inches. Included among the reprinted strips were Dirks's *The*

They Raced Across the Lawn

Above: This suspenseful scene from Junior G-Men is a typical Big Little Book illustration. Opposite: A selection of Big Little Books and Better Little Books. Kids loved the books' handy size, action-packed narratives, and exciting illustrations.

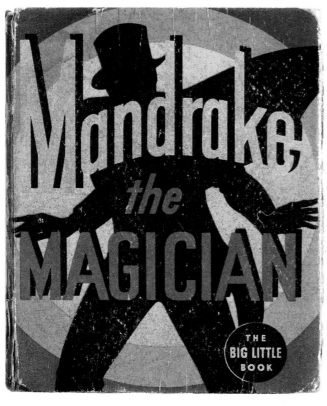

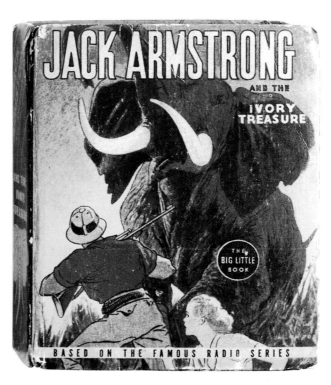

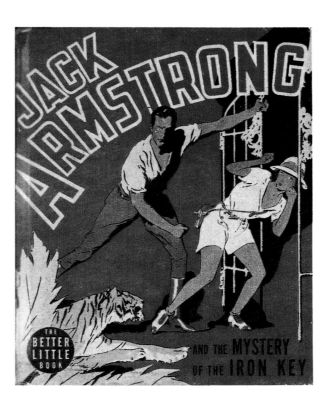

A typical sampling from the *Hairbreadth Harry* series in *Famous Funnies*. The first comic book in the modern format, *Famous Funnies* got off to a shaky start, but eventually revolutionized the publishing industry.

©1937 by Famous Funnies, Inc.

Captain and the Kids and Merrill Blosser's *Freckles and his Friends*. As late as 1941, long after Whitman had gone into the four-color comic book business, the company introduced a Better Little Book series called *All Picture Comics*. These titles, which printed one unaltered strip panel per page, included *Dan Dunn, Smitty*, and *Smokey Stover*.

The first regularly published comic book in the standard format was *Famous Funnies*. Remember that title; although *Famous Funnies* got off to a shaky start and didn't climb out of the red until it had been in business for more than six months, it became the cornerstone of what was to become one of the most lucrative branches of magazine publishing. Not only was *Famous Funnies* the first comic book in the modern format, it was also the first, with the exception of *The Funnies*, to feature more than one character. For anyone who had a dime in the Depression year of 1934, *Famous Funnies* offered dozens of characters, all of them from the newspapers. The lineup included *Joe Palooka, Dixie Dugan, Connie, Hairbreadth Harry* and the perennially popular *Mutt & Jeff. Buck Rogers* was added in the third issue. The covers promised "100 comics and games," which was good enough to eventually attract legions of faithful readers.

The creator of *Famous Funnies*—which is esentially the comic book as we know it today—appears to be a man named Harry I. Wildenberg. The reason there's no shock of recognition when you hear Wildenberg's name is because he came up with his innovative idea while working for someone else. He worked for the Eastern Color Printing Company of Waterbury, Connecticut, as sales manager. One of the things Eastern Color did was print the Sunday comic sections of several East Coast newspapers. Having an advertising background, Wildenberg first thought of using the comics as advertising premiums. He sold Gulf Oil the idea of giving away a tabloid-size book of comics at its gas stations. The gimmick was a successful one, and Wildenberg continued to refine the idea. While contemplating extensions of the funnies as a premium, Wildenberg and some of his associates noticed that reduced Sunday pages they had made as a promotion for the Philadelphia *Ledger* would fit two to a page on a standard tabloid-size sheet of paper. Further fiddling and figuring enabled Wildenberg to work out a way to use Eastern's presses to print sixty-four-page, color comic books.

The next problem was what to do with the resultant magazines. Wildenberg, with the help of an Eastern salesman named M. C. Gaines, first interested other advertisers in using comic books as premiums. Eastern produced books for Procter & Gamble, Canada Dry, Kinney Shoes, Wheatena, and other manufacturers of kid-oriented products. These giveaway editions usually had print runs ranging from 100,000 to 250,000, but some went as high as one million copies. ▶

M.C. Gaines

M. C. Gaines was a publishing veteran with an astute sense of what youngsters wanted to read. *Picture Stories from the Bible* was just one of Gaines's many successes.

©1942 by M. C. Gaines

His full name was Maxwell Charles Gaines, but most people called him Charlie. A natural entrepreneur, Gaines was an important figure in the development of modern comic books. He played a part in launching *Famous Funnies*, packaged such early reprint titles as *Popular Comics*, helped discover Superman, and published the comic books that introduced heroic characters like Hawkman, the Flash, the Atom, the Green Lantern, and Wonder Woman.

Born in 1896, Gaines first worked as a salesman. While employed by Eastern Color, he teamed with Harry Wildenberg to get *Famous Funnies* going and onto the newsstands. In the middle 1930s, while working at the McClure Syndicate, he used McClure's color presses to print a line of comic books for Dell. Aided by youthful cartoonist/editor Sheldon Mayer, Gaines put together *Popular Comics*, *The Funnies*, and *The Comics*. At Mayer's suggestion, he advised DC to print *Superman*. Finally, late in 1938, Gaines entered into partnership with DC to produce comic books. His titles eventually included *All-American Comics*, *Flash Comics*, *All Star Comics*, and *Sensation Comics*.

Despite his association with some of the most successful superheroes of the Golden Age, Gaines never was especially fond of that type of character. He believed comic books could be used for educational purposes. While still with DC, he persuaded the company to issue *Picture Stories From The Bible*. The seven issues of this series, begun in 1942, eventually sold several million copies. Gaines donated part of his profits from the enterprise to religious groups, telling them he considered the Bible comic books not a business venture but rather "a public service."

Gaines parted with DC in 1945 to found Educational Comics, Inc. By concentrating on comic books devoted to history and science, EC racked up some impressive sales. Unfortunately, the first part of the EC story came to an end in the summer of 1947, when M.C. Gaines was killed in a boating accident. The company was inherited by his son, William, who went on to make some comic book history of his own.

Wildenberg and Gaines then considered sticking a 10-cent price tag on their comic books and selling them directly to children. With this, one of the great ideas of publishing history had been hatched. The pair approached the Woolworth's chain as a possible outlet but were told that sixty-four pages of old comics didn't offer sufficient value for a dime. Eventually, in 1934, Wildenberg persuaded the American News Company to distribute a monthly comic book to newsstands across the country. He called the new magazine *Famous Funnies*, a title he'd originally thought of for a soap company premium. The initial issue sold ninety percent of its 200,000 copies. Although Eastern Color lost over $4,000 on that one, by issue #12 *Famous* was netting $30,000 a month. Wildenberg admitted, in a profile of him that appeared years later in *The Commonweal*, that he never read the funnies himself. He "didn't understand how anyone else could, but he could see [the funnies'] commercial possibilities."

Editorial offices for the fledgling magazine were set up in Manhattan. Although Harold A. Moore, a longtime Eastern Color employee, was listed as editor, the actual working editor of *Famous Funnies* was Stephen A. Douglas. Brooklyn born, Douglas was working as a professional cartoonist before he even reached his teens. He was in his late twenties when he went to work as an editor and production manager for *Famous*. Among Douglas's responsibilities was to take the syndicate proofs

of the strips and get them ready to be printed. This involved, unfortunately, relettering, enlarging, and sometimes cutting the copy in the balloons and captions so that the whole package wouldn't reproduce too small. Minuscule lettering became a source of criticism for the early reprint comic books, where Sunday pages usually ran at one-fourth of their intended newspaper size. The first original-material magazines that came along a year or so after the debut of *Famous Funnies* stressed the fact that their comics were ones "you can read without hurting your eyes." Douglas also had to extend a panel here and there to make it fit the pages just right, and he would white out any dot patterns that might interfere with the laying on of color.

During its early days, *Famous Funnies* reprinted mostly Sunday pages. Among the few exceptions were a sports strip called *Ned Brant* and an aviation strip, *Flying to Fame*. Besides those mentioned earlier, some of the other Sunday pages reprinted were *Tailspin Tommy*, *The Bungle Family*, *Jane Arden* (complete with paper dolls), *Toonerville Folks*, and *The Nebbs*. Except for the two-page text story at the center of each issue, there was no original material to be found in the first few issues.

Gradually some original filler pages started to show up, though none were drawn by Douglas, who didn't have a chance to use his own work in the magazine for several years. The earliest contributor was Victor E. Pazmino. A man with an affinity

Seaweed Sam, the Rhyming Rover, sails with his pal Tiny into a potentially dangerous situation.

©1941 by Famous Funnies, Inc.

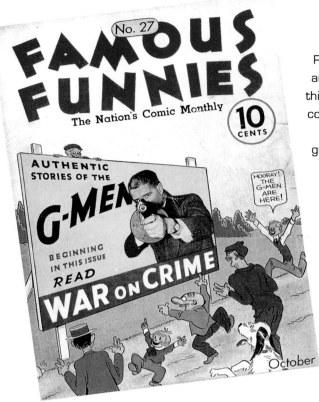

Public interest in the FBI and in "G-Men" prompted this 1936 *Famous Funnies* cover, in which the war on crime is heralded by a group of newspaper-strip stars.

©1936 by Famous Funnies, Inc.

Famous Funnies heralds the coming of the new year, 1937, with a nod to America's "G-Men."

©1937 by Famous Funnies, Inc.

for being present at the creation of significant things, VEP had been a contributor to *The Funnies* in 1929. For *Famous Funnies* he drew a monthly page of gag cartoons as well as a page about Seaweed Sam, a bubble-nosed, hard-traveling sailor who was fond of speaking in verse. Nearly all the covers during the magazine's first seven years were drawn by VEP. He had an appealingly loose, simple style, one that looked as though it had probably stopped developing when he was about ten years old. Other early fillers were supplied by Bob Bliss, who contributed a page about a little girl named Queenie, and M. E. Brady, who brought two cartoon lads named Buttons and Fatty over from the Brooklyn *Eagle* and rechristened them Butty and Fatty.

As it moved into its third year, *Famous Funnies* made considerable changes in its contents. Several of the top Associated Press-syndicate strips, including *Scorchy Smith*, *Dickie Dare*, *Oaky Doaks*, and *The Adventures of Patsy*, were added. That meant the magazine was now offering artwork by some of the most gifted newspaper artists of the 1930s—men such as Noel Sickles, Milton Caniff, Ralph B. Fuller, Mel Graff, Coulton Waugh, and Bert Christman. Late in 1937, when the Register & Tribune Syndicate and the McNaught Syndicate decided to go into the comic book business on their own (the result was *Feature Funnies*), *Famous Funnies* lost *Joe Palooka*, *Dixie Dugan*, *Jane Arden*, and several other popular features. By the

Dick Calkins's *Buck Rogers* (above, left) is one of the classic science fiction newspaper strips. *Oaky Doaks* (above, right) was appealingly drawn by Ralph B. Fuller. Both strips were popular features of *Famous Funnies*.

end of the decade, *Famous Funnies* had a lineup that included—in addition to the Associated Press strips and *Buck Rogers*—*Roy Powers, Eagle Scout* by Frank Godwin, *Skyroads* by Russell Keaton, and *Big Chief Wahoo* by Allen Saunders and Elmer Woggon.

In issue #62 (September 1939) two pages of *Lightnin' and the Lone Rider* dailies were added to each issue. This cowboy strip, which differed from *The Lone Ranger* only in that its hero didn't ride a white horse or have an

Indian companion, was drawn by a young fellow who used the snappy pen name of Lance Kirby. As "Jack" Kirby he'd produce work of much greater originality, and win countless fans over a span of five decades.

Famous Funnies also reprinted *Lone Rider* strips by Kirby's successor, Frank Robbins. *Speed Spaulding* was eventually added to the magazine's lineup, in four-page chunks. This was science fiction based on the Edwin Balmer-Philip Wylie novel *When Worlds*

Collide; the feature was illustrated by Marvin Bradley, who later graduated to *Rex Morgan, MD.*, a long-running newspaper strip. Another fantasy strip, Russell Stamm's *Invisible Scarlet O'Neil*, bowed in *Famous Funnies* #81 (April 1941).

By this time the superhero deluge had hit comic books and *Famous Funnies* was starting to worry about the competition. The magazine's sales figures climbed to a peak of over 400,000 copies a month in 1939, but by 1941 had skidded to just a little

over 250,000. Until then the covers had been whimsical, showing various characters in gag situations. But the cover on issue #81 was a dramatic one, depicting Scarlet O'Neil rescuing a child from a fire. Artwork was by H. G. Peter, who would go over to DC in 1942 to draw *Wonder Woman*.

This new approach would be the start of a trend and the next nine *Famous Funnies* covers were all serious and showed the likes of Buck Rogers, Scorchy Smith, and Dickie Dare in action

Famous Funnies also got mileage out of M. E. Brady's innocuously amusing kid strip *Butty and Fatty* (above, left) and Elmer Woggon's *Big Chief Wahoo* (above, right).

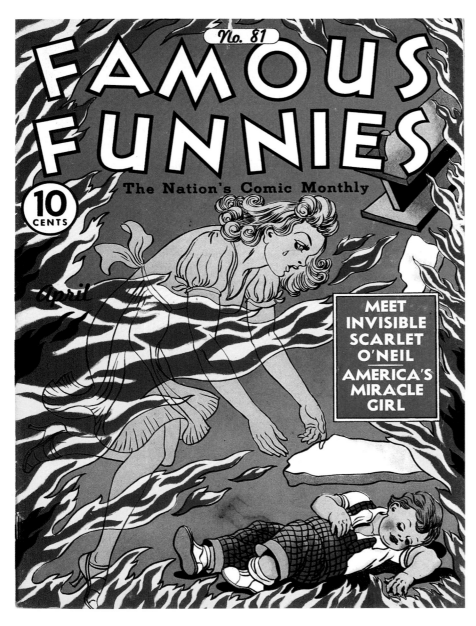

No. 81

FAMOUS FUNNIES

The Nation's Comic Monthly

10 CENTS

April

MEET INVISIBLE SCARLET O'NEIL AMERICA'S MIRACLE GIRL

H. G. Peter drew this vivid cover featuring Invisible Scarlet O'Neil.

©1941 by Famous Funnies, Inc.

situations. Two of these actionful covers were by Bill Everett, creator of Sub-Mariner.

Going even further in trying to hold its own against Superman, Batman, and the hordes of other costumed heroes who were taking over the newsstands, *Famous Funnies* came up with a superhero of its own for issue #89, dated December, 1941. Created by Douglas and drawn by Peter, the character was named Fearless Flint, a fellow who started life as an ordinary guy named Jack Bradley. Bradley had one of the more proletarian backgrounds among the heroes and was not the usual bored playboy or mild mannered reporter. When first encountered, he was operating a jackhammer on the Mt. Rushmore sculptures. An explosion transformed him into "A MAN FROM FLINT . . . with the strength of 10 men." Flint's costume consisted of a pair of white riding pants and boots. He went around bare-chested, the better to show off the fact that his skin turned a bright crimson when he went into his heroic phase. If this sounds dubious to you, don't worry—it didn't go over any better with readers in the early forties. Creating topnotch heroes just wasn't Douglas's forte; Flint was extinguished after *Famous Funnies* #109.

For most of the remainder of its days *Famous Funnies* concentrated on comic strip reprints. There were fewer strips now and they were being run larger and allowed to retain their original lettering. A typical 1947 issue, for example, contained eight pages of *Steve Roper* (formerly *Big Chief Wahoo*), six pages of *Invisible Scarlet O'Neil*, six of *Dickie Dare*, six of *Scorchy Smith*, and six of *Oaky Doaks*. Four pages of *Napoleon* Sunday strips were scattered through the book. Marty Links's *Bobby Sox* panel was added in 1948, with the issue's cover admonishing readers, "Don't be an 'ICK,' be a 'FOX.' Get 'IN THE GROOVE' with BOBBY SOX." A later addition, in October of 1949, was *Ben Friday*, scripted by gag cartoonist and mystery novelist Lawrence Lariar and drawn by former Will Eisner assistant John Spranger.

An ailing bimonthly by 1950, *Famous Funnies* dropped *Buck Rogers* and replaced him with an inept science-fiction feature entitled *Barney Carr, Space Detective*. Barney's interplanetary career was short and he vanished after only two issues. Buck finally returned in #209 and the event was celebrated with the first of a series of eight Buck Rogers covers by the gifted fantasy illustrator Frank Frazetta.

The final issue of *Famous Funnies* was #218 (July 1955). It was a slim thirty-two pages, just half as thick as it had been when the title began, and contained no reprints except those of *Buck Rogers*. The rest of the issue was made up of three brand new kid features, two by Dave Gantz and one by Jack Berrill. Times had changed but *Famous Funnies* had not changed enough to maintain its audience. Significantly, perhaps, a television set figured prominently on the final cover.

By the early 1940s, the covers of *Famous Funnies* emphasized adventure rather than humor. This dramatic illustration is by Bill Everett, the creator of Sub-Mariner. Everett was still producing fine comic book work in the 1970s.

CHAPTER TWO

THE BANDWAGON STARTS TO ROLL

The most successful of the early, modern-format comic books prospered because they offered reprints of popular newspaper strips in convenient packages. *The Funnies* was one of numerous titles that, beginning in 1935, arrived to give *Famous Funnies* some competition. The enthusiastic reception given to these and other reprint comics paved the way for all-new characters and features, and the continued growth of the comic book industry.

©1939 by Dell Publishing Co.

The comic book business didn't hit high gear right away. *Famous Funnies* had the field to itself for all of its initial year and then, starting in 1935, a few other titles began to show up on newsstands. Some, inspired by *Famous*, offered reprints of popular newspaper strips. Others offered brand new material—an approach that proved to be a wise one. Readers responded so dramatically that, by 1938, the combined monthly sales of all available comic book titles were well over 2,500,000 copies. In this chapter we'll see how the fledgling industry got to that first plateau.

Late in 1935 Dell Publishing introduced Popular Comics (cover-dated February 1936), the first reprint title to compete with *Famous Funnies*. Although the early statements of ownership list Dell of 149 Madison Avenue, New York City, as the publisher and a gentleman named Arthur Lawson as editor, they don't tell the real story. *Popular Comics* was packaged for Dell at the offices of the McClure Syndicate, where M. C. Gaines was utilizing color presses to cash in on what he surmised would be a comic book boom. Two of the presses had been purchased from the defunct *New York Graphic*, Bernard Macfadden's impressively sleazy daily tabloid. Gaines had figured out a way to adapt the pair of two-color presses to print four-color comic books. As noted earlier, Gaines had been in on the birth of *Famous Funnies*, and now he was involved in something nearly as significant.

Popular needed an editor and Gaines's choice was a teenage cartoonist named Sheldon Mayer. "I went to work for M. C. Gaines in January of 1936," Mayer once recalled. "I had been up to see him the previous summer, and half a year later he gave me a call and offered me a few days' pasteup work." The few days stretched into a few years and Mayer was eventually editing *Popular* as well as *The Funnies* and *The Comics*. To fill his pages, Mayer used both syndicate proofs and original strip art. The syndicates were paid about five dollars a page for reprint rights. Even though comic books were a fat sixty-four pages at that time, the pay scale didn't demand that the publisher make an enormous outlay of money.

The premiere issue of *Popular Comics* was very much in the *Famous Funnies* format, although the color was better and brighter and none of the copy had been relettered to make it larger. Only Sunday pages were reprinted. There was no original material except for the mandatory filler story at the center of the book. *Dick Tracy*

led off the issue, in the midst of his tussle with the brutal Boris Arson. Strips from several rival syndicates were used, including *Skippy, Tailspin Tommy, Mutt & Jeff* (who'd also been in *Famous Funnies*), *The Gumps, Don Winslow, Little Orphan Annie, Bronc Peeler, Smokey Stover, Terry and the Pirates*, and *Believe It Or Not*. No attempt was made to start the reprinted sequences at the beginning of a continuity, although *Terry* did happen to commence with the first pages of the second adventure. Better-known features got four pages each month; lesser ones got two.

By the end of the first year a few changes had been made to the *Popular Comics* lineup. *Tiny Tim, Reg'lar Fellers, Smilin' Jack*, and Garret Price's handsome and imaginative *Skull Valley* had been added, and Mayer was using his own artwork to illustrate the fiction fillers. *Tom Mix* was appearing, through the courtesy of licensing-merchandising man Stephen Slesinger; the Mix adventures appear to be adaptations of Whitman Big Little Books.

By the time Mayer and Gaines ended their association with *Popular*, somewhere toward the end of 1938, the title was running fewer reprints and had added a smattering of original material. All the Chicago Tribune-New York News Syndicate pages—*Terry, Dick Tracy, Annie,* et al—had shifted over to *Super Comics* (first issue cover-dated May 1938) and been replaced by mostly original features. One such was a series of six-page adaptations of western B-movies, mostly the

Popular Comics reprinted Sunday newspaper-strip pages only. Its roster was culled from more than one syndicate. Here, chinless Andy Gump makes a resolution he won't be keeping for long.
©1937 by Dell Publishing Co.

product of Monogram Pictures, starring such cinema cowpokes as Tex Ritter, Gene Autry, and Jack Randall. Slesinger was represented by a true-crime G-Men feature drawn by his protege, Jim Gary.

Popular was now being printed by the Whitman division of Western Printing & Lithographing Company at its Poughkeepsie, New York, plant as part of a new agreement with Dell. Editorial work was done in the Manhattan office under the direction of Oskar Lebeck. A former stage designer and book illustrator, Lebeck served the magazine as artist, writer, and editor. He drew covers, wrote scripts, and initiated more new features. Among them were *The Hurricane Kids, The Masked Pilot*, and *Gang Busters*.

As the forties progressed the magazine gradually returned to its old reprint ways. By issue #90 (August 1943) the only original feature that remained was *Gang Busters,* which shared the pages with *Smilin' Jack, The Gumps, Toots and Casper*, and *Terry. Popular Comics* remained essentially a reprint comic book until the end of its days in the summer of 1948; by then it was a thin bimonthly.

The second monthly packaged for Dell by Gaines and Mayer was *The Funnies*. The first issue arrived on the stands late in the summer of 1936 (cover-dated October 1936) and was devoted to newspaper strip reprints. As mentioned in the previous chapter, Dell had already used *The Funnies* as a title for its unsuccessful original-material tabloid of 1929.

Optimistic about success in a changed market, Dell resurrected the name for the new monthly. Early issues drew heavily on the stable of the Cleveland-based NEA syndicate, reprinting *Alley Oop, Captain Easy, Boots, Out Our Way, Myra North*, and *Salesman Sam*. Among the other reprints were *Dan Dunn, Tailspin Tommy, Don Dixon*, and *Bronc Peeler. Mutt & Jeff* was also in the lineup, suggesting that Gaines may have been superstitious about the strip; it had also been in *Famous* and *Popular*.

In the second issue of *The Funnies* editor Mayer finally got to draw a feature. It was a new one called *Scribbly*, a strip about a boy cartoonist—an appropriate character, in that Mayer himself was a "boy cartoonist." The two or three *Scribbly* pages that appeared in each issue were laid out like Sunday pages, each sporting its own logo. Mayer did this so his upstart creation could comfortably rub shoulders with the real Sunday pages being reprinted. The strip dealt with Scribbly Jibbet, who was young, small, and possessed of a head of hair resembling an untidy haystack. Mayer focused on Scribbly's efforts to break free of the bonds of home and school and into the charmed world of newspaper cartooning. Mayer has said that the strip is a blend of autobiography and fantasy, and that some of the truest-seeming elements are the most unreal. The pages mixed lower middle class apartment life with wacky excursions into the worlds of newspaper publishing, radio, and even Hollywood. It was an

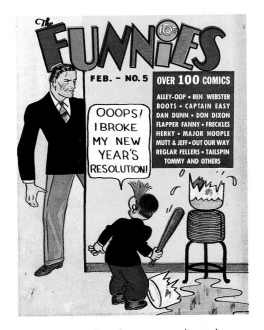

The Funnies was packaged for Dell Publishing by M. C. Gaines and a young cartoonist named Sheldon Mayer. As seen on the cover of the fifth issue, another New Year's resolution comes to naught.

©1937 by Dell Publishing Co.

In time, the good mix of whimsy and adventure reprints offered by *The Funnies* was augmented by original strips. The lineup seen on this cover suggests the diversity that readers could expect.

©1940 by Dell Publishing Co.

exuberant creation, rendered in the youthful Mayer's appealing, scribbly cartoon style.

By the end of its first year *The Funnies* had added two new, or nearly new, features. These were *G-Men on the Job* and *Og, Son of Fire*, both two-pages-per-issue adaptations of already-published Big Little Books. After Gaines and Mayer ended their association with Dell, *The Funnies* underwent further changes in content and added several original strips.

The third and final magazine produced by the Gaines-Mayer team for Dell was *The Comics*. It made its debut with the March 1937 issue and, although billed originally as a monthly, took until March of 1939 to reach its eleventh issue. *The Comics* was a hodgepodge of reprints, reruns, and original works. The earlier issues offered reprints of *Wash Tubbs*, but the other newspaper strips that showed up in the magazine's pages were considerably less well known. From the Brooklyn Eagle's syndicate came *Bill and Davy*, a seagoing adventure done in comically exagerrated, "bigfoot" cartooning style by James McCague, and *Gordon Fife*, a strip dealing with intrigue in mythical European kingdoms. From a sparsely distributed ready-print Sunday section turned out by the George Mathew Adams Service came a cowboy strip, *Ted Strong*, by Al Carrelno; a kid adventure titled *The Enchanted Stone* by Adolphe Barreaux; and *Rod Rian of the Sky Police* by Paul Jepson. *The Comics* also reprinted *Deadwood Gulch, My Big Brudder*, and

No. 55   November

Tip Top Comics

Tm. Reg. U. S. Pat. Off.

10¢

NOW I PICK OFF DER RED ONE!

VILYUM TELL IN PERSON!

ADDING
The TRIPLE TERROR
The MIRROR MAN
And IRON VIC
To Your Favorites

ALSO — LI'L ABNER — TARZAN — FRITZI RITZ — JIM HARDY — ELLA CINDERS —
BRONCHO BILL — ABBIE an' SLATS — FRANKIE DOODLE — LITTLE MARY MIXUP

Tip Top Comics: Hans and Fritz— those irrepressible
Katzenjammer Kids—take aim at the snoozing Captain; plenty
of screaming is sure to follow. *Tip Top* was the first comic
book published by United Features Syndicate.

©1940 by United Feature Syndicate, Inc.

Clancy the Cop, all of which had appeared originally in the 1929 version of *The Funnies*.

In 1936 the newspaper syndicates, which up to that time had been content to sell reprint rights to enterprising publishers, now began to take an active part in the funny book business. William Randolph Hearst's King Features Syndicate, for example, entered into an agreement with the David McKay Company to produce a comic book titled *King Comics*. United Features Syndicate, part of the Scripps-Howard communications empire, went King one better and published its own magazines. The first of these was *Tip Top Comics*, which appeared in the spring of 1936.

The earliest *Tip Top* covers were drawn by Mo Leff, a United staff artist, and depicted gatherings—usually improbable —of the magazine's various characters. On the cover of the very first issue Tarzan and Li'l Abner face off in a boxing ring. Joe Jinks serves as referee and Mammy Yokum is her son's second. Among those gathered at ringside are Ella Cinders, Fritzi Ritz, and Hans, Fritz, and the Captain. Strange bedfellows, all! Inside these first issues were a potpourri of features, mostly reprinted Sunday pages.

Some of the pages were several years old; others, like the *Li'l Abner* Sundays, were relatively fresh. Each issue offered three *Tarzan* pages, taken from an impressive 1933 Hal Foster sequence dealing with a lost civilization patterned after ancient Egypt. Harry O'Neill's *Broncho Bill* and Leff's own boys' ▶

BE A CARTOONIST!

Harvey Kurtzman
2166 Clinton Ave.
Bronx, New York

A runner-up in a 1939 *Tip Top* "Cartoon Club" contest was a talented young fellow named Harvey Kurtzman, who went on to create *Mad.*

©1939 by United Feature Syndicate, Inc.

One of the most interesting features in the early issues of *Tip Top Comics*, at least to the would-be cartoonists in the audience, was the section devoted to fledgling artists. It was headed with the lines—"Be a cartoonist! Join the Tip Top Cartoon Club now—it's fun!" Originally this was just a place for young cartoonists to submit their sample strips, but with issue #21 a new section was added. This involved a mustachioed western character called Buffalo Bob, who got himself into a dire predicament each month. A typical panel showed Bob falling off his ladder while painting a barn and about to land on the sharp tines of a pitchfork being held by a daydreaming farmer. "Merely draw a solution . . . find a novel way of saving poor Buffalo Bob . . . you have a chance of being a 'winner.'" As if the prospect of fame and an opportunity to save Bob's bacon weren't suffficient motivation, a one dollar prize was offered for winning solutions and original strips.

The Cartoon Club was usually given three pages each issue—a leadoff page that set up the latest Buffalo Bob dilemma, one for the winning solutions of the previous month's problem, and one for a quartet of amateur strips. The set-up page also offered news, drawing tips, and words of encouragement: "Some of the cartoons . . . are pretty close to professional standards. The improvement can be noted all down the line."

Sometimes, however, the eager young artists went too far, causing warnings to be posted. "The December BUFFALO BOB Contest taxed the imaginations of members more than usual. Entrants were asked to submit their own problems and in doing so many of them used what are know as 'editorial taboos.' We are listing them here so that other members may not make the same mistakes. 1. The use of snakes is prohibited. 2. The use of underworld characters is not allowed. 3. Solutions that point ridicule to any race, color or creed should not be used. 4. In some instances, humor due to embarrassing situations is taboo. One member sent a problem showing Buffalo Bob in shorts. It is better to steer clear of such solutions as in most cases they are unacceptable."

Because it was one of the few such outlets around (*Open Road For Boys* magazine ran a similar section), the Tip Top Cartoon Club attracted just about every aspiring cartoonist in the country. Looking back at those old pages now, one finds the names and early work of quite a few youngsters who eventually made it into professional ranks. These include Bill Yates, Jack Davis, Dan Heilman, Harvey Kurtzman, Mort Walker, and Warren Tufts. (Tufts actually managed years later to sell the strip *Casey Ruggles* to United Features, the publishers of *Tip Top*.) *Beetle Bailey*'s Mort Walker, when asked if he recalled sending in his work and how he felt about seeing it in print, replied that he did indeed remember. Most important to him was that he got paid, which meant he was a pro.

Comics on Parade was United Feature's companion title to *Tip Top*. This seaside scene drawn by Mo Leff includes Li'l Abner, Nancy, Tarzan, Ella Cinders, and other popular newspaper-strip stars.

©1938 by United Feature Syndicate, Inc.

Sis Sez was a continuing feature of *King Comics*. It was written by Ruth Thompson, Royal Historian of Oz, and drawn by Marge Buell, who later created Little Lulu.

©1940 by David McKay Publications

adventure fantasy, *Peter Pat*, provided the only serious fare. The rest of the magazine was given over to humor, supplied by the likes of *Ella Cinders, Fritzi Ritz, Looy Dot Dope, Joe Jinks, Cynical Susie, Danny Dingle, Little Mary Mixup, Benny, Billy Make Believe, Grin and Bear It*, and *The Captain and the Kids*. United seemed determined to get just about every strip and panel on its list packed into *Tip Top's* sixty-four pages.

Tip Top's first editor was Lev Gleason, who'd worked with Harry Wildenberg at Eastern Color. Gleason would eventually publish a number of aggressively innovative comic books, including *Boy, Daredevil,* and *Crime Does Not Pay*—none of which were exactly in the *Tip Top* vein. Still, by the end of its second year, *Tip Top* was leaning more toward adventure. *Tarzan* was now getting five pages and active strips like *Frankie Doodle* and Dick Moore's *Jim Hardy* had been added.

By 1945, the magazine was down to forty-eight pages and was even thinner by the late 1940s. When *Tip Top* folded in 1961, with its 225th issue, it was being published as a quarterly by Dell. The Dell issues contained brand new (and not very well done) adventures of *Nancy, The Captain and the Kids*, and similar fare.

United Features's second monthly, *Comics On Parade*, was launched early in 1938. The lineup was similar to what was found in *Tip Top*, except that daily versions of the strips rather than the Sundays were reprinted. *Tarzan*, in fact, started at the very beginning of its run, with reprints of Hal Foster's handsome 1929 dailies. There were also *Fritzi Ritz, Li'l Abner*, and *Ella Cinders* dailies, all suitably colored for their comic book appearance, plus the rare daily *The Captain and the Kids* strips from the early 1930s. The strip was originally drawn by Rudolph Dirks and was subsequently taken over by Bernard Dibble. Wildly melodramatic plots were added, and punched up with dialogue that mixed Dirks's stage German with lines what would fit into a Marx Brothers movie.

After its twenty-ninth issue (August 1940) *Comics On Parade* underwent a format change. The remaining seventy-five issues were devoted to one character per book. *Li'l Abner, The Captain and the Kids*, and *Nancy & Fritzi Ritz* alternated for several years and then the frazzle-haired Nancy became the sole star until the title ceased publication in 1955. A very similar companion comic, *Sparkler Comics*, was introduced by United in the summer of 1941.

King Comics, the first McKay-Hearst title, hit the stands at the same time as *Tip Top*. Both magazines were dated April 1936 and, by chance, both used the same basic cover idea, a prizefight. On the *King* cover, Popeye wallops a gorilla while Jiggs referees. Inside, the new magazine offered a somewhat stronger lineup than its rival. On the adventure side there were Sunday pages of *Flash Gordon*, complete with *Jungle Jim* topper, *King of the Royal Mounted, Mandrake*, and *Tim Tyler's Luck*.

Also crowded in were lesser-known adventure pages such as *Curley Harper, Radio Patrol, Little Annie Rooney, Ted Towers*, and *Ace Drummond*. Derring-do outweighed humor in the earliest issues of *King Comics*. Laughs were provided by Popeye in Segar's *Thimble Theatre, Henry, Bringing Up Father*, and Otto Soglow's *The Little King*. (Soglow's red-coated monarch also appeared in the magazine's logo.)

The production of *King Comics* was a joint effort that involved the Philadelphia editorial offices of the McKay Company and the King Features syndicate bullpen in Manhattan. Alexander McKay was the business manager and Ruth Plumly Thompson was the Philadelphia-based editor. Joe Musial, Bud Sagendorf, and other artists handled the New York end of things, pasting up the pages, doing covers, and so on.

Philadelphia-born Ruth Thompson is best known as the "official" successor to L. Frank Baum, writer of the *Wizard of Oz* books. Picked by Baum's publisher, Reilley & Lee, in 1921 (two years after Baum's death), Thompson turned out an Oz book a year until retiring as Royal Historian of Oz in 1939. By 1938, *King Comics's* second year, she was writing poems and text fillers for the magazine. The poems, which ran under the title *Sis Sez*, dealt with the misadventures of a freckled teenage girl and were illustrated by Marge Buell, the creator of *Little Lulu*. Buell also drew the pictures for the Thompson

The star of *Thimble Theatre* was Popeye, the rough 'n' ready swab whose popularity has continued undiminished for seven decades. These newspaper panels were reprinted in *King Comics* in 1939.

©1939 by King Features Syndicate, Inc.

Jimmy Thompson's *Redmen*, a well-crafted feature created expressly for *King Comics*, attempted to create an honest portrait of Native Americans.

fiction, which was in the Oz vein and featured such whimsical characters as King Kojo and Her Highness of Whyness.

As *King Comics* progressed, some of the marginal features were dropped and new ones were added. *Ming Foo* and *Ted Towers* left, replaced by *Barney Baxter, The Phantom*, and *The Lone Ranger*. Besides Miss Thompson's efforts, there was very little original material to be found in the magazine. Bob Dunn, in the days before his memorable *They'll Do It Every Time* gag panel, was in the King Features office from the middle 1930s on. When he wasn't ghosting for Milt Gross and handling other chores, he found

time to provide a monthly gag page entitled *Dun-dums*. The only serious original feature to find its way into *King Comics* arrived during the magazine's second year. Laid out like a Sunday page, Jimmy Thompson's nicely done *Redmen* ran in the exact middle of the book.

Exactly a year after introducing *King Comics*, McKay introduced a title that, like *King,* was devoted to Hearst strips. Perhaps thinking of an ideal poker hand, the publisher named the new magazine *Ace Comics.* The emphasis in *Ace* was initially on the funny side. Early issues offered H. H. Knerr's expert version of the venerable *Katzenjammer Kids*, plus *Blondie,*

IN THE INTENSE COLD, FLASH DRIVES HIMSELF AND HIS COMRADES TO THE LIMIT OF THEIR ENDURANCE REPAIRING MACHINERY AND EQUIPMENT WRECKED IN THE AVALANCHE

Tillie the Toiler, Barney Google, The Pussycat Princess, and *Krazy Kat*. For adventure buffs, *Ace* provided heroes brought over from *King Comics*. Alex Raymond's *Jungle Jim* was the standout of a group that included *Tim Tyler, Curley Harer*, and Lee Falk's *The Phantom*. Hardcore students of comics will be interested to learn that McKay's own engravers were responsible for coloring the pages, which probably explains why Falk's masked mystery man wears a brown costume in comic books and a purple one in the funny papers.

Ace Comics #26 brought another actionful feature, *Prince Valiant*. In all, *Ace* survived until

fall of 1949.

McKay's third reprint magazine came along in the summer of 1939 and was called *Magic Comics*. The star, as the title may imply, was *Mandrake the Magician*. Besides offering *Mandrake* dailies by Falk and artist Phil Davis, the early issues were used as dumping grounds for some of King Features's less popular daily strips. *Inspector Wade* was to be found there, along with *Barney Baxter* and *Secret Agent X-9*. In the humor department were *Henry, Blondie*, and *Thimble Theatre* dailies. Jimmy Thompson drew another of his admirable features, this one called *Indian Lore*. Later issues added the dependable

Alex Raymond was one of the greatest (and most influential) newspaper-strip artists ever, and his *Flash Gordon* became an American institution. Reprints of Raymond's Sunday pages were enthusiastically received by the readers of *King Comics*.

©1939 by King Features Syndicate, Inc.

Lone Ranger and Roy Crane's *Buz Sawyer. Magic Comics* disappeared late in 1949, right after *Ace. King Comics* held on until the end of 1951.

The first issue of *Super Comics* had a cover date of May 1938 and was published by Whitman. All its reprints were from the Chicago Tribune-N.Y. News Syndicate roster. Many of the strips had already been running in *Popular* and then were switched to the new magazine, so they weren't brand new even to comic book readers who didn't have access to Trib-News funnies. The stars of *Super* were *Dick Tracy* and *Terry and the Pirates*, backed up by *Smilin' Jack, Moon Mullins*, and *The Gumps*. In *Super's* early years most of the reprinted strips were newly colored dailies, some of them from as far back as 1935.

By the second year of *Super Comics*, Sunday pages only were being used. Since most of the continuity strips had stories that ran daily and on Sundays, this practice resulted in some perplexing gaps in the narratives. The reprints were doled out in snippets of from two to four pages per issue. Oskar Lebeck was *Super's* first editor, and also drew some of the original-material filler pages.

Toward the end of 1939, Whitman must have concluded that *Super* would have to be overhauled if it were to meet the competition from the ever-increasing number of original-material comic books. With issue #21 (February 1940), three, all-new adventure features were introduced— *Magic Morro* by Ken Ernst, *Jack Wander* by Ed

Mandrake the Magician pops in to say hello on the cover of *Magic Comics* (above), one of many all-reprint comic books that was inspired by the success of *Famous Funnies*. Opposite: The reprinted newspaper strips that appeared in *Super Comics* came from the Chicago Tribune-N.Y. News Syndicate. The lineup was a potent one, as this 1940 cover attests.

©1941 by King Features Syndicate (Magic Comics); ©1940 by R. S. Callender (Super Comics)

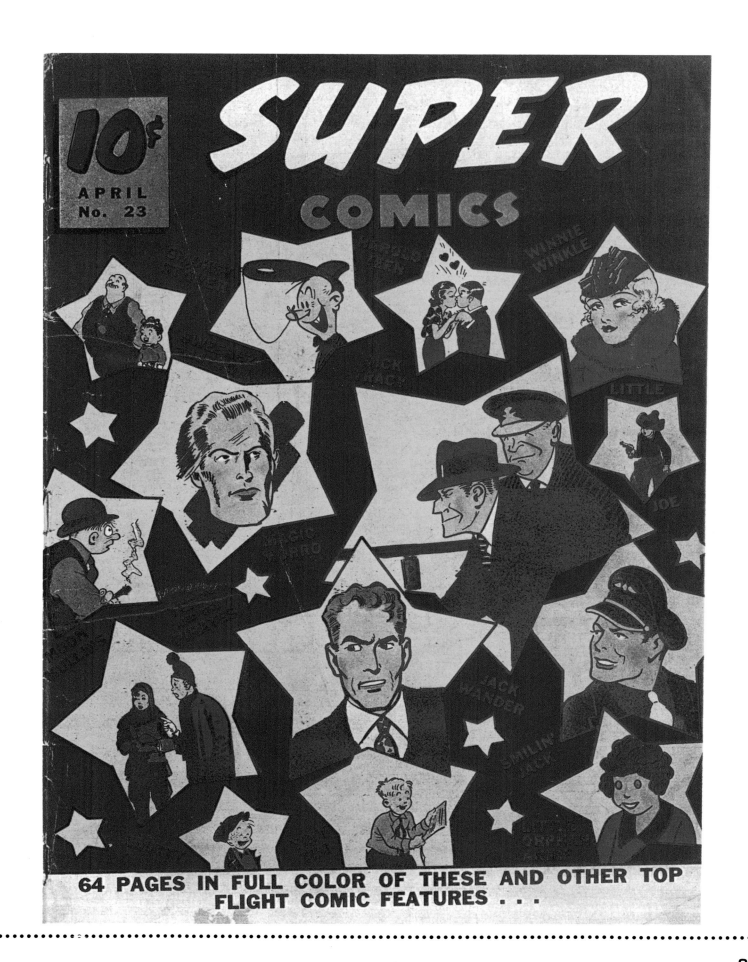

Opposite: The crimefighting
Owl made his debut in
Crackajack Funnies. This
moody 1941 cover is by
Frank Thomas. Above: The
naval adventures of Don
Winslow had first appeared
in newspaper-strip form.

©1941 by K. K. Publications, Inc.
(Crackajack Funnies);
©1940 by Whitman Publishing Co., Inc.
(Don Winslow)

Moore, and *The Thief of Bagdad*
by Erwin L. Hess. The latter
strip, which was based on neither
of the movies of that name, was
soon replaced with Richard M.
Fletcher's *Jim Ellis*.

As early as the spring of
1941, Whitman apparently
decided that their original
characters were no match for the
livelier heroes and heroines
being offered by DC, Marvel,
and other comic book
publishers. Whitman kept most
of their characters but swung
back to reprints. Beginning with
issue #35 (April 1941), the tried-
and-true *Dick Tracy* was featured
on every cover for the next
several years. By the late 1940s
Super was again just a reprint
book; the final issue, #121, was
published early in 1949.

Whitman introduced
Crackajack Funnies in the spring
of 1938. The early issues had
covers of uncoated, nonglossy
stock, making them stand out a
bit from most of the competition.
Unlike some of the earlier Dell
and Whitman titles, this one
offered more original material
mixed with reprints right from
the start. The original stuff was
pretty tame and revolved mainly
around movie cowboys. The
reprint side relied considerably
on the NEA syndicate. In fact,
with the exception of *Alley Oop*,
the new magazine used just
about the entire NEA package.
*Wash Tubbs, Boots, Freckles,
Out Our Way, Red Ryder*, and
Myra North were all featured
in *Crackajack*'s pages. Other
syndicates provided *Don
Winslow, Dan Dunn*, and *Apple
Mary*, the latter a maudlin strip
that found its widest audience

after changing its name to *Mary
Worth*.

Saturday matinees inspired
cartoon versions of western
heroes Tom Mix and Buck
Jones. Their adventures—
rehashed BLB stories laid
out in imitation Sunday-page
style—had enticing titles like
"The Rock Creek Cattle War"
and "Kidnappers of Cholla
Wash." Art was by Jim
Chambers, Jim Gary, and Ken
Ernst. Alden McWilliams's
Stratosphere Jim began in
Crackerjack #19 (January 1940),
and Oskar Lebeck provided
Time Marches Back—"The time
machine is the famous invention
of Looney Luke. With a simple
twist of the dial it can transport
him over a span of years into
any age."

In *Crackajack* #23 (May
1940) the sleuth Ellery Queen
made his four-color debut. The
June 1940 issue introduced a
costumed crimefighter, a
mysterious figure of the night
known as the Owl. Frank
Thomas, who drew both bigfoot
and straight adventure features,
illustrated the Owl's nocturnal
adventures beginning with the
second episode.

Crackajack Funnies died with
issue #43 (January 1942). Eight
pages of Milton Caniff's *Terry
and the Pirates* reprints were
added for the last go-round and a
blow-up of a Caniff panel served
as the final cover. After the
collapse of *Crackajack,* the Owl
set up shop in *Popular Comics*,
where he held on for fourteen
more adventures. The success
(however marginal) of this all-
new character signaled the
beginning of a new era in comics.

"EVERYTHING IS BRAND NEW."

Sometime in the autumn of 1934 Major Malcolm Wheeler-Nicholson, an erstwhile cavalry officer and pulp-magazine writer, got an idea. He made numerous notes, which he carried around Manhattan in an impressive-looking briefcase. After renting office space on Fourth Avenue, Nicholson began recruiting artists and writers and seeking financing. What he had in mind was a line of comic books that would feature nothing but original material. The company the major founded would eventually, under the name DC, earn countless millions of dollars. But Nicholson, like many a pioneer, went broke within a few years and never partook of any of these riches. They say that old soldiers just fade away, and that's what finally happened to Major Nicholson.

Initially, though, Nicholson's idea seemed full of promise. His first magazine was called *New Fun* and had a cover date of February 1935. Touted as the "big comic magazine," it was a 10- by 15-inch tabloid, taller and wider than *Famous Funnies* but nowhere near as colorful. The cover, which consisted of Lyman Anderson's *Jack Woods* cowboy page, was in full color and bordered in bright red. The thirty-two interior pages, however, were black and white. All the new strips were laid out like Sunday funnies and none, with a single exception, were given more than one page.

This package was an eclectic one that offered several pages of text material along with the humor and adventure strips. In addition to comics, readers got a two-page western yarn, a sports page, radio and movie news, and a popular-science page. Readers of a mechanical bent no doubt appreciated the comic's instructions for building a model plane and model boat.

The major had managed, probably through his pulp magazine (so-named for the cheap pulpwood on which they were printed) connections, to gather together quite a few ads. Not exactly aimed at kids, these included an invitation from the Gem Razor people to join the Shav-Easy Foundation, an offer from the Coyne Electrical School to divulge an "Amazingly Easy Way To Get Into Electricity," and also to send along a free booklet explaining, among other things, how to "get in on the ground floor of television." There were solicitations from two of the decade's leading mail-order musclemen, Charles Atlas and George Jowett. These advertisers, and others like them, had been longtime staples of the pulps.

Among *New Fun*'s to-be-continued adventure features were *Sandra of the Secret Service*;

Jack Andrews, All-American Boy (possibly a distant cousin of Jack Armstrong); *Cap'n Erik*; and *Buckskin Jim*. Lawrence Lariar contributed *Barry O'Neill*, a strip in the Fu Manchu tradition that pitted pipe-smoking Barry against the insidious Oriental villain Fang Gow. Lariar, a gag cartoonist and mystery novelist, later became cartoon editor of *Liberty* and compiler of the annual *Best Cartoons* albums. Henry Kiefer, a Europe-trained artist who would become one of the most prolific of comic book hacks, drew *Wing Brady*. This one combined two popular genres by offering a Foreign Legionnaire who was also an aviator. Adolphe Barreaux, who drew the risqué filler strip *Sally the Sleuth* that appeared in the *Spicy Detective* pulp, produced *The Magic Crystal of History*, a very tame, educational time-travel fantasy. Clemens Gretter took care of science fiction, drawing *Don Drake of the Planet Saro* and *2033/Super Police*.

Because Major Nicholson didn't neglect the classics, the first issue of *New Fun* contained the initial installment of an adaptation of *Ivanhoe*. Charles Flanders, in his late twenties and a fixture in the King Features bullpen, did the drawing. He abandoned the Sir Walter Scott epic after a few issues and moved on to *Treasure Island*. This adaptation must originally have been intended for publication elsewhere, since the pages ended by urging readers to "see next week."

The humor pages in *New Fun*'s premiere issue were not exactly hilarious. There was a

The "all-original" *New Fun* was the maiden effort of publisher Malcolm Wheeler-Nicholson. Pictured here is the cover of the third issue.

Artist Charles Flanders adapted Sir Walter Scott's *Ivanhoe;* the handsome result was serialized in *New Fun.* This page appeared in *New Fun* #1.

"funny animal" strip called *Pelion and Ossa* (perhaps the only comic book feature to take its name from mountains that figure in Greek mythology), *Caveman Capers*, and a college humor strip called *Jigger and Ginger*. Artist Jack Warren, who had an appealing style but a not very inventive comic mind, was represented by *Loco Luke*, a cowboy page. Bert Whitman, who'd be a name to reckon with in the comic books of the early 1940s, drew a page featuring a character called Judge Perkins.

Tom McNamara, a veteran newspaper cartoonist, was cartoon editor on the early issues of *New Fun*. His own work was represented by a kid page called *After School*, which was similar to the *Us Boys* strip he'd done for Hearst in the teens and twenties. McNamara's success with *Us Boys* had earned him an invitation from movie producer Hal Roach to participate in the creation of the Our Gang series of two-reel comedies in the early twenties. Working for Roach director-general Charley Chase, McNamara wrote and illustrated title cards and even directed a few of the earliest shorts in the series. Unfortunately, a serious drinking problem reduced him to scuffling for cartoon work by the time Major Nicholson sent out his call.

For a topper to his kid page, McNamara added *My Grandpa*. Drawn in kid style, this was supposed to be a boy cartoonist's account of his grandfather's wild and wooly youthful adventures. McNamara later drew a similar strip, called *Grandpa Peters*, for various DC comics in the early

1940s. In all versions, it was quiet but genuinely funny.

Because of the shaky state of Nicholson's finances, he often didn't get around to paying his artists the small fees—usually five dollars a page—he'd promised them. Besides considerable ill will, this produced noticeable staff turnover. Lyman Anderson quit and was replaced by fellow pulp illustrator W. C. Brigham; Lariar left and Leo O'Mealia eventually inherited characters Barry O'Neill and Fang Gow; Barreaux gave way to Monroe Eisenberg.

New artists and writers were also lured into the fold. Vincent Sullivan started by doing a cartoony kid adventure page called *Spike Spalding* and Whitney Ellsworth contributed an *Orphan Annie* imitation named *Little Linda*. Contributions began coming in over the transom, too. From Cleveland came material created by a pair of youngsters named Jerry Siegel and Joe Shuster. The first feature of theirs to see print was *Doctor Occult*, which started in *New Fun* #6 (October 1935). The youthful partners signed the strip with the pen names Leger and Reuths. Dr. Occult, a ghost detective who "has sworn to combat supernatural evil in the world," gets right down to business. In the very first panel, "while passing an alley one evening," he runs into a tuxedo-clad vampire about to siphon some blood from his latest victim. Occult uses a magic symbol to scare the fiend away.

One of the reasons Major Nicholson was having money

Artist/writer Tom McNamara had worked on Hal Roach's *Our Gang* movie shorts in the early 1920s. *New Fun* ran McNamara's *After School* feature a decade later. Here, kid-type mischief escalates into a battle of the sexes.

©1935 by National Allied Publications, Inc.

A pair of youngsters from Cleveland, Ohio—writer Jerry Siegel and artist Joe Shuster—created Dr. Occult for *New Fun*. By the time these panels appeared in 1937, Siegel and Shuster were struggling to sell another of their creations—Superman.

©1937 by DC Comics, Inc.

troubles was that his new magazine simply wasn't selling. The comic book boom hadn't yet begun when he first offered *New Fun* to the world in 1935. In fact, the only other comic book on the newsstands was the fledgling *Famous Funnies*. Distributors were still reluctant to handle comic books and newsstands were even more reluctant to give them valuable rack space. Tom McNamara once recalled that Nicholson's Fourth Avenue loft was usually piled high with unsold, returned copies.

By 1936, as already noted, *Popular*, *Tip Top*, *King*, and *The Funnies* would all be in business. They, of course, all offered reprints of popular, well-established newspaper comics. The major, on the other hand, was trying to gain a foothold with a tabloid-size magazine full of unknown characters. A stubborn, if not overly practical man, he held on.

The sixth issue of the struggling magazine was cover-dated October 1935 and the seventh January 1936—a long time between issues for a comic book that was trying to build an audience and pass itself off as a monthly. In the interval it had shrunk in trim size, moving closer to the comic-book standard. It had also changed its name to *More Fun*. Color had been added and, as it entered its second year of life, the comic looked fairly presentable. The major and his editors, by this time Whitney Ellsworth and Vincent Sullivan, promoted the magazine's new look and title by utilizing the venerable advertising gambit of making

liabilities seem like assets and differences seem like strengths. The leadoff page in their first standard-size issue, after explaining that the magazine had changed because "so many people wrote in asking for *More Fun* in a smaller, handier size," went on to extol the book's virtues. One was that "everything between these covers is BRAND NEW, never before published," and another was the fact that "all the pictures, type, and lettering are clear and legible . . . no eyestrain."

The magazine now appeared much less like a compilation of rejected newspaper Sundays. Most of the strips filled two pages, usually of six panels each. The straight features outnumbered the humorous ones and just about every adventure strip ended with the words "to be continued." Some of the characters from *New Fun* were still kicking, including *Sandra of the Secret Service*, *Don Drake*, and *Little Linda*. Siegel and Shuster were continuing their *Doctor Occult* and had added *Henri Duval*, a musketeer saga starring a fellow who closely resembled the creators' boyhood idol, Douglas Fairbanks, Sr.

Red-headed hero Barry O'Neill was keeping up his battle with the Chinese villain Fang Gow, who also was known as "the inscrutable and vengeful enemy of the human race." Leo O'Mealia, who was rendering O'Neill's adventures, was in his fifties at the time and a veteran of several decades as a newspaper strip artist. He drew this Yellow Peril epic in a meticulous, melodramatic style perfectly suited to its flamboyant plots and prose. No stranger to sinister Orientals, O'Mealia had drawn the *Fu Manchu* newspaper strip that had had a modest two-year run in the early 1930s. He'd obtained further practice at depicting fog-shrouded streets and master villains when he drew the even less successful *Sherlock Holmes* comic strip in 1930. For *More Fun* O'Mealia also produced *Bob Merritt and His Flying Pals*. Handsome, clean-cut Bob was described as a "gentleman adventurer and inventor." If O'Mealia was getting only five dollars per page, he did an impressive amount of pen work to earn it.

Features came and went, as did cartoonists. Alex Blum took over *Ivanhoe*; an artist calling himself Sven Elven carried on *Treasure Island* and added *The Three Musketeers*; Siegel and Shuster abandoned *Henri Duval* for a new cops and robbers strip, *Radio Squad*. Tom Hickey assumed the drawing of *Wing Brady* and a science fiction tale called *Brad Hardy*.

Creig Flessel began working for *More Fun* with issue #12 (August 1936). In his middle twenties, he had been doing illustrations for pulp magazines for the past two years. Flessel had heard about the major's comic book activities by way of an ad in the *New York Times*. He remembers that Nicholson had "a continental air. Spats, a cane, a beaver hat, cigarette holder clenched between rotten teeth. He always bowed when he shook hands with you." Flessel drew *Pep Morgan*, about a college

Leo O'Mealia had illustrated the *Fu Manchu* newspaper strip in the early 1930s, and had become adept at drawing sinister Orientals. In this 1937 *Bob Merritt* page that ran in *More Fun*, our hero is at the mercy of some "silent Asiatics."

©1937 by DC Comics, Inc.

GEE, HE GOT LOOSE! HE'S GOING OVER THE BANK.

HEY?

PEP HURTLES HEAD OVER HEELS DOWN A 20 FOOT BANK—LANDING RIGHT SIDE UP!!!—

THE FINISH! PEP IS UNABLE TO OVERTAKE THE WINNER—BUT FINISHES SECOND GIVING HIS TEAM THE NEEDED 3 POINTS TO WIN THE MEET.

—FLESS—

College athlete Pep Morgan takes a tough fall in a 1937 *More Fun* adventure. Art is by Creig Flessel.

©1937 by DC Comics, Inc.

athlete, and *The Bradley Boys*, concerning two youths roughing it in the wilderness. He also began doing covers. A polished artist even then, Flessel displayed a slickness that many of his contemporaries lacked.

By the spring of 1937, *More Fun* was running fewer features but daring to innovate by giving most strips four entire pages. All of the adventure features continued, but each hero and heroine had been given more room to move around in. Because the major couldn't afford full color throughout, a dozen of his sixty-four pages were black and white, and another eight were three-color: black, white, and red. The December 1937 issue offered an eight-page western yarn titled *The Ucca Terror*. It was drawn by Homer Fleming, another veteran cartoonist, and was a complete, self-contained story. From then on, four-, six-, and eight-page stories dominated *More Fun*.

Undaunted by the lack of success of his tabloid-sized *New Fun Comics*, the intrepid Major Nicholson added a second magazine, *New Comics*, late in 1935. In shape, size, and general appearance, the premiere issue was close to what would become the standard format for comic books, except that *New Comics* contained eighty pages, sixteen more than the usual amount, and had an uncoated, non-glossy paper cover. Like its predecessor, the new comic book was not full color throughout, and offered a hodgepodge of adventure and comedy strips, and a variety of text features. As the title evolved, adventure fans could enjoy

Castaway Island, Slim and Tex, Captain Quick, Dale Daring, and *Federal Men*. On the light side were strips like *Dickie Duck, Sagebrush N' Cactus*, and *J. Worthington Blimp, Esq.* The obligatory text story often ran to six pages or more and there were columns devoted to radio, movies, puzzles, book reviews, magic tricks, cartooning tips, and letters from readers— "Marjorie Callaghan of 584 4th St., Brooklyn, says that getting a copy of NEW COMICS is like buying all the Sunday papers in the city just for the funnies, except that you get more in NEW COMICS."

New Comics was dubbed the "international picture story magazine" by its enterprising publisher. Included among the staffers responsible for living up to this lofty claim were business manager John Mahon and managing editor William Cook; Vincent Sullivan was initially assistant editor. Cook and Mahon, as we'll see, soon defected to start a comic book of their own. With the sixth issue, *New Comics* dropped to sixty-four pages and with the seventh started using heavier stock for covers.

The dynamic duo from Cleveland, Siegel and Shuster, came up with another feature, *Federal Men*, which began in *New Comics* #2 (January 1936). This was a serial strip starring Steve Carson, whose grim, sharp-featured profile probably made even Dick Tracy envious. Almost from the start, the young writer-artist team, unlike most of their peers, encouraged reader response to their feature. At the

Another sample of splendid *More Fun* artwork by Leo O'Mealia, as hero Barry O'Neill works to thwart the evil Fang Gow.

conclusion of the four-page episode in issue #3 they promised a "FREE original drawing of Steve Carson along with a personal message" to the fan who sent in "the most interesting and constructive letter." The magazine's fifth issue brought the Junior Federal Men Club; there was no charge to join at first, but dues eventually were set at a dime.

Very soon in *Federal Men*

Siegel and Shuster betrayed the fact that they were longtime science fiction enthusiasts. After introducing a gang of villains who operated a mysterious submarine, they tweaked the plot to include a criminal invasion of Washington, D.C. with a gigantic tank. Next came a mammoth robot, a metal colossus built along the lines of King Kong—"Populace Terrified by Nightmarish Invader!" Steve

Carson helps defeat "the scientific criminals who sought to capture America," and then it was back to machine guns and dope rings for a while.

Since the major's fondness for classics, and near classics, hadn't abated, *New Comics* offered an adaptation of Dickens's *A Tale of Two Cities* in two-page doses, from #4 onward. Commencing in #6, H. Rider Haggard's *She*, illustrated by ▶

MALCOLM WHEELER-NICHOLSON

Perhaps the most colorful figure in comic book history is Major Malcolm Wheeler-Nicholson, a onetime cavalry officer and prolific adventure writer who became one of the first moguls of the comic book industry.

©1930 by Argosy

Born in 1890, Malcolm Wheeler-Nicholson was at various times in his life a major in the U.S. Army cavalry, a fairly successful writer of action and adventure yarns for pulp-fiction magazines, and a not-so-successful publisher of comic books. Dapper and well-groomed, he had an erect military bearing, carried a cane, and wore spats. "I was born in the South," he once explained, "raised on a western ranch, worked for a while as a cub newspaper reporter, became a second lieutenant of cavalry in the regular army, chased bandits on the Mexican border, fought fevers and played polo in the Philippines, led a battalion of infantry against the Bolsheviki in Siberia, helped straighten out the affairs of the army in France, commanded the headquarters cavalry of the American force in the Rhine, and left the army as a major equipped with a select assortment of racing and polo cups, a saber, and a battered typewriter."

Nicholson's parting with the service in the early 1920s was not an especially amicable one.

An outspoken fellow, he'd made an assortment of charges against his senior officers and gone so far as to accuse them of Prussianism. These charges he also put into a letter to President Harding. That caused him considerable discomfort in the form of various charges brought against him by the army. It wasn't until 1924, after hearings and countercharges and threats of lawsuits by Nicholson, that the controversy ended. Nicholson, who'd already written professionally on military matters, took up that battered typewriter and embarked on a career as a writer of fiction. He was soon selling to many of the most popular pulps, especially to *Adventure* and *Argosy*. His specialties were stories of military action around the world and historical tales of intrigue and swordplay. His was a name that editors would showcase on their covers.

After the major was eased out of the comic book company he had founded, he returned to the writing of both fiction and nonfiction. He gradually dropped from sight and died in 1968.

Sven Elven, was serialized. More cultural uplift was provided by an adaptation of the King Arthur legend and a long-running Viking saga.

Comic books' first Tarzan impersonator appeared in *New Comics* #5. By the time the character, Sandor, set up shop in the jungle, the choices for animal surrogate parents had become restricted—other jungle heroes had been raised by apes, wolves, tigers, and lions. "In the deep jungles of Northern India lives a strange white youth known as Sandor," the copy gamely explained, "raised from infancy by a pack of wild dogs that now acknowledge him as their leader." Despite his humble upbringing, the golden-skinned Sandor did a commendable job as "the deadly enemy of Rajah Marajah, ruler of the people of the Lost Civilization." Homer Fleming was the artist.

Issue #5 also brought the debut of *Steve Conrad*. Nicely drawn by Creig Flessel, the initial episodes were printed in black and white. Steve, described as an "adventurer, scientist and inventor of the Cyanogen Cruiser," was involved in exploring Dolorosa Isle, "a tropical island with a mountain range, treacherous swamps, dense jungles, and an abundance of vegetation . . . it is not inhabited by man or beast!" That initial appraisal of real estate conditions on Dolorosa proved to be wildly inaccurate and soon Steve and his comrades, including a pretty blonde stowaway named Myrna, were up to their elbows in murderous savages and an evil ruler known

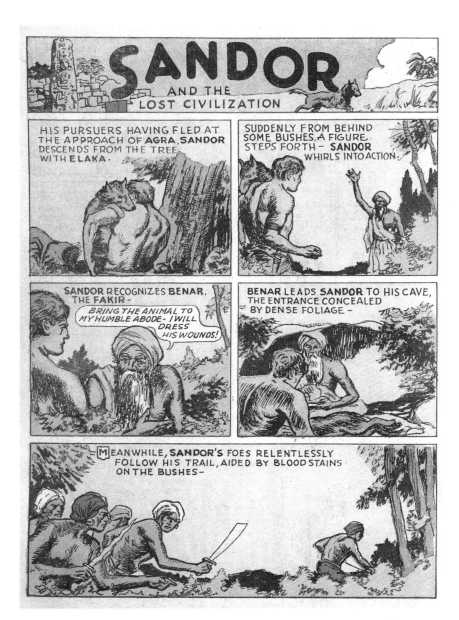

Tarzan, created by novelist Edgar Rice Burroughs, was wildly popular, and inspired countless comic book imitators. One of them was Sandor, who was featured in *New Comics*. Homer Fleming drew the adventures of this jungle lord, who had been raised by wild dogs.

©1937 by DC Comics, Inc.

Major Nicholson's *New Comics* #10, with cover art by Whitney Ellsworth. Two issues later, the comic's title would change to *New Adventure* and later still to *Adventure*.

©1936 by Nicholson Publishing Co., Inc.

as the Great Devachan. When color was added to the strip a few issues later, readers were unsettled to discover that most of the natives of the isle were a bright green.

The best funny material in the first issues of *New* was supplied by teenage Brooklyn cartoonist Sheldon Mayer. When asked how he first got together with the major, he replied, "I just walked into the office, because I saw the stuff on the newsstands and I wrote down the addresses. I'd been doing that all along with all sorts of things." Even though Major Nicholson never paid him, Mayer has said, "You couldn't hate him. He was a charmer." After showing his samples and getting an okay to do some features, the boy cartoonist asked if he might have a small advance with which to buy bristol board, ink, and other supplies. The major promptly wrote out a check for one dollar. When Mayer asked Cook and Mahon where he might cash it, Mahon took the check from him and handed him a dollar from his own pocket. Mayer has always believed the dollar was one that had come in from a reader that day for a subscription.

Mayer drew two features, both adapted from unsold newspaper strip ideas. *J. Worthington Blimp, Esq.*, as its title suggests, starred a plump windbag of a fellow who shared some of the attributes of W. C. Fields and Popeye's chum Wimpy. The continuity had to do with Blimp's attempts to cross the country on a bicycle. The strip had some of the freewheeling and rowdy flavor of

Billy DeBeck's *Barney Google*. In the other feature, *The Strange Adventures of Mr. Weed*, Mayer played with fantasy and time travel. Weed is a scholarly young fellow who teams up with a plump inventor to journey back to 1835 in a time machine the inventor has put together in his basement. The stories and dialogue in both strips were bright and Mayer, even at eighteen, was drawing like a pro.

With the twelfth issue *New Comics* became *New Adventure Comics*. For years one of the best markets for Major Nicholson's fiction had been the prestigious pulp *Adventure*, whose untrimmed pages he shared with Talbot Mundy, Harold Lamb, and scores of other top-rank pulp-fiction writers. Nicholson borrowed the successful pulp's name for his struggling comic, which soon began to transform itself. The most obvious change occurred on the cover. The word *New* waned and slid over to the far left; *Adventure* became dominant. The earliest covers that came after the name change were whimsical instead of flat-out funny. Less than ten issues later, though, dramatic action became the predominant cover element.

During its second year, *New Adventure* overhauled its interior, as well. While almost all the adventure features were carried on, they now filled from four to eight pages as opposed to the mere two favored earlier. In 1938 the magazine grew even more action oriented, and after #31 (October 1938) *New* was dropped from the logo entirely; with the next issue the magazine became simply *Adventure Comics*,

signaling the beginning of one of the longest-running titles in comic book history.

Another long-lived title, and the cornerstone of the DC empire, is *Detective Comics*, which got off to a modest start early in 1937. This was the last title the enterprising but underfunded Major Nicholson had his name attached to. The premiere issue was dated March 1937, and sported a cover featuring a sinister-looking Oriental, who glowers at the reader from against a crimson background. The new title had been hyped in December 1936 issues of Nicholson's other two titles, in ads that promised that *Detective Comics* was going to be "the most thrilling narrative-cartoon magazine in the comic field." The major's financial problems, however, were worsening and publication was delayed three months.

It was at about this time that Harry Donenfeld became more actively involved with Nicholson. An aggressive and gregarious man in his late thirties, Donenfeld had been involved in several aspects of the magazine business for most of the decade. He published pulp magazines under several company names and was a partner in the Independent News Company distribution operation. He also owned the printing plant that ran off covers for Major Nicholson's comics. Nicholson, who owed money for those covers, had also been advanced funds from Donenfeld's distribution wing. In order to get *Detective* launched, Nicholson was obliged to take on Donenfeld as a partner.

This issue of Major Nicholson's *New Adventure* features a cover embellished with a typically dramatic action scene.

©1938 by DC Comics, Inc.

As this *New Comics* ad explained, the comic was not only fun to read, but healthful, too: "YOU CAN READ WITHOUT DANGER OF HURTING YOUR EYES!" Art is by Vincent Sullivan.

A new company was formed to publish the latest title—Detective Comics, Inc.—and its owners were listed as Nicholson and J. S. Liebowitz. Liebowitz was Donenfeld's accountant. Contrary to most previously published accounts, Nicholson stayed on with *Detective Comics* throughout its entire first year and didn't give it up, along with his other titles, until 1938. Vincent Sullivan served as editor of *Detective*. A former newspaper sports cartoonist, he'd been with the major's shaky organization from almost the start. When asked many years later if he'd drawn that first cover of the magazine, he replied that he was pretty sure he had, since he'd been fascinated with the Fu Manchu brand of villainy at that time.

As implied by the comic's title, the initial issue featured nothing but detectives—more than a half dozen of them plus humorous fillers dealing with mystery and sleuthing.

Like the pulp detective fiction magazines and the movies that inspired it, *Detective Comics* dished out plenty of action, suspense, and violence. Many of the stories attempted formal mystery plotting, offering an array of suspects and clues. There was a little bit of everything, from tough cop to dapper amateur investigator. Speed Saunders, a plainclothes cop who covered the waterfront, occupied the leadoff spot. He was a clean-cut fellow with a fondness for trenchcoats. When the able Creig Flessel gave up the ace investigator in the spring of 1938, Fred Guardineer took over the drawing and Gardner Fox the scripting. Speed became tougher, abandoned the waterfront, and took to wearing plaid suits. His cases grew more violent and sometimes became downright gruesome.

Major Nicholson himself wrote the adventures of Brad Nelson, the "crack amateur sleuth" whose first adventure was entitled "The Claws of the Red Dragon." The storyline went on for eight issues and involved Nelson with unscrupulous Orientals, a lovely blonde, and a great deal of violence. Later Nelson cases included "The Blood of the Lotus," "Murder in the Clouds," and "The Song of Death." Tom Hickey, a disciple of newspaper-strip stars Alex Raymond and Milton Caniff, supplied the artwork.

An even suaver detective was Cosmo, also known as the Phantom of Disguise. He was a handsome fellow who solved cases all over the world. When the Manhattan police or the best brains of Scotland Yard were baffled, they turned to him— "Ah! Cosmo! Why didn't I think of him before? Let's call him in!" And for readers who liked a touch of sagebrush in their mysteries, the magazine offered Buck Marshall, who was a range detective by trade.

Although stuck at the tail end of the first issue, the closest thing to a star that *Detective* had was Slam Bradley. Billed as an "ace freelance sleuth, fighter and adventurer," he was another Siegel and Shuster creation. Slam's first case involved him in mystery and murder in the bowels of Chinatown. As his

name suggests, Slam was a rough and tumble operative who used his fists more often than he used a magnifying glass. He owed as much to Roy Crane's freewheeling soldier of fortune, Captain Easy, as he did to the private eyes of pulps and movies. And just as Easy had the diminutive Wash Tubbs as a sidekick, Slam had Shorty Morgan. They teamed up, after a considerable show of reluctance on Slam's part, during the first case.

Unlike many fictional private detectives, Slam rarely used a gun, relying instead on his fists and his nerve to arrive at a solution. One early investigation begins with his chasing a suspect circus performer right up onto the fellow's trapeze, another with Slam crashing through a roof after a parachute jump. He and Shorty solved crimes and misdemeanors in Hollywood, on Broadway, in Mexico, and the frozen North. Deeply enamored of science fiction, Siegel and Shuster eventually involved Slam and Shorty with rocket ships, magic, and even time travel. And it was on this feature that the creative team began experimenting with the use of full-page splash panels at a time when most comic book layouts were still as sedate as those of newspaper Sunday pages.

Spy was another Siegel & Shuster creation. The initial episode, which looks as though it was made up from unsold Sunday pages, introduced Bart Regan and his fiancée, Sally Norris. Working together each month in the give-and-take manner of Nick and Nora

Charles in the Thin Man movies, the couple led a fast-paced life in locations around the world while combating spies, saboteurs, and other enemies of Uncle Sam.

Despite its emphasis on detectives, *Detective Comics* wasn't all gloom and violence; quite a bit of comic crimebusting was going on, too. Sullivan and Whit Ellsworth, a co-editor on early issues, provided pages of gag cartoons. During the magazine's second years, cartoonist Bob Kane (remember that name) began a one-page filler featuring Oscar the Gumshoe.

The most sinister Oriental of all time set up shop in *Detective* #18 (July 1938). Departing from its policy of using only original material, the magazine began reprinting the *Fu Manchu* newspaper strip. This heady blend of Yellow Peril melodrama and flowery romance vanished after issue #27.

Detective got its first costumed hero in issue #20. The Crimson Avenger owed a great deal to a hero of another color, the Green Hornet. The Hornet had first taken to the air over Detroit's radio station WXYZ in 1936, and by the spring of 1938 was being heard nationwide on the Mutual radio network. Whereas the Hornet was Britt Reid, daring young publisher of the *Daily Sentinel*, the Crimson Avenger was Lee Travis, daring young publisher of the *Globe Leader*. The only person who knew the Hornet's true identity was his faithful valet, Kato. The Crimson Avenger's secret was shared only by his Chinese servant, Wing. Like the Hornet,

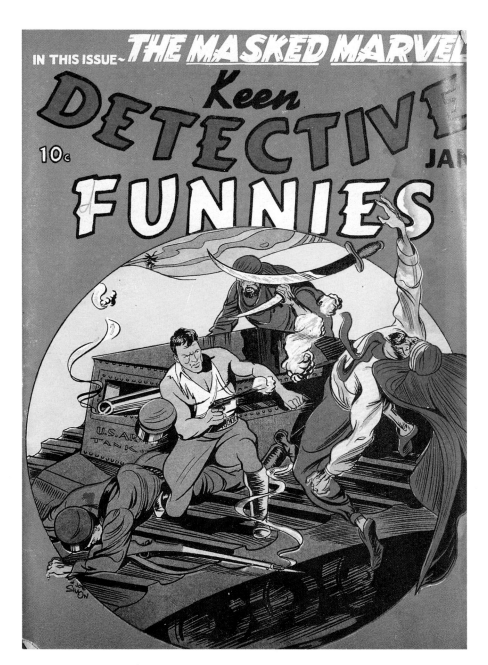

Centaur Pubications's *Keen Detective Funnies* had started as a Comics Magazine publication called *Detective Picture Stories*. This dramatic cover, from issue #13, was drawn by Joe Simon in 1938, before his momentous teaming with artist Jack Kirby.

the Crimson Avenger never used a deadly weapon, preferring instead to put his adversaries to sleep with a blast from his gas gun. As drawn by Jim Chambers, he wore a dark blue slouch hat, a domino mask, and a crimson, Inverness-style cape. Much flashier than the private eyes and cops with whom he shared the magazine, the Crimson Avenger had a moment of stardom when he was featured on the cover of *Detective* #22. Unfortunately for him, a new and more original costumed hero came along a few issues later. We'll talk more about this new character in Chapter 5.

As noted earlier, William Cook had worked briefly as managing editor on *New Fun* in 1935. In 1936 he and John Mahon, another defector from Major Nicholson's camp, formed the Comics Magazine Company, Inc. Their first title was *The Comics Magazine* (within a few months it became *Funny Pages*), and had a May 1936 cover date on the debut issue. Cook and Mahon promised their readers that everything was original and new and that "the creators of the features in this issue have established themselves with fans in all parts of the world." The early issues offered the same mixture of adventure and comedy as the major's magazines. In fact, some of the strips were unpublished *New Fun* and *New Comics* material. Sheldon Mayer was there with two strips, Siegel and Shuster's Dr. Occult was practicing his ghost detecting as Dr. Mystic, and *New Comics*' Federal Men feature was altered and issued as

Federal Agent. Later in 1936, *Funny Picture Stories* appeared, promising "Mystery Thriller, Ace Adventure, Western," and introducing George Brenner's character, the Clock, the first mystery man in comics.

The Clock was a natty fellow who did his detecting in tuxedo and gray fedora. He covered his face with a black silken mask and carried a gold-headed cane. Brenner, who wrote and drew the feature, was quite probably influenced by Leslie Charteris's Saint as well as by such dapper pulp crime fighters as the Phantom Detective. Just as the Saint left behind a card adorned with a haloed stick figure, The Clock left a card with the depiction of a timepiece and the slogan *The Clock Has Struck.*

Detective Picture Stories was the next offering from Comics Magazine Company, and was devoted to the single theme of crime detection. "Here is a magazine crammed full of color, action, plot and punch," promised a subscription ad. "You'll see why crime does not pay, why the police always put the finger on the criminal." The stories were longer than those in the Nicholson magazines, up to ten pages, and all were self-contained. There were no regularly featured "star" detectives. Story titles were reminiscent of those in pulp magazines: "Murder in the Blue Room," "The Diamond Dick," "The Phantom Killer." Among the artists were Bert Christman, Ed Moore, and George Brenner. Although the first issue's cover promised a Clock story, none showed up inside. The fourth

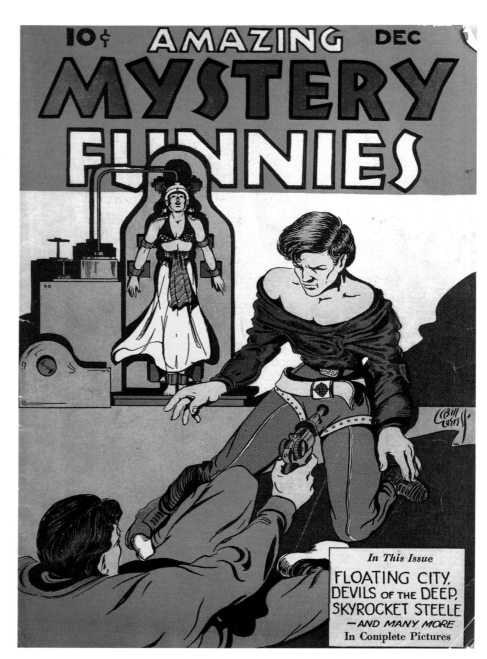

Amazing Mystery Funnies was another Centaur comic book. The cover of this issue, #3, is by Bill Everett, and features Skyrocket Steele.

©1938 by Centaur Publications, Inc.

issue contained *Muss 'em Up*, an early effort by writer-artist Will Eisner.

Despite a line of three titles, Cook and Mahon did not do well. By the middle of 1937 they had sold out to an outfit called Ultem Publications. Ultem in turn sold its interests the following year to Joseph Hardie, who made the magazines the basis of his Centaur Publications, Inc. *Detective Picture Stories* became *Keen Detective Funnies* (a snappy title!) in the summer of 1938. Lloyd Jacquet, another Nicholson alum, was the editor. The retitled magazine's first star was the Clock. Of the sleuths who appeared in support, a character with one foot in the costumed-adventurer camp was the Masked Marvel. Most of *Keen*'s other detectives were more prosaic. These included Thurston Hunt, Terry Taylor, and Rock Baird. In the sixth issue a scientific sleuth named Dean Denton joined the lineup.

Over time, a variety of detective characters continued to check in and out of the magazine. There were Stony Dawson, TNT Todd of the FBI, and Little Dynamite. This last one was the first adventure feature by artist Jack Cole to see print—Cole would go on to do brilliantly clever work in the forties and fifties.

A farsighted entrepreneur named Harry "A" Chesler was one of the first to suspect that there was going to be a comic book industry in America. His initial by the way, didn't stand for anything and was stuck into the middle of his name and set off by quotes for no other reason than

Chesler liked the way it looked. In 1936 Harry "A", who neither drew nor wrote, opened an office at 276 Fifth Avenue in Manhattan and set up what was the first comic art shop. Hiring artists and writers who'd work cheaply, he began to produce features for the original-material comic magazines. The field being what it was at the time, the pioneering shop initially had only two customers—Major Nicholson and the renegade Cook-Mahon outfit. Late in 1936 Chesler decided to branch out into publishing and the result was two new titles, *Star Comics* and *Star Ranger*, both cover-dated February 1937. These were initially slightly larger than their newsstand rivals, measuring 8 inches by 11, but running just forty-eight pages.

Star Comics offered a blend of adventure and humor features, most of them one to three pages in length. The exceptions were *Dan Hastings*, which went to eight, and *The Mad Goddess*, which came in at seven. The *Hastings* opus was laid out in Sunday-page style and bears a 1935 copyright date, indicating that Chesler had made an unsuccessful attempt to peddle it as a newspaper feature. A science fiction adventure, *Dan Hastings,* was first drawn by Clemens Gretter and carried on by Fred Guardineer.

The Mad Goddess was set "in the jungles of South America," and drawn by Robert L. Golden. It was billed as "a complete adventure story." Other artists in the first issue were Creig Flessel, Fred Schwab, Henry C. Kiefer, and Dick Moores, who was

represented by *King Kole's Court*, another unsold Sunday page. Moores eventually took over the *Gasoline Alley* newspaper strip.

Star Ranger, filled entirely with cowboys, both serious and whimsical, was the first comic book devoted entirely to the West. Ken Fitch served as editor and wrote many of the stories. Several prolific pulp-fiction writers also got credits, including Norman Daniels and Tom Curry. Among the early artists were Flessel, Guardineer, Schwab, and Rafael Astarita.

After publishing a half dozen issues of each of the magazines, Chesler sold them. Eventually they came under Joseph Hardie's Centaur banner. *Star Comics* continued to concentrate on short material, an average issue containing as many as three dozen different features. Among the other contributors were artists Jack Cole, Ken Ernst, Bob Wood, and Charles Biro. Robert Winsor McCay, signing himself Winsor McCay, Jr., revived his father's best-known creation and drew some sadly uninspired *Little Nemo* pages for the magazine. In its latter-day issues *Star Comics* included Tarpé Mills's *Diana Dean in Hollywood*, Paul Gustavson's *Speed Silvers*, and Carl Burgos's *The Last Pirate*. All of these artists went on to better things.

Star Comics survived for twenty-three issues before expiring in the summer of 1939. *Star Ranger*, after undergoing a couple of title changes (*Cowboy Comics*, followed by *Star Ranger Funnies*), folded in the fall of the same year.

CHAPTER FOUR

T he original-material comic books gradually moved away from imitating the look of their reprint rivals. In addition to fewer panels per page, Major Nicholson and his followers came increasingly to use complete stories and ones that ran from six to eight pages. They also realized the importance of recurring characters in building reader loyalty. Interestingly enough, however, both kinds of early comic books tended to stress the *quantity* of features available and to avoid giving any one character favored treatment.

The reprint titles, such as *Famous Funnies*, *Tip Top*, and *Crackajack*, featured bunches of characters on their covers. *Comics on Parade*, for instance, didn't allow a character to solo on a cover until Li'l Abner was given the nod for the seventh issue. *Ace Comics* didn't disperse the crowds until the cover of the fourteenth issue, when the aggressively nonheroic Katzenjammer Kids began a several-year run as cover boys. During its initial year in business, *New Comics* used only funny covers, most of them

Comic books did not spring full blown from a vacuum. Pulp magazines, movie serials, Big Little Books, and other forms of popular entertainment influenced comic books' development. Here, it's cross and doublecross as a trio of miscreants falls under the watchful eye of pulp avenger the Black Bat.

©1939 by Better Publications, Inc.

drawn by Whit Ellsworth. Issue #15 (May 1937) marked the first time the magazine, now titled *New Adventure*, sported a straight adventure cover. Creig Flessel drew that as well as the next one, which depicted Steve Carson of *Federal Men*. Flessel did the next sixteen covers in a row, none of which made use of any of *Adventure*'s characters. It was not until the advent of Sandman in #40 (July 1939) that a hero from within the magazine showed up again on its front.

Detective Comics followed a similar policy, although all of its covers stressed mystery and action rather than humor. With issue #18 (August 1938), that top-seeded Oriental menace, Fu Manchu, became the first interior character to be shown on a cover. The cover of issue #22 (December 1938) featured the masked crimebuster called the Crimson Avenger, who had the distinction of being the first *Detective hero* to rate a cover.

The situation was no different with DC's competition. For example, Centaur's *Funny Pages* utilized nothing but comedy covers for twenty-nine issues, few of which made use of characters to be found inside the magazine. *Funny Pages* didn't depict a hero, a chap named the Arrow, until the summer of 1939. *Funny Picture Stories* showcased the Clock on the cover of its first issue, then switched to adventure covers that highlighted detectives, explorers, Royal Mounties, and similarly generic heroes. After that came a dozen gag covers.

By imitating the Sunday comic sections and some pulp magazines of the anthology type, such as *Adventure* and *Argosy*, the early comic book titles of the 1930s overlooked two of the basic rules of catering to a young audience. Namely, that kids like larger-than-life heroes and they don't usually like them in bunches. In time, comic book publishers got the hint, and joined in on the wholesale manufacture of fictional heroes that was already going on in other, competing media.

Fictional heroes had become increasingly accessible to the broad American public in the 19th century. From the early 1800s onward, Americans grew more literate and printing methods became faster and cheaper. As the century progressed, more and more people were able to, and wanted to, read about famous men—politicians, soldiers, and celebrities. Besides stories of real-life men of accomplishment, the unfolding 19th century offered a growing number of made-up heroes. Somewhere in between were larger-than-life figures such as Daniel Boone, Davy Crockett, Kit Carson, and Buffalo Bill, who entered the public consciousness via published adventures that were partly real and a good deal fictitious.

Magazines blossomed and so did inexpensive books; adolescents were especially fond of the many five-cent fiction weeklies and the ubiquitous "dime novels." Fictional heroes continued to multiply right on through the end of the 19th century and into the next. Readers responded to figures

Man overboard as the Sandman does his bit for justice in 1939.

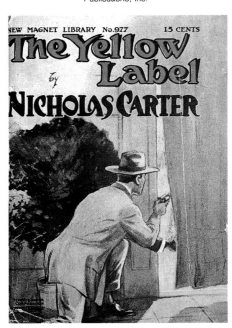

A 1915 "dime novel" (of the fifteen-cent variety) featuring hero Nick Carter.

FRANK READE

WEEKLY MAGAZINE.

Containing Stories of Adventures on Land, Sea & in the Air.

Issued Weekly—By Subscription $2.50 per year. Application made for Second-Class Entry at N. Y. Post Office.

No. 57.   NEW YORK, NOVEMBER 27, 1903.   Price 5 Cents.

FROM TROPIC TO TROPIC !

OR, FRANK READE, JR.'S TOUR WITH HIS BICYCLE CAR.

By "NONAME."

Frank Reade, Jr. hits the jungle trail with his fabulous bicycle car. This adventure was devoured by young readers in 1903.

©1903 by Frank Tousey

like Old Sleuth, Frank Reade, Jr., Nick Carter, Frank Merriwell, Deadwood Dick, Young Wild West, and Roaring Ralph Rockwood the Ruthless Ranger.

Gradually, pulp magazines supplanted the dime novels and fiction weeklies. Heroes were plentiful in the pulps. Like the comic books that came later, pulps usually sold for ten cents a copy. They sported colorful, often lurid covers and usually measured 9½ by 7½ inches. Page counts ranged from 114 to 162.

One of the earliest and most influential of the pulp mystery men appeared in 1914 in Street & Smith's *People Magazine*. Jimmie Dale, alias the Gray Seal, was the creation of Canadian author Frank L. Packard. Inspired by such earlier figures as Raffles and Jimmy Valentine, Jimmie Dale did them one better. He had an alternate identity, that of the Gray Seal, a mysterious, masked avenger who prowled the midnight streets of Manhattan. Hunted by the law, yet actually a man dedicated to justice, he struck swiftly and left behind only a small sticker, the notorious gray seal. In the everyday world Jimmie Dale was a wealthy playboy, but he had several other identities as well. "As Larry the Bat, the dope fiend, he slinks through the dens of Chinatown," explained one blurb. "As Smarlinghue, the artist, he cadges beers in the Bowery, and as the Gray Seal . . . he uses clues and tips gathered in these disguises to battle and confound the underworld."

The leading creator of phantom detectives and mystery

men was a onetime newspaper reporter from the Midwest named Johnston McCulley. Although he created one of the most famous masked men of the 20th century, McCulley is little remembered and seldom written about. Regardless, McCulley made his mark, for it was in the spring of 1919 that his serial "The Curse of Capistrano" began in Munsey's *All-Story Weekly*. This five-part story introduced Zorro to the world.

While Zorro was McCulley's best-known character and one about whom the ex-newsman wrote more than sixty novels and stories, Zorro was only one of the many dual identity characters McCulley created. He also introduced a hooded villain called Black Star and a mysterious criminal known as the Spider (a very popular name through the years for both heroes and villains). In the 1920s, McCulley created a gallery of masked good guys, including the Thunderbolt, the Man in Purple, and the Crimson Clown.

The most important pulp mystery man of the thirties was the Shadow. His first adventure was published early in 1931, and was the creation of a young man named Walter B. Gibson. Using the pen name Maxwell Grant, Gibson wrote nearly three hundred novels about the scourge of crime over the next two decades. While the Shadow was somewhat similar to earlier pulp avengers, such as Zorro and the Gray Seal, he dressed much more like a sinister villain, in black cloak and slouch hat. His weapons of choice were twin .45

automatics. Several comic book heroes, most notably Batman, would also use their costumes to strike fear into the hearts of their foes. (Interestingly, Batman packed a pistol in his earliest adventures.)

The Shadow was not an easy man to get to know. In the first novels, in fact, even Gibson didn't seem quite sure who the Shadow was. Unlike the Jimmie Dale novels, there were no interludes in the Shadow stories that showed the real Shadow relaxing with friends before slipping into a disguise. The Shadow never appeared before the reader undisguised. Often he lurked in the background, emulating the sinister menace of a horror film. He had a love of obfuscation and dim lighting and came across as a man who would wear a mask even when he's alone in a pitch black room.

The early Shadow stories were heavy with disappearances, fireworks, surprises, and mysterious atmosphere. The Shadow novels, especially those of the early 1930s, were usually about the people the character worked through, the crooks he destroyed, and the agents he manipulated. Gradually the Shadow acquired an assortment of alter egos that opened up the stories and gave the character more room to move about. His best-known pseudo-identity was that of Lamont Cranston, millionaire playboy. He was also fond of appearing as Fritz, the janitor at police headquarters. Eventually, in the late thirties, it was revealed that the Shadow was actually a noted aviator named Kent Allard, though by

The Shadow, omnipresent and fearless, held the criminal world in his thrall.

©1933 by Street & Smith Publications, Inc.

Cover art from the January 1, 1933 issue of the Shadow pulp (above) was recycled seven years later for the Shadow comic book.

©1933, 1940 by Street & Smith Publications, Inc.

Pulp hero Doc Savage—
seen here on the cover of a
1935 issue of his
magazine—strongly
influenced the creators of
Superman.

©1935 by Street & Smith Publications,
Inc.

The Shadow, the most
memorable of all pulp
avengers, prepares to mete
out justice from an
unexpected hiding place.

©1933 by Street & Smith Publications,
Inc.

The well-heeled pulp hero
known as the Phantom
Detective spent a day at the
races in 1946.

©1946 by Standard Magazines, Inc.

that time most readers thought he was actually Lamont Cranston.

Street & Smith, publisher of *The Shadow*, scored again in 1933 with *Doc Savage*. The brilliant, overpoweringly strong Doc—known to all as the Man of Bronze—was to have a considerable influence on the development of Superman. Quick-witted, muscular, and phsyically fearless, Doc had devoted his life to "striving to help those who needed it, punishing those who deserved it." Unlike the Shadow, Doc was

not a killer but a nobler, less frightening figure. Written by Lester Dent under the pseudonym Kenneth Robeson, the Doc Savage adventures were frequently science-fictional and filled with outlandish gadgets—futuristic weapons or tools that Doc could count on to get him out of tight spots.

Doc and the Shadow—each defining "hero" in a way completely different from the other—were perhaps the preeminent pulp heroes. Most of the other successful pulp heroes of the decade fell into the

mystery man category. These included the Spider and the Phantom Detective, both of whom began to stalk and fight crime in 1933. Secret Agent X first showed up on the scene (in disguise) in 1934. His "ability as an impersonator is a combination of superlative voice mimicry, character acting that great Thespians might well envy, and a sculptorlike skill in modeling plastic material over his own features so that they resemble those of another man." The Whisperer came along in 1936 and the Avenger in 1939. Finally,

Issue #1 of the *Whisperer* pulp. The character—the alter ego of police commissioner "Wildcat" Gordon—first appeared as a backup feature in the *Shadow* pulp.

©1936 by Street & Smith Publications, Inc.

The Black Bat gets the drop on a killer on this gory *Black Book Detective* pulp cover from 1939.

©1939 by Better Publications, Inc.

Outfitted with pith helmet and .45 automatic for his adventure in the Canal Zone, the Masked Detective was a particularly rugged pulp hero.

©1942 by Better Publications, Inc.

in 1940, the Green Lama arrived.

Most of the mysterious avengers of the pulps, except for Secret Agent X, had alternate civilian identities. An unusually large percentage were wealthy, big-city playboys. Not surprisingly, perhaps, a great many comic book crimefighters and superheroes would be recruited from the playboy class. Other elements of the pulp hero milieu that were carried over into comics were the Criminal Mastermind and the Fiendish Plot. The Shadow contended, for instance, with recurring villains like the notorious Voodoo Master and the sinister Shiwan Khan. The Spider had to deal with such problems as "a city swept by Bubonic Plague"; with an epidemic that turns America's finest families into a "set of swanky thieves and killers"; with the Emperor of Hades, who "scattered his scarlet, slaying devil-dust" over Manhattan; with five thousand mad dogs who go on a rampage in Cologne, Ohio (!); and with dozens of equally unsettling villains and situations. Doc Savage had his hands full, too: He met the Thousand Headed Man, the Red Skull, the Thing that Pursued, and others.

Such carryings-on were the stuff of vivid, highly salable adventure, so the pulp fiction magazines did not hesitate to frequently feature a leading hero on a cover, or to devote an entire magazine to a single character. But comic books, as noted earlier, were slow to follow.

Fictional heroes weren't restricted to the printed page, of course; they had been a longtime staple of the movies, and one form of packaging that especially appealed to youth was the serial.

These "continued-next-week" chapter plays had started showing up in movie theaters during the second decade of the 20th century. Many of the earliest cliffhangers were built around the exploits of heroines—*The Adventures of Kathlyn*, *The Perils of Pauline*, *The Hazards of Helen*, *The Exploits of Elaine*, and other silent serials tickled audiences with edge-of-the-seat predicaments of beautiful, daring women.

Serials quickly grew in popularity; film historian Alan G. Barbour estimates that more than 250 of them were released between 1913 and 1930. During the thirties, an era that saw the advent of the double bill and the flourishing of the Saturday and Sunday matinee, serials continued to be an important Hollywood product. In that decade well over a hundred sound serials were produced. They ran from twelve to fifteen chapters, with each chapter lasting about fifteen to twenty minutes. In order to follow a 1930s serial hero from his first moment of peril to the final unmasking of the villain a kid had to attend every weekend matinee at the local movie house for three to four months—a pretty long time to be kept in suspense!

Movie screens overflowed with serial heroes of every stripe and job description. Cowboys were popular and often were played by B-movie favorites such as Tim McCoy, Tom Mix, Buck Jones, and Gene Autry. There were also explorers, wonder dogs, G-Men, aviators, Marines,

The crimefighting Spider spins his web on the cover of his first issue.

©1933 by Popular Publications

Pulp magazine covers did not shy away from grue, as this 1938 *Spider* cover attests.

©1938 by Popular Publications

and Royal Canadian Mounted Policemen.

The mask was an important chapter play prop, useful to both bad guys and good guys. Included among the masked crimefighters were the Phantom Rider, Zorro, the Lone Ranger, the Copperhead, the Green Hornet, The Shadow, and the Spider. These last two, of course, were adapted from the pulps.

Several serials were inspired by the exploits of newspaper-strip heroes. Flash Gordon and Buck Rogers, both played by Buster Crabbe, were featured in successful movie cliffhangers, as were Dick Tracy, Tailspin Tommy, Don Winslow, Secret Agent X-9, and Mandrake the Magician.

Moviemakers weren't the only ones to take an increased interest in kids during the 1930s. Advertisers, too, saw dollar signs when they looked at youngsters. The favored medium for reaching them during this Depression decade was radio. In those long ago years radio provided much more than just the music and information that are staples of today's broadcasts. There was also an infinite variety of drama and comedy.

A great many radio programs were designed to appeal to children and many of these were built around adventure heroes. The shows, usually in a serial format and aired five times a week in fifteen-minute segments, were heard chiefly during the children's hour. That was a period that might start as early as 4:30 in the afternoon and run as late as 6:00. Just as women's daytime serials were sponsored

One thin dime brought pulp readers the latest adventure of Doc Savage. This advertisement is from 1934.

©1934 by Street & Smith Publications, Inc.

Olympic swimming champion Larry "Buster" Crabbe (second from right) became a Hollywood star when he took the lead in three exciting *Flash Gordon* serials. Lively and full of fun, these chapter plays remain popular today.

©1936 by Universal Pictures

primarily by the makers of soap and other domestic products, the kids' serials were sponsored by breakfast-food manufacturers and other makers of things to eat and drink.

Among the earliest kid radio serials were *Skippy, Little Orphan Annie*—both adapted from newspaper comics—and *The Air Adventures of Jimmy Allen*. One of the first mystery men to take to the airwaves was the Lone Ranger. Originating at the studios of WXYZ in Detroit, the adventures of the masked rider of the plains were aired after the children's hour, in complete half-hour episodes three times a week. The show was first broadcast in January of 1933 and eventually was heard on stations throughout the country. It was sponsored regionally, by an assortment of bread companies.

WXYZ did so well with their first masked man that they introduced another one in 1936, a contemporary urban avenger known as the Green Hornet. With his mask, gas gun, powerful automobile, faithful chauffeur, and vigilante ways, the Hornet was to prove an important influence on later creators of comic book heroes.

An equally inspiring figure of radio mystery was the Shadow, heard once a week in a half-hour format, commencing in 1937. Portrayed originally by twenty-two-year-old Orson Welles, the radio Shadow differed from his pulp counterpart. His civilian identity was definitely that of wealthy man about town Lamont Cranston, his friend and companion was the lovely Margo Lane and, a definite plus, he had

the ability to become invisible. Less a coldblooded avenger than his pulp counterpart, the radio Shadow dealt not only with crooks and criminal masterminds but with madmen, monsters, and an entertaining variety of occult terrors. Though he also appealed to an adult listening audience, the Shadow had a large youth following and was obviously highly thought of by several of the artists and writers who were earning their living in comic books.

Of the other popular kid radio shows of the 1930s, some were adapted from the funny papers and some were created expressly for radio. All told, the kid shows comprised a large list that included *Jack Armstrong, Tom Mix, Dick Tracy, Tarzan, Buck Rogers, Chandu the Magician, Smilin' Jack, Terry and the Pirates*, and *Captain Midnight*. Wheaties, Ovaltine, and Hot Ralston were typical of the sponsoring products.

By the late 1930s, popular media in America encompassed film, radio, and pulp magazines. The modern-format comic book had been established and the number of regularly issued titles was increasing. Although most editors, writers, and artists were freely assimilating types of characters and storytelling methods of newspaper funnies and other media, some of them were beginning to realize that the comic book was a separate medium altogether. It was a canny observation, but what was needed now to turn the blossoming business into a full-scale industry was the right kind of hero.

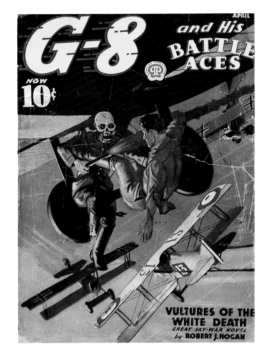

The world of aviation provided the springboard for many adventure stories— in print, on radio, and on film. *G-8 and His Battle Aces*, a popular pulp magazine, featured some of the best and most imaginative. Here, G-8 faces terror in a 1937 adventure.

©1937 by Popular Publications, Inc.

Another great aviator— seen here on the cover of a 1942 Big Little Book—was Captain Midnight, the star of a popular radio show aimed at youngsters.

©1937 by General Mills, Inc.

"IT'S . . . SUPERMAN!"

Comic books needed help—it was definitely a job for Superman. The trouble was that no comic book publisher seemed to realize that the Man of Steel was exactly the sort of hero that was needed to revolutionize the business. The creation of a pair of teenagers—writer Jerry Siegel and artist Joe Shuster—Superman was born in Cleveland, Ohio in the early 1930s. He languished there for several years, making occasional assaults on Manhattan and trying to get somebody to pay attention to him. Finally, in 1938, the big guy got a break and started appearing in *Action Comics*. Single-handedly he (and alter-ego Clark Kent) turned comic books into big business, changing their look and content forever. He also made several of the people associated with him impressively rich. For a while, even his creators prospered.

The notion of a superman was, obviously, not a new one; tales of super men date back to antiquity. Siegel and Shuster certainly drew from classical influences, but also took cues from Philip Wylie's 1930 novel *Gladiator,* which had introduced a contemporary version of the superman concept. The book's hero, Hugo Danner, possesses exceptional physical strength and is very nearly invulnerable. According to Wylie's biographer, Truman Frederick Keefer, "One of the main challenges to Wylie in writing *Gladiator* was the need to devise spectacular feats for Hugo to perform and then to make them seem probable. Our exposure to the *Superman* comic strip unfortunately obscures the originality of many of these inventions, which, according to Wylie, as well as recent scholars, were 'borrowed' from *Gladiator*. Hugo hurtling across a river in a single leap, bounding fifty feet straight up in the air, holding a cannon above his head with one arm, killing a shark by ripping its jaws apart, felling a charging bull with a fist between the eyes, lifting an automobile by its bumper and turning it around in the road—all of these were, in 1930, fresh and new and very exciting to read about."

Superman was influenced by other fictional heroes, as well. There were earlier dual-identity heroes like Zorro and the Shadow, and there was Doc Savage, whose first name was Clark. Siegel told the *Saturday Evening Post* that he'd conceived the character this way—"I am lying in bed counting sheep when all of a sudden it hits me. I conceive a character like Samson, Hercules and all the strong men I ever heard of rolled into one. Only more so."

Siegel was also aware of the tremendous appeal of his basic concept. "You see, Clark Kent

The rescue of attractive young women who had fallen from windows became a familiar part of Superman's daily routine.
©1940 by DC Comics, Inc.

Superman was an almost immediate success, and quickly proved himself as useful under the sea as on land and in the air.
©1939 by DC Comics, Inc.

grew not only out of my private life, but also out of Joe's," Siegel told an interviewer a few years ago. "As a high school student, I thought that some day I might become a reporter, and I had crushes on several attractive girls who either didn't know I existed or didn't care I existed. It occurred to me: What if I was real terrific? What if I had something special going for me, like jumping over buildings or throwing cars around or something like that? Then maybe they would notice me."

Indeed, it is the mild-mannered Clark Kent who gives Superman such great and enduring appeal. Worthy but underappreciated, Kent is the alter-ego not just of Superman, but of many of Superman's fans. Siegel nailed it when he remembered that he had wanted to be noticed. Superman provided Clark with a way to be noticed, and provided the same thing, vicariously, to the comic's readers.

Initially, it was syndicates and comic book editors who failed to notice *Superman*. A typical rejection letter for the strip read, "We are in the market only for strips likely to have the most extraordinary appeal, and we do not feel that *Superman* gets into that category." Sheldon Mayer was a bit more astute. "What happened was this," he once explained. "It came into the McClure Syndicate, offered as a strip. I went nuts over the thing; it was the thing we were all looking for. It struck me as having the elements that were popular in the movies, all the elements that were popular in

This Superman page is from *Superman* #1, and originally appeared in the first issue of *Action Comics,* the comic book in which Siegel and Shuster's immortal hero made his first appearance. Note that Superman's flying was initially more akin to leaping, and that his familiar "S" crest had not yet taken its final form.

©1939 by DC Comics, Inc.

novels, and all the elements that I loved."

The problem was Mayer couldn't convince M. C. Gaines or any of the McClure officials to sign on the feature. "They asked me what I thought of it. I thought it was great. And they kept sending it back." Mayer's persistence got Gaines interested enough to look the material over again. "He took it and looked at it and read it, and he said, 'You think this is good?' And I said, 'Yeah!'"

Rather than persuade the syndicate to use *Superman*, Gaines "had a better idea. He was going to take it up and offer it as a comic book so we could get the printing out of it. In other words, he was a proper businessman. He knew where he stood."

Just before his departure from the company, Major Nicholson had worked with his staff on a fourth title. It was to be called either *Action Funnies* or *Action Comics*. The major didn't get to see that one through and by the time DC's *Action Comics* was ready to roll, he was out on the street. Legend has it that Gaines showed the *Superman* strips to Harry Donenfeld himself and persuaded the publisher to add the feature to the forthcoming magazine. Vincent Sullivan, who was editor of *Action*, recalled things somewhat differently. "Donenfeld had little or nothing to do with the selection of features and things of that nature," he once explained. The samples were shown directly to editor Sullivan. "When they showed this thing to me that

Beautiful in its power and simplicity, the cover of *Superman* #1 captures much of the character's timeless appeal.

©1939 by DC Comics, Inc.

The panels read:

AS THE LAD GREW OLDER, HE LEARNED TO HIS DELIGHT THAT HE COULD HURDLE SKYSCRAPERS . . .

. . . LEAP AN EIGHTH OF A MILE . . .

. . . RAISE TREMENDOUS WEIGHTS . . .

. . . RUN FASTER THAN A STREAMLINE TRAIN --

. . . AND NOTHING LESS THAN A BURSTING SHELL COULD PENETRATE HIS SKIN!

WHAT TH' — ? THIS IS THE SIXTH HYPODERMIC NEEDLE I'VE BROKEN ON YOUR SKIN!

TRY AGAIN, DOC!

THE PASSING AWAY OF HIS FOSTER-PARENTS GREATLY GRIEVED CLARK KENT. BUT IT STRENGTHENED A DETERMINATION THAT HAD BEEN GROWING IN HIS MIND.

CLARK DECIDED HE MUST TURN HIS TITANIC STRENGTH INTO CHANNELS THAT WOULD BENEFIT MANKIND AND SO WAS CREATED--

SUPERMAN
CHAMPION OF THE OPPRESSED, THE PHYSICAL MARVEL WHO HAD SWORN TO DEVOTE HIS EXISTENCE TO HELPING THOSE IN NEED!

Superman was not merely the "champion of the oppressed," but a bona fide publishing phenomenon.

they'd been trying to sell, it looked good to me, and I started it. That's how *Superman* got going."

The story that appeared in *Action Comics* #1 (June 1938) offered a one-page introduction to the new hero, listing his birthplace only as "a distant planet" and making no mention of his real or adoptive parents. Page two began in the middle of the story, with Superman carrying a pretty nightclub singer through the air. The story ends with the words "to be continued." Siegel and Shuster's final panel said, "And so begins the startling adventures of the most sensational strip character of all time: SUPERMAN!" The grammar may have been weak, but the predictive aspect was dead on.

That first adventure was, according to Shuster, "taken directly from the newspaper strip. They were in a rush to meet the deadline on the first issue. Everything happened very fast. They made the decision to publish it and said to us, 'Just get out and turn out 13 pages based on your strip.' It was a rush job. . . . The only solution Jerry and I could come up with was to cut up the strips into panels and paste the panels on a sheet the size of the page."

The first *Action* cover was adapted from a panel in the story. "When Harry Donenfeld first saw that cover of Superman holding that car in the air," Mayer recalled, "he really got worried. He felt that nobody would believe it, that it was ridiculous . . . crazy." Possibly because of that, the next few covers didn't show Superman or even mention him. Drawn by Leo O'Mealia, they showed scenes of plausible adventure involving airplanes, Arabs, and Mounties. At the time, no one except Siegel, Shuster, and Mayer had great expectations for *Superman*. Vince Sullivan, when asked if he'd anticipated the new hero's success, replied, "No, I don't think anybody did." He said he'd simply bought the feature because "it looked good. It was different and there was a lot of action. This is what kids wanted."

The public, heavily weighted with Depression-reared kids who wanted the most they could get for their dimes, was far quicker than DC to grasp the new character's appeal. From the moment the youngsters saw Superman lift that car over his head, they recognized that he was something special. But according to John Kobler's profile of Siegel and Shuster in the June 21, 1941 issue of the *Saturday Evening Post*, the sales on the first three issues of *Action* were not particularly impressive. "But with the fourth, *Action Comics* spurted mysteriously ahead of its fellow publications," Kobler related. "Donenfeld heard the rumble of distant drums. 'We better have a newsstand survey,' said he. The survey quickened his brightened hopes. Children were clamoring not for *Action Comics*, but for 'that magazine with Superman on it.' Quivering with excitement, Donenfeld ordered Superman splashed all over the cover of succeeding issues. They sold out."

The sales of *Action* quickly rose to 500,000 a month and by 1941 the magazine was selling 900,000 copies of each issue. The *Superman* magazine, started in 1939, soon reached a circulation of 1,250,000 and grossed $950,000 in 1940.

Superman continued to proliferate. He got a newspaper strip of his own, syndicated by McClure. It was here, in this newspaper strip, that a detailed account of the destruction of the planet Krypton was given for the first time, along with scenes of the baby Superman being rocketed to Earth, like a streamlined Moses, in a ship of his father's invention. The strip devoted two whole weeks to Superman's parents, Jor-L and Lora, and to all the dire seismic events leading up to his emigration. By the third week Superman, in his guise of Clark Kent, was seen working as a mild-mannered reporter and had met co-worker Lois Lane.

Some of the best-known dramatic lines associated with the character originated not in the comics but on the radio show. This program, inaugurated on a national basis early in 1940, was heard mostly in the eastern United States during its first few months. Eventually, three fifteen-minute episodes were broadcast each week from New York, airing in most parts of the nation on Monday, Wednesday, and Friday sometime between five and six in the evening. Clayton "Bud" Collyer starred; the adventures were narrated by Jackson Beck.

It was the radio show that introduced such memorable phrases as, "Up, up and away!" and "This is a job for . . . Superman!" The show's opening

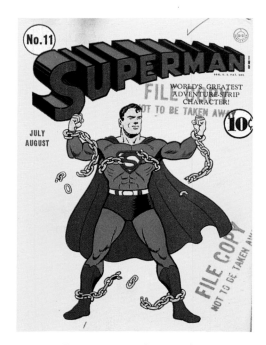

The stocky and muscular Superman of the early 1940s seems very much a hero for the common man.

©1941 by DC Comics, Inc.

A democratic sort of crimefighter, Superman was equally
willing to deal with petty thugs as with criminal masterminds.

©1941 by DC Comics, Inc.

was built around two other unforgettable bits of copy. "Faster than a speeding bullet, more powerful than a locomotive, able to leap tall buildings at a single bound. . . ." is one of them. This was chiefly a variation on introductory copy Siegel had written for the first issues of *Action* and *Superman*. The speeding bullet doesn't appear there, though, and the locomotive was called a "streamline train." The radio program's extolling of Superman's abilities was followed by, "Look! Up in the sky! It's a bird! It's a plane! It's . . . Superman!" If there is an art to the writing of radio copy, it reached its zenith here.

In order to meet the increasing demand for Superman comic book stories and maintain *Slam Bradley*, *Federal Men*, *Spy*, and their other features, Siegel and Shuster had to hire additional artists. In 1938 ads began running in artists' and writers' magazines: "Help wanted. Artist with ability to draw action-adventure strips; assist on nationally established features. Send samples. Joseph E. Shuster, 10905 Amor Ave., Cleveland, Ohio."

Wayne Boring, who'd worked as a salesman of advertising art and put in a stint assisting on the *Big Chief Wahoo* comic strip, responded to the ad with samples. Shortly thereafter, he found himself working in Cleveland in a shop with other new recruits, Paul Cassidy and Leo Nowak. "We had an office 12 by 12 with four drawing boards set up there," Boring recalled. "Jerry had a desk in the ▶

SIEGEL & SHUSTER

Jerry Siegel (left) and Joe Shuster flank their great creation, Superman, in this 1942 caricature.

©1990 by DC Comics, Inc.

Writer Jerry Siegel and artist Joe Shuster met while attending Cleveland's Glenville High School. The pair always knew that their creation, Superman, was destined for great things. Long before they'd received so much as a friendly nibble from a publisher or syndicate editor, they were working on merchandising details. "One day I read an article in some leading magazine about how Tarzan was merchandised by Stephen Slesinger so successfully," Siegel once recalled. "And I thought: Wow! Superman is even more super than Tarzan. The same [merchandising] could happen with Superman. And I mentioned it to Joe. He got real enthusiastic, and I walked in a day or so later, and he had made a big drawing of Superman, showing how the character could be merchandised on boxtops, T-shirts, and everything." Shuster added, "In this drawing we just let our imagination run wild. We visualized Superman toys, games and a radio show—that was before TV—and Superman movies. We even visualized Superman billboards. And it's all come true."

Both the partners were avid movie and pulp magazine buffs, and shared an abiding interest in science fiction. In 1932, they began to collaborate on a mimeographed fanzine, entitled simply *Science Fiction,* that mixed articles and fiction. The January 1933 issue of the shortlived effort contained a story, written by Siegel and illustrated by Shuster, called "The Reign of the Superman." In it, the superman of the title was a villain.

"A couple of months after I published this story," Siegel has said, "it occurred to me that a superman as a hero rather than a villain might make a great comic strip character in the vein of Tarzan, only more super and sensational than that great character. Joe and I drew it up as a comic book—this was early in 1933. We interested a publisher in putting it out, but then he changed his mind, and that was the end of that particular version of Superman." In this early incarnation, Superman had super powers but no costume—"he was simply wearing a T-shirt and pants."

The first adventure of Superboy appeared in *More Fun Comics* #101 in 1944. Siegel and Shuster had to go to court in order to be compensated by DC for use of the character.

©1944 by DC Comics, Inc.

Eventually, of course, Superman found a home and became a publishing phenomenon. As the years passed and the team's creation piled up profits, Siegel and Shuster grew increasingly unhappy. In 1947, when their joint annual income had dropped to $46,000, they decided to go to court. The April 14, 1947 issue of *Newsweek* reported, "In the New York Supreme Court in Westchester County [Siegel and Shuster] had filed suit seeking (1) to regain the rights to their brainchild, (2) to cancel their newspaper syndication contract with McClure and their contract with [publisher Harry] Donenfeld on the ground that they have been violated, and (3) to recover about $5,000,000 they say Superman should have brought them over a nine-year period."

Newsweek went on to note a conflict over the Superboy character. "When Siegel was in the army, Superboy made his debut under the double byline. Siegel claimed he never authorized such use of his name and has never received a cent for the strip."

Siegel and Shuster did not fare well. While the court eventually ruled that "Detective Comics, Inc. acted illegally" as far as Superboy was concerned, DC did indeed own Superman. The partners were paid for Superboy, in a settlement rumored to be around $50,000 to each, but they were fired by Donenfeld. Siegel and Shuster had been separated from their creation.

The team turned their attention to other projects. *Funnyman,* which was both a newspaper strip and a comic book in the late 1940s (the latter published by their old *Action* editor, Vincent Sullivan), did not succeed. The pair devoted nearly the next three decades to various legal actions intended to help them regain ownership of Superman. It wasn't until 1975, with the first of the multimillion-dollar Superman movies in the preproduction phase, that DC, by then owned by Warner Communications, agreed on a financial settlement with the creators. In recent years Siegel and Shuster have had what's been reported as "a good relationship with DC."

anteroom . . . it was the smallest office in Cleveland. At first Joe would sketch out pretty lightly, and we'd work over it." Later, as Shuster's eyesight worsened, the assistants did more and more of the work.

Siegel and Shuster's dreams about *Superman* were now coming true. But they were finding that creating a character that earns millions of dollars doesn't always mean you'll make millions yourself. When DC bought *Superman*, Jack Liebowitz had explained to the pair that they had to sign a release giving all rights to the feature to the publisher. "It is customary for all our contributors to release all rights to us," he wrote. "This is the businesslike way of doing things." Liebowtiz wasn't trying to con the boys—this was indeed the common practice throughout the comic book field and the situation didn't change at all until fairly recently. The partners were paid $130 for that first *Superman* job—ten dollars a page. That meant, as journalist John Kobler pointed out back in 1941, they would "be relinquishing their equity in all possible future profits from syndication, radio, movies, and so on, and that Harry Donenfeld, as sole owner of *Superman*, could even hire some other team to draw him." Conflict loomed.

As their character's popularity increased, Siegel started asking for more money. At first Liebowitz contended that the success of *Action Comics* was only partially due to the Man of Steel. When it became impossible to deny the impact

Menacing robots became just so much scrap iron at the hands of the Man of Steel.

©1941 by DC Comics, Inc.

As international events moved to involve the United States in World War II, Superman established himself as a defender of the American way of life.

©1942 by DC Comics, Inc.

anc
No. 5

FUNNYMAN

by JERRY SIEGEL JOE SHUSTER

JULY 1948

10c

Fired by DC for asking for fair compensation as the creators of Superman, Jerry Siegel and Joe Shuster hoped for success elsewhere. *Funnyman,* the team's 1947-48 attempt to duplicate the success of Superman, failed; the title lasted just six issues.

Superman was having, the situation changed. "It was only after anguished appeals that Siegel and Shuster finally managed, in 1940, to wangle sizable profits for themselves," reported the *Post* article. "$75,000, of which $16,000 goes in staff salaries and overhead. . . . Their syndicate profits have leaped to $600 a week. . . . Next year, with their revenues from radio, movies, and licenses coming in, they stand to make $150,000. Their ten-year term of service, however, is not reciprocal. Donenfeld remains free at any time to discharge them."

The importance of *Superman* was noticed by the business community fairly quickly. As early as 1942, *Business Week* reported that comics had become big time and that kids were spending an estimated fifteen million dollars a year on them. The weekly stated, "Superman has shown the way in a new field of publishing."

For the rest of the year following the advent of the Man of Steel, though, no further superheroes were introduced, not even by DC. And only two new costumed crimefighters, neither of whom had a single super power, entered comics.

The earliest costumed hero to venture onto the newsstands in the wake of *Superman* was not especially impressive. He possessed no special powers and wore a baggy costume that resembled a hooded business suit. Fighting crime with a bow and arrow, he called himself the Arrow and could be found in *Funny Pages* from #21

The Arrow, whose adventures were written and drawn by
Paul Gustavson, was the first costumed superhero to arrive
on the scene following the initial appearances of
Superman. This panel is from *Arrow* #1.

©1940 by Centaur Comics

(September 1938) onward. Paul Gustavson was the artist and writer. The Arrow was one of those mysterious fellows who just seemed to know when a crime was taking place. If a lovely blonde heiress was about to be attacked in a mansion at midnight by a "huge, grotesque figure," the Arrow would suddenly leap into the room and his bowstring would start twanging. Should a handsome couple be stranded in a mad doctor's mysterious house "high in the Rocky Mountains, miles away from civilization," you could be certain the Arrow would save the day with a well-placed shaft.

The Crimson Avenger, whom we met previously, was the only other dress-up crimebuster to come forward in 1938. He commenced wielding his gas gun in *Detective Comics* a month after the Arrow first dipped into his quiver.

The first authentic *super*hero to set up shop in competition with Superman was created by the unlikely team of Victor S. Fox and Will Eisner, and first appeared in the spring of 1939. The British-born Fox had spent twenty years on Wall Street and left it, with a less than spotless reputation, to go to work as an accountant for Detective Comics,

Inc. at 480 Lexington Avenue in Manhattan. While contemplating the increasingly impressive sales figures of *Action Comics*, he decided to start his own funny book company. After moving to gloomy offices on another floor of the same building that housed DC, Fox got in touch with the Eisner-Iger shop. Jerry Iger handled the business details, Will Eisner handled the creative end. "We were," Eisner has said, "delivering instant comic books to publishers."

According to Eisner, Fox had in mind a comic book that would star a character to be called Wonder Man. This new hero was to have a red costume, but the rest of the specifications "were almost identical to Superman," Eisner has said. "We knew it was very much like Superman, that it was imitative, but we had no idea of its legal implications."

Eisner wrote and drew Wonder Man's first and, as it turned out, only adventure and signed it with the name Willis. Unlike Superman, Wonder Man was blond and he was not an extraterrestrial. He picked up his many impressive abilities— which included leaping over tall buildings in a single bound, catching explosive shells in his bare hands, smashing through solid walls, and so forth—in Tibet, the magical-powers capital of the world. An ancient mystic trained him and gave him a special ring "as a symbol of the Herculean powers with which you are endowed. As long as you wear it you will be the strongest human on Earth and will be impervious."

In everyday life Wonder Man was Fred Carson, "a timid radio engineer and inventor." The fourteen-page story in *Wonder Comics* #1 (May 1939) found Fred journeying, along with the debutante daughter of his boss at the IBC network, to a mythical European country to cover a war. Before too long he "removes his outer garments and becomes Wonder Man, mightiest human on Earth." Subsequently he behaves in a Superman-like manner.

Or so Harry Donenfeld, the head man at DC, contended. "[Donenfeld] hit Fox real hard," Eisner has recalled, "and right away." Detective Comics, Inc.

sued Fox for infringement of copyright. The case reached the federal district court for New York City, in 1940. At that time the judge ruled in favor of DC. But Wonder Man was a long time dead by then, since Fox never risked the character's second appearance. But the enterprising Fox, whom Eisner remembers as having the manner and morals of the sort of movie gangster portrayed by Edward G. Robinson, didn't give up his dream of cashing in on what he was certain would be a superhero boom. Victor Fox would return.

Detective Comics #27 appeared at just about the same time as the first issue of *Wonder* and contained DC's next entry in the superhero derby. There on the cover was a costumed fellow called The Batman, swinging over the rooftops with an armlock around the throat of a hoodlum in a green pinstripe suit. Inside, the new hero led off the issue in a short, six-page story. Although the pointy ears on his cowl were a little lopsided, and his batwing cape didn't fit exactly right, there was something intriguing about him.

Batman typified the ability of the original-material comic books to deliver pulp magazine and movie elements in a funny paper format. The popular entertainments the artists and writers of this growing new industry had enjoyed as children were now recycled and turned into comic book stories. Batman is one of the most successful examples of this, inspired by movie melodramas and pulpwood yarns but becoming a ▶

DC's second-most important superhero was Batman, the mysterious avenger who patrolled Gotham City with his young partner Robin, the Boy Wonder. Seen here is the alluring cover of Batman #1.

©1940 by DC Comics, Inc.

BOB KANE and BILL FINGER

Bob Kane, the acknowledged creator of Batman.

Batman was the creation of a young man from the Bronx who'd drawn gag cartoons and humorous fillers before trying his hand at more serious fare. He had considerable help from a young shoe salesman who aspired to be a writer. Eventually, the production of the adventures of their increasingly popular hero would require a whole crew of artists, writers, and editors.

For artist Bob Kane, Batman has meant more than five decades of public recogniton and accolade. Kane began his professional career in 1936, drawing *Hiram Hick*, a funny feature that appeared in Henle Publishing's short-lived *Wow Comics*. The editor there was Jerry Iger and when Iger and Will Eisner formed a shop in the following year, the twenty-one year old Kane was invited to join the staff. He drew *Jest Laffs* and other gag cartoons, and a comedy-adventure strip titled *Peter Pupp*. These ran in Fiction House's *Jumbo Comics*. The Pupp feature, which was probably at least partly inspired by Floyd Gottfredson's *Mickey Mouse* newspaper strip, allowed Kane to deal for the first time with some of the elements he'd later treat more seriously in *Batman*. Pete was a daring little fellow; a typical four-page sequence sent him up in a fighter plane to combat a giant robot. The robot was controlled by a satanic villain whose forehead was adorned with a single eye.

Kane's first sales to DC were also in the humor line—one- and two-page comedy fillers. These were *Professor Doolittle*, a pantomime effort for *Adventure Comics; Ginger Snap*, about a wise little girl, for *More Fun*; and *Oscar the Gumshoe* for *Detective*.

In the Bob Kane entry in Jerry Bails's *Who's Who of American Comics*, Kane lists the artists who were major influences on him: Alex Raymond, Billy DeBeck, and Milton Caniff. Kane's first serious feature, *Rusty and His Pals*, shows the Caniff influence clearly. *Rusty* started in *Adventure* in 1938 and dealt with three boys and their Pat Ryan-type mentor, Steve Carter. Like Terry of Caniff's *Terry and the Pirates*, Rusty and company tangled with pirates and sinister Orientals. Kane's drawing on the early episodes was cartoony, but picked up a more serious look as *Rusty* progressed, even emulating Caniff's bold style of inking.

The scripts for Kane's first attempt at adventure were provided by his Bronx neighbor, Bill Finger. Two years older than Kane and working at selling shoes, Finger was a dedicated movie fan and reader of the pulps. The two met at a party and later decided to collaborate.

Kane and Finger followed *Rusty and His Pals* with *Batman*. Next came *Clip Carson*, which began in *Action Comics* #14 (July 1939). "I've always liked Rider Haggard's *King Solomon's Mines*," Finger once explained. "So I thought we might have a great white hunter type—one whose adventures would take him anywhere, Africa, South America, anywhere."

Finger never received a byline on any of the Kane features. It wasn't until he helped create the Green Lantern for DC in 1940 that his name began to appear in comic books. Except for a period in which he wrote for television, Bill Finger remained in comics for most of his life. He died in 1974.

This crude but dynamic page is from *Detective Comics* #27—the comic book that introduced Batman to the world. Writer Bill Finger and artist Bob Kane had created a truly great fictional hero.

©1939 by DC Comics, Inc.

distinctive character in his own right.

Bill Finger, the original writer of the feature, once said, "My first script was a take-off on a *Shadow* story . . . I patterned my style of writing *Batman* after the *Shadow*. Also after Warner Bros. movies, the gangster movies." Bob Kane, Batman's original artist, has mentioned that another source of inspiration was a 1926 movie called *The Bat*, "in which the villain wore a batlike costume which was quite awesome."

In its earliest incarnation, *The Bat* was a highly popular Broadway play by Avery Hopwood and Mary Roberts Rinehart. It was filmed for the first time in 1926 and again in 1931 under the title *The Bat Whispers*, with tough guy Chester Morris taking top billing. Basically an "old dark house" story, it had to do with stolen money, secret rooms and hidden passages, and a crazed killer who dresses up like a bat. The night-stalking Bat of the 1931 version certainly seems to be an ancestor of Batman, particularly when prowling the rooftops and casting his weird shadow across walls. Kane is on record as having been influenced by this movie.

In civilian life Batman was Bruce Wayne, "a bored young socialite." When night fell, however, playboy Wayne became "powerful and awesome," a "weird menace to all crime." Unlike his more sedate contemporaries in the private investigator line, Batman didn't wait for cases to come to him. He prowled the city—New York in the earliest adventures and later Gotham City—looking for trouble. He always found it, dropping down to shock the bejeesus out of burglars, kidnappers, and murderers. Although not above wisecracking while tangling with groups of a half dozen or more gunmen, Batman was a pretty grim vigilante in his early days. Besides his gadget-laden utility belt, he carried a .45 automatic and wasn't reluctant to use it. A trained athlete and acrobat, he was capable of breaking a man's neck with a well-placed kick.

Batman's origin, the inside story of "who he is and how he came to be," didn't appear until *Detective* #33 (November 1939). In a terse two-page account readers were told that fifteen years earlier Bruce Wayne's parents were gunned down on the street by a stickup man. The boy, a witness to the crime, vowed to dedicate his life to "warring on criminals." Having no supernatural powers, Wayne had to work at becoming a hero. He devoted years to preparing for his crimefighting career, turning himself into both a master scientist and crackerjack athlete. Deciding that he'd need a disguise capable of striking terror into the hearts of criminals, he was inspired by the intrusion of a bat into his den. "It's an omen . . . I shall become a BAT!"

Another major event in Batman's life was recounted in *Detective* #38 (April 1940): He acquired a sidekick. "An exciting new figure whose incredible gymnastic and athletic feats will astound you," a blurb

"I shall become a bat!" Batman's origin was first revealed in *Detective Comics* #33.

©1939 by DC Comics, Inc.

Batman's acrobatic skills were the focus of the action of many memorable covers and stories. This 1941 cover was probably drawn by Jerry Robinson.

©1941 by DC Comics, Inc.

proclaimed. "A laughing, fighting young daredevil who scoffs at danger like the legendary Robin Hood whose name and spirit he has adopted . . . Robin the Boy Wonder." Bob Kane once explained, "In my subconscious mind I longed to be like Robin when I was his age, fighting alongside his idol Batman (or, in my case, Doug Fairbanks, Sr.). I figured Robin would appeal to all children of his age group as an identifiable person for their inner fantasies."

Bill Finger amplified, "Batman was a combination of Fairbanks and Sherlock Holmes. Holmes had his Watson. The thing that bothered me was that Batman didn't have anyone to talk to, and it got a little tiresome always having him thinking. I found as I went along that Batman needed a Watson to talk to. That's how Robin came to be. Bob called me over and said he was going to put a boy in the story to identify with Batman. I thought it was a great idea."

Jerry Robinson, Kane's assistant at the time, had a few more facts to add about the dynamic youth's gestation. "I thought of Batman's new partner as a sort of young Robin Hood . . . I remember plugging the name Robin against the others that didn't seem quite as good," he recalled. "Once we agreed on the name, I suggested adapting Robin Hood's costume for the new character."

Why exactly did Batman and Robin succeed where so many other superheroes failed? For one thing, there was the look of Bob Kane's art work. His primitive, cartoony style, carried

Lou Fine, one of the best artists of the comic book "Golden Age," drew this exciting *Mystery Men* cover.

©1940 by Fox Publications, Inc.

on and polished by Robinson, fit the sort of melodramatic, nighttime stories he and Finger loved to spin. "Batman's world took control of the reader," Jules Feiffer has observed. "Kane's was an authentic fantasy, a genuine vision, so that, however one might nitpick the components, the end product remained an impregnable whole: gripping and original." The stories, particularly in the World War II years, were good, borrowing from writers O. Henry and Damon Runyon, and from the movies. And, of course, Batman and Robin battled some of the all-time best villains in comics—bizarre figures like the Joker, the Penguin, the Riddler, and Catwoman.

In the summer of 1939 the unconquerable Victor Fox came back into the fray. He introduced not one but three new costumed heroes. The third issue of *Wonderworld* (July 1939), which is what Fox was now calling *Wonder*, introduced the Flame, another product of the Eisner-Iger packaging establishment. The initial adventures of the yellow-clad superman were handsomely rendered by Lou Fine, a fine draftsman with a gift for classically heroic figure work. A slow starter, the Flame took several issues to really ignite. When he first showed up, he didn't appear to have any superpowers at all. Confused racketeers asked him questions like, "Who are you? What do you want?" In subsequent issues he displayed an ability to materialize out of smoke and flame. A while later he really started living up to his name, revealing a hitherto unsuspected knack for bursting into flame, burning through walls, and performing similarly fiery stunts. In *Wonderworld* #30 (October 1941) the Flame acquired a female companion. Known as Flame Girl, she stuck with him until the magazine died only three issues later.

Fox's second magazine was *Mystery Men Comics* and in this one he offered two costumed heroes. The intended leading man was the Green Mask, who wore a blue costume and cape and a green headrag mask. The artist was Walter Frehm, who'd been Will Gould's assistant on *Red Barry*. The Green Mask feature had the same cartoony-adventure look of that cops and robbers newspaper strip— blazing automatics, fast cars, sinister Orientals, snarling gangsters, big city backgrounds. "The Green Mask wasn't much of a mystery man," comics historian Robert Jennings has observed, "since he had no secret identity, no background, and no unusual powers. He did wear a pretty bizarre costume, but he relied more on a blazing automatic pistol than super strength to solve his problems."

Several issues, and artists, later the Mask did acquire a few more of the accouterments of his trade. A caption informed readers, "Michael Selby, placed in a vita-ray machine, discovers that the supercharged shocks have made him a miracle man. He can zoom through the air and perform super-human feats." The Mask also picked up a boy companion named Domino. Although never a particularly engaging character, The Mask

Artist Charles Wojtkowski adopted the pen name Charles Nicholas when drawing the adventures of the Blue Beetle. This panel is from a 1939 issue of *Mystery Men Comics*.

©1939 by Fox Publications, Inc.

Lou Fine illustrated the adventures of the Flame for publisher Victor Fox.

©1940 by Fox Features Syndicate

did look appropriately heroic on early covers by Lou Fine.

Soon, however, the Mask lost his star slot to the book's other resident superhero, the Blue Beetle. This unusually named character started out near the back of the book, biding his time in short four-page adventures. Until his second appearance, he didn't even have a crimefighting costume. Eventually he started showing up for work in the distinctive blue, chain mail outfit and black domino mask that became his trademark. Wisely, he abandoned the bug antennae he'd briefly worn on his cowl.

The Blue Beetle's early escapades were drawn by Charles Wojtkowski, who'd adopted the pen name Charles Nicholas. The Beetle was one of the few superheroes who acquired his powers through attention to his diet—captions continually reminded readers that he was "given super-energy by vitamin 2X." His chain mail outfit, by the way, made him "almost invulnerable." Once powered by 2X, the Blue Beetle would run around for eight or ten pages, cracking skulls and making wisecracks, while he hunted down a crazed scientist called Doc and other, peculiarly named villains: the Wart, Scrag, the Eel, and Mr. Downhill.

The Blue Beetle became Fox's most popular character. He moved to the front of *Mystery Men* and was showcased on every cover beginning with issue #7 (February 1940). He got a magazine all his own before a year was out and for awhile appeared in a newspaper strip drawn by Jack Kirby. Victor Fox even managed to promote a Blue

The Blue Beetle won his own book in 1939. This is the cover of *Blue Beetle* #1.

©1939 by Fox Publications, Inc.

PAGE 64   BIG·3

THE BLUE BEETLE
COAST TO COAST

Thrilling
Drama of
the Avenging
Gang Smasher

Twice-a-Week

On
Your
Favorite
Radio
Station

CONSULT YOUR LOCAL NEWSPAPER, OR BETTER

CALL YOUR FAVORITE LOCAL STATION, FOR

THE SCHEDULE OF THIS SUPER-THRILLER. IF IT

IS NOT SCHEDULED IN YOUR LOCALITY, ASK

YOUR FAVORITE LOCAL STATION TO HAVE THE

BLUE BEETLE ON THE AIR.

The Blue Beetle's popularity had inspired a radio show by the early forties. This ad page is from an issue of *Big-3*.

©Fox Publications, Inc.

Beetle radio show starring character actor Frank Lovejoy—"Thrilling Drama of the Avenging Gang Smasher . . . Twice-a-Week."

Centaur Publications' Amazing Man, an early creation of artist Bill Everett, first appeared in the fall of 1939. *Amazing Man Comics* skipped the first four issues and commenced with #5. The character's origin came about this way—"25 years ago, in the mountains of Tibet, the Council of Seven selected an orphan of superb physical structure, and each did his part to develop in the child all the qualities of one who would dominate the world of men with his great strength, knowledge and courage . . . His friend Nika, the young chemist, endowed him with the power to make himself disappear in a cloud of green vapor, and extracted from him the promise to always be good and kind and generous."

Before graduating and being sent to America to combat evil, A-Man had to undergo a series of tests that made your average college midterm or IRS tax audit look like a cinch. Among the hurdles he overcame were a tug-of-war match with a bull elephant and a tussle with a cobra—while his hands were tied behind his back. The main snag to an uncomplicated career of crime-stopping was a rogue member of the Council of Seven itself. A sinister hooded figure with the power of telepathy, this villain, the Great Question, "covets plans of dire evil for the boy." Needless to say, Amazing Man had his work cut out for him.

Marvel Mystery became synonymous with wild, nonstop action. The comic's stars, Sub-Mariner and the Human Torch, were two of the most vivid comic book characters of the 1940s.

©1941 by Timely Comics, Inc.

Timely (later Marvel) Comics came up with *Marvel Comics* (*Marvel Mystery Comics* as of issue #2), which went on sale late in 1939. This title offered a pair of superheroes who would enjoy long popularity, the Human Torch and the Sub-Mariner. The Human Torch, who grabbed the cover of the premiere issue, wasn't actually human. Rather, he was a "synthetic man—an exact replica of a human being." His origin story is not exactly coherent, but it seems that one Professor Horton, who had been working to create a synthetic human, holds a press conference to announce that, although he's succeeded, he has some doubts. "I call him THE HUMAN TORCH," Horton explains as he unveils a large airtight glass cylinder that contains his blond, red-suited creation. "Something went wrong with my figuring somewhere—every time the robot . . . contacts oxygen in the air, he bursts into flame!" Sure enough, as soon as Horton allows air into the cage, the Torch's figure is engulfed by fire. The gathered reporters, obviously lacking the true spirit of scientific inquiry, shout unhelpful things like, "Destroy that man!"

Although Horton does try to incapacitate his android by burying him in cement, that doesn't work and before long "the HUMAN TORCH is on the loose again!" Appropriately enough, the Torch gets mixed up with arsonists and cleans up their dirty racket. By the end of the yarn he's learned to melt iron bars, throw fireballs, and turn his flame on and off at will. When the old professor suggests that the two of them might be able to make a fortune, the now-altruistic Torch informs his misguided creator, "No, Horton, I'll be free and no one will ever use me for selfish gain—or crime!"

What Carl Burgos, the artist-creator of the strip, had stumbled on was a basic idea that had tremendous appeal to kids. Most of us go through a phase in our youth where we're touched with a little pyromania—we play with matches, we yearn for fireworks, we attempt to concoct fiery explosives with our chemistry sets. With the Human Torch readers had a hero who could play with fire and get away with it. The character's basic appeal was so strong that even Burgos's less-than-masterful drawing couldn't smother it.

Beyond a doubt, two of the things that contributed to the early success of *Marvel Mystery Comics* were the battles and subsequent team-ups of the Torch and the Sub-Mariner. Bill Everett's waterlogged Prince Namor, who'd first appeared in the extremely short-lived *Motion Picture Funnies Weekly*, had been raising hell from the very first issue of *Marvel*. Coming to Manhattan from his decimated undersea kingdom, Sub-Mariner was determined to get revenge. "You white devils have persecuted and tormented my people for years," he explains to policewoman Betty Dean, the pretty brunette with whom he carries on a love-hate relationship. Once in New York City, Namor behaves in the manner of an earlier and larger visitor named King Kong.

"He was an angry character," reflected Everett some years later. "He was probably expressing some of my own personality." With the angry Namor cutting up in the Big Apple and the Human Torch freshly arrived to work as a cop, a confrontation was inevitable. "That was an idea Carl [Burgos] and I dreamed up," Everett once explained. "We considered the fact that the two characters and their opposing elements had separate stories and wondered what would happen if we got them together as rivals to fight each other." What happened was a battle royal that raged through *Marvel* #8 and #9 and wound up in a standoff in #10. But the next time these representatives of fire and water met, they were "fighting side by side!" As a caption in the 26-page team-up saga in *Marvel Mystery Comics* #17 (March 1941) explained, "The Human Torch and the Sub-Mariner are together again. Not to destroy each other but to form an alliance that will stop the gigantic plans for an invasion of the United States!"

Not to be outdone by Timely, Victor Fox was back yet again at the end of 1939 with another new magazine, *Fantastic Comics*, and another new superhero, Samson. This time the creative minds at the Eisner-Iger shop turned to the Bible for inspiration—"Out of the mist of history comes the mighty Samson. . . . Like his ancient forebears Samson pits his tremendous strength against the forces of evil and injustice." A "yellow-haired giant" whose

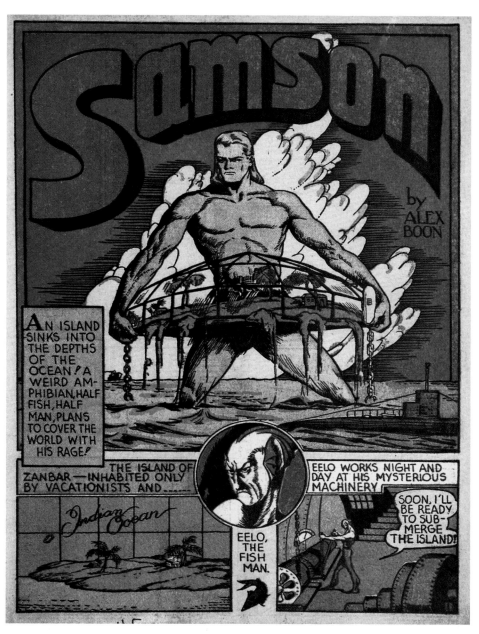

Hey, Samson—don't turn your back on Eelo, the Fish Man. Eisner-Iger employee Alex Blum (signing his work as Alex Boon), drew Samson's adventures in *Fantastic Comics*.

©1940 by Fox Features Syndicate

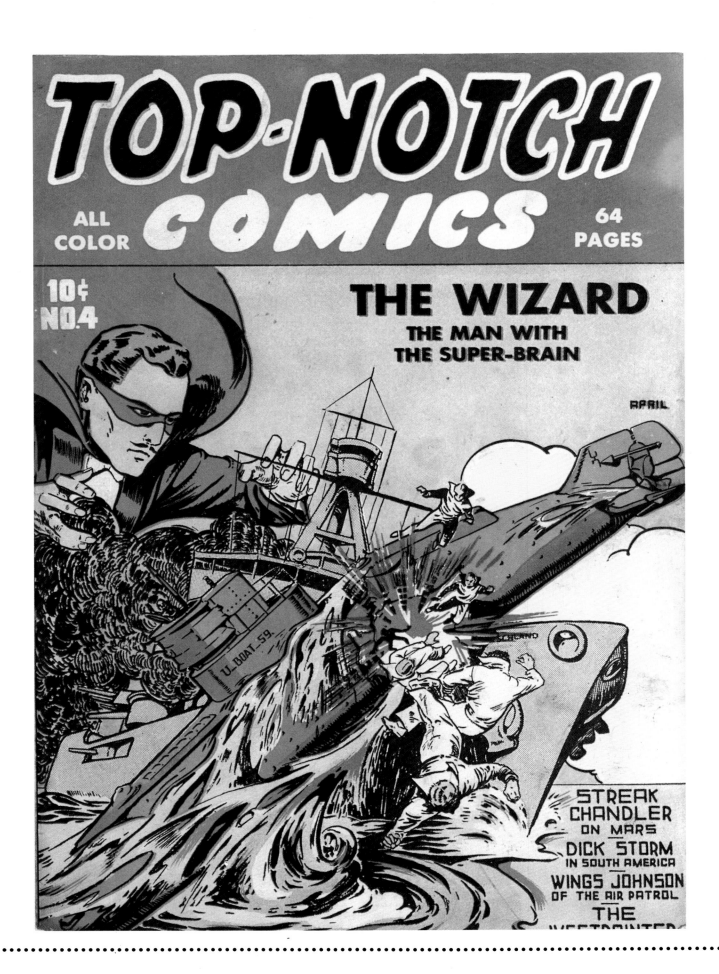

costume consisted of thonged sandals and a pair of shaggy shorts, Samson's early adventures found him roughing up warmongers in mythical European countries. A humorless, dedicated chap who was driven by a compulsive need to "fight against crime and corruption," Samson favored a stunt in which he pulled down the pillars of a building and caused the walls to come tumbling down. Like his Biblical namesake, Samson's weak spot was his hair, and now and then he would be temporarily incapacitated when a giant robot or other rampaging bully tugged at his golden locks.

A year later, in the autumn of 1940, Samson followed the latest trend in comics by teaming up with blond lad named David. Since this feature was always of the no-frills sort, neither Samson nor his sidekick had a civilian identity. Most stories simply opened with them in shorts, ready to spring into action. A typical adventure gets rolling with the pair standing on a city street. "Samson! Look!" cries David, pointing upward. "A man falling from that building!" "Oh, Oh!" responds the yellow-haired giant. "I've got to work fast!" He picks up a nearby truck and holds it up over his head to catch the plummeting man. "Good thing this load of hay is handy!" And how. Alex Blum, a workhorse of the Eisner-Iger shop, was the first to draw mighty Samson's prosaic escapades; he was succeeded by Joe Simon, Al Carreno, and others.

MLJ Magazines' The Wizard, who first appeared in *Top-Notch*

#1 (December 1939), was much better dressed than Samson and probably smarter, too, for he was known as the Man With The Super Brain. Dapper as well as bright, the Wizard originally performed his deeds wearing black tie and tails, a cape, and a red domino mask. In that clean-shaven era, he was one of the few comic book heroes who wore a moustache. The Wiz's specialty was handling invasions and "plots against the government." In civilian life he was Blane Whitney, polo-playing scion of one of America's first families. "With his super-brain and photographic mind the Wizard is able to visualize far-away happenings. With these mental powers and his super-strength he ferrets out plots against the U.S."

In the Wizard's earliest battles, against such foreign scourges as the Jatsonian invaders and the equally nasty Borentals, he made use of many amazing weapons of his own invention. These included Secret Formula F 22 X, the H2-VX-O Ray, and his Dynamagno-Saw Ray Projector. Edd Ashe, Jr., was the first artist to bring all of this life; Al Camy took over after a few issues and in #7 gave the Wizard a new costume. The outfit consisted of a blue tunic and tights, red shorts, and cape. The red mask was retained, along with the moustache.

Such was the state of the superhero business in the months following the debut of Superman—some interesting characters, some silly ones, but hardly more than a trickle of them. And then, in 1940, the deluge came.

Because few magazine publishers could ignore the amazing success of Superman, the 1940s were marked by a profusion of superhero comic books. Scores of colorfully costumed male and female do-gooders strode forth to battle the forces of evil. The energetic high spirits of this "Golden Age" of comic books is expressed by this 1942 *Adventure Comics* cover by Simon and Kirby, featuring Sandman and Sandy.

©1942 by DC Comics, Inc.

The comics boom continued, not only with new titles, but with more and more publishing companies joining in. In its June 1941 issue, *Writer's Digest* exclaimed, "The number of comics on the stands continues to grow in unbelievable fashion. It is reported that there are 115 of them on the stands now, and that by September this will be increased to 135!" That was only the beginning, and hundreds more titles would come and go as the forties progressed. A few of the outfits turning out magazines had been in business at least as long as DC, but most of them were newcomers. And just about all of them did well—for a while, anyway.

The most popular and best selling superhero of the decade proved to be not Superman but rather a red-clad upstart who didn't even take his profession seriously. Created by cartoonist C. C. Beck and editor-writer Bill Parker, Captain Marvel came along early in 1940. Within a very few years this beefy, perpetually grinning superhero was outselling not only Superman but also every other crime-

Fawcett's Captain Marvel—known to his admirers and
enemies alike as The Big Red Cheese—may have been the
most purely likable superhero of the 1940s. He was the
most popular, too, and outsold even Superman.

© 1940 by Fawcett Publications, Inc.

fighter who'd followed in the wake of the Man of Steel, from Amazing Man to the Zebra.

Late in 1939 Roscoe K. Fawcett of Fawcett Publications, Inc. sent out a promotion piece to magazine distributors across the country. It announced the impending debut of *Whiz Comics*, which would star Captain Marvel—"another character sensation in the comic field!" Until then, the Fawcett folks had been known for such magazines as *Real Life Story*, *Motion Picture*, *Mechanix Illustrated*, and *Captain Billy's Whiz-Bang*. Now they were promising wholesalers a comic book, one that was "here to stay." The forthcoming title would lead the parade and bring "permanent profits." Many comic book publishers would make similiar claims and fail to live up to them, but in the case of Fawcett, all the advance hyperbole turned out to be true.

The original name selected for Fawcett's first superhero was Captain Thunder, and he was going to be the leader of a group of heroes. According to Ralph Daigh, then editorial director at Fawcett, Bill Parker's initial suggestion was "that our superhero feature a team, probably four, under the command of one hero Bill identified as Captain Thunder. The 'captain' was to have a squad of lieutenants, each possessing a singular attribute traceable to such heroes as Hercules, Atlas, Zeus, Achilles and Mercury."

In time, the group notion and the Captain Thunder name were discarded. And Parker, perhaps with suggestions from the Fawcett staff, came up with a

C.C. Beck's drawing style was simple and pleasing. This *Whiz Comics* splash panel features a fearsome gorillion and the evil Dr. Sivana (bottom right).

© 1940 by Fawcett Publications, Inc.

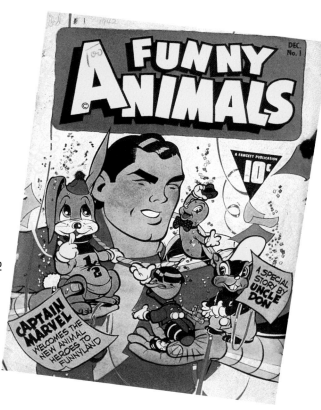

So great was Captain Marvel's popularity by 1942 that he was utilized by Fawcett to herald a new title, *Funny Animals*.

© 1942 by Fawcett Publications, Inc.

variation on the dual identity theme—a variation that turned out to be as powerful and compelling as the dual identities of Dr. Jekyll and Mr. Hyde, Zorro, and Superman: Captain Marvel was really a teenage boy named Billy Batson. Young readers—most of them young *boy* readers—loved it.

By saying the magic word "SHAZAM!" (revealed to him by a mysterious wizard in a long-forgotten section of subway), Billy could transform himself into the red-clad Captain Marvel, the World's Mightiest Mortal. Just for the record, the letters of the magic word stood for the wisdom of **S**olomon, the strength of **H**ercules, the stamina of **A**tlas, the power of **Z**eus, the courage of **A**chilles, and the speed of **M**ercury.

Despite the fact that Captain Marvel was invincible, it was Billy Batson who quietly dominated the stories. Captain Marvel was the one who duked it out with the villains, but he always returned to his true identity of Billy (by shouting "Shazam!") when the trouble had passed.

Parker's basic premise, a boy with the power to change into a full-grown superhero, was beautiful in its simplicity and inherent appeal. Youngsters were snared because the adventures were about a kid who could take a shortcut to adulthood when he needed help with a serious problem. In a sense, Billy became his own helpful big brother or protective father. And all it took was the magic word, not years of growing up or even months of rigorous exercise.

The captain's adventures also had great visual appeal. This was provided by Charles Clarence Beck, a young cartoonist who had been a Fawcett staff artist since the middle 1930s. A cantankerous gentleman with a strong sense of humor, he was influenced not by serious illustration but by such comic strips as *Little Orphan Annie*, *The Gumps*, and, especially, *Barney Google*. "The basis I go on is never to put in a single line that isn't necessary," he once explained. "Don't try to show off." His *Captain Marvel* stories exemplified his philosophy and were models of simplicity, clarity, and appealing design. They were as much fun to look at as they were to read.

Although Beck's friendly, cartoony style had a great deal to do with the success of the captain, he maintained, "The stories were what put Marvel over, not the drawings." And indeed, Captain Marvel's adventures were consistently well scripted, and leavened with as much wit and whimsy as action. There was nothing stuffy about the captain, who didn't seem too terribly offended whenever his enemies referred to him as "The Big Red Cheese."

Otto Binder, an established pulp science fiction writer, became the chief Captain Marvel scripter during the feature's second year. "My first *Captain Marvel Adventures* script was written in December, 1941 and appeared in the ninth issue, April, 1942," Binder once said. "The end result of this, some twelve years later in 1953, was a total of 529 stories about the Big

Red Cheese alone." Binder was responsible for just about all the stories that dealt with time travel, space travel, and other science-fiction staples. He also invented Mr. Tawny, the nattily dressed talking tiger who turned out to be one of the feature's most charming and popular supporting characters.

The pulps provided Beck with not just a convivial scripter, but with with his first art assistant, as well. Pete Costanza had been a pulp illustrator before switching to comic books. "When Pete left his 'straight illustration,'" Beck said, "he turned out to be a remarkably fine cartoonist with a great sense of humor." Costanza quickly made his presence felt; his hand is already evident during the first year of *Whiz*.

As the demand for Captain Marvel stories increased—the character was appearing in *Whiz Comics* (which he shared with such stalwarts as Spy Smasher, the Golden Arrow, and Ibis the Invincible), *Captain Marvel Adventures*, and *America's Greatest* in the early 1940s— Fawcett first went to outsiders to fill the pages, and then had Beck set up a shop of his own. Among the outside artists were Jack Kirby, who produced a hurried-looking first issue of *Captain Marvel Adventures*, and George Tuska. Beck's shop employed Morris Weiss, Al Fagaly, Chic Stone, Dave Berg, Kurt Schaffenberger, and Marc Swayze.

In *Whiz* #25 another addition was made to the Marvel family. After an encounter with the odious Captain Nazi, teenage

An ingenious and appealing variation on Captain Marvel was Captain Marvel, Jr., a young crimefighter who remained a boy whether in his normal or superhero guise. The very talented Mac Raboy drew the cover of Jr.'s debut issue.

©1942 by Fawcett Publications, Inc.

Another of Mac Raboy's handsome depictions of Captain Marvel, Jr.

©1942 by Fawcett Publications, Inc.

Mary Marvel—wholesome, pretty, and as dedicated to crimefighting as her big brother, Captain Marvel—won her own magazine in late 1945.

Freddy Freeman is left near death. Billy Batson decides to do something. "Deep in a forgotten section of the subway, known only to Billy himself, the boy carries his unconscious burden aboard a weird vehicle." Soon the two youths are face to face with Shazam, the wizard who had provided Billy with his alter ego nearly two years earlier—or, rather, they're face to face with Shazam's ghost, since the bearded warlock expired after performing that earlier feat. Shazam works a switch on the original trick, arranging things so that Freddy will become a superhero by shouting, "Captain Marvel!" Since this particular magic phrase isn't quite as powerful as "Shazam!" Freddy won't turn into a super adult but a super boy. Decked out in a blue version of the Marvel costume, Captain Marvel, Jr. whizzed over to *Master Comics* for a long and successful career. Mac Raboy, an impressively talented artist, drew the young hero's first adventures. It says something about how firmly the tradition of dual identity was by now established in comic books that Freddy, crippled after his encounter with Captain Nazi, chose to return to that role when he wasn't fighting crime.

Lightning struck again at Fawcett a year later. This time it was Mary Marvel, who first flashed into being in *Captain Marvel Adventures* #18 (December 1942). Her real name was Mary Batson and she turned out to be Billy's long-lost sister. After learning her brother's secret, Mary says, "Shazam!" and—w*hoom!*—she changes, too. ▶

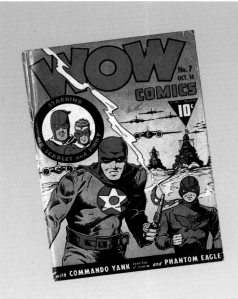

BOY WONDERS

Shortly after Batman hooked up with Robin, adolescent boy wonders became all the rage. *Wow* #7 (left) features Mr. Scarlet's Pinky and Commando Yank's Phantom Eagle. *Prize Comics* (right) offered a *pair* of boy wonders, Yank and Doodle.

©1942 by Fawcett Publications, Inc.
(*Wow*)
©1942 by Feature Publications, Inc.
(*Prize*)

Robin the Boy Wonder teamed up with Batman in the spring of 1939, becoming the first of what was to be a long line of youthful sidekicks. In 1940 and 1941, especially, established costumed heroes and those just embarking on careers of super-altruism began showing up for work with kid companions. In the early 1950s the zealous critic of comic books, psychiatrist Dr. Fredric Wertham, would charge that "only someone ignorant of the fundamentals of psychiatry and the psychopathology of sex can fail to realize a subtle atmosphere of homoeroticism which pervades the adventures of the mature 'Batman' and his young friend 'Robin.'" Despite Wertham's observations, it seems unlikely that any of the editors who started adding boy wonders to their magazines had anything more sinister than plagiarism in mind— and an easy way to appeal to youthful readers, who could identify with the kid heroes.

Among the earliest wonder boys were Toro the Flaming Kid, who joined the Human Torch in the summer of 1940, and Roy the Super Boy, who started palling around with the Wizard at about the same time. Nicknames ending in the letter Y were especially popular and in the early 1940s Buddy, Rusty, Dusty, Speedy, and Pinky could be found teamed up with, respectively, the Eagle, Captain Aero, the Shield, the Green Arrow, and Mr. Scarlet. There were also Bucky, who was Captain America's partner, and Sandy, who worked side by side with Sandman.

Now and then a certain amount of whimsy was in evidence. A minor hero called Airmale had a boy companion named Stampy, a fellow known as Nightmare worked in tandem with Sleepy. On at least one occasion the usual situation was reversed, when the pint-sized Star-Spangled Kid traveled with a lantern-jawed adult sidekick called Stripesy.

Not satisfied with just one kid companion, several heroes worked with bunches of them. The original Daredevil hung out with the Little Wise Guys and Captain Commando guided the Boy Soldiers. Joe Simon and Jack Kirby, who'd created such successful kid gangs as the Young Allies and the Boy Commandos, came up with the Newsboy Legion in 1942 and gave them a costumed adult partner known as the Guardian. Fun and lively, the kid heroes allowed the comics' young readers to cast themselves in the adventures: "If Robin can do it, so can I!"

"I feel strong—powerful," she exclaims, not at all disappointed that she's been transformed into a super teenager and not a full grown woman.

Mary, by the way, had a separate but equal version of the magic word. Whereas Billy's Shazam stands for Solomon, Hercules, Atlas, Zeus, Achilles, and Mercury, Mary's stands for Selena, Hippolyta, Ariadne, Zephyrus, Aurora, and Minerva. (It's not difficult to visualize old Shazam off in limbo somewhere, tugging at his whiskers as he works out these lists of gods and mythical figures to match the initials of his name.) Mary Marvel went on to become the leading character in *Wow Comics* with issue #9 (January 1943).

Fawcett's other early comic book titles had been more experimental. *Slam-Bang Comics*, which followed *Whiz* by a month, was an attempt to do a magazine without a single costumed superhero. Instead readers were offered a lackluster lineup of plainclothes good guys—Jim Dolan, Hurricane Hansen, Lee Granger. Although a character named Diamond Jack did have a little magic going for him, he went about his business in civvies. The contents of this ill-fated magazine were provided by the Chesler Shop. After just seven issues, *Slam-Bang* folded.

Master Comics was an attempt to succeed where Dell and Major Nicholson had failed and to make a success of a tabloid-sized comic book. "Now you have MASTER, the only 15¢ Comic Magazine!" Roscoe Fawcett told distributors. "One that makes its own

Displays!—Cover . . . is 10¼ by 14 inches!—48 Big pages of 4-Color, Sure-Fire Comics." Better still, they'd make "2 cents per copy profit!" There was a superhero in this one, a blond fellow known as Master Man. Billed as the World's Greatest Hero, he was a dull fellow who didn't even have an alternate identity. Phooey! Sharing the oversized book with him were Shipwreck Roberts, the White Raja, Frontier Marshall, the Devil's Dagger, and El Carim, Master of Magic—"whose name printed backwards spells 'miracle.'"

Fawcett's ambition was apparently boundless, for the next thing the company attempted was a *weekly* comic book. Not only that—the comic would sell for just five cents. The first issue of *Nickel Comics* appeared with a May 17, 1940 cover date and the next issue appeared two weeks later. "We are able to give you a five cent comic on an every other week production schedule," explained Roscoe Fawcett to the wholesalers. "And the promise that if NICKEL COMICS clicks it will be made a weekly." Apparently, some resistance was anticipated, since several paragraphs of Fawcett's news release struck a reassuring tone. "If we felt for one minute that a 5¢ comic would contribute to the detriment of the comic field, we would be foolish indeed to jeopardize the profitable one million monthly circulation now maintained on the comic publications which we distribute." (The figure of one million is explained by the

Mary Marvel hooks up with Mr. Scarlet's pal, Pinky, in these *Wow Comics* panels from 1944. Art is by Jack Binder.

At five cents a copy, Fawcett's *Nickel Comics* was the least expensive comic book of the forties. The title lasted just eight issues. Cover art is by Jack Binder.

©1940 by Fawcett Publications, Inc.

Oversized and selling for fifteen cents instead of a dime, *Master Comics* was a bold experiment by publisher Roscoe Fawcett. The experiment failed, and *Master* eventually assumed the traditional size and price.

©1940 by Fawcett Publications, Inc.

Fawcett organization's distribution of magazines of other publishers.)

The featured hero in each thirty-two-page issue of *Nickel* was Bulletman. He wore a scarlet tunic, blue sash and boots, and lemon yellow riding breeches. Bulletman lived up to his name in dramatic fashion, thanks to a tapered helmet that gave him that enviable streamlined look as he flew through the air.

Despite appealing characters and innovative sizes and prices, neither *Nickel* nor *Master* succeeded, at least not in their original formats. The five-center expired after eight slim issues; the fifteen-center dropped to conventional size and price with its seventh. Bulletman replaced Master Man as *Master* cover-boy, and characters from the defunct *Slam-Bang* were also assimilated. As noted earlier, Captain Marvel, Jr. was later installed as *Master*'s leading man.

Fawcett's *Wow Comics* began life late in 1940 as a quarterly; most of the characters were leftovers from *Slam-Bang*. The exception was Mr. Scarlet, a brand new, satanic-looking crimson avenger drawn initially by Jack Kirby. Ad copy described him this way: "Special prosecutor by day, Brian Butler discards his legal robes at midnight to become the mysterious 'Mister Scarlet,' an underworld legend—a myth who strikes with merciless reality and brings to justice those who escape the law through its legal loopholes." *Wow* eventually went monthly, added Mary Marvel to its lineup, and continued until 1948.

Fawcett's biggest hit was always Captain Marvel, but life was not easy for the red-clad Shazam-shouter. In 1941 DC Comics undertook legal action against Fawcett. DC's contention was that Captain Marvel was so close in concept to Superman that he infringed on DC's copyright. The lawsuit was fought throughout the 1940s and into the 1950s. Finally, in the middle fifties, Fawcett gave up and quit publishing Captain Marvel in any shape or form. Lawyer-comics historian Robert M. Ingersoll, writing in the *Comic's Buyer's Guide* weekly newspaper, has said, "Fawcett has sometimes been criticized for his decision to give up the fight. But it didn't really give up the fight; it had already lost it. The trial court had ruled that Captain Marvel infringed on Superman's copyright, and that issue could not be litigated again. So the result of any new trial was a foregone conclusion; Fawcett would lose. Rather than spend useless time and effort fighting a losing battle, Fawcett settled out of court. An aesthetically unpopular but legally wise choice."

Captain Marvel returned to the newsstands twenty years later, under the DC banner. Artist C. C. Beck came back, too, for a while. But the captain's comeback was not exactly triumphal and Beck soon quit after an argument over scripts.

Captain Marvel's first flush of success was indicative of the public's eagerness for new superheroes. Well aware of the trend it had initiated, DC plunged more enthusiastically

Jerry Siegel and Bernard Bàily's the Spectre is certainly the most intimidating of all superheroes. As much a figure of horror as a good guy, the Spectre meted out frightful retribution to wrongdoers. This splash panel is from *More Fun Comics* #57.

Bulletman and, later, Bulletgirl showed up in *Nickel* and *Master* comics. The splash panel seen here is from *Master* #14, and was drawn by Jack Binder.

into the superhero business in 1940. *More Fun* #52 (February 1940) introduced an eerie character called the Spectre. Written by Jerry Siegel and drawn by Bernard Baily, the new feature was about a redheaded cop named Jim Corrigan who, after being murdered by gangsters, returns to walk among the living as a crimebuster, cloaked in green and sporting a pasty white complexion. He had the ability, shared with Orphan Annie, of making the pupils of his eyes disappear. As all of this might suggest, the Spectre's early adventures were pretty odd. He had frequent conversations with the Almighty and made occasional trips to the hereafter to get clues from departed souls. Once, he even stalked a supernatural villain "into the depths of infinity," a peculiar void made up mainly of clouds. He could walk through walls, turn crooks into skeletons and, on the *More Fun* covers, at least, grow as tall as a downtown office building. A grim, uniquely talented chap, the Spectre didn't just collar crooks—he enjoyed himself by *destroying* them. After one instance of brutal vigilantism, the Spectre observed, "One less vermin to peril decency."

More Fun added another weird hero a few months later, in issue #55—Dr. Fate, a Gardner Fox invention, drawn in a stylized but spooky fashion by Howard Sherman. "Dwelling apart from mankind in his lonely tower north of ghost-ridden Salem is the mysterious Dr. Fate," an early caption explained, "who called upon secret and ancient sources for the power with which he fights unusual crimes." Unusual for sure. Fate, who wore a blue and gold superhero suit and a metal helmet that completely hid his face, specialized in besting ancient Mayan gods, combating "globemen" from outer space, defeating horrors summoned from the cosmic void, and counseling young women who suspected they might be wereleopards. In one adventure with his recurrent enemy Wotan the Wizard, Fate first goes to Hell for a chat with the skeletal boatman on the River Styx and then shoots up to talk to God, who is depicted as a blinding light. Although never a top-rank hero, Dr. Fate gained a loyal coterie of fans, and remains an active character to this day.

The first honest-to-goodness superhero to grace the pages of DC's *Adventure Comics* was Bernard Baily's Hourman, who was introduced in issue #48 (March 1940). The introductory story's first caption informed readers that a young chemist named Rex "Tick-Tock" Tyler had recently discovered "Miraclo, a powerful chemical that transforms him from a meek, mild scientist to the underworld's most formidable foe . . . with Miraclo he has for *one hour* the power of chained lighting-speed . . . But unless he performs his deeds of strength and daring within one hour, the effects of Miraclo wear off and the Hourman becomes his former meek self."

Adventure's next superhero was auspiciously launched in early 1941, when he got the cover and leadoff position of issue #61. This was Starman, who was quite a bit like the similarly named Skyman, who'd first taken to the air the previous year in Columbia Comics's *Big Shot Comics*. Neither had the benefit of an origin, and both were first-rate scientists who pretended to be laconic and cowardly playboys until duty called. The Skyman flew around in a super plane of his own invention; Starman flew by holding tight to his Gravity Rod—"For thousands of years men have spoken of the mysterious powers of the stars—but I am the first to discover that RADIATED STARLIGHT can be harnessed and used scientifically." The resemblances between the two heroes are accounted for by the fact that both were written by Gardner Fox.

Artwork on *Starman* was by Jack Burnley, who had been a syndicated sports cartoonist while still a teenager and an uncredited artist on *Superman* since 1940. Despite Burnley's impressive drawing and the feature's interesting fantasy stories—in which the red-clad Starman met invisible men, mad scientists who make their victims teenie weenie, and a host of other challenging villains—he failed to live up to DC's obvious great expectations.

Starman's loss of his favored status was indicated by *Adventure* #69 (December 1941), in which the Sandman got a new look—an updated costume with yellow tunic and tights, purple cowl, cape, and boots, and a boy

DC had a lot of hopes for Starman, but despite good scripts by Gardner Fox and splendid artwork by Jack Burnley, the character failed to seize the imaginations of readers. This page is from *Adventure Comics* #67.

©1941 by DC Comics, Inc.

The adventures of Ultra-Man were set in the year 2239. Despite Ultra-Man's impressive physique, his popularity was only middling, and he was not even featured on every cover. Artwork seen here is probably by Jon L. Blummer.

©1939 by All-American Comics, Inc.

companion named Sandy. The artist who converted Sandman into a costumed crimebuster was Chad Grothkopf. Paul Norris drew the revised hero for the next two issues and was replaced by Joe Simon and Jack Kirby. This imaginative, very talented team proceeded to do for Sandman what they'd just done for Captain America over at Marvel; quickly, Sandman became the hit of the magazine.

Under new management and with the help of Superman and their new bunch of heroes, DC prospered. The line didn't fully assume a group identity until the spring of 1940, when DC's familiar logo, a small circle proclaiming "a DC publication," began to appear on all covers. The seal was amended to read "A Superman DC Publication" in the fall of the following year. By that time Detective Comics, Inc. was publishing well over a dozen titles. *Superman* had been added in 1939, *Batman* in 1940, and *World's Finest*, a continuation of the earlier *World's Fair* annuals, in 1941.

Late in 1938 M. C. Gaines had entered into an agreement to produce a series of comic books that would appear under the DC umbrella. The initial titles, edited by the youthful Sheldon Mayer, were *Movie Comics* and *All-American Comics*. Both appeared the next year with cover dates of April 1939. While *All-American* featured some original material, it did not contain a single superhero and relied on newspaper reprints to fill many of its pages. Of the several characters shown on the bright yellow covers, only Mayer's

Scribbly was not a newspaper reprint. The cover blurb of the first issue began by announcing, "The only comic monthly with all your old favorites: Mutt & Jeff, Ben Webster, Tippie, Reg'lar Fellers, Skippy. . . ."

Mayer once explained *All-American*'s dearth of superheroes by revealing that Gaines, despite being instrumental in the discovery of Superman, didn't believe the public would be interested in any additional superheroes. So it was that the magazine's early, original features were pretty straightforward, and reminiscent of strips that had gone before: *Red, White and Blue*, about a spy smashing trio made up of a soldier, a sailor, and a marine; *Hop Harrigan*, Jon L. Blummer's aviator strip; *Adventures into the Unknown*, adaptations of the juvenile science-fiction novels of Carl H. Claudy. About the closest thing to a superhero in the first year of *All-American* was *Ultra-Man*, a futuristic adventure strip that started in issue #8 (November 1939). Set in the United States of North America in the year 2239 and starring a heroic fellow in red tunic, green shorts, and eagle-crested metal helmet, the strip was handled by *Hop Harrigan*'s Jon L. Blummer.

All-American finally succumbed to superhero fever in the summer of 1940, when it introduced the Green Lantern in issue #16. The creation of artist Mart Nodell, with considerable help from Mayer and writer Bill Finger, GL was a hit from the start. (A good deal of the early artwork was ghosted by Irwin Hasen, who was much later

Green Lantern received his marvelous crimefighting abilities from a mysterious power ring. Cover art is by Shelly Moldoff.
©1941 by DC Comics, Inc.

So fast was the Flash that he could save lives by outrunning speeding bullets. Cover art on the debut issue of the Flash's own comic is by Shelly Moldoff.
©1940 by DC Comics, Inc.

DC's super-speedster, the Flash, gave criminals fits, but also proved his mettle on busy city streets.
©1941 by DC Comics, Inc.

DC's *More Fun Comics* was a long-running title that featured many superheroes. On the cover of issue #101, Green Arrow and sidekick Speedy let fly against an unusually large foe.

©1945 by DC Comics, Inc.

DC's *Green Lantern* has proved himself one of DC's most enduring superheroes. Cover art for GL's debut issue is by Howard Purcell.

©1941 by DC Comics, Inc.

involved with the *Dondi* newspaper strip.) Helped out by his magical power ring and Brooklynesque sidekick Doiby Dickles, Green Lantern was a hit, and (with some revision over the years) has proved to be one of the most enduring superheroes in comic book history.

Once *All-American* opened its doors to the Green Lantern, other crimefighters and superheroes began to move in. The Atom arrived in #19 (October 1940), followed by Dr. Mid-nite in #25 (April 1941) and Sargon the Sorcerer in #26 (May 1941). The cast remained stable for the next several years. Even *Mutt & Jeff*, long one of Gaines's favorites, hung around for almost the entire life of the magazine.

DC tried something new with *Movie Comics*, which began at the same time as *All-American*. *Movie Comics* offered comic book versions of current movies and used still photos with captions and balloons. It sounds appealing, but what resulted were fuzzy, poorly colored, and impossibly truncated versions of such films as *Stagecoach*, *Gunga Din*, *Son of Frankenstein*, and *A Chump At Oxford*. *Movie* died after six issues. (Fiction House launched a comic of the same title in 1946; though the films were drawn in standard comic book style, this second incarnation of *Movie Comics* lasted just four issues.)

Flash Comics premiered with the January 1940 issue. With it, DC offered two superheroes plus a masked avenger and, for good measure, a comedy character with magical powers. Edited by Sheldon Mayer, much of the

magazine was written by Gardner Fox. His major creations were the Flash, also known as the Fastest Man Alive, and the winged avenger known as the Hawkman. Rounding out the early crew were the Whip, a Zorro impersonator; and Johnny Thunder, a nitwit who was looked after by a somewhat snide, anthropomorphized thunderbolt. Newspaper veteran Ed Wheelan drew another of the title's features, *Flash Picture Novelets*, which eventually became *Minute Movies*, a comic book version of his once-famous comic strip.

The final Gaines-Mayer DC monthly was *Sensation Comics*. The first issue bore a January 1942 cover date and showcased a star-spangled heroine named Wonder Woman. The feature was written by psychologist William Moulton Marston under the pen name Charles Moulton and drawn by veteran illustrator Harry G. Peter. Revolutionary in a quiet way, Wonder Woman demonstrated that a woman could be every bit as heroic as a man.

Among the other characters in *Sensation* were Mr. Terrific, the Gay Ghost, and Little Boy Blue. One of the more novel characters was Hasen and Finger's Wildcat, a boxing champ who donned an animal skin to fight crime.

One of Sheldon Mayer's more enduring inventions was *All Star Comics*. Originally a quarterly, it brought together characters from both the DC and M. C. Gaines's old All American branches of the family. The bright yellow cover of the first ▶

WONDER WOMAN AND HER SISTERS

Wonder Woman is the greatest female crimebuster in comic book history. On this whimsical *Sensation Comics* cover by H. G. Peter, WW leads the Holliday Girls on a Halloween adventure.

©1948 by DC Comics, Inc.

A half-century after her debut, Wonder Woman remains the preeminent female crimebuster of comic books. So enduring has been her appeal that it is difficult to realize that there was a time when no comic book superheroines existed at all. In fact, there were few female characters of any kind in the original-material comic books of the 1930s.

New Fun offered Sandra of the Secret Service and *New Adventure* made room for a lady daredevil named Dale Daring. Sheena, a product of the Eisner-Iger shop, made her jungle debut in *Jumbo Comics* #1 in the summer of 1938. She wore a skimpy leopard-skin outfit—attire that wasn't considered unusual by readers who'd grown up with Tarzan. The first true costumed lady crimefighter was Lady Luck. A Will Eisner creation, she debuted in June of 1940 as a back-up feature in his weekly *Spirit* newspaper comic book. Several artists drew the blonde, green-clad crimebuster over the next few years. Lady Luck had no superpowers and was similar to such male characters as the Crimson Avenger and the Green Hornet.

The earliest costumed heroine who actually had supernatural abilities was the Black Widow, who debuted in Tinely's *Mystic Comics* #4 (Aug-

ust 1940), billed as the "strangest, most terrifying character in action picture comics." Writer George Kapitan and artist Harry Sahle were responsible for her. The Widow dressed in a skin-tight black costume, gold-trimmed boots, and a green and blue cape. She had an impressive list of powers, including the ability to fly, to materialize at will, to strike her opponents dead, and to turn the pupils of her eyes into images of skulls. Rather than working on the side of law and order, the Black Widow was in the employ of Satan himself; she had died and was subsequently sent to Earth to track down sinners, kill them, and escort their souls safely to Hell. Not surprisingly, the morbid Ms. Widow didn't catch on and appeared only twice more in *Mystic* and two more times elsewhere.

Nineteen-forty saw few other new heroines. The Woman in Red began in *Thrilling Comics* #2 (March 1940), but a new year had begun before any further costumed ladies showed up. Among the earliest were two who signed on as companions to already established male characters. The Owl had been in *Crackajack* for several months when he was joined by Owl Girl in issue #32 (February 1941). Likewise, Bulletman was well-established by the time Bulletgirl joined him

Active and fearless, Wonder Woman (left) appealed equally to boys and girls. H. G. Peter drew the cover of her first issue. Bulletgirl (right) joined Bulletman in many adventures. Cover art is by Mac Raboy.

in *Master Comics* #13 (April 1941). In both instances the women were longtime friends of the heroes, and eventually discovered the heroes' true identities.

Harry Sahle gave it another try with a lady known as the Silver Scorpion, who was considerably better natured than the Black Widow. Hoodlums, unaccustomed to distaff do-gooders, tended to exclaim when they saw her—"G-gosh! It's a goil!" Introduced in Timely's *Daring Mystery Comics* #7 (April 1941), the Scorpion lasted two more issues and was gone.

Six more ladies went into business in magazines cover-dated August 1941: Miss America, Miss Victory, and Pat Patriot, as well as the Phantom Lady, the Black Cat, and Wildfire. This last character began in *Smash Comics* and possessed "the power to use flames for any purpose she desires, as a gift of the fire-god." Spider Queen, Madame Strange, and Lady Fairplay all appeared briefly in late 1940.

Dr. William Moulton Marston, a psychologist who'd lectured and taught at Radcliffe, Tufts, Columbia, and the New School of Social Research, was nearly fifty when he assumed the pen name Charles Moulton to begin scripting DC's *Wonder Woman*. The

rationale he put forth makes him sound like a pioneering feminist: "Women's strong qualities have become despised because of their weak ones," he wrote. "The obvious remedy is to create a feminine character with all the strength of a superman plus all the allure of a good and beautiful woman." As to whether boys would go for a strongwoman the doctor asserted, "Give them an alluring woman stronger than themselves to submit to and they'll be proud to become her willing slaves!" Marston certainly seems to have tipped his psychosexual hand with statements like that one.

The early Wonder Woman yarns are rich with the sort of bondage and submission fantasies that had hitherto been seen only in under-the-counter publications. Moulton's scripts were some of the wackiest continuities of the era; Wonder Woman offered wartime readers a heady brew of whips, chains, and cockeyed mythology. To bring all this to life Harry G. Peter was brought in as artist. A professional cartoonist since early in the century, he gave the feature a slightly decadent, entertainingly unsavory feel. His thick pen lines, blocky figures, and Rubenesque women added up to a unique comic-art style.

The thick linework employed by artist H. G. Peter gave
Wonder Woman a heavy, substantial look.

© DC Comics, Inc.

Wonder Woman was introduced at the back of *All Star* #8 late in 1941—"At last in a world torn by the hatreds and wars of men, appears a woman to show the problems and fears of men are mere child's play." The nine-page intro story began in the manner of some of the Dorothy Lamour sarong movies of the thirties, with a handsome blond aviator crashing on the "shores of an uncharted isle set in the midst of a vast expanse of ocean." Captain Steve Trevor is seriously hurt in the crash and is nursed back to health by Diana, the daughter of the Queen of Paradise Island. The island is an all-female enclave and the Amazons have been living there, immortal, since before the Christian era. They are dedicated, because of unfortunate past experiences, to keeping "aloof from men." But the power of love proves to be too strong for Princess Di and she leaves her island and forsakes her immortality to escort Steve back to America.

When *Sensation Comics* #1 (January 1942) appeared, Wonder Woman was its leading character. She arrives in the United States with Steve, flying her transparent airplane (nobody ever explained the advantage of an invisible plane in which the pilot remains visible). WW assumes the identity of a lovelorn nurse named Diana

Prince so that she can be close to Steve while he convalesces. The real Diana Prince has gone off to South America to be married. "By taking your place," she explains to the real Diana Prince, "I can see the man I love and you can marry the man you love." Suddenly, Wonder Woman sounds not quite as liberated as she had on her home turf. As with most dual identity situations, Steve never pays much attention to Diana the nurse and is enamored of Wonder Woman, whom he persists in calling "my beautiful angel."

In the second issue of *Sensation* readers met the sweets-loving Etta Candy and the girls of the Holliday College for Women. The students all seemed to attend classes wearing sweaters and shorts, but one of them criticizes Wonder Woman's costume for being too skimpy: "The Dean . . . insists on more above the waist."

Aided by Etta and the girls, Wonder Woman went on to wage war on spies, crooks, and assorted bizarre villains. There was hardly a story in which women weren't tied up with ropes, manacled with chains, and spanked. Sheldon Mayer, editor of *Sensation,* has said that the stuff would've been even wilder if he'd allowed Moulton to include all the plot elements and symbolism that the psychologist tried to sneak in.

issue, showing panels ripped from four of the strips, was designed by Mayer, who also drew the lively, star-spangled logo. In issue #3 (Winter 1940) the first meeting of the Justice Society of America (JSA) was held—with Sandman, the Atom, the Spectre, the Flash, Hawkman, Dr. Fate, the Green Lantern, and Hourman attending.

All Star #4, the first bimonthly issue, was also the first to feature a unifying theme that ran through all the stories. As devised by the inventive Gardner Fox, novel-length JSA adventures were divided into separate chapters, each featuring a particular hero; each hero's regular artist illustrated that chapter. From then on, the JSA teamed up in each issue to travel to other planets, defend the country against spies, feed the starving peoples of Europe, and defeat an impressive assortment of villains such as the Brain Wave, the Psycho-Pirate, and Degaton. By defying the conventional wisdom that kids don't like groups of heroes, *All Star*'s JSA concept paved the way for numberless superhero groups.

Not everything at DC was superhero-oriented. Like Major Nicholson before him, M. C. Gaines had a yearning to educate as well as entertain. As implemented by Nicholson, this yearning resulted in adaptations of the classics in *More Fun* and *New Adventure*. In Gaines's case, the result was *Picture Stories From the Bible*. The first issue appeared in 1942, with art by Don Cameron. Mayer never

Sheldon Mayer conceived *All Star Comics* and designed the cover of the first issue, seen here. By issue #3, the book had begun to chronicle the adventures of the Justice Society of America.

©1940 by All-American Comics, Inc.

thought much of the project and tried to have as little to do with the project as possible. But Gaines was determined to make the idea work, and followed his first title with *Picture Stories from American History*, in 1946. By the time *Picture Stories from World History* appeared in 1947, Gaines had parted with DC and founded his own EC line. Mayer stayed on at DC, stepping down as an editor in 1948 but continuing to draw for the company.

Late in 1939 pulp publisher Martin Goodman ventured into comic books. He called his outfit Timely Publications and the first issue of his new magazine was just plain *Marvel Comics*. While everything that the Funnies, Inc. shop dreamed up for the premiere issue wasn't first-rate, they did manage to include the Human Torch, Sub-Mariner, the Angel, and the jungleman Ka-Zar. As discussed in Chapter Five, *Marvel Comics* became *Marvel Mystery Comics* with the second issue. To most fans the magazine was always simply *Marvel* and it is the cornerstone of today's large Marvel Comics empire.

Timely introduced other titles, including *Daring Mystery Comics* and *Mystic Comics*, but never settled on a stable cast of characters. Over the ensuing months the publisher's heroes included the Fiery Mask, the Laughing Mask, the Phantom Bullet, Zephyr Jones and his Rocket Ship, Trojak the Tigerman, the Marvel Boy, the Thunderer, the Fin (another aquatic hero by Bill Everett, creator of Sub-Mariner), Blue Diamond, the Silver Scorpion, Citizen V, the Falcon, Blue Blaze,

Sub-Mariner first appeared in *Marvel Comics* and later graduated to his own title. Here, Subby inadvertently puts a pretty girl in peril; Namora speeds to the rescue.

©1947 by Manvis Publications

The ultimate patriot, Captain America is one of the greatest comic book characters of all time. His comic book adventures from the war years are thrilling and memorable. This typically frenetic cover was drawn by Alex Schomburg.

©1945 by Complete Photo Story Corp.

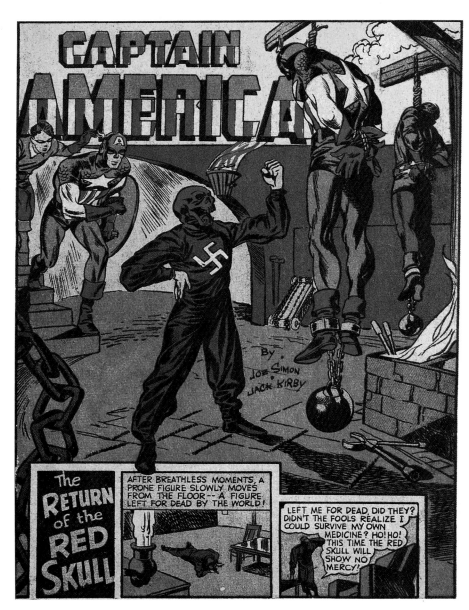

Captain America's most frightening (and persistent) nemesis was the Red Skull—murderer, betrayer, agent of Hitler. In this Simon and Kirby story from *Captain America #3*, the Skull cheats his would-be executioners.

©1941 by Timely Comics

Dynamic Man, Flexo the Rubber Man, the Black Marvel, Super Slave, the Blazing Skull, and the Destroyer. This lengthy roster of colorful heroes kept Timely's arists and writers busy, but did not inspire long-lasting reader interest.

The situation changed in 1941, when Timely introduced Captain America. Until Cap's debut in 1941, characters who got whole comic books of their own had first had a successful tryout elsewhere—Superman in *Action Comics*, Batman in *Detective Comics*, Captain Marvel in *Whiz*. Captain America was the exception, cooked up for Timely by the recently formed team of Joe Simon and Jack Kirby and introduced to the world in *Captain America Comics #1*. "Captain America was created for a time that needed noble figures," Kirby once recalled. "We weren't at war yet, but everyone knew it was coming. That's why Captain America was born; America needed a superpatriot." As to their new hero's appearance, Kirby said, "Drape the flag on anything, and it looks good. We gave him a chain mail shirt and shield, like a modern-day crusader. The wings on his helmet were from Mercury. . . . He symbolized the American dream." Obviously a superhero with that much going for him couldn't fail. Indeed, Captain America was a smash hit right from the start. The first issue provided not only his origin but also introduced Bucky, his boy companion.

Kirby had a good deal of help with the art chores. Simon did some of the inking, but pencilling and inking were also handled by Al Avison, Syd Shores, and Reed Crandall. Still, the book's visual tone really came from Kirby, whose flair for dynamic action and fluid anatomy set the tone not just for *Captain America*, but for two generations of superhero artists.

Kirby thought big; one identifying trademark of the art he did for Cap was his love of spacious panels that often stretched across two pages. "Movies were what I knew best," Kirby has said, "and I wanted to tell stories the way they do." When Simon and Kirby were lured over to DC, the Captain and Bucky were taken over by Avison, Shores, and others.

Throughout the magazine's glory days during World War II, its colorful, actionful covers made it instantly recognizable. Simon and Kirby set the style with the covers of the book's earliest issues, which placed Cap and Bucky in the midst of a wild variety of Axis death traps. They were menaced by stretch rack, fire, crushing, stabbing, and numerous other horrific methods. Throughout 1942, Al Avison's flair for the grotesque manifested itself in a cover gallery of fiendish Nazi hunchbacks and inhuman Japanese dwarfs. These howling fiends enjoyed their work, but then, Cap and Bucky enjoyed theirs, too!

Many of the best *Captain America* covers were by Alex Schomburg, a versatile artist who painted serious works in the contemplative style of Thomas Hart Benton, but who drew comic book covers with wild

abandon. As depicted by Schomburg, Cap and Bucky pursue evil by leaping from tram cars, locomotives, and the roofs of buildings. In scenes in which every bit of cover space is filled with hurtling figures, the pair slug it out with saboteurs, fifth columnists, gorillas, even Hitler himself. Inside and out, then, *Captain America* summed up all the energy and reckless fun of comics in the forties.

Captain America wasn't Timely's only success. The company put together a popular ensemble when it mixed a little of the Justice Society idea with Hollywood's Dead End Kids concept, to come up with the Young Allies. The first issue of the group's quarterly was published in the summer of 1941. The story filled the whole book and teamed Bucky and Toro—the Human Torch's boy pal—with three everyday kids—Knuckles, "formerly a dead-end kid," a fat boy named Tubby, and a black youth, Whitewash ("Yeah man! I is also good on de watermelon!") Well, what the comic lacked in racial understanding it tried to make up for with action. In the first story, the Young Allies join forces with a British secret agent, do combat with the formidable Red Skull, and even have a brush with Hitler in Berlin. At the end, after Captain America and the Human Torch have lent a hand, readers were asked, "Do you want to see more of the Young Allies?" The response was positive and the "small band of daring kids" went on to appear in twenty issues of their own magazine as well as in *Kid Komics*, *Amazing*, *Mystic*, and

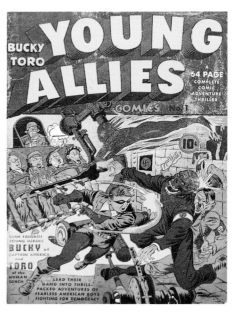

Rowdy (but patriotic) kid gangs were a staple element of comic books of the forties. Timely's *Young Allies* was a particularly action-packed example. Simon and Kirby drew the cover for issue #1; Alex Schomburg did #8.

©1941, 1943 by USA Publications

Three of Timely's greatest superheroes—and some lesser ones, too—adorned the cover of the first issue of *All Winners.*

©1941 by Comic Magazine Corp.

Marvel. As with *Captain America, Young Allies* was distinguished by fast, improbable action and wild covers by Simon and Kirby, Alex Schomburg, and Al Gabrielle.

The summer of '41 also brought Timely's answer to DC's *All Star: All Winners.* Unfortunately, the new magazine had to fudge a bit to come up with five heroes who could be labeled winners. Undoubtedly the Human Torch, Sub-Mariner, and Captain America fit the bill, but the Angel was a second stringer and the Black Marvel was known only to the few readers who had happened to notice him in the sporadically printed issues of *Mystic.* He was replaced in the second issue by the Destroyer and the oddly named Whizzer, a fellow who'd gained his super speed by way of a transfusion of mongoose blood.

Not until 1946 did Timely get around to imitating the Justice Society. At that time, it introduced a group known as the All Winners Squad. Consisting of the Human Torch, Sub-Mariner, Captain America, the Whizzer, and a lady known as Miss America, the squad had two book-length adventures, in *All Winners* #19 and #21 (there was no *All Winners* #20).

The country's fervent interest in superheroes meant that there was no dearth of entrepreneurs who wanted a piece of the comic book action that had been staked out by DC and Timely. One of them, Everett M. "Busy" Arnold, was a graduate of Brown University and had worked in the printing business since leaving college.

Tiny but tough—that was Quality Comics's Doll Man. A creation of Will Eisner, Doll Man debuted in *Feature Comics* and later gained a title of his own. Art for the cover of *Feature* #54 is by Gill Fox.

He'd printed the Cook-Mahon Comics Magazine titles (see Chapter Three) and in 1937 went into publishing himself. Possibly made cautious by the far from conspicuous success of Cook and Mahon's *Funny Pages* and *Funny Picture Stories*, Arnold made sure he had solvent partners in his own attempt. These included Frank J. Markey, who was an executive with the McNaught Syndicate and also ran a subsidiary syndicate using his own name, and the Cowles family. These latter worthies owned the Register & Tribune Syndicate, the Des Moines newspaper of that name, and *Look* magazine. For his editor Arnold brought in a cartoonist named Ed Cronin. Arnold called his company the Quality Comics Group, and his first title was *Feature Funnies*, a good example of the effect of the appearance and subsequent success of Superman. The comic book began life in the autumn of 1937 and was devoted mainly to reprinting newspaper strips. By early 1940 it had changed its name to *Feature Comics* and was showcasing a superhero of its own on the covers. This hero was a diminutive do-gooder known as Doll Man, created by Will Eisner and drawn in his earliest adventures by Lou Fine.

Quality's first companion to *Feature* came along in the summer of 1939, and was called *Smash Comics*. Despite the fact that *Smash* went on sale a year after *Action Comics* and was made up entirely of original material, the first issue had no superheroes. The closest thing was a robot named Bozo, the invention of a diligent but second-rate artist named George Brenner. Finally, in the fourteenth issue, the Ray arrived. Described as the "new sensation of the comic magazines," he had mysterious powers that included the ability to fly, to materialize out of a beam of light, and to convert himself by mystical means from a business-suited newsman to a yellow-costumed hero. The stories weren't especially compelling, alternating between crook sequences and fantasies involving pirates and monster-ridden castles, but Lou Fine's impressive artwork made the Ray worth following.

Despite his less than terrific storylines, the Ray might have remained the head man in *Smash Comics* had not a supremely inventive artist named Jack Cole come along with Midnight in *Smash* #18 (January 1941). Midnight—a character with physical similarities to Will Eisner's The Spirit—was a crimefighter who went to work wearing a suit, a fedora, and a domino mask. Cole's layouts were bold and unconventional, utilizing incredible long shots, overhead shots, close-ups, and other approaches that utilized the framing tricks of action movies and animated cartoons. Cole also had a strong and active sense of humor. He never took anything too seriously in his hero strips, including violence, death, and vast destruction.

By 1940, America's newsstands were becoming crowded with comic books. There still was room for more, however, so Quality introduced

Jack Cole's invigorating hero, Midnight, was introduced in an early issue of *Smash Comics*. On this lively Cole cover, Midnight and friends show that they're not going to be intimidated by Father Time.

©1949 by Everett M. Arnold

The Ray was a rather mystical fellow whose adventures were beautifully drawn by the talented Lou Fine. This page is from a *Smash Comics* adventure.

©1941 by Comics Magazine, Inc.

three new titles—and a new batch of super heroes and heroines. Counted among these new characters were a superpatriot, a man who could fly like a bird, a woman cop . . . and the only female impersonator in comic books.

The first of the new Quality titles, the explosively titled *Crack Comics*, appeared in the spring of 1940. Its features included *The Space Legion*, *The Red Torpedo*, and an old Cook-Mahon character, *The Clock*, who was having another go-round in comics. Artist Paul Gustavson contributed *Alias the Spider*, featuring an archer who fought crime and lawlessness with "his deadly bow." *Crack*'s most unusual strip, *Madam Fatal*, dealt with a famous character actor who dressed up like a little old lady to go after crooks. Crimebusting of the more familiar sort was provided by the Black Condor, a sturdy superhero whose dark blue costume included a cape that could be made to look like wings. In his youth he'd picked up the ability to fly and he used that ability in his war on crime. The most attractive thing about the feature was, as with the Ray, Lou Fine's art.

The first issue of Quality's *National Comics*, aptly enough, had a patriotic cover date of July 1940. Its star was Uncle Sam, enlisted from political cartoons and recruiting posters to fill a new role: superhero. Uncle Sam was billed on the cover as "America's Greatest Comic Character." The contents of *National* came from the Eisner-Iger shop; Eisner himself drew

the "9 action packed pages" that introduced Uncle Sam. Besides Uncle Sam, the new magazine offered such strips as *Prop Powers*, featuring a daredevil pilot; *Sally O'Neil*, concerning a pretty brunette policewoman; *Merlin the Magician*, which dealt with an idle playboy who inherits the cloak of the original Arthurian Merlin and becomes a dedicated super magician; *Wonder Boy*, who comes to earth "from the vacuous depths of outer space" and uses his "strength of a thousand men" to work as the first teenage superhero in comics; *Pen Miller*, starring a "famous comic magazine cartoonist who is also an amateur detective of wide reputation"; and *Kid Patrol*, a crimefighting variation of Hollywood's Our Gang (Little Rascals) concept.

Hit Comics arrived in the same month as *National* but never managed to live up to its name. The book had a dozen characters but not one was a winner. The leadoff story dealt with a blond good guy called Hercules. Then there was the Red Bee. The degree of seriousness involved with this character was best indicated by the pen name attached to it: B. H. Apiary. Any kid who knew what an apiary was could guess that the gentleman's initials must stand for Bee Hive. In real life the Bee was Rick Raleigh, an assistant DA in crime-infested Superior City. Impatient with the delays of the law, he decided to undertake a "one man fight on crime." Concealed in the buckle of his belt was a trained bumblebee, who came buzzing

Black Condor was carefully drawn by Lou Fine, a mainstay of the Quality Comics art staff throughout the 1940s.

©1942 by Comic Magazines, Inc.

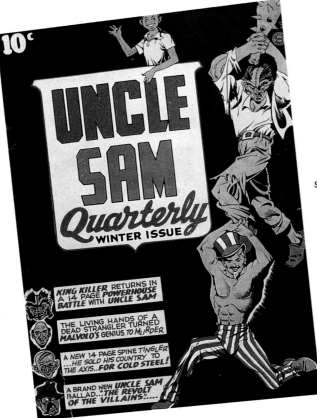

During World War II, Quality Comics turned venerable old Uncle Sam into a barrel-chested superhero. Cover art is by Lou Fine.

©1941 by Comic Magazines, Inc.

Plastic Man's remarkable physical abilities delighted readers, and allowed Plas's creator, artist Jack Cole, to indulge his own antic sense of humor.

©1948 by Comic Magazines

out on cue to sting criminals. A novel concept, yes, but not one that was destined to excite many readers.

The last two Quality monthlies bowed side by side in the summer of 1941. *Police Comics* #1 featured "the mysterious figure who fights for justice as the Firebrand." Fred Guardineer contributed *The Mouthpiece*, about "newly elected District Attorney, young Bill Perkins," who wore a black mask along with his business suit to go after "evasive figures beyond the law." Unlike most of the comic books of the period, *Police* found room for a woman character. "The society columns record the activities of Sandra Knight, debutante daughter of Senator Henry Knight. . . ." No one suspected that the frivolous Sandra was also the fabulous Phantom Lady, whose battles against spies and public enemies constantly made the headlines.

Plastic Man began his career in the middle of the first issue of *Police*. Another creation of Jack Cole, the red-suited rubberman had only six pages in which to introduce himself, get through the obligatory origin, and establish himself with the reader. He did an impressive job and by issue #5 he was also appearing on the covers. Readers loved the character's uninhibited physicality—he could elongate his fingers and turn them into the bars of a cage; he could flatten his body and skim through the sky like a kite; he could even bounce across the ground like a rubber ball. By *Police* #9 Plas had ousted Firebrand from the title's lead spot and had nine pages to himself. Less than six months after that poor Firebrand had departed and Cole's flexible hero had thirteen pages. Little wonder, for Cole had a strong sense of what the fast-growing new comic book business was all about. He knew how to package his work and how to communicate directly with the reader. Indeed, there is a freshness and an immediacy about Cole's Plastic Man that is matched by very few characters of the era. Wildly exaggerated, howlingly funny, and unafraid to bend the sometimes stolid "rules" of the superhero genre, Plastic Man is one of comics' all-time great creations.

During his heyday Plastic Man's only real competition came from the Spirit. Will Eisner's streetwise masked man first appeared in *Police* #11 (September 1942). The character was already two years old by that time, since the weekly *Spirit* booklets had first appeared in newspaper Sunday comic sections in June of 1940. For the comic book reprint of the first story, by the way, Eisner added the Spirit's domino mask to the full-face title panel portrait; he'd left that out the first time around. That initial episode was the origin story, but from then on the stories were not reprinted in sequence.

The Spirit was a strip of great inventiveness, distinguished by Eisner's moody, shadowed drawings (strongly reminiscent of Hollywood *film noir* crime thrillers), and by his flair for affecting, often bizarre characterizations, plot, and

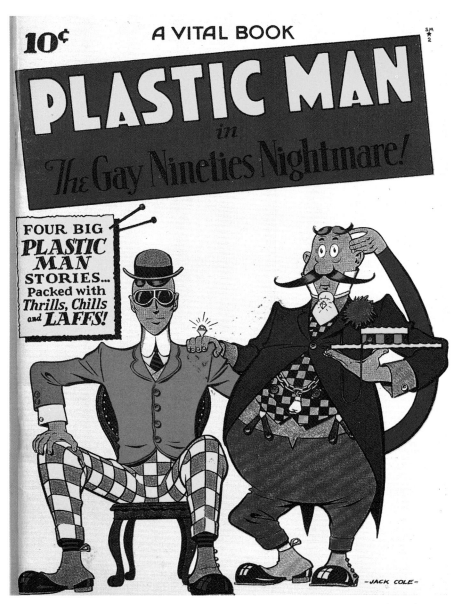

Plastic Man and artist Jack Cole offer their interpretation of the Gay Nineties on the cover of *Plastic Man* #2.

©1944 by Vital Publications, Inc.

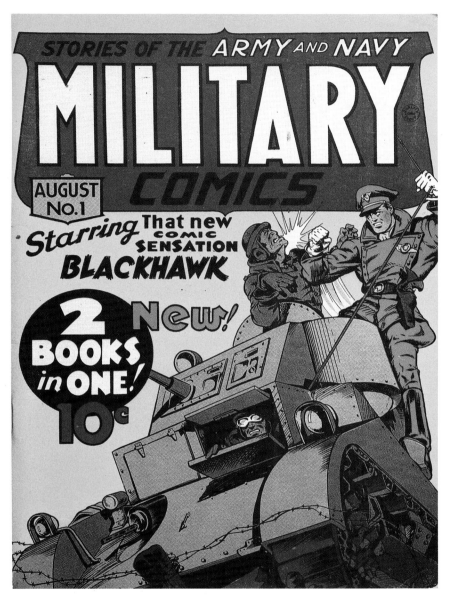

The indomitable Blackhawk—the only Polish superhero— dominated the pages of Quality's *Military Comics*. Blackhawk remains a popular character to this day. The cover of *Military* #1 was drawn by Blackhawk's creator, Will Eisner, who also created the Spirit.

©1941 by Comic Magazines, Inc.

dialogue. If Orson Welles had been a comic strip artist, he might have created The Spirit.

Quality's *Military Comics* was launched just a few months after the United Stated entered World War II. The magazine was edited by Eisner, who'd ended his partnership with Jerry Iger to start a shop of his own, and offered its readers "Stories of the Army and Navy." That cover slogan was rather loosely interpreted and some fairly unconventional warriors were to be found doing battle within.

The undisputed star of *Military* was Blackhawk. Created by Eisner and drawn by Charles "Chuck" Cuidera, he had the leadoff slot in every issue. In the first adventure readers learned that Blackhawk was a Polish aviator whose brother and sister had been killed by the Nazis. Escaping his occupied homeland, he acquired a mysterious island to use as a base. There, he recruited a band of freedom-minded outcasts and fugitives to carry on aerial guerilla warfare against Nazi Germany. With *Military* #12 Reed Crandall, with an assist from Alex Kotzky in that issue only, took over the drawing. A gifted draftsman with a keen sense of drama, Crandall was one of the best comic book illustrators of the period. Although adept at any genre, he seemed more at home with the Blackhawk crew than he had with any of the superheroes Quality had saddled him with. Crandall's *Blackhawk* work is excellent and he remained with the feature, off and on, for the next several years.

The good-looking cover for
America's Best #19 was
drawn by Alex Schomburg.

America's Best ©1946 by Visual Editions

Doc Strange owed his
amazing powers to a
chemical compound called
Alosun. Alex Schomburg
drew this, the Doc's last
appearance on a *Thrilling*
cover.

Thrilling ©1947 by Standard Magazines,
Inc.

Military Comics offered a lot more than just *Blackhawk*. The title also featured *Loops and Banks*, about a team of flyers; *Shot and Shell*, concerning a big blond hayseed pilot teamed with a diminutive con man named Colonel Shot; and *The Blue Tracer*, about a super plane that was the "newest and earliest flying engineer of war."

Military also featured *Death Patrol*, brightly written and drawn by Jack Cole. The strip dealt with "five convicts and one Del Van Dyne, former airlines pilot, thrown together by fate. They fly to England and fight for the RAF! THE DEATH PATROL, most daring of all British warbirds!" The group came by its nickname because in each of the earliest adventures one of them was killed and replaced by a new recruit. Cole turned out only three stories before turning things over to Dave Berg, an artist-writer who found popularity many years later with his "The Lighter Side of . . ." feature in *Mad* magazine.

The fullness of the *Military* lineup makes clear that one of the biggest differences between today's comics and those of a half-century ago is the number of features. Nowadays there is usually only one character, or a single team of characters, in each issue of a comic book. But in the old days a selection of anywhere from eight to a dozen separately featured characters was typical. All comic books boasted sixty-four pages (today's standard is thirty-two) and individual stories ran from four pages to thirteen.

As profits increased more and more publishers hopped onto the comic book bandwagon. One of them was Ned Pines, who had entered publishing in the 1920s. In the 1930s he and his editor-in-chief, Leo Margulies, were running the Thrilling Group of pulp magazines. Pines's list of pulp titles was a long one that included *Phantom Detective*, *Thrilling Detective*, *Thrilling Love*, *Thrilling Western*, *Startling Stories*, *Thrilling Wonder Stories*, *Black Book Detective*, and *The Rio Kid*. The Pines outfit also published *Screenland*, *Silver Screen*, and *Your Daily Horoscope*. Pines wanted to get into comic books. After a false start in 1939-40 with *Best Comics*, an eccentric, oversized magazine that had to be read sideways, Pines issued a more conventional title cover-dated February 1940. It was called, as might have been expected, *Thrilling Comics*. This was followed by *Exciting Comics* and *Startling Comics*.

Half of the first issue of *Thrilling* was devoted to the origin of Dr. Strange (not to be confused with the later Marvel mystery man). Created by writer Richard Hughes and drawn initially by Alexander Kostuk, Strange was a gifted scientist who'd invented a compound called Alosun. This elixir endowed him with a wide range of powers, including "the ability to soar through the air as if winged." By the fifth issue, no doubt under the influence of pulp hero Doc Savage, he changed his name to Doc Strange. He subsequently shed his civilian suits for a costume consisting of boots, red T-shirt, and blue riding breeches. Doc Strange was joined in *Thrilling* by the

Alex Schomburg created this Doc Strange action scene for *Thrilling* #11. Once again, the Nazis come out on the short end.

Ghost, the Rio Kid, and the Woman in Red.

Pines's next title, *Exciting Comics*, debuted with an April 1940 cover date, and offered a mix of features that included *The Space Rovers*. This science fiction opus was drawn, anonymously, by Max Plaisted, one of the leading illustrators of the *Spicy Detective* pulp. In its ninth issue (May 1941) *Exciting* introduced the Black Terror, yet another superhero who got his powers from a magic potion—"Bob Benton discovers titanic strength in a solution of formic ethers!" The science might have been shaky, but with his black hair, black domino mask, blue and red cape, and black costume adorned on its chest with a white skull and crossbones, the Black Terror was certainly one of the more intimidating-appearing of all the early superheroes.

Startling Comics originally starred Captain Future, who bore no resemblance to the Pines pulp hero of the same name. In issue #10 (September 1941) a superpatriot called the Fighting Yank was installed as the leading hero. Other characters included the Masked Rider; Mystico; and Biff Powers, Big Game Hunter.

Another important company to join the fray in this period was MLJ. Less formal than the movie studio MGM, the MLJ company took its name from the *first*-name initials of its proprietors, who had backgrounds in the pulps and in magazine distribution. They were Morris Coyne, Louis Silverkleit, and John Goldwater, who entered the burgeoning funny book field together at the end of 1939. The artwork and

SUPERPATRIOTS

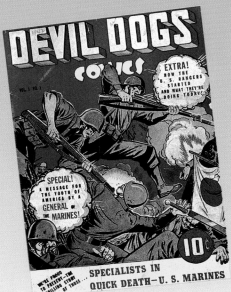

The patriotic fervor that was stirred by America's entry into World War II was immense, and was immediately reflected in comic books. Here, the *Devil Dogs* avenge Pearl Harbor.

©1942 by Street & Smith Publications, Inc.

The United States officially entered the Second World War in December of 1941, following the Japanese attack on the U.S. naval base at Pearl Harbor, Hawaii. In the tense years leading up to that event, as war jitters increased, over two dozen superpatriotic heroes and heroines showed up in American comic books. All wore costumes that utilized the stars and stripes in their design, all fought spies, saboteurs, and would-be invaders. The concerns of Americans—especially kid readers—as Hitler's war spread across Europe were reflected in comic books and especially in superpatriotic features.

As the 1930s ended, America was swept by a growing patriotic fervor. "Americans had dragged their patriotism out of the closet," reported *Life* in its July 22, 1940 issue, "and were wearing it in the streets as they had not done since 1918. Every musical show on Broadway featured the national anthem as a curtain-raiser or finale. Red, white and blue gallantly gleamed on lapels, umbrellas, hats and suspenders. Patriotic pins, pendants, clips and bracelets 'walked off the counters' of department and five-and-dime stores as fast as they could be stocked."

The Selective Service Act, better known as the draft, was passed in the autumn of 1940. Un-

doubtedly it was of more interest to the young writers and artists producing the comic book stories than to most of their readers. Many of the creators now had to face the possibility of being put into uniform—a khaki, or maybe navy blue, uniform and not one that was emblazoned with stars and stripes and accented by a flowing cape. That comic book creators grasped the reality of being drafted may account for the fact that some of the comic book superpatriots didn't exactly volunteer for their jobs.

The first superpatriotic hero was the Shield, who did volunteer. His star-spangled costume, adapted from the flag, set the style for what the well-dressed ultrapatriotic superhero should wear. Created by Harry Shorten and Irv Novick, he debuted in MLJ's *Pep Comics* #1 (January 1940). His avowed purpose was to "shield the U.S. government from all enemies." He was followed by Uncle Sam, who appeared in Quality's *National Comics*. Thanks to creator Will Eisner, the comic book Uncle Sam was a muscular superman rather than the aging, avuncular fellow most people knew from billboards and recruiting posters.

Next came Minute-Man, who debuted in Fawcett's *Master Comics* #11 (February 1941).

Superheroes did their bit for the war effort in a big way. At left, the Silver Streak takes on Hitler himself, while Major Victory (right) puts the brakes on some Nazi mischief.

©1941 by New Friday Publications, Inc. (*Silver Streak*)
©1944 by H. Clay Glover Co. (*Major Victory*)

After being drafted into the Army, Jack Weston is asked by his guardian, General Milton, to combat "an enemy who strikes from within. Sabotage and wholesale destruction will follow in the wake of the draft. To combat that I have chosen you. You are strong, brave and alert. You'll be more than a soldier. You'll be a MIN-UTE-MAN." No superpowers went with the job, but Jack got a red, white, and blue star-spangled costume that he wore beneath his Army private uniform. Dubbed the "One Man Army," Minute-Man specialized in fighting the usual assortment of spies, saboteurs, and foreign invaders.

Captain America also entered the field early in 1941, in his own magazine. His alter-ego, blond Steve Rogers, tries to enlist in the service but is turned down "because of his unfit condition." It isn't clear in the introductory episode whether he willingly takes an experimental injection from Professor Reinstein, but he does seem to go along with Reinstein's scheme to create a super-soldier. The "strange seething liquid" works like a magical Charles Atlas course and turns Rogers from a 97-pound weakling into a superhuman. Reinstein has envisioned a "corps of super-agents whose mental and physical ability will make them a terror to spies and sabo-

teurs!" But the prof is gunned down by a Gestapo agent after creating just one superman, who takes the name Captain America.

It would seem, if you think about it at all, that carrying on a double life while a private in the United States Army would be extremely difficult. Nonetheless Rogers, like Jack (Minute-Man) Weston, tried just that. He pulled it off, too, and even met Bucky Barnes, an energetic, fearless youngster who's described as the "mascot of the regiment." The two teamed up against the "vicious elements who seek to overthrow the U.S. government!"

Several women became superpatriots in 1941. A lady named USA, the Spirit of Old Glory, commenced her brief career in Quality's *Feature Comics* #42 (March 1941). She wasn't exactly a person, but rather a sort of mystical figure who personified the spirit of the American flag. A blonde in a short, blue dress, she carried a large flag that was able to flutter on its own. When it didn't, that meant trouble and prompted USA to utter the memorable line, "My flag droops . . . danger lurks!" The danger might be a subversive school teacher or an invasion by a foreign army decked out in purple uniforms. USA was a novel character, but she had just seven adventures.

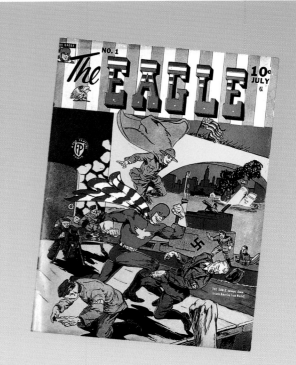

Captain Battle (left) used an amazing array of inventions in his ceaseless fight for "freedom and decency." Art is by Jack Binder. The Eagle (right) laughs off Nazi machine gun fire on the cover of the first issue of his own comic.

©1941 by New Friday

Quality tried again with Miss America, who bowed in *Military Comics* #1 (August 1941). A similarly named heroine, Miss Victory, showed up in the first issue of Holyoke's *Captain Fearless* (August 1941). Over at Lev Gleason, Pat Patriot was working in an aircraft factory when, suspecting her bosses of sabotage, she donned a red, white, and blue costume and became "America's Joan of Arc." She appeared in *Daredevil* from #2 (August 1941) through #11 (June 1942). The very talented Reed Crandall was the first of several artists to draw Pat's adventures.

Male superpatriots continued to proliferate during 1941. Captain Battle was the invention of Jack Binder and various members of his art and editorial shop. The captain, who first appeared in Lev Gleason's *Silver Streak Comics* #10 (May 1941), stood out from all the others because he wore a black patch over his left eye. As his origin story explained, the captain had been the youngest combatant in World War I, and had lost his eye in battle. According to an introductory caption, Battle "has given his life to the scientific perfection of inventions which he uses to overcome evil and aggressive influences. His curvoscope, his luceflyer and his dissolvo give him

power possessed by no other mortal alive." Captain Battle was armed for bear, and a good thing, too, for he coped with somewhat more exotic villainy than that faced by his colleagues. In his initial adventure he notes some strange doings in Europe by way of his curvoscope, a telescope that "allows him to see anywhere on Earth, because its lenses follow the Earth's curves." It seems a race of giant birdmen is invading Europe. Captain Battle races over there in his luceflyer, which travels at "almost the speed of light," and defeats the plan.

Marvel offered two superpatriots in *U.S.A. Comics*, the Defender and Mr. Liberty, and added the Patriot to *Marvel Mystery Comics* after the character had tried out in the Human Torch's magazine. Among the others from various publishers were Captain Courageous, the Conqueror, Man of War, the Lone Warrior, Captain Freedom, Captain Flag, the Stars and Stripes (a patriotic trio), the Flag, Flagman, Major Victory, the Fighting Yank, Stormy Foster, the Great Defender, Yankee Doodle Jones, U.S. Jones, and the Star-Spangled Kid. Ironically, few new superpatriots were introduced after America actually entered the war.

Nazi dictator Adolf Hitler turned up on an occasional comic
book cover, but never as vividly as here, on *Daredevil* #1. Our
hero gives Der Fuehrer plenty to think about. Art is by
Bob Wood and Charles Biro.

scripts for the earliest issues of their new titles were provided by the Harry "A" Chesler shop. While talented people did work for Chesler, it's evident he didn't send in his first team to turn out material for Morris, Louis, and John; the MLJ line got off to a rather shaky start with *Blue Ribbon Comics*. The first issue bore a November 1939 cover date and its star was not a costumed hero but a dog. Rang-A-Tang, billed as the Wonder Dog, gnaws on a villain's wrist on the cover and leads off the issue with a six-page adventure. *Blue Ribbon*'s first superhero appeared in the second issue. He wore a green costume, a green cowl with wings over the ears, and a scarlet cape. His name was Bob Phantom, which isn't a particularly striking name for a fellow who fancied himself "the Scourge of the Underworld." A crimefighter with a first name is just too folksy to strike terror in crooked hearts. (How do you suppose bad guys would react to Bill Batman or Fred Superman?)

Artist Charles Biro—soon to become a major force in the industry—was the most talented contributor to the second issue of *Blue Ribbon*. His *Scoop Cody*, dealing with an ace newsman, ended after two issues, but *Corporal Collins*, about a "two-fisted American in the French infantry," fared somewhat better.

MLJ quickly wised up to the poor quality of work that the Chesler shop had provided. The company quit Chesler and hired some of his better staffers away from him. *Blue Ribbon* #4 (June 1940) introduced a batch of new characters, including Hercules,

Rang-A-Tang the Wonder Dog was the original star of MLJ's *Blue Ribbon Comics*. Cover art for issue #8 was drawn by Ed Smalle.

©1940 by M.L.J. Magazines, Inc.

The Shield & Dusty team up with Hangman on the cover of *Pep Comics* #8, drawn by Irv Novick.

©1941 by M.L.J. Magazines, Inc.

Bob Montana, the creator of Archie, drew the cover for *Top-Notch Laugh* #30, one of the first issues of the revised *Top-Notch*. MLJ had (temporarily) given up on superheroes.

©1942 by M.L.J. Magazines, Inc.

the Fox, the Green Falcon, and Ty-Gor. The ninth issue (February 1941) signed on Mr. Justice. Created by writer Joe Blair and artist Sam Cooper, he was, like DC's Spectre, dead. And like the Spectre, Mr. Justice had those blankly staring, Orphan Annie eyes. Off duty, his peepers reverted to normalcy and he assumed "the form of a mortal man," a handsome blond fellow in a conservative business suit. *Blue Ribbon*'s last hero, Captain Flag, bowed in issue #16 (September 1941).

The second MLJ title was *Top-Notch Comics*, and only one superhero was dreamed up for its December 1939 debut issue—the Wizard, the fellow with the Super Brain. Bob Phantom became part of the cast in issue #3. The Firefly, creation of writer Harry Shorten and artist Bob Wood, was added in #8 and in #9 (October 1940) came the Black Hood, another of those impatient officers of the law who became a vigilante. In addition to the intimidating hood that give him his name, he wore a yellow tunic, black shorts, and yellow tights.

In the summer of 1942 *Top-Notch* converted to humor. With the bold slogan, "We dared to do it!! A Joke Book That's Really Funny!" issue #28 appeared under the revised title *Top-Notch Laugh*. The Black Hood stayed on for a time but most of the other heroes were dumped and replaced by allegedly funny stuff the caliber of *Dotty and Ditto*, *Pokey Oakey*, and *Senor Siesta*.

MLJ's *Pep Comics* had a January 1940 cover date on its first issue. At the outset, the

Joe Simon and Jack Kirby
illustrated the adventures of
the Black Owl in *Prize
Comics*. This handsome
page is from *Prize #9*.

©1940 by Feature Publications

The faintly menacing Green
Lama was a terror to
crooks everywhere.

©1940 by Feature Publications, Inc.

The Black Owl swings into
action to thwart wartime
saboteurs.

©1941 by Feature Publications, Inc.

magazine boasted two
superheroes— one of them, the
Shield, was the first of that breed
of comic book superpatriots who
wore red, white and blue. Harry
Shorten was the scriptwriter and
Irving Novick the artist on these
adventures of "the G-Man
Extraordinary." *Pep*'s other
super-powered character was
Jack Cole's the Comet. When the
Comet was killed by gangsters'
bullets, his brother, the
Hangman, replaced him in issue
#17.

The MLJ folks inaugurated
their fourth and last monthly as
1940 was starting. Over at *Action
Comics*, Superman was known as

the Man of Steel, but that didn't
bother the upstart of *Zip Comics*,
Steel Sterling. A red-costumed,
abundantly muscled fellow, the
character was a joint effort by
artist Charles Biro and the
magazine's editor, Abner Sundell.
Since Biro had been doing cute
comedy fillers until a few months
earlier, he still was not
completely at home with straight
adventure. But he had a strong
sense of action and his early
pages, though often crudely
drawn, had movement and life.
Throughout his career, in fact,
Biro's potent techniques for
grabbing and holding the
readers' attention would always

America's Fighting Twins,
Yank and Doodle, battle
Japanese agents atop the
Statue of Liberty. Cover art
is by Jack Binder.

©1942 by Feature Publications, Inc.

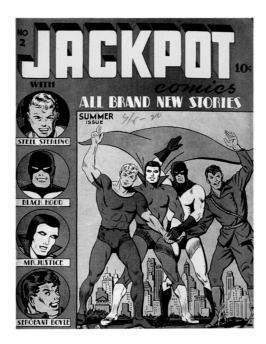

MLJ's big guns strike a
friendly pose on the cover
of *Jackpot Comics* #2,
drawn by S. Cooper.

©1941 by M.L.J. Magazines, Inc.

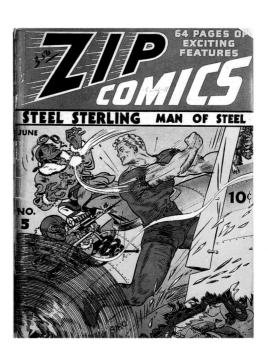

Steel Sterling was artist
Charles Biro's first attempt
at a "serious" feature. As
this action-packed *Zip
Comics* cover suggests,
Biro picked up the knack
pretty quickly.

©1940 by M.L.J. Magazines, Inc.

be several paces ahead of his
actual drawing ability. Besides
Steel Sterling, *Zip* offered other
costumed heroes—Scarlet
Avenger, Mr. Satan, Black Jack,
and the Web.

The deluge of new
companies and new titles
continued through the early
forties. Crestwood offered *Prize
Comics*, with the Black Owl, the
Green Lama, and Dick Briefer's
Frankenstein. Vincent Sullivan
left DC to edit Columbia
Comics's *Big Shot Comics*, the
home of Skyman, the Face, and
Sparky Watts. The Hillman
Company, a pioneer in paperback
books, introduced *Air Fighters*

starring "America's Ace," Airboy.
The Harvey Brothers were
responsible for *Speed Comics*,
Green Hornet, and *Champ* and
such characters as Captain
Freedom, Shock Gibson, and the
Black Cat, the last a long-legged
beauty who was one of the most
successful of lady crimefighters.

The Curtis Publishing
Company of Philadelphia,
publisher of both the *Saturday
Evening Post* and *Ladies Home
Journal*, unobtrusively went into
the comics business in 1940, too.
Calling itself Novelty Press, Inc.
and operating out of editorial
offices on West 52nd Street in
Manhattan, Curtis issued *Target*

Writer Ed Gruskin came up with a winner when he created Supersnipe, the musclebound alter ego of Koppy McFad, the boy with the most comic books in America. The cover of *Supersnipe* #13, probably drawn by C. M. Payne, depicts one of Koppy's dreams of glory.

©1944 by Street & Smith Publications

Comics and *Blue Bolt*. The former featured Carl Burgos's the White Streak, Basil Wolverton's eccentric Spacehawk, and Bob Wood's the Target. The hero of the second title was Blue Bolt, a character that represented the first collaboration of the formidable team of Joe Simon and Jack Kirby.

Also available on newsstands in the early 1940s were Nita Publications's *Whirlwind Comics* (with Cyclone), Bilbara Publishing's *Cyclone Comics* (featuring Tornado Tom), Lev Gleason's *Silver Streak* (starring the title character and the villainous Claw), Holyoke's *Cat-Man*, Hyper's *Hyper Mystery* (starring Hyper the Phenomenal), and dozens more.

Inevitably, the novelty value of costumed superheroes faded, and the genre became ripe for parody. The comic book industry produced a number of mock heroes in the early 1940s, including Sparky Watts, Al T. Tude, Stuporman, and Powerhouse Pepper. By far the best—and most insightful—sendup of the superhero genre was Street & Smith's *Supersnipe Comics*. Written by Ed Gruskin, the feature had trial runs in *Shadow Comics* and *Doc Savage Comics* before graduating to a bimonthly title of its own in the fall of 1942. The charming central character was Koppy McFad, also known as "The Boy with the Most Comic Books in America." An imaginative, well-meaning lad, Koppy was driven by dreams of glory that were fueled by the enormous quantities of comic

books he read. Above all else, he longed to be a superhero. Undaunted by reality, Koppy put together a costume from his grandfather's red flannels, his father's lodge cape, and his own tennis shoes. Thus attired, he set out to fight crime as Supersnipe. Koppy's heroic alter-ego had no super strength, however, and couldn't fly, either, so he got around mainly on foot or by bicycle.

Now and then Koppy would have dream-sequence adventures in which Supersnipe was a real, grown-up superman, complete with rippling muscles, skin-tight costume, and flowing cape. Curiously, though, Supersnipe's head remained that of a small boy. George Marcoux, who had assisted on the *Skippy* newspaper strip and drawn a kid strip of his own, *Toddy*, was the artist for Koppy's real-life adventures. The amusing dream sequences were illustrated by another newspaper veteran, C. M. Payne.

Supersnipe was refreshing because it poked fun at the whole idea of costumed heroes and youthful aspirations to adventure. Often, the situations that Koppy perceived to be dire crimes turned out to be far less sinister, and when he did encounter crooks, they were petty small-timers who were far removed from the evil masterminds of the boy's imagination. Most of the stories had a pleasant undertone of the sort of smalltown-America humor that typified radio shows like *Fibber McGee and Molly* and *The Great Gildersleeve*. *Supersnipe* enjoyed a respectable forty-four-issue run that

With popular characters the caliber of Captain Marvel and Captain Midnight, Fawcett Publications enjoyed healthy sales throughout the 1940s.

©1942 by Fawcett Publications, Inc.

The mystical Ibis was Fawcett's "Miracle Man," and indeed, the entire comic book industry had enjoyed miraculous growth during the 1940s.

©1942 by Fawcett Publications, Inc.

concluded in 1949.

The success of *Supersnipe* proved that readers were willing to laugh at superheroes but, by the middle 1940s, the even greater success of many of the "straight" superheroes meant that the comic book industry was enjoying its best years to date. For example, in 1944 DC was publishing nineteen different titles and running up combined monthly sales of over 8,500,000 copies. In 1945 Fawcett, with eight titles, reported sales of nearly 4,500,000 each month. Their *Captain Marvel Adventures* alone averaged over 1,300,000 copies per issue. That same year MLJ's five titles had combined sales of nearly 2,000,000 monthly, Quality's nine titles sold over 1,500,000, and the American Comics Group's (ACG) two funny animal books, *Giggle Comics* and *Ha Ha Comics*, sold over 650,000 combined.

A publisher usually made six cents on every ten-cent comic book sold. On a book such as *Captain Marvel*, Fawcett would take in about $78,000 per issue for a total of around $936,000 a year. DC's gross for 1945, when they'd increased their roster to twenty-one titles, was in the neighborhood of $6,500,000, and that doesn't include profits from toys, movies, radio shows, and other forms of licensing and merchandising. Even ACG, with only *Giggle* and *Ha Ha* at that point, could count on an annual gross take of almost $500,000. Sales figures like these are what inspired the continuing expansion of the comic book industry during the war years and after.

LAFF IT UP!

In the 1930s and 1940s there was a good deal more to be found in comic books than just superheroes and costumed crimefighters. During those years, when the comic book market was still expanding, quite a few comic books really were comic. All sorts of funny stuff was available, from relatively sophisticated satire to knockabout burlesque to the kind of bunny-rabbit whimsy that produced giggles in the nursery. The decade of the forties, especially, was a period when publishers sought to expand their audience in both directions, luring older readers with such things as true crime and sexy women and enticing younger readers with more wholesome fare. Most of the titles aimed at tots were humorous, and a great many of them featured funny animals.

The king of the animals since the late 1920s was Walt Disney, and his screen characters had begun appearing on newsstands in the middle 1930s. *Mickey Mouse Magazine* was issued in the summer of 1935 by K.K. Publications. This company represented a partnership between the

Whitman Publishing Company and Disney's Kay Kamen. A former Kansas City department store executive and advertising man, Kamen had been hired by the Disney studio in 1932 to set up a New York-based merchandising department and handle the licensing of the Disney cartoon animals. It was during Kamen's early years with the organization that the Walt Disney name and familiar stylized signature began showing up on products that bore the likenesses of Mickey, Donald Duck, and the rest of the cartoon family. This merchandising provided a visual link between Walt Disney himself and the characters his company controlled. It also helped to make Disney one of the best-known men in America.

Mickey Mouse Magazine was not exactly a true comic book. With the debut issue measuring 10¼ by 13¼ inches, it was slightly larger than what would later become the industry standard. With the second issue, dimensions were trimmed to 8½ by 11½, and a heavier paper stock was used. In the early issues readers got no more than four pages of comics; the rest of each issue consisted of text stories about Mickey, fairy tales, poems, puzzles, a "Wise Quacks" joke page edited by Donald Duck, and sundry other features and fillers. Oskar Lebeck contributed an assortment of original strips and stories, most notably a feature starring Peter the Farm Detective. By 1940 five pages of reprints, including the *Mickey Mouse* daily and, usually, a *Donald Duck* Sunday page were highlights of each issue.

Donald Duck revels in the holiday spirit on the cover of *Mickey Mouse Magazine* #52.

©1940 by K. K. Publications, Inc.

Walt Disney's Comics & Stories featured the work of artist/writer Carl Barks, who created dozens of brilliant Donald Duck adventures.

©1952 by Walt Disney Productions

Walt Kelly, the creator of Pogo, brought his delightful cartoon style to this 1943 *Pat, Patsy and Pete* adventure that appeared in *Looney Tunes*.

©1943 by R. S. Callender

Looney Tunes #6. Note the signature of cartoon producer Leon Schlesinger, who neither wrote nor drew.

©1942 by Leon Schlesinger Productions

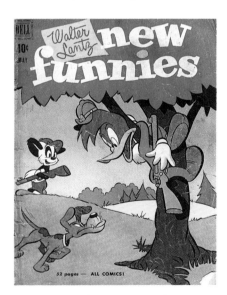

Animated-cartoon producer Walter Lantz never achieved the stature of rival Walt Disney, but two of his creations, Andy Panda and Woody Woodpecker, have retained much of their popularity through the years. This is the cover of *New Funnies* #171.

©1951 by Walter Lantz Productions

Walt Disney's Comics & Stories replaced Mickey's mag in the fall of 1940, with Dell now joining in as publisher. The new book was originally made up almost entirely of newspaper reprints—Floyd Gottfredson's splendid mock-adventure *Mickey* dailies, Al Taliafero's funny gag-a-day *Donald Duck* strips, and various Sundays, including the *Silly Symphony* pages. A change was made in 1943 when the magazine's leadoff stories became original Donald Duck adventures. The artist and writer was an ex-gag cartoonist and animator named Carl Barks (see sidebar), whose energetic drawing style and whimsical, imaginative stories won him two generations of loyal fans.

The Disney stable proved to be a gold mine, so Dell went on to license the Warner Brothers animated cartoon characters. The first issue of *Looney Tunes and Merrie Melodies* appeared late in 1941 with individual stories devoted to Porky Pig, Elmer Fudd, and Bugs Bunny. In the comic's early days, the artwork was produced on both coasts. Chase Craig (who drew Porky) and Roger Armstrong (Mary Jane and Sniffles) were based in Southern California; George Storm (Bugs Bunny) was in Manhattan. So was a talented cartoonist named Walt Kelly, who'd returned to the East after toiling in the Disney studios as an animator. In time, he'd find international fame as the creator of the *Pogo* newspaper strip, but his early work was more modest. His first feature for *Looney Tunes* was *Kandi the Cave Kid* and it was credited, as were all the

stories in each issue, to Leon Schlesinger, the non-drawing (and, by all accounts, generally uncreative) producer of the Warner movie cartoons.

Win Smith, a former Disney employee who'd done early artwork on the *Mickey Mouse* daily, drew the very first *Bugs Bunny* story before Storm tried his hand for a few issues. *Looney Tunes* also gave space to an alternating variety of other characters, such as Chester Turtle, Ringy Roonga, and Charlie Carrot, one of the few vegetables ever to appear in a comic book feature of his own; logically enough, Charlie's girlfriend was a tomato. *Pat, Patsy and Pete*, about two kids and a talking penguin, was not a Warner property, but it ran in the magazine for several years. Smith started the feature and eventually handed it to Storm. Kelly drew six episodes in 1943, converting it into a raucous slapstick comedy.

Andy Panda, a product of the Walter Lantz animation studios, wound up in *The Funnies* #61 (October 1941) when the magazine was still playing it straight; Andy's earliest co-workers were Captain Midnight, Phantasmo, and Philo Vance. With the sixty-fifth issue (July 1942) the book's title was changed to *New Funnies* and offered a potpourri of Lantz characters and comedy and fantasy characters from other sources. Lantz was represented by *Andy, Oswald the Rabbit, Li'l Eightball*, and his most popular and enduring creation, *Woody Woodpecker*. From the estate of onetime political cartooonist Johnny Gruelle came *Raggedy* ▶

CARL BARKS

Anonymous for years, writer/artist Carl Barks today receives his due as one of the greatest creative talents in comic book history.

Unsung and anonymous during his active years in comic books, Carl Barks is now acclaimed as one of the medium's authentic geniuses. He gained his fame by drawing ducks, but because the ducks were the property of Walt Disney, Barks was never allowed to sign his work. Yet, because of the quality and individuality of what he did, he gradually became one of the most well-known and admired cartoonists in the world.

Carl Barks was born in a remote part of eastern Oregon in 1901, and by the late 1920s had started to sell his cartoon drawings. He avoided the crowded New Yorker-style market by aiming lower, selling gags to *College Humor* and *Judge*. He was even more successful with markets that were receptive to mildly risque material. Gags of this sort, which Barks built around well-endowed ladies in various states of undress, were especially well received by a Minneapolis-based magazine called *The Calgary Eye-Opener*. Barks accepted a staff job there in 1931 and stayed with the magazine until 1935,

when he got a job with the Walt Disney studios in Los Angeles.

Although hired for twenty dollars a week as an animated cartoon "in-betweener" (an artist who creates the drawings that fill in the movement between key drawings made by more experienced animators), Barks quickly displayed an inventiveness that convinced the studio he was better suited to the story department. He remained there until the early 1940s, when he decided to quit Disney and try his hand at something else.

"Something else" turned out to be comic books. Before leaving Disney, Barks (along with artist Jack Hannah) had worked on a one-shot 1942 comic called *Donald Duck Finds Pirate Gold,* written by Bob Karp. Based on a never-produced animated cartoon, it was the first original Donald Duck comic book. Late in 1942 Barks heard that Dell-Western wanted somebody to do original ten-page stories to be added to the lineup of *Walt Disney's Comics & Stories*. He was hired and his first work appeared

Barks's pricelessly funny Donald Duck and Uncle Scrooge
adventures are models of effective plotting, characterization,
and visual storytelling.

in issue #31 (April 1943).

Soon after, Barks was writing as well as drawing. His most notable innovation was to broaden Donald Duck's character. "Instead of making just a quarrelsome little guy out of him, I made a sympathetic character," Barks has recalled. "He was sometimes a villain, and he was often a real good guy and at all times he was just a blundering person like the average human being."

Donald's three nephews—Huey, Dewey, and Louie—underwent changes, too, becoming resourceful and inventive. "I broadened them like I did Donald, started out with mischievous little guys and ended up with little scientists, you might say."

Barks added full-length Donald books to his schedule in 1943. It was with the stories produced from this point onward—"The Mummy's Ring," "Frozen Gold," "Volcano Valley"—that Barks hit his stride. With plenty of space to move around in, he created carefully plotted graphic novels. The stories were full of adventure, action, comedy, and satire. They were set in exotic locales and featured some of the best cartooning and visual storytelling ever to be found in comic books.

A 1947 adventure called "Christmas on Bear Mountain" introduced Barks's major creation—Uncle Scrooge. Penurious, paranoid about protecting his vast fortune from the scheming Beagle Boys and other menaces, yet gruffly fond of Donald and the nephews, Uncle Scrooge is at once whimsical and delightfully real. Other characters that Barks vividly brought to life include inventor Gyro Gearloose and the supremely insincere Gladstone Gander.

Barks retired at the age of 65 and has devoted himself since to painting. These works, many of which feature, yes, ducks, are eagerly sought by collectors. His comic book work has been continually reprinted and, since Walt Disney's death in 1966, Barks's important contribution to the Disney family has been publicly acknowledged by comic book publishers and by the Disney organization.

Ann and *Mr. Twee Deedle*. For good measure there were reprints of *Felix the Cat* and the *Peter Rabbit* Sunday page, plus *Billy and Bonny Bee* by Frank Thomas and an updated version of the venerable *Brownies*.

The Whitman-Dell coalition continued its assault on the kid market with the bimonthly *Animal Comics*, which commenced late in 1941. It was here that Walt Kelly's Pogo began his long and successful career. Although the original star of the magazine, from the second issue on, was meant to be Howard Garis's venerable rabbit gentleman Uncle Wiggily, Pogo and his swamp-dwelling pals eventually pushed Unc into a secondary position. The first all-Pogo comic book came along in the spring of 1946, under the title *Albert the Alligator & Pogo Possum*. By 1949 a *Pogo Possum* magazine was being issued on a fairly regular basis. Finally, in 1949, the *Pogo* newspaper strip started running nationally, and Kelly gained his widest and most enthusiastic audience.

Dell's *Our Gang Comics* and *Raggedy Ann and Andy*, and Western's *Fairy Tale Parade* all arrived in 1942, offering a mixed bag of animal and human characters. In *Our Gang* Kelly drew the adventures of the kids featured in the MGM comedy shorts, blending melodrama and slapstick far more agreeably than in the shorts themselves. The film series, produced with care by the Hal Roach studio beginning in 1922, had shifted to MGM in the late thirties and was on its last legs by the time Kelly was given the comic book

assignment. His success with the feature is a splendid example of the power of his imagination and sense of whimsy.

More Kelly was on view in *Fairy Tale Parade*, in which the artist would typically draw about half of each issue. In addition, he contributed to *Santa Claus Funnies* and *Easter with Mother Goose*, both irregularly issued titles.

Also adapted from MGM properties were Tom & Jerry, Benny Burro, and Barney Bear. Carl Barks eventually took over Benny and, later, the burro teamed up with the bear. These stories were milder and more innocuous than those Barks was creating for the Disney ducks.

In addition to Ann and Andy stories by veteran artist George Kerr, the *Raggedy Ann* magazine offered *Billy and Bonny Bee* and *Egbert the Elephant*. Most issues of the above-mentioned titles were edited by Oskar Lebeck.

Marvel's earliest funny animal title was *Krazy Komics*, first published in the summer of 1942. Editor Vince Fago and a staff that included Kim Platt, George Klein, Dave Gantz, and Stan Lee offered an all-new crew of animated cartoon-type characters. Even at this early date, the funny animal formula was looking a bit threadbare, and there were no surprises in such characters as Posty Pelican, Toughy Tomcat & Chester Chipmunk, and Al Jaffee's Silly Seal & Ziggy Pig. *Krazy*'s most unusual feature was an oddity called *The Creeper & Homer*, starring a mysterious villain and a not-too-bright rabbit. It managed now and then to work

Krazy Komics was Marvel's first funny animal title. On the cover of issue #9, Ziggy Pig and Silly Seal indulge in a little wartime propaganda at the expense of Toughy Tomcat.

©1943 by Jest Publishing

Animator Paul Terry's most enduring creation is Mighty Mouse, seen here on the cover of *Terry-Toons* #49.

©1946 by Timely Comics, Inc.

Uncle Wiggily and Albert the Alligator go fishing on the cover of *Animal Comics* #14, beautifully drawn by Walt Kelly.

most of the magazine's artists and writers into the stories and on one occasion publisher Martin Goodman himself appeared to complain, "Ah, woe is me! Krazy Komics is 14 months late, and my laundry hasn't come back from [writer] Stan Lee's." Later in the year, Marvel's *Terry Toons*, adapted from Paul Terry's rather dull movie cartoons, provided a home for Gandy Goose, Oscar Pig, Dinky Duck and, in 1945, Terry's biggest star, Mighty Mouse.

Originally Fawcett announced that its entry in the animated-character derby would be called *Animal Funny Stories*, but when the magazine finally appeared toward the end of 1942 the title was livelier: *Fawcett's Funny Animals*. This being Fawcett's first venture away from straight heroes, the company went to someone with experience in the animated cartoon field to help produce the new comic book. Chicago-born Chad Grothkopf was in his late twenties at the time and had worked in California for Disney. Grothkopf had come east in 1938, when NBC had asked him to work on the very first animated show for the network's fledgling television operation. "There were only fifty sets in the area," he's recalled, "and we'd call up people and tell them we were going on the air. We'd stay on until we ran out of film." To supplement his income, Grothkopf started working in comic books, initially on adventure features like DC's *Sandman* and *Radio Squad*.

In 1942 Roscoe Fawcett, knowing of Grothkopf's

Funny Stuff #2, featuring Sheldon Mayer's blustery J. Rufus Lion.

©1944 by All-American Comics, Inc.

The Fox and the Crow—headed for conflict once again—in a story from *Comic Cavalcade* #52. Art is by James F. Davis.

©1952 by National Comics Publications

animation background, called him and asked, "Can you make a book for us?" The artist sat down with editorial director Ralph Daigh and worked out a batch of characters. These included Sherlock Monk, Billy the Kid—a goat cowboy—and Willie the Worm. This last character had originally been created by Grothkopf for NBC television animation. The new book's leading character was to be yet another member of the Marvel family, Hoppy the Marvel Bunny. Like Captain Marvel, he just had to shout, "Shazam!" in order to turn into a red-clad superhero—albeit a long-eared one. The Captain himself appeared on the cover of the first issue of *Fawcett's Funny Animals*, along with Hoppy and the rest of the animal gang.

Grothkopf had a distinctive, appealing style in the animated cartoon tradition. He's said that he enjoyed complete freedom at Fawcett and that the publishers gave him no trouble. He worked with a freelance staff of five or six in a studio on 20th Street in Manhattan, "catty-corner from [drummer] Gene Krupa's." While he was working on Hoppy and his friends, "I had the most fun I ever had in my life."

The All-American branch of DC Comics, under the editorship of Sheldon Mayer, produced DC's first funny animal title. This was *Funny Stuff*, a quarterly that appeared in the summer of 1944. Mayer himself drew J. Rufus Lion, an animal-kingdom version of newspaper-strip star Major Hoople. Blackie Bear, the Three Mouseketeers, and Bulldog Drumhead were also in the troupe. One of the most interesting characters was McSnurtle the Turtle, alias the Terrific Whatzit. McSnurtle was a parody of DC's superhero-speedster, the Flash, and even wore a miniature Flash costume, winged helmet and all. Martin Naydell, who drew McSnurtle, was also one of the artists on the real Flash at the time.

The benchmark issue of *Funny Stuff* was #5. That one Mayer drew entirely by himself, cover and interior. "I had such a yen to sit down and draw pictures again," he explained to readers, "that I drew this whole issue before I could get it out of my system." It was a noble, and funny, effort.

DC turned to movie cartoon characters in 1945 with *Real Screen Comics*. This starred the *Fox and Crow*, a team that had been appearing in a series of animated shorts released by Columbia Pictures. The Fox was a perennial patsy, the Crow the eternal con man who foiled, flimflammed, hoodwinked, and otherwise took advantage of his hapless companion. "[Editor] Whit Ellsworth came out looking for a cartoon subject," animator James F. Davis has explained. "The only thing available was Columbia."

Davis, in addition to working as an animator, was heading up the West Coast branch of the Manhattan-based Ben Sangor shop. Sangor was in partnership with Fred Iger; the pair eventually called themselves the American Comics Group (ACG) and published many successful titles of their own, but the shop also turned out artwork and packaged comics for other publishers. The Sangor specialty was funny animals and, in Hollywood, Davis took over the drawing of the *Fox and Crow* in 1948 and rode herd over a bunch of moonlighting animators and writers. "Well, there were 65 of us working on those things at one time," he once told an interviewer, "and we used to send back sheets of Strathmore two feet high every month." Eventually DC added *Funny Folks* and other animal titles, and converted hero books like *Comic Cavalcade* and *Leading Comics* to funny stuff; the revamped *Leading Comics* featured a character with the spiffy name of Peter Porkchops.

The Sangor shop also provided the contents for the Pines line of animated comics— *Barnyard*, *Happy*, *Goofy*, and *Coo Coo*. The last title featured Supermouse, whose "great powers, you know, stem from his SUPERCHEESE." This super rodent, created and drawn initially by Kim Platt, appeared on the scene in the autumn of 1942 and was the first animal character to burlesque the more serious human superheroes. Fawcett's Hoppy followed a couple of months later and early in 1943 Marvel made Super Rabbit the star of *Comedy Comics*. Super Rabbit appeared in several short-lived titles, including *Comic Capers* and *All Surprise*, before getting a book of his own in 1944. MLJ's entrant was Super Duck, also known as the Cockeyed Wonder, who waddled into view in the summer of 1943 in *Jolly Jingles*. The MLJ folks lost interest in supermen much ▶

Pines Comics's Supermouse (upper left) was featured in *Coo Coo Comics*.

©1945 by Nedor Publishing Co.

Basil Wolverton

Powerhouse Pepper is bedeviled by girl trouble in these panels from "The Face from Space," written and drawn by Basil Wolverton, probably in the early 1940s. Even the most inattentive reader could not help noticing Wolverton's fondness for rhyme and alliteration.

©1971 by Marvel Comics

Basil Wolverton was perhaps the most eccentric cartoonist America ever produced, a master of fine-line detail who had a penchant for the bizarre and the hilariously grotesque. He came to national attention in 1946 after winning *Life* magazine's "Ugliest Girl in the World" art competition. This was a highly publicized "search" for Lena the Hyena, a character who had been featured but never completely revealed in Al Capp's satiric comic strip, *Li'l Abner.* Wolverton's winning interpretation of Lena, complete with hideously protruding teeth, rotted gums, and pocked skin, amused the nation and marked him as a unique talent. His comic book work, much of which pre-dates Lena, showed him to be as adept at grim horror and science-fiction as

with wild humor. He worked occasionally for *Mad* and even created powerful, often apocalyptic illustrations for religious publications.

Although Wolverton's *Powerhouse Pepper* owed something to such newspaper strips as *Smokey Stover* and to movies like Olsen and Johnson's *Hellzapoppin,* it was still ninety-nine percent pure Wolverton—lowbrow yet strangely brilliant, inventive and audacious, very much in tune with the baggy-pants burlesque comedy that flourished during World War II.

One of Wolverton's favorite devices was alliteration, and before *Powerhouse* was many issues old the artist-writer had given way to his compulsive fascination to such a degree that he could no longer sign his name straight; stories were

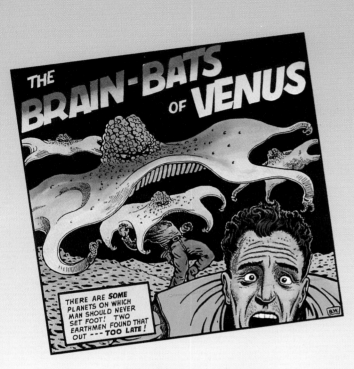

Wolverton made his name with humorous drawings, but his dramatic-style cartooning is equally memorable. This bizarre science fiction story originally appeared in *Mr. Mystery* #7 in 1952.

©1987 by Monte Wolverton

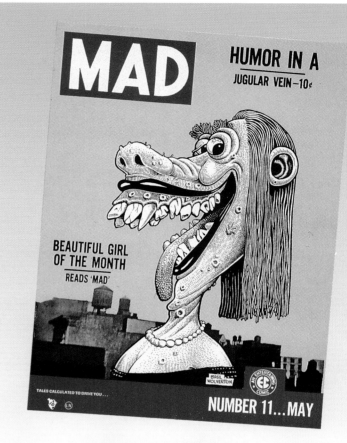

No magazine spoofed *Life* the way *Mad* did, and no one drew women with quite the same loving touch as Basil Wolverton.

©1954 by Educational Comics, Inc.

credited to Basil Weirdwit Wolverton, Basil Bleakbrain Wolverton, Basil Baboonbrain Wolverton, and innumerable variations.

Wolverton was equally fond of internal rhyme. His dialogue, as well as numerous signs and posters that cluttered almost every inch of wall space (and often the floors and ceilings, too) were full of the stuff. A lout about to drop a safe out of a window onto Powerhouse's dome would exclaim "Ah! This is gonna give that little dolt a terrific jolt!" After being insulted, a typical Powerhouse response would go, "That remark makes me sore, bore, and when I get sore, there's war!" Ending up in Egypt in one episode (sign in the sand: Will Sara wear a Sahara tiara?), Powerhouse encounters a reanimated mummy and escorts him back to America. After viewing the joys of modern civilization (which includes a visit to a restaurant named simply Crude Food, wherein are offered such delicacies as blue blackbirds broiled in brown bovine butter and buzz bugs basted in bilge water), the mummy decides he'd be better off in his sarcophagus.

Wolverton's backgrounds were as lively as the foregrounds. He had a fondness for advertisements for dreadful-sounding products and services—"Head hurt? Hog a heap of Hank's Headache Hominy!" "Troubled with a tired, tilted torso? Try tying a timber to your trunk!" "Blue? Blow out your brains with a Bloop and Blinch Brand Blunder-buss!" So it went in the Weirdwit World of Wolverton.

Super Duck (the Cockeyed Wonder) looked natty in spats, but lacked the enduring appeal of Donald. Art on this 1949 story is by Al Fagaly.

©1949 by M.L.J. Magazines, Inc.

Super Rabbit, Marvel's super bunny, meets the Creeper in a 1943 story from *Comedy Comics*.

©1943 by Comedy Publications

Superkatt mingles with his public in this 1946 story, nicely drawn by Dan Gordon.

©1946 by Creston Publications Corp.

earlier than any of their competitors and were retooling for humor far ahead of the rest; until the Duck's debut *Jolly Jingles* had been known as *Jackpot Comics* and was home to no-nonsense characters like Steel Sterling and the Black Hood.

Giggle Comics, published by ACG as a companion to *Ha Ha Comics*, introduced Superkatt in the spring of 1944. Contrary to his name, the well-meaning feline had no exceptional powers at all. He didn't look particularly heroic, either, since his costume consisted of a baby bonnet, a large bow tie, and a diaper. Dan Gordon, a former animator working in Manhattan, drew Superkatt's adventures; a prolific editor-writer named Richard Hughes provided the scripts.

Funny animals weren't necessarily the only way to mine laughs. Marvel tried humor with (more or less) human characters in 1942 when it launched *Joker Comics*—modestly billed as "Loaded with Laffs." Headlining *Joker* was Basil Wolverton's Powerhouse Pepper (see sidebar), the only bald superhero of his day. Besides being hairless, Powerhouse didn't need a superman suit to combat evil. Instead, he wore a striped turtleneck sweater, slacks, and heavy work shoes. At last, a hero for the common man! The character's success won him his own comic, as a one-shot in 1943, and as a regular (though short-lived) series five years later.

Powerhouse Pepper was joined in *Joker* by Al Jaffee's *Squat Car Squad*, a screwball police strip; *Snoop and Dr. Nutzy,* a detective burlesque; *Tessie the Typist*, a working-girl saga; and an assortment of other funny fillers.

DC brought out its first all-funny title in 1943 and called it, logically enough, *All Funny Comics*. A quarterly, it boasted that its sixty-four pages contained "12 Big Laugh Features!" Some of the characters, such as the impecunious private eye Penniless Palmer and the costumed human encyclopedia Genius Jones, had been borrowed from other DC titles. New characters included Two-Gun Percy, Hamilton & Egbert, and Buzzy. Several of the cartoonists recruited for this humor project were newspaper and magazine veterans, some of whom had been turning out funny stuff since before the first world war. These veteran contributors included Tom McNamara, Jack Farr, Jack Callahan, Jimmy Thompson, Paul Fung, and George Storm.

Ray McGill produced *All Funny*'s *Hayfoot Henry*, one of the few cops and robbers features ever written in verse— "I'll take it home and check it for prints. Maybe it'll give me a couple of hints." Well, no one ever claimed it was *great* verse. Paul Fung contributed *Hamilton & Egbert* and an occasional *Penniless Palmer*. He'd assisted Billy DeBeck on the *Barney Google* newspaper strip and drawn such forgotten strips of his own as *Gus & Gussie* and *Dumb Dora*. The younger *All Funny* contributors included Bernard Baily, original artist on *Two-Gun Percy*; Henry Boltinoff,

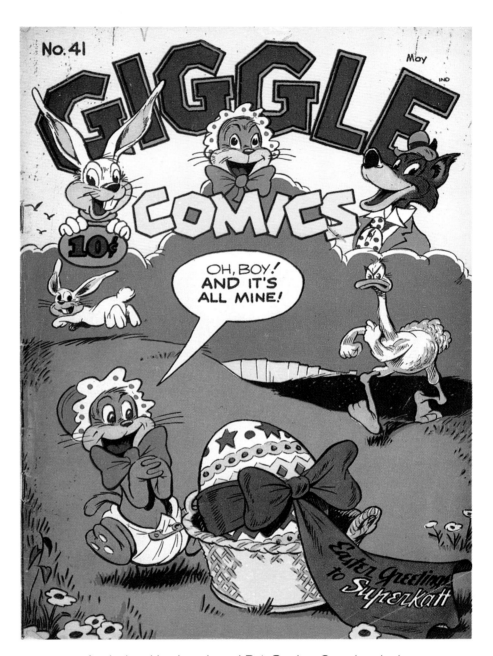

As depicted by the talented Dan Gordon, Superkatt is the image of delight on this 1947 *Giggle Comics* cover.

©1947 by Creston Publications Corp.

The Pie-Face Prince takes possession of a Dingabus in a
1942 *Jingle Jangles* story written and illustrated by the
delightfully imaginative George Carlson.

©1942 by Eastern Color Printing Co.

who drew the cases of a team of
dimwitted detectives named
Dover & Clover; and Stan Kaye,
illustrator of the mock
adventures of Genius Jones.

Early in 1942 Famous
Funnies Inc. introduced *Jingle
Jangle Comics*, a kid-oriented title
that provided a mix of human
and funny animal features. Steve
Douglas was the editor and
George Carlson the star
cartoonist. A veteran children's
book illustrator and puzzlemaker,
Carlson was in his middle fifties
by the time he ventured into
comic books. He'd had a varied
career that included painting the
dust jacket for Margaret
Mitchell's *Gone With the Wind*
and ghosting the *Reg'lar Fellers*
newspaper strip for credited

artist Gene Byrnes. Carlson had
been kicking the *Jingle Jangle
Tales* idea around for several
years (the "Jingle Jangle" title
was his creation), and had
already tried it as a children's
book and, unsuccessfully, as a
newspaper Sunday page. Each
issue of *Jingle Jangle* contained
two of his features—*Jingle Jangle
Tales* and *The Pie-Face Prince*.

Carlson was a one-man band
of a cartoonist who did scripting,
pencilling, inking—the works.
Apparently dedicated to these
stories, Carlson always
submitted a one-page synopsis of
each one to Steve Douglas. After
getting an okay, he would
prepare a detailed outline that
mixed typed copy and handsome
full-color pencil sketches. For his

conscientious dedication,
Carlson eventually earned
twenty-five dollars per page for
the twelve pages of material he
turned out for each issue. The
tales mixed burlesque, fantasy,
and word play with his own,
individualistic brand of nonsense.

Carlson brought a
sophisticated approach to fairy
tales, turning out multileveled
material in which the visual and
verbal elements worked
together. The dialogue in his
work demonstrated his
fascination with language: it
contained left-handed puns, and
stock phrases twisted into new
and unexpected shapes. Quite
obviously he was amusing
himself first and foremost. And,
like Walt Kelly, he had in mind

AMERICA'S PIN-UP QUEEN

OH, DOCTOR KILDEAR, THAT'LL BE WONDERFUL GOING TO A COSTUME BALL WITH YOU BUT WHAT SHOULD I WEAR?

Leggy, sweet, and a slave to fashion—that was Katy Keene, "America's Pin-Up Queen." Art is by Katy's creator, Bill Woggon.

©1984 by Close-Up, Inc.

Most comic book fans agree that Katy Keene epitomized four-color glamour and wholesome sex appeal. Although the largest part of her audience was composed of teens and pre-teens, Katy wasn't a teenager herself. She was a full-grown young woman who worked initially as a model and later as a Hollywood starlet.

Apparently just about every girl in America goes through a phase where she wants to be a model and/or fashion designer. Katy, whose life was given over chiefly to modeling, posing, and dating, had immediate appeal for an audience that had been unmoved by superheroes, cowboys, or funny animals. Added reader involvement was ensured by Katy's mischievous little sister, Sis, a pig-tailed mischief maker who acted as Katy's accomplice, conscience, and cheerleader. Katy's boyfriends included boxer K.O. Kelly, millionaire playboy Randy Von Ronson, and movie idol Erroll Swoon.

Especially important to Katy's success was the way the feature encouraged reader participation—youngsters were invited to send in designs for Katy's outfits. These designs, rendered by artist Bill Woggon and other staffers, credited each contributor by name and hometown. As cartoonist and longtime Katy fan Trina Robbins has pointed out, "Each episode featured countless costume changes, with every outfit designed by a different reader."

Bill Woggon, who had assisted his brother Elmer on the *Big Chief Wahoo* newspaper strip, created Katy in 1945. The big-eyed beauty made her debut in MLJ's *Wilbur* #5, as a backup feature. Her appeal soon became apparent and she was added to the lineups of *Laugh, Pep,* and *Suzie.* In 1949, Katy got a magazine of her own. The book appeared just once that year, once in 1950, and twice in 1951. *Katy Keene* became a quarterly in 1952 and went bimonthly a year later. Nineteen fifty-five brought two new titles, *Katy Keene Fashion Book Magazine* and a 25-cent comic, *Katy Keene Pin-up Parade.*

Woggon, who drew in a simple and direct cartoon style, has said that he was influenced by comic strips like *Fritzi Ritz, Brenda Starr,* and *Tillie the Toiler.* The work of George Petty, the airbrush artist who painted pin-ups for *Esquire* magazine, was another influence. [The] Petty Girl was indeed my favorite," Woggon has said, "and inspired me to create . . . Katy Keene." Significantly, each of the three comic strips cited by Woggon occasionally included paper dolls, and would give credit to readers who submitted fashion designs.

Woggon employed several assistants over the years, including Hazel Marten, Cassie Bill, Floyd Norman, Bob MacLeod, Tom Cooke, and Bill Ziegler. Katy's career ended in 1961, but she made a modestly successful comeback in 1983.

not only the kids who were buying the funny books but the grown-ups who were going to be cajoled into reading the stories aloud.

Among the characters who did turns in Carlson's *Jingle Jangle Tales* were the Youthful Yodeler, who lived on a newly painted mountain and sold all kinds of weather by the yard; the Half-Champion Archer, who wasn't the full-time champ because he never hit the king's special Tuesday target; the Very Horseless Jockey, who became rich from a flavored snowball business and then set out, via steamed-up steam engine, to buy a fine mahogany horse for himself. A delightful variety of unusual props, people, and creatures wandered through Carlson's lively, cluttered pages—a freshly toasted sandwich board, a young idea "with its buttons all neatly sewed on the wrong side," a four-footed yardstick maker, a zigzag zither, a lovely blonde mazurka, and a trio of jellybeans, "all slicked up, with shoe-laces neatly pressed," who go forth into the world to seek their fortune.

Pretzleburg, ruled over by King Hokum without much help from his pie-face offspring Prince Dimwitri, was a place that brought an inspired silliness to the conventions of light opera. The recurrent players were Princess Panetella Murphy, who was more or less the object of Dimwitri's affections and could sometimes be found residing in "her left-footed uncle's second-best castle"; the Raging Raja, billed as the Prince's "favorite enemy"; and the Wicked Green

The Pie-Pace Prince's encounter with the Dingabus continues, in a misadventure that was related with typical whimsy by artist/writer George Carlson.

©1942 by Eastern Color Printing Co.

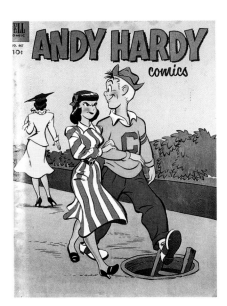

Four Color #447, featuring
Andy Hardy. By the time
this comic book appeared
in 1953, the popularity of
"traditional" teen comics
had faded noticeably.

©1952 by Western Printing &
Lithographing Co.

Witch (a longtime resident of
Connecticut, Carlson was no
doubt inspired here by the
common mispronunciation of
Greenwich). Prince Dimwitri's
interests and adventures were
wide-ranging. In one issue he set
out to find the coveted
Doopsniggle Prize with his corn-
beef flavored cabbage plant; in
another he went aloft in an
eighteen-carat balloon in search
of a missing bass drum.

Jingle Jangle certainly
appealed to children and
probably captivated more than its
share of adults, too. But there
was another audience that a
comic like *Jingle Jangle* could not
reach: the teenage audience.
Fairly early in the forties comic
book publishers discovered that
teenagers liked to read about
themselves, and that stories
about teenagers could be highly
salable. Adolescents had only
recently been discovered to be a
separate tribe. Publishers, film
producers, and other
entrepreneurs looked at
adolescents and saw a large
segment of the population whose
antics and rituals could be
exploited for entertainment
purposes and who had money of
their own to spend.

College youths inspired
popular images in the 1920s,
when artist John Held, Jr. and his
many imitators started depicting
short-skirted flappers and flask-
toting "sheiks" in raccoon coats.
High school kids, though, didn't
really get much public notice
until the 1930s, when swing
music and the jitterbug dance
craze helped put them on the
map. Suddenly, the high-energy
antics of high-school boys and

girls were noted by newspapers,
magazines, and newsreels, which
in turn piqued the interest (and
sometimes dismay) of grown-
ups. More notably, this rush of
attention caught the fancy of
younger children, who couldn't
wait to be teenagers themselves.
So it was that teenagers, adults,
and young kids provided a large
audience in the late thirties and
early forties for teen-based
entertainments.

Henry Aldrich, the well-
meaning but bumbling teen who
was the prime inspiration for
most of the early comic book
high schoolers, had first
appeared in 1938 in Clifford
Goldsmith's Broadway play *What
a Life*. Henry and his pal Homer
soon made the leap to radio and
then to the movies. Jackie
Cooper was the first screen
Henry; Jimmy Lydon, a gawkier,
more overtly comic young fellow,
took over the role in the early
1940s. Although B-films, the
Henry Aldrich pictures were
produced by Paramount with a
modest gloss, much as MGM
brought appealing production
values to their own teen
comedies—the Andy Hardy
series with Mickey Rooney.
Preoccupied with girls, cars, and
school, Henry and Andy saw no
reason why they shouldn't have
all the rights and perks of
adulthood—after all, they'd be
grown up any day now! But their
elaborate schemes and dreams
of glory led them into all sorts of
unforeseen complications. The
boys' parents, of course, rarely
understood them. Mothers and
fathers tried to be understanding,
but often acted as though Henry
and Andy had contracted some

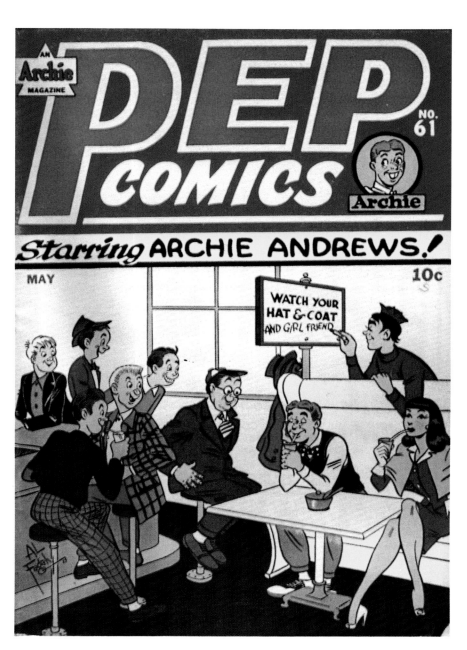

MLJ produced some creditable superheroes during the forties, but found its greatest and most enduring success with a redheaded kid named Archie Andrews. This 1947 *Pep* cover is by Al Fagaly.

©1947 by M.L.J. Magazines, Inc.

rare disease that had caused them to run amok.

Parental disquiet aside, the Henry Aldrich and Andy Hardy comedies were very successful, and spurred comic book publishers into offering funny teens of their own. MLJ was the first to be influenced by the newly emergent American teeenager. Beginning in 1941, the company began adding characters to titles that had previously contained nothing but superheroes, masked marvels, and similarly violent vigilante types. MLJ's most successful kid star was Bob Montana's Archie, who changed not just the company's fortunes, but its very name, as well.

Archie arrived in *Pep Comics* #22 and *Jackpot Comics* #4, accompanied by his wholesome blonde girlfriend, Betty, and his deceptively dimwitted pal, Jughead. The dark-haired Veronica came slinking into Archie's life a few months later. Montana had an attractive, cartoony style and most of the Archie plots were breezy, formulaic, and spiced with agreeable doses of slapstick.

The Archie version of teen life was one that a great many readers took to and the character's star began to rise. The first issue of Archie's own magazine came out in the fall of 1942 and by late 1947 he'd nudged all the serious heroes out of *Pep*. Bob Montana had left the Archie comic books in the middle forties to take care of the new *Archie* newspaper strip; artists who carried on in the comic books included Harry Sahle, Bill Vigoda, and Dan ▶

JOHN STANLEY'S LITTLE LULU

John Stanley's *Little Lulu* brought wit and genuine insight to kid comics. Told in a direct, unpretentious manner, the stories are just as rewarding for adult readers as for youngsters.

©Marjorie Henderson Buell

Created by cartoonist Marge Henderson Buell for a series of gag panels that began in *The Saturday Evening Post* in 1935, it is as a comic book character that Little Lulu is most fondly remembered. The clever little girl with the corkscrew curls, bright red dress, and tiny red hat made her comic book debut in Dell's *Four Color* #74 in 1945, and stepped up to a title of her own late in 1947. The long-running comic, though officially titled *Marge's Little Lulu,* was masterminded by artist-writer John Stanley.

What Stanley provided, after having written and drawn the first couple of *Little Lulu* issues by himself, were rough storyboards for artist Irving Tripp to follow. Comics historian Mike Barrier explained, "To say that Stanley 'wrote' *Little Lulu* is actually a little deceptive, since he was responsible for more than the plots and the dialogue. He sketched each story in rough form, so that he controlled the staging within each panel and the appearance and attitudes of the characters." Stanley's penciled pages would be enlarged, inked by Tripp (with occasional assists from Gordon Rose and others), and lettered.

Stanley inherited Lulu's boyfriend/antagonist Tubby from the original gag cartoons (where the fat boy was named Joe), but he invented most of the other characters. These include truant officer Mr. McNabbem, Wilbur Van Snobbe, Witch Hazel & Little Itch, and the bullying West Side Boys. As Mike Barrier has pointed out, Stanley's conception of Lulu is quite different from the bratty kid of the *Post* era. Eventually, "Lulu . . . became a 'good little girl' who outsmarted the boys instead of triumphing through sheer brass, as she had in the past. Many of the stories built around the [boy vs. girl] rivalry theme are ingenious and funny, and the best of them spiral upward until the boys become the victims of comic catastrophe."

Lulu's adventures were intelligent and refreshingly low key. These attributes, coupled with Stanley's simple storytelling style, entertained a generation of kids and inspired many of them to remain fans into their adult lives.

Stanley worked on *Little Lulu* until 1961; in all, he was responsible for about 150 issues. The comic book continued without him (many post-Stanley issues simply reprint his earlier stories) and was published until 1984. Today, the best of Stanley's Lulu stories are available in quality hardcovers published for the collector market.

DeCarlo. (An ironic side note to the Archie success story is that Archie Comics has made periodic attempts since the 1960s to revive the original MLJ superheroes and to introduce wholly new superhero characters; each attempt has failed.)

The Quality Comics Group's most successful teenager showed up in late 1944 in, of all places, *Police Comics*. Starting with issue #37, sexy, chestnut-haired Candy rubbed shoulders with Plastic Man, the Spirit, and the Human Bomb. Candy was the creation of Harry Sahle, who had recently left Archie. Although sweet and wholesome, Candy was much more liberated than the girls to be found at MLJ. She saw to it that she got her way and was very adept at managing her blond boyfriend, Ted, and her plump businessman father. Candy was much like the energetic young ladies who were featured in *A Date with Judy*, *Meet Corliss Archer*, and other established radio shows. (Both Judy and Corliss, by the way, would have comic books of their own later in the forties). Candy won her own comic in the summer of 1947 and enjoyed a run of sixty-four issues. Like all her sisters, she was expert with the latest slang—"But definitely," "I know you're pooched," "all reet," and so forth. She doted on her boyfriends and her collection of jitterbug platters—hobbies that caused her parents no end of consternation.

DC's earliest entry in the teen sweepstakes was also a jive cat, but nowhere near as hep as Candy. His name was Buzzy and

BUZZY No.1 WINTER ISSUE — THE RIB-TICKLING MISADVENTURES OF AMERICA'S FAVORITE TEENSTER!

A SUPERMAN PUBLICATION

BUZZY

TEN CENTS

DADDY MUST BE A BIT OFF THE BEAM, BUZZY— HE ACTUALLY SEEMS TO *LIKE* YOUR TOOTING!

Against all odds, Susie's dad seems to be enjoying the bleat of Buzzy's trumpet; one wonders how long the peace will last. This copy of *Buzzy* #1 was once owned by the feature's artist, George Storm.

©1944 by National Periodical Publications, Inc.

The American Comics Group offered *Hi-Jinx*, a peculiar mix of the teen and funny animal genres. Art on this 1948 cover is by Dan Gordon.

©1948 by B & I Publishing Co., Inc.

HI-JINX FLEA CIRCUS

IN THIS ISSUE NEW SURPRISE LAFF FEATURES!

I'VE BEEN ROBBED!

JULY-AUG.

TRAINED FLEAS

ADMISSION 10¢

Gay Comics #31: Flicker's in love, but few readers cared by the time this issue appeared in 1948. Another, more "adult" sort of comic book had already begun to dominate the industry.

©1948 by USA Comic Magazine Corp.

he came along late in 1943 in *All Funny*. Not only did he collect phonograph records, he played the trumpet, too. His pretty girlfriend, Susie, adored this facet of Buzzy's personality, but her portly businessman father couldn't stand the sound of the kid's bleating horn. Just a few toots and the old guy would boot Buzzy from the house and attempt mayhem on the boy's scrawny body—a frenzied reaction that caused Susie to frequently exclaim, "Popsy is killing Buzzy!" Written and drawn in kinetic style by the admirable George Storm, the feature had a certain wacky appeal. Buzzy, however, wasn't exactly a reasonable facsimile of a 1940s adolescent. He seemed stiff in his suit and tie and the junky, slogan-covered jalopy he drove looked like something that might have been driven a decade earlier by newspaper-strip star Harold Teen. Even so, Buzzy graduated to a magazine of his own by 1944, and although Storm abandoned his offspring not long after, *Buzzy* hung on until 1958.

The American Comics Group brought added slapstick to the teen formula with Cookie, a diminutive, wide-eyed kid who first surfaced in *Topsy-Turvy Comics*, a one-shot that came out in the spring of 1945. Exactly a year later he returned in his own bimonthly. Cookie may not have been as tall as his fellow teen stars, but he did have the requisite supporting cast— irascible businessman father, understanding mother, beautiful blonde girlfriend (named Angelpuss, no less), slang-

spewing pal (named Jitterbuck), and a tall, conniving rival (named Zoot). What made Cookie stand out from Buzzy and all the rest was that he was drawn by Dan Gordon, a former cartoon animator who produced a version of teen life that had the flavor of the eccentric wildness of cartoon director Tex Avery or the Warner Bros. Looney Tunes. Gordon's stories were full of violent pratfalls, lowbrow jokes, and gags involving outrageous props.

Teen titles continued to proliferate into the later 1940s, and were one of the factors that contributed to the (temporary) demise of superheroes. Binky, Kathy, Ozzie, Ginger, Jeanie, Junior, Mitzi, Patsy Walker, Georgie, and dozens of others were to be found on the roster of just about every comic book publisher.

Beyond doubt the most unusual attempt to cash in on the teenage craze was made by ACG in 1947, when it introduced *Hi-Jinx*. "A brand-new idea in comics," the magazine promised the public. "Teenage animal funnies." Even the invitation to "meet some real hepcats," didn't save this one and, despite contributions from Dan Gordon and Milt Gross, the comic expired after just seven issues.

By the end of World War II, the innate innocuousness of teen comics had become apparent to the reading public. Even Dell's *Henry Aldrich* comic, introduced in 1950, could not stop the comic book industry's gravitation to a new, rougher sort of fare that would dominate the first decade of the postwar era.

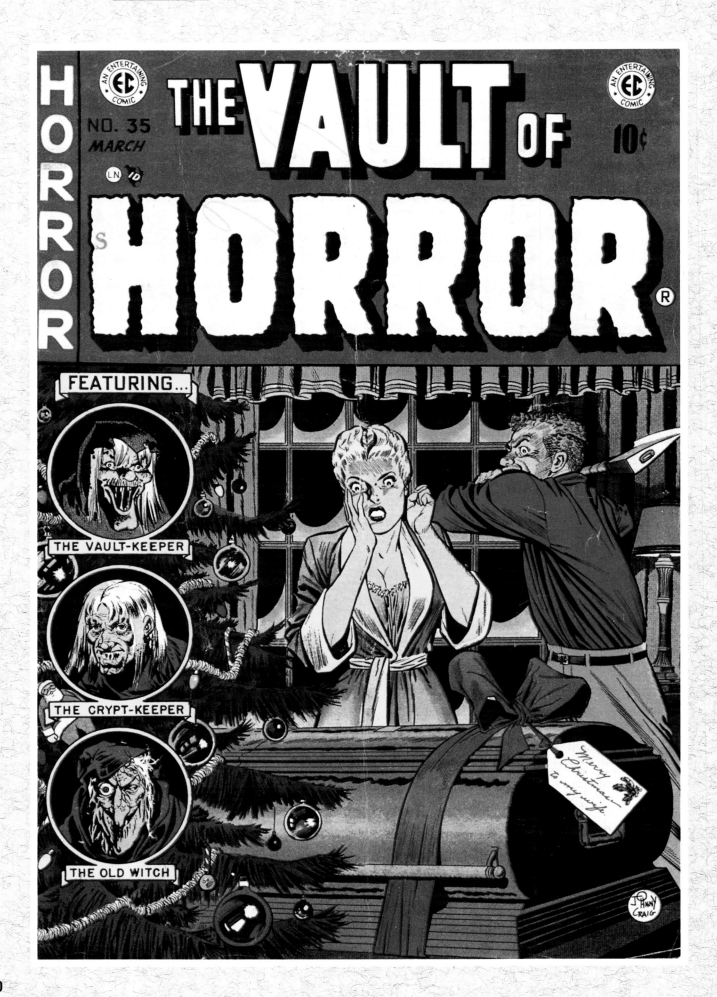

CHAPTER EIGHT

GIRLS! ROMANCE! HORRORS!

Overall sales of comic books continued to increase during the middle and late 1940s. In 1945 the combined annual sales of ten of the top publishers amounted to approximately 275,000,000 copies. By 1947 the figure had climbed to 300,000,000 and in 1949 it was nearly 340,000,000. What these fantastic sales figures don't show is the desperation that plagued comic book publishers, and the anxious, industry-wide retooling for new product. The supermen and wonderwomen, in particular, had a difficult time adjusting to the postwar era. America's four years of war had produced an audience that was older and more sophisticated; the caped, long-underwear crowd suddenly seemed passe.

Even though interest in costumed crimefighters was waning, there was still big money to be made in comic book publishing. All that was needed was some rethinking. The audience for comic books had grown impressively throughout the war years, particularly among adults. Most of the millions of new, adult readers were servicemen,

Horror comics from a multitude of publishers sold in tremendous numbers in the early 1950s. Few titles delivered the goods more effectively than EC Comics's *The Vault of Horror*. Johnny Craig provided the crisp artwork for this touch of EC-style Christmas cheer.

©1954 by L. L. Publishing Company, Inc.

whose tastes account for many of the changes that took place in comic books beginning in the middle 1940s. In an effort to appeal to the huge Post Exchange readership, publishers had added more sex, violence, and humor to their comics, and had also introduced new varieties of comics.

Basic fact: One way to appeal to a young male readership is to offer pictures of young, voluptuous females. In the days when mildly risqué "cheescake" pin-up magazines enjoyed healthy circulations, comic books were one more place to girl watch. The chief source of what dedicated collectors now refer to as "good girl" art in the 1940s was the comics published by the Fiction House company. Good girl art doesn't refer to *Wonder Woman* or to reprints of the *Mary Worth* newspaper strip, but rather to the spicy stories tailored for teenage boys and GIs. Fiction House, the undisputed champ of this sort of material, was headquartered on Eighth Avenue in Manhattan. It turned out a line of comic books with deceptively mild titles—*Planet*, *Wings*, *Jungle*, *Fight*, *Jumbo*—and fairly steamy contents.

As the names of the magazines suggest, the Fiction House gang was able to introduce sexy ladies into every sort of situation and locale. Fiction House's readers encountered amply constructed and sparsely clad young women on the land, the sea, and in the air. Deep in the jungles, beautiful blondes wore leopard-skin undies, while off on a remote

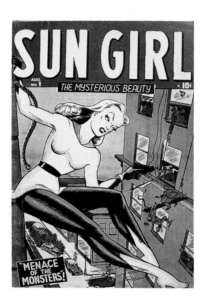

The popularity of superheroes faded after World War II, but the genre did not die out completely. Marvel's *Sun Girl* combined superheroine adventure with cheesecake in 1948.

©1948 by Comic Combine Corp.

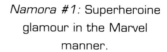

Namora #1: Superheroine glamour in the Marvel manner.

©1948 by Prime Publications, Inc.

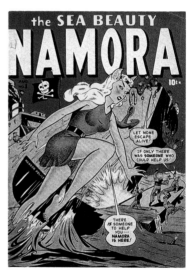

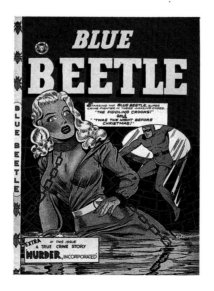

By the late forties, some superhero comics had to rely on partially clad women and even bondage to ensure respectable sales.

©1948 by Fox Feature Syndicate

Good-looking women were featured on the covers of innumerable comics published by Fiction House. *Planet* #44 suggests that even purple fellows with snouts on the ends of their arms can have an eye for the ladies.

©1946 by Love Romances Pub. Co.

Fiction House had a knack for combining jungle thrills with half-dressed women. This cover for *Jungle Comics* #34 was drawn by Dan Zolnerowich.

©1942 by Glen Ken Pub. Co.

planet a lovely redhead might sport a chrome-plated bra, flimsy skirt, and little else. Although the East Coast street jargon of the time dubbed these magazines "headlight comics," the artists turning out the product were fascinated not only with breasts, but also with buttocks, thighs, and just about any other portion of the female anatomy that could be thrust excitingly against—or through— provocative clothing.

The artists had an easier time than the scriptwriters, who had to continually devise new excuses for introducing nearly naked girls into yarns that allegedly dealt with prizefighting, delivering the airmail, exploring Mars, or fighting the Japanese in the Pacific. Not surprisingly, the writers' ingenuity proved boundless, and the gals showed up in story after story, just like clockwork.

Fiction House had begun life in the 1920s as a publisher of pulp fiction. Owned by the Two Jacks—Kelly and Glennister—the Fiction House lineup included *Action Stories*, *Wings*, and *Fight Stories*. Publication of all titles was suspended at the end of 1932 but a few years later T. T. Scott, who'd been the company's secretary, revived the Fiction House pulp line and added *Jungle Stories* and *Planet Stories*. Persuaded by the Eisner-Iger shop to go into comic books, Scott introduced his first, *Jumbo Comics*, in the summer of 1938. Most of his later comics were adaptations of the Fiction House pulps. By the early 1940s Eisner was on his own and Iger was

The Jerry Iger studio turned out a small mountain of "good girl" art for Fiction House and other publishers. Artist Marcia Snyder worked in the Iger shop, and was one of the few women artists in comics. Her *Camilla* page (above) dates from the mid-forties. Lily Renee also worked for Iger. The good-looking panel seen below is from Renee's 1945 Fiction House story, "Lost World."

heading up the shop, providing the material for all of Scott's comics. Interestingly enough, quite a bit of the shop's good girl art was drawn by women. Lily Renee, Fran Hopper, and Marcia Snyder were all employed by Iger, and illustrated the adventures of such characters as the jungle girl Camilla, Glory Forbes, and Senorita Rio.

The Fiction House preoccupation with sex became obvious with only a glance at their front covers. Of all the hundreds of gaudy covers that graced the company's comic books throughout the forties, there is hardly a one that doesn't prominently feature a pretty girl somewhere in the action. A typical *Planet Comics* cover, for instance, might depict the Lizard Tyrant of the Twilight Worlds or the Raiders of the Red Moon, but there's also a distressed damsel flashing considerable amounts of flesh in the foreground. The formula was the same with the covers of *Wings Comics*, *Fight Comics*, *Jungle Comics*, and the rest. Readers would enjoy an authentic World War II aircraft, realistically rendered, or believable African flora and fauna, but there also would be a pretty girl with her skirt hiked above her garters and her blouse torn down to her midriff.

Since Fiction House was an equal opportunity employer, a whole flock of female characters starred in features of their own. The resident sexpot in *Fight Comics* for a couple of years was Senorita Rio, "once in Hollywood, now a U.S. secret agent," who fought Axis spies in South America. Her investigations invariably called for several changes of costume and her faithful readers were allowed to watch every one of them. *Ranger Comics* boasted two female stars. One was Glory Forbes, yet another secret agent type, and the other was Firehair, a red-haired lass who played Lone Ranger games in the Old West while wearing a short buckskin dress and not much else. The artist who drew more Firehair adventures than anyone else was Bob Lubbers, who later moved on to good girl newspaper strips such as *Long Sam* and *Robin Malone*.

Fiction House offered quite a few other fetching female strips—*Mysta of the Moon, Gale Allen and the Girl Squadron, Patsy Pinup, Sky Girl, Futura,* and *Camilla*. Their most successful and best remembered female character was Sheena, Queen of the Jungle, who debuted in *Jumbo Comics* in 1939 and continued in the title (and on nearly every cover) until its final issue, published in 1953. Leggy, buxom, and blonde, Sheena was the quintessential jungle girl. Young female readers may have appreciated her fearlessness against lions, crocodiles, and surly natives, but Sheena's most ardent fans, undoubtedly, were boys and young men. (This fan interest was fervid enough, in fact, to inspire a syndicated *Sheena* television series that aired in 1955, two years after the demise of *Jumbo Comics*; statuesque Irish McCalla starred as the jungle girl.)

Since being a jungle girl afforded obvious opportunities for going around with a

Sheena made her debut in 1939 and got her own book three years later. Her sexy good looks had a profound influence on the look and tone of comic books of the forties and fifties.

©1942 by Fiction House Magazines

Artist Bob Lubbers demonstrated his skill with "leg art" on the cover of Wings #92.

©1948 by Fiction House Magazines

Fiction House's Sheena, Queen of the Jungle—drawn here by Bob Webb—set new comic book standards of ladylike attire.

©1942 by Real Adventure Publishing Co.

Sheena inspired many leggy imitators. One of them, Judy of the Jungle, knocked the superhero Black Terror off the covers of Standard's *Exciting Comics*. This cover was drawn by Alex Schomburg, who occasionally signed his work "Xela."

©1948 by Better Publications, Inc.

minimum of clothing, Fiction House could not resist the temptation to offer another besides Sheena. The company's variation was Tiger Girl, who turned out to be one of the most successful of the industry's Sheena surrogates. She first appeared in *Fight Comics* #32 (June 1944) and was drawn originally by Matt Baker (see sidebar), one of the stars of the Iger shop and a master of the good girl style. Also known as Princess Vishnu, the blonde Tiger Girl wore a two-piece tiger-skin bathing suit, lived in a hidden temple, and served as a guardian of the people and animals who lived in her part of India. Tiger Girl was also very handy with a bullwhip. The character remained in *Fight* until 1952 and appeared, battling a variety of wilderness threats, on every cover from issue #49 through #81.

A modest wave of other new jungle girls came along in the immediate postwar years, many of them in the Pines line of comics. Princess Pantha began in *Exciting Comics* #56 (October 1946) and soon nudged Doc Strange out of the title's star spot. Drawn initially by Ralph Mayo, the feature dealt with "a mere girl" who worked as a big game hunter. The dark-haired Pantha did her hunting clad in a two-piece leopard-skin bathing suit, accompanied by a blond explorer-writer-hunk named Dane Hunter. Equally at home in any of the jungles of the world, Pantha prowled not only in Africa but in Central Asia, Mexico, and New Guinea. After the departure of Ralph Mayo, Pantha's ▶

MATT BAKER

Matt Baker's skill at drawing pretty girls is apparent in this 1947 illustration of the lively character Flamingo.

©1984 by The Caplin-Iger Co., Ltd.

A prolific and very influential comic book artist, Matt Baker enjoyed a flourishing career from the middle 1940s until his death in 1955. One of the few blacks employed in comics in those days, he was a leading creator of what comic book collectors refer to as "good girl" art.

Baker was born around 1918 and went to work for the Iger shop early in 1946. His arrival on the comic book scene coincided with the beginning of the decline of the superhero genre. The companies that tied their futures to pretty-girl comics found Baker's work marketable and highly appealing. Fox and Fiction House, in particular, showcased his art. Baker's pages, filled with his immediately identifiable slim, large-breasted, and long-legged heroines, appeared frequently in titles from both companies.

It was for Fox that Baker drew his most famous character, Phantom Lady. Though that title survived less than two years, the character—busty, athletic, and skimpily costumed—made a lasting impression on readers and collectors. Baker's pin-up-style interpretation of Phantom Lady is boyishly enthusiastic, and doubly interesting because of its unabashed bondage elements. These attributes have turned the Fox/Baker *Phantom Lady* into a valuable collector's title.

Baker also drew material that was more sedate, including the *Classics Illustrated* adaptation of *Lorna Doone* that appeared in issue #32 (December 1946). As comic books turned away from sexy material in the mid-fifties, Baker switched to westerns, war stories, and true crime. In addition, he did particularly fine work for St. John's *Teen-Age Romances* and *Going Steady*, and other romance titles. He even drew three issues of Dell's *Lassie*. According to comic book artist Jay Disbrow's book, *The Iger Comics Kingdom*, Baker died of a "congenital illness" at age 37. Some sources speculate that the culprit was heart failure brought on by overwork.

adventures were illustrated by Artie Saaf and Rafael Astarita, who, like Mayo, were alumni of Fiction House. Pines added two more jungle girls in the spring of 1947—Tygra in *Startling Comics* and Judy of the Jungle in *Exciting Comics.*

Never one to miss an exploitable trend, publisher Victor Fox branched out into jungle girls at about the same time as Ned Pines. Rulah, Jungle Princess, who wore a two-piece bathing suit made of what looked to be giraffe skin, took over as leading lady of *All Top Comics* with issue #8, published toward the end of 1947 (the comic had previously been a funny animal book that starred a super feline named Cosmo Cat). Rulah also appeared briefly in *Zoot Comics.* In 1948 Fox introduced Tegra, Jungle Empress, in a magazine of her own. After one issue her name was changed to Zegra and she retired after four more issues. Rulah and Tegra/Zegra were products of the Iger studio.

The jungle genre persevered into the early and middle fifties. Fox was represented during this period by *Jungle Jo* and *Jungle Lil*, both of which began and ended in 1950. Marvel, which called itself Atlas at the time, introduced Lorna the Jungle Girl in her own magazine in the summer of 1953 and added *Jungle Tales* in 1954. Brunette Jann of the Jungle was sufficiently successful in the latter title that the magazine changed its name to hers with the eighth issue (November 1955). Magazine Enterprises offered a slight variation on the jungle girl theme with *Cave Girl*

in 1953; talented Bob Powell provided the artwork. Fetching though they were, however, none of these characters survived the decade.

Sheena's closest competition as most popular sex object in comic books of the 1940s was a superheroine, Phantom Lady. She'd begun her career, as noted in Chapter 6, in the pages of Quality's *Police Comics* in 1941. Victor Fox got hold of her in 1947 and gave her a magazine of her own. Going out solo changed her somewhat—her costume became even skimpier and her bosom grew impressively larger. She also developed a marked propensity for being tied up and chained, and frequently appeared in these states, especially on the comics' covers. If 1950s cult photo model Betty Page had a fictional predecessor in the bondage stakes, it's Phantom Lady. The art during this kinky heyday was provided by the dependable Matt Baker.

Not every good-girl temptress was a superheroine. Torchy was a sexy, teasing lady who didn't bother with crimefighting or other strenuous activities—she seemed content merely to display herself. She wore the frilliest black lingerie in the business and first showed up in issue #53 (September 1946) of Quality's *Modern Comics*, home of Blackhawk. She got a magazine of her own three years later. Torchy was created by good girl specialist Bill Ward, whose outrageously sexy men's magazine cartoons would later make him a cult figure. Ward adapted the Torchy character from a strip he'd drawn while in

Bill Ward's Torchy was one of the most popular glamour girls in comics. Long-legged and brimming with sex appeal, she was concerned mainly with her boyfriends and wardrobe. The *Modern Comics* panel seen here dates from about 1947.

©Quality Comics Group

"Beautiful but dumb"—such was the state of comic book humor in 1949. Suzie was just one of many pretty girls who showed up in comics published by MLJ.

©1949 by M.L.J. Magazines, Inc.

the service; the long-legged blonde's later exploits were rendered by Gill Fox.

Most of the other provocative ladies in the comics of the immediate postwar years were shapely crimefighters like Lady Luck, the Blonde Phantom, and Lee Elias's Black Cat, or they were just plain pretty girls like Suzie, Tessie the Typist, and Millie the Model.

The pretty girl comics maintained their popularity into the early 1950s and helped to supplant the superhero genre. Unfortunately for the comic book publishers, not everyone liked

what the industry was producing. More to the point, sexy women were capable of arousing even more ire and criticism from unsympathetic observers than crimebusting musclemen had ever inspired.

Comics did have a "softer" side at this time—one that demonstrated that if pretty girls meant sex and action, they also meant romance. As the 1940s drew to a close, there was an enormous outpouring of love. It began as a provocative tickle in 1947 and 1948, and then more than a hundred different romance titles hit the stands in 1949,

followed by nearly half a hundred more in 1950. All the major publishers, and quite a few of the minor ones, had gone mushy for dollars. Love was everywhere. Marvel, once the home of heroes, offered about thirty romantic comic books, ranging from *Girl Confessions* to *Romances of the West*. Quality, Fawcett, Lev Gleason, Avon, and DC all joined the love parade. The ever-enterprising Victor Fox was responsible for over two dozen romance comics, seventeen of which contained the word *my* in the title—*My Desire, My Secret, My Secret Affair, My Great Love*, et al.

Romantic Picture Novelettes was probably the first romance comic book. Although a one-shot, it encouraged a tidal wave of love comics in the late forties and early fifties.

©1946 by Magazine Enterprises, Inc.

Love comics were inspired by confession magazines such as *True Story* and *True Confessions*, by radio soap operas, and by such increasingly popular newspaper strips as *Mary Worth* and *Rex Morgan, M.D.* In fact, an early precursor of the later wave of love comics was *Romantic Picture Novelettes*, a one-shot (one issue only) issued in 1946 by Vincent Sullivan's Magazine Enterprises. Hiding behind the title were reprints of the *Mary Worth* strip, which revolved around the lovelorn characters encountered by Mary, a kindly, silver-haired lady who was always ready with some good advice. *Mary Worth* and the other soap strips were full of domestic strife, heartache, and, yes, love. "Realistic" in their subject matter, they were drawn in the slickly illustrative Milton Caniff (*Steve Canyon*) manner. All of these elements were adopted by the romance comic books.

The romance comic book format was devised by the team of Simon and Kirby, heretofore noted mainly for their best-selling superheroes (Captain America) and kid gangs (Young Allies). Joe Simon has recalled that he got the love-comic idea while serving in the Coast Guard. "I noticed that there were so many adults, the officers and the men and the people in town, reading kid comic books," he's said. "I felt sure there should be an adult comic book." Intent upon packaging the entire concept, Simon drew sample title pages and a sample cover for his proposed magazine, which he called *Young Romance*, the "Adult Comic Book." When asked why

Secret Romances #14:
Trouble in paradise.

©1953 by Superior Publications

Simon & Kirby's *Young Love* was a smash hit that revolutionized the comic book industry.

©1951 by Crestwood Publications, Inc.

he'd picked the love genre, Simon answered, "It was about the only thing that hadn't been done."

After returning from the service Simon resumed his partnership with Jack Kirby. "[Kirby] loved the idea," Simon recalled. "So we decided, since we weren't working, we would make up the whole book. We spent money on the features, we did part of it and we had [artist] Bill Draut and others doing part of it." As to the scripts—"We wrote the whole thing. We couldn't afford writers."

Simon was surely aware of the soap opera newspaper strips, but he was more influenced by the somewhat darker tone of the confession magazines. The finished package was taken to Maurice Rosenfeld, managing editor of the Prize Group—*Prize Comics, Headline, Frankenstein.* Rosenfeld and the company's owners, Mike Bleir and Teddy Epstein, were enthusiastic and "we worked out a fifty percent arrangement." Sharing of the profits was unusual at the time and Kirby has said, "We were the first to get percentages."

The first issue of *Young Romance* was published in the fall of 1947 with an impressive S & K cover showing an eternal triangle unfolding in the studio of a handsome young artist. The line "Designed For The More ADULT Readers of Comics" ran beneath the title. The first issue sold out a print run of 500,000 copies. The circulation soon jumped to one million per issue, as did that of its companion title, *Young Love,* which came along at the tail end of 1948. "The things made millions," Simon has recalled.

By the end of the 1940s sales were truly impressive for almost all the love books. According to a report in the August 22, 1949 issue of *Time*, the love comics were "outselling all others, even the blood and thunder variety." Fawcett's *Sweethearts*, for example, was another title that was selling a million copies an issue; the same publisher's *Life Story* accounted for 700,000 copies. Interestingly, the romance comic books were hurting more than just the superhero comics—they also were cutting into the sales of the pulps and the true confession magazines. The venerable *True Story* went so far as to admit that its sales were being hurt by the upstart comics.

Not everyone was favorably impressed by the sales power of the romance comics; *Time* was especially unsympathetic, concluding its love comics piece by asserting, "For pulp magazines the moral was even clearer: no matter how low their standards for fiction, the comics could find lower ones."

Time magazine's criticism of love comics was nothing compared to the firestorm that would be unleashed by another upstart genre: the horror comic. During World War II, Charles Biro's *Crime Does Not Pay* had proved that comic books didn't need heroes in order to sell in big numbers. Meantime, other publishers, notably the Harvey brothers, experimented with more sedate magazines that used no continuing characters. *All-New* and the oddly titled *Hello*

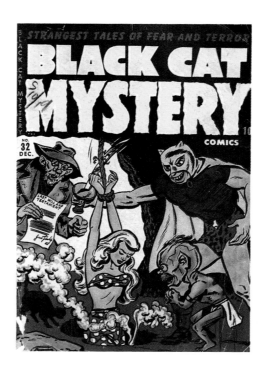

Pal, both inaugurated in 1943, featured short stories in comic book form. So did Harvey's *Front Page* in 1945 and *Strange Story* in 1946. These latter titles introduced Bob Powell's Man in Black, who narrated unusual and spooky yarns. By utilizing a sardonic host who would introduce and comment upon the action of the story, Powell was borrowing a device from popular radio shows such as *Inner Sanctum*, *The Whistler*, and *Suspense*. *Suspense*, in fact, used a narrator called the Man in Black during several seasons.

Avon's *Eerie*, the first out-and-out horror comic book, emerged late in 1946. Published as part of the company's long-lived series of one-shots, it offered six stories, fairly adult in attitude though tame in the overt depiction of blood and gore. The leadoff story dealt with a man haunted by the ghost of a stuffed tiger, another with a shipwreck on an island of man-eating lizards, a third with a fellow who thinks he's murdered his wife by shoving her in the path of a subway train and then is hounded by her bloody corpse. The names of the issue's scriptwriters are lost to history, but the artists included Fred Kida, George Roussos, and Joe Kubert.

Eerie, after establishing the horror genre, went into a cataleptic state and didn't return until 1951, when it showed up as a regularly published comic. In the interim, the American Comics Group had come along with *Adventures Into the Unknown*, which was introduced in the fall of 1948. A fairly

restrained title, it offered a wide range of horror material each issue—witchcraft, ghosts, monsters, even an adaptation of Horace Walpole's 18th century Gothic novel *The Castle of Otranto*. *Adventures Into the Unknown* was the first regularly issued horror comic book and it remained in business for nearly twenty years.

The Marvel/Atlas folks, sensing a trend, began to convert to horror in 1949. *Marvel Mystery* became *Marvel Tales* and for two issues (#74 and #75) *Captain America* was known as *Captain America's Weird Tales*. Many of Marvel's superhero titles had been rich in horrors, especially during the World War II years, when costumed crimebusters were menaced not only by stretch racks and boiling lead, but by zombies, vampires, and werewolves who labored in the employ of the Nazis and Japanese. What Marvel did now was keep the horror elements and dump most of the heroes. Harvey followed suit in 1951 by discarding its longtime crimefighter the Black Cat, and converting her magazine to *Black Cat Mystery*.

Young William Gaines was another comic book publisher who noted the new interest in horror. He had inherited the Educational Comics company from his father, M.C. Gaines, in 1947. Among the EC magazines then being published were *Tiny Tot Comics* and the various *Picture Stories* titles. The younger Gaines favored a more blatantly commercial emphasis. He changed the meaning of the EC acronym to Entertaining

Comics and added such titles as *Crime Patrol*, *Gunfighter*, *Modern Love*, and *Saddle Justice*. In 1948 Gaines hired artist-writer Al Feldstein, a graduate of the Iger shop. Feldstein soon became an editor and in 1950 the EC horror line was born.

Gaines has recalled, "Feldstein and I were working along, putting out this crap, and suddenly talking—because we talked a lot, of course—realized that we both had similar interests in suspense and horror stuff. I grew up on horror pulps and *The Witch's Tale* on the radio and things like that, and at that point they had things on television like *Suspense*, *Lights Out*, *Inner Sanctum*, so we just started doing that kind of story in our crime books." Real horror comics soon followed for EC.

EC's *Weird Fantasy*, *Weird Science*, *The Haunt of Fear*, *Tales From the Crypt,* and *The Vault of Horror* were all born in 1950. The last three featured sardonically funny, and ugly, hosts—The Old Witch, the Crypt Keeper, and the Vault Keeper, respectively—who introduced each issue's quartet of tales, and who showed up again at the conclusion of each to make an appropriately ironic comment. Feldstein did most of the early scripting (he had help later from Carl Wessler, Jack Oleck, and others) and the artwork was provided by the likes of Jack Kamen, Johnny Craig, Graham Ingels (who signed his horror stories "Ghastly"), Wallace Wood, Quality Comics veteran Reed Crandall, Jack Davis, Bernard Krigstein, and Harvey Kurtzman. Actually, Kurtzman limited his

EC Comics publisher William Gaines always claimed to have been proudest of his science fiction titles. *Weird Science* #17 features striking cover art by Wally Wood, one of the giants of comic book history.

©1952 by Fables Publishing Co., Inc.

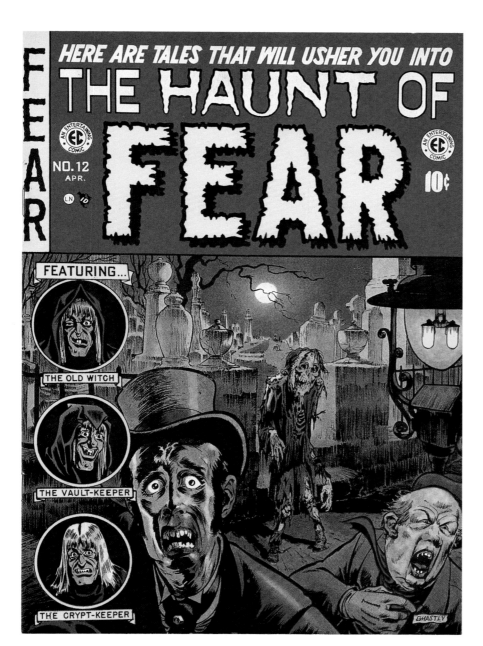

"Ghastly" Graham Ingels drew this atmospheric cover to illustrate his story, "Poetic Justice." Genuinely eerie, the illustration is typical of Ingels's spidery style.

©1952 by Fables Publishing Co., Inc.

early EC work to the science-fiction titles, refusing to work on the horror books. He's said, "The business of playing with dead bodies—stories about chopping people into baseball fields and making their intestines into Christmas ribbons. That's not the kind of thing that I liked to subject my child to."

Kurtzman's reservations aside, Al Feldstein quickly settled into a groove of writing a story a day. He and Gaines had a facile way with the O. Henry style of twist endings, and a love of poetic justice—usually taken to absurd extremes. The archetypal EC horror story was, in fact, called "Poetic Justice" (*Haunt of Fear* #12, April 1952). In it, a kindly junkman is driven to suicide after being sent cruel, anonymous Valentines by a rich man and his sneering son. The junkman is buried, but rises from his grave one year later to avenge his own death. In the story's last panel, the rich man unwraps a Valentine package containing the sticky heart of his son.

Feldstein's variations on this sort of story were ingenious, and although many of the EC horror stories were well written (a few were even adapted from the works of Ray Bradbury) and handsomely illustrated, they did tend to cross boundaries hitherto uncrossed in comic books. As EC historian E. B. Boatner has pointed out, "EC horror opened new vistas of death from sources previously unimagined by the reader. Victims were serial-sectioned by giant machines, eaten by ghouls, devoured by rats—from inside and ▶

THE EC ARTISTS

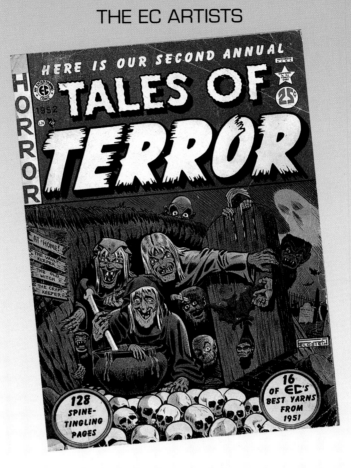

Unsold EC horror comics were stripped of their covers, stapled together beneath a new cover in bunches of four, and sold as annuals. Fans loved them. This spookily funny 1952 cover was drawn by the multi-talented Al Feldstein.

©1952 by Educational Comics, Inc.

While many fans admire EC Comic's well-crafted scripts, it is the exceptional artwork that piques the interest and admiration of collectors. Publisher William Gaines and his editors, Al Feldstein and Harvey Kurtzman, gathered together an impressive crew.

One of the earliest recruits was Johnny Craig, who signed on in the late 1940s after a stint as assistant to artist Sheldon Mayer. Craig started out on *War Against Crime* and Bill Gaines's other early magazines, and later contributed to such titles as *The Vault of Horror* and *The Haunt of Fear*. He drew in a sophisticated, crisply illustrative style that showed the influence of Milton Caniff as well as of the slick magazine illustrators of the period. Craig drew a great many of the EC covers, including the infamous severed head image that graced the cover of *Crime SuspenStories* #22 (May 1954).

The enormously talented Wally Wood went to work for EC in the late 1940s, initially in tandem with artist (and later science-fiction novelist) Harry Harrison. Wood had worked for numerous publishers, but once said he knew he'd "found a home" at EC. Although not an outstanding draftsman, Wood was a master storyteller whose affinities for action and the dramatic interplay of light and shadow were unparalleled. The science-fiction stories he drew for EC's *Weird Science* and *Weird Fantasy* are particularly impressive, and are filled with elegantly rendered rocketships, gruesomely tentacled monsters, and—most memorably—the curvy, full-lipped "Wood women" that became one of his trademarks. He was an able parodist, as well, as he demonstrated in the pages of *Mad*. There, he aped the styles of Walt Kelly, the Disney artists, and many others, to hilarious effect. A true giant

THE PUTRID ODOR OF THIRTY-TWO DECAYING CORPSES BURNED THE TRAPPED COUNCILMEN'S NOSTRILS ...

OH, LORD! HELP US!

WE'RE TRAPPED! AND THEY'RE COMING...

EEEEEAAAA!

Jack Davis illustrated "Graft in Concrete," a tale in *The Vault of Horror* #26 that concerns murderous councilmen who get what's coming to them.

of comic book history, Wood made important contributions to the superhero revival of the 1960s and '70s, and remained active until failing eyesight curtailed his output in the late 1970s. He died in 1981.

Jack Davis is the most prolific graduate of EC. An eccentric cartoonist with a flair for caricature, he came to EC in the early 1950s, after having worked as an inker on *The Saint* newspaper strip. His bold, exaggerated style was equally suited to EC's horror, war, and humor comics. "I'm a cartoonist, not an illustrator," he has always insisted. Since the early 1960s Davis has had a very successful career in commercial art, drawing movie posters, cartoons for print advertisements, and covers for such magazines as *Time* and *TV Guide*.

The greatest of EC's horror artists was Graham Ingels, a quiet, reserved man who had logged many years for other comic book publishers before coming to EC in the late forties. He'd drawn everything from cowboys to spacemen in that decade, but found his niche in the EC horror titles. His spidery renderings of decaying mansions, wizened old crones, and scheming husbands and wives are the stuff of nightmare. If comic books have produced a talent equal to Bosch, it is Graham Ingels.

Among the many other artists who enhanced their reputations by working for EC were science-fiction specialist Al Williamson, manic humorist Will Elder, "good girl" artist Jack Kamen, horror and aviation specialist George Evans, the brilliant draftsman Reed Crandall, and onetime Wally Wood assistant Joe Orlando. In addition, the company occasionally used Russ Heath, Alex Toth, Frank Frazetta, Gene Colan, and Joe Kubert.

EC may have been way out in front in terms of horror-comic quality, but no publisher could touch Marvel (Atlas) for sheer quantity. *Strange Tales* . . .

©1952 by Comic Combine

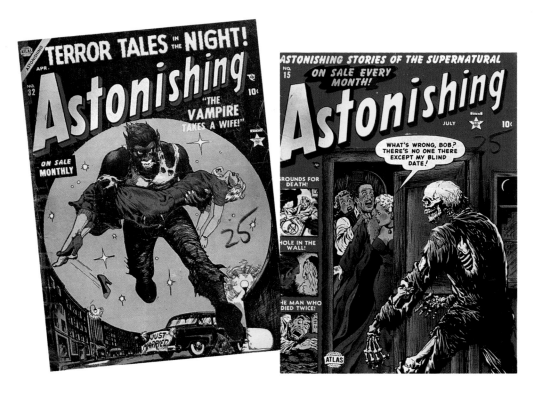

. . . and *Astonishing* were just two of more than a dozen horror titles published under the Atlas imprint.

©1952, 1954 by 20th Century Comics

out—pecked by pigeons, stuffed down disposals, skewered on swords, buried alive, dismembered and used as baseball equipment, hung as living clappers in huge bells, made into sausage and soap, dissolved, southern-fried, hacked up by maniacs in Santa Claus suits, and offed in unusually high percentages by their wives or husbands."

EC had pioneered a new kind of horror comic based not in myth and fantasy but in the banal horrors that, just maybe, could be taking place behind the closed doors of any business or suburban home. These powerfully illustrated melodramas especially appealed to adolescents and young adults who may not have read other, milder comics. Feldstein's scripts were wordy and caption-heavy—more like short stories than comic book tales. Even at their best, though, EC's horror stories were models of blunt simplicity. The value system apparent in Feldstein's scripts was one that had no shadings of gray, no ambiguity. Good people were totally good and evil people were irredeemably, consistently evil. Innocents often suffered, but the guilty suffered even more. To unsophisticated readers—particularly adolescents who felt buffeted by teachers, bullies, and other forces beyond their control—this sort of hamfisted morality was like manna.

After sales figures had established that the EC horror formula was a success, fright comics came creeping onto the stands from a horde of

The quality of Harvey's *Witches Tales* was variable, but readers could always count on plenty of lurid fun.

©1952, 1953 by Witches Tales, Inc.

DC's *House of Mystery* was vaguely suspenseful, but it's a sure thing that no kid ever got nightmares from it.

©1951, 1952 by DC Comics, Inc.

publishers, making the early 1950s the heyday of horror. *Weird Adventures*, *Weird Horrors*, *Weird Thrillers*, *Weird Terror*, *Weird Mysteries*, and *Weird Tales of the Future* could be found crouching beside *Web of Evil*, *Web of Mystery*, *Tomb of Terror*, *Horrific*, *Fantastic Fears*, *Journey into Fear*, *Strange Tales*, *The Horrors*, *Witches' Tales*, and *Uncanny Tales*. Additional horror titles numbered in the dozens.

A great many of the stories recounted in this swarm of magazines were dreadful, and frightening only in their lack of merit and restraint. The more unimaginative publishers took only the roughest, most obvious elements of the EC formula and mated them with wretched scripting and crude, ugly drawing. "Horror comics began to show more gore, more violence, ever more explicitly," science fiction writer and horror comics authority Lawrence Watt-Evans has observed. "It became a matter of topping what had come before; if one issue showed a man killing his wife, the next would top that by having him hack his wife to pieces, and the next would top *that* by having him eat her corpse!"

Parents had not paid much attention to Junior's reading habits when he was absorbed in *Superman* and *Jingle Jangle*. But when rough horror comics began showing up under Junior's bed, parents took a second look. Educators, too, began to grow concerned. Transparent, half-hearted attempts from within the comics industry to regulate its own product in the very early 1950s had come to naught. Like

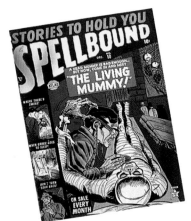

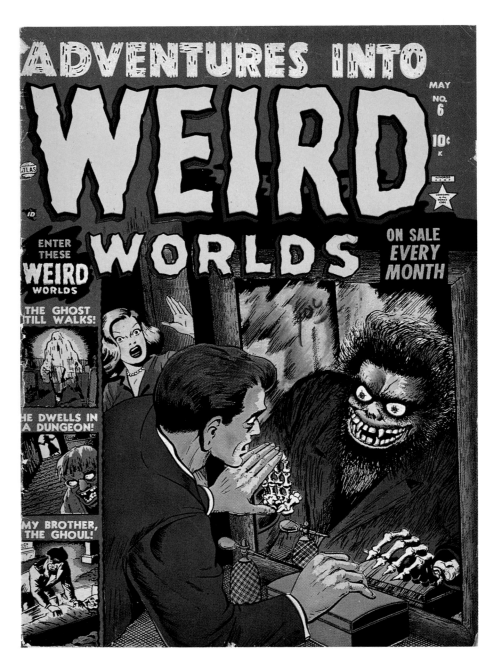

Mummies, demons, the living dead, sudden death. These were among the most familiar elements of horror comics of the early 1950s. Parents didn't appreciate all the grue, but kids ate it up.

©1952 by Animirth Comics, Inc. *(Spellbound)*; ©1951 by DC Comics, Inc. *(Sansation Comics)*; ©1954 by 20th Century Comics *(Mystery Tales)*; ©1953 by Prime Publications, Inc. *(Uncanny Tales)*; ©1952 by Animirth Comics, Inc. *(Adventures Into Weird Worlds)*

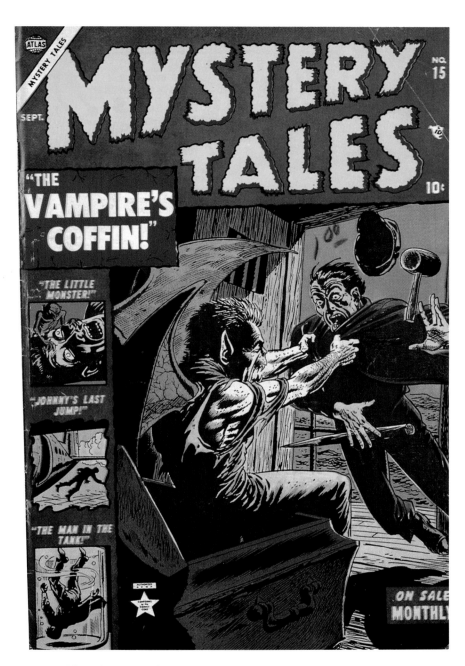

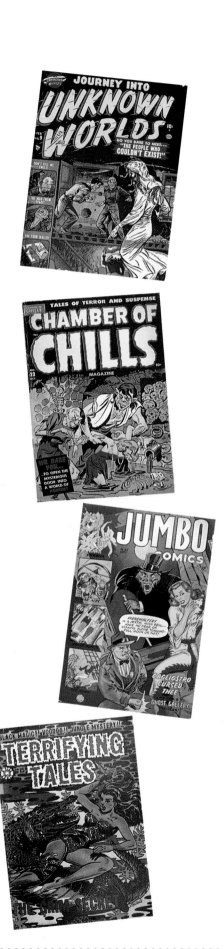

Vampires and phantoms were popular, too, but not nearly as salable as underdressed young women. Artist L. B. Cole's colorful cover for *Terrifying Tales* #15 (bottom, right) is a prime example.

"Foul Play" appeared in *The Haunt of Fear* #19. The story was powerfully illustrated by Jack Davis, but Al Feldstein's script went beyond the boundaries of what was acceptable even by the liberal standards of horror comics.

©1953 by Fables Publishing Co., Inc.

some cow town in the Old West, comic books were wide open.

A portent of bad times to come was sounded in 1953, when EC stepped over the line it had itself defined, running a story called "Foul Play" in *Haunt of Fear* #19 (June 1953). In it, an unscrupulous baseball star takes out an opposing player by sliding into the man while wearing poisoned spikes. The victim dies and his teammates discover who's responsible. The story's final panels show a peculiar baseball game, played at midnight beneath the light of the moon. The only players are the teammates of the murdered man. The killer is there, too: His intestines mark the baselines and his legs are the bats. His torso is worn by the catcher as a chest protector. The murderer's scalp is used to brush off home plate, and his head—one eye hanging from its socket—is the ball. This lapse into bad taste shocked even the artist, Jack Davis.

The excesses of "Foul Play" and the decapitations, stabbings, burnings with acid, and sparsely clad young women who were the victims in most of the industry's horror comics didn't go unnoticed by unsympathetic eyes. Ironically, it was the readers of horror novels and viewers of monster movies who probably knew better than anyone else what might befall the publishers of horror comics. Much like the fictional mad scientists who create uncontrollable monsters, the horror publishers had tampered with forbidden things—a transgression that always leads to retribution. Bela Lugosi and

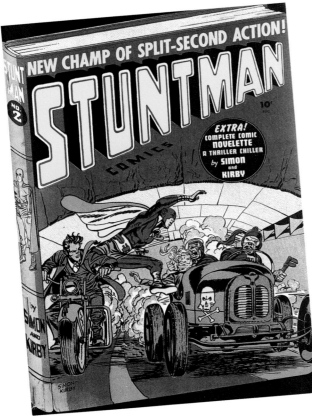

This exceptional cover done by Simon & Kirby for *Stuntman* #2 sums up the kinetic appeal of the team's flamboyant postwar superhero.

©1946 by Harvey Features Syndicate

The Korean War created an audience for war comics. Marvel's *Man Comics*, previously a potpourri of crime and adventure stories, became a war title with issue #9.

©1951 by Newsstand Publications, Inc.

Boris Karloff always got their comeuppance, and so would the comic book industry.

In the meantime, sales figures were high and the comic book business was booming. Joe Simon and Jack Kirby, who never completely turned their backs on heroes, tried to buck the trend toward violence in 1946, when they produced two issues of *Stuntman* for Harvey. Their red-clad hero specialized in crimes that centered around Hollywood. This was bravura, slam-bang material, with two-page splash panels that outdid anything the pair had offered in *Captain America*. Sadly, *Stuntman* folded after just three issues.

Simon and Kirby also produced two issues of *The Boy Explorers* in 1946, but only the first issue received proper distribution. The pair's hero product was as inherently appealing as before, but the times were no longer sympathetic to this sort of thing. S & K's *Boy's Ranch*, combining the kid gang idea with the western, followed in 1950 and lasted less than a year.

As superheroes declined, categories that had previously been neglected were expanded. The Korean War began in the summer of 1950 and this inspired a flood of combat comic books. Before the conflict came to a negotiated end in 1953, several dozen war comics, by no means devoted exclusively to the fighting in Korea, had come into being. Where there had earlier been just a handful—such as Dell's *War Comics* and *War Heroes* and Famous Funnies's *Heroic* in the 1940s—there were

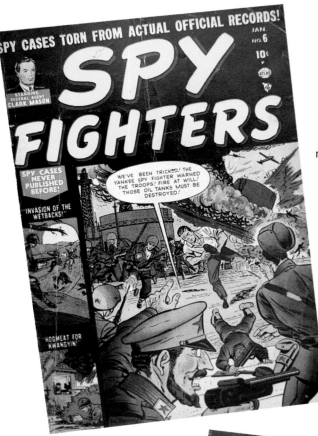

War comics were quick to seize upon the anti-communist fervor that swept America in the early fifties. Here, Red soldiers receive their comeuppance.

©1952 by Classic Syndicate, Inc.

The enemy takes a bazooka hit on the bluntly effective cover of *Battle Report* #1.

©1952 by Excellent Publications, Inc.

now many. Marvel publisher Martin Goodman's war effort was especially impressive. Among the more than two dozen war titles he published in the early 1950s, usually under the Atlas colophon, were *Battle Action*, *Battlefield*, *Battle Brady*, *Marines In Action*, *Navy Tales*, and *Young Men on the Battlefield*. DC offered *Our Fighting Forces*, *Our Army At War*, *Star Spangled War Stories*, and *All-American Men of War*.

EC, with Harvey Kurtzman editing, was responsible for the industry's most politically liberal and literate war titles, *Frontline Combat* and *Two-Fisted Tales*. These were carefully researched and believably drawn by such top-notch talents as John Severin, Reed Crandall, George Evans, and Kurtzman himself. The EC war titles and many of those from other publishers eventually faded from the scene, but the genre had been so firmly established that many of the combat books remained successful sellers until the Vietnam War.

Comic book supermen were also besieged by cowboys. DC turned *All Star* and *All-American* (later to be a war book) into western titles and added *Western Comics*, *Jimmy Wakley*, and *Dale Evans*. No piker, Marvel gave the public over fifty different cowboy comics. These included *Kid Colt*, *The Ringo Kid*, *The Texas Kid*, *The Rawhide Kid*, *The Outlaw Kid*, *The Two-Gun Kid*, *The Arizona Kid*, *The Apache Kid* and *The Kid From Texas*. Kid stuff, to be sure, but plenty profitable. Fawcett and Dell emphasized movie cowboys such as Roy Rogers, Bill Boyd, Gene Autry,

One of the bright spots of the American experience in Korea was the impressive combat performance of U.S. jet fighters. Superior's *Fighting Air Force* celebrated the exciting new machines.

©1952 by Superior Publishers Limited

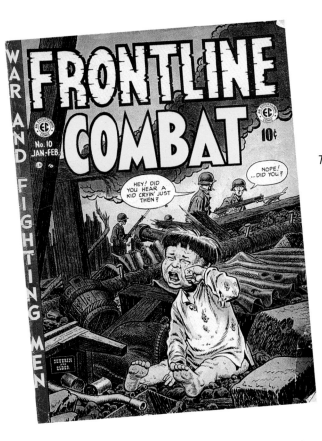

The best (and most humanistic) war comic books were *Two-Fisted Tales* and *Frontline Combat*, both published by EC. This dramatic cover was penciled by John Severin and inked by Bill Elder.

©1952 by Tiny Tot Publications

Gabby Hayes, Tom Mix, Ken Maynard, Monte Hale, Rocky Lane, and Lash LaRue. By the time Victor Fox got around to licensing a cowboy, he had to settle for Hoot Gibson.

Satirical humor became another salable commodity in the early 1950s. EC blazed the way in the autumn of 1952 when it introduced *Mad*. Edited by Kurtzman, this was a comic book version of the college humor magazine of the day as filtered through the eclectic mind of its editor. Early on, *Mad* specialized in hilarious spoofs of famous characters from newspaper comic strips and comic books. Soon, the focus of the magazine's humor broadened to include TV and movies, politics, and daily life.

"Ever since *Mad* started, I've heard twenty stories about who was responsible for *Mad*'s creation," Harvey Kurtzman once said. "As I remember it, I became desperate to do a quick comic. I wasn't making any money with the war books. . . . So I somehow convinced Gaines that I should do something else that was easier. He said 'Go ahead.' Now, I'd always been doing satire in school, in the streets; it was my kind of clowning. . . . The format would make fun of comic books as they were at that particular period."

EC publisher William Gaines has concurred with Kurtzman's recollection of the comic's genesis. "Our official reason for publishing *Mad* was, we were tired of the horror, weary of the science fiction, we wanted to do a *comic* comic. That was not true; it was just publicity. It was so ▶

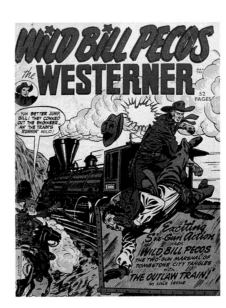

Fueled by the growth of television, western comics flourished throughout the 1950s. Some, such as *Roy Rogers* and *Gene Autry*, featured movie and TV cowboy stars. Others, like *Ghost Rider,* offered characters unique to comics. Collectors will note that the cover of *Ghost Rider* #3 (top row, third from left) was drawn by famed illustrator Frank Frazetta.

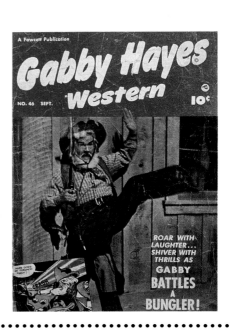

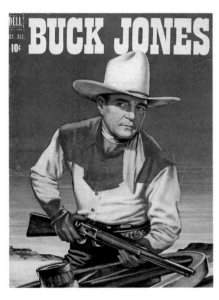

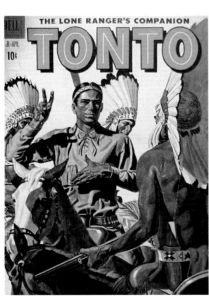

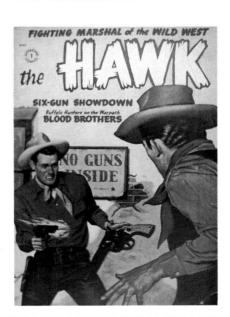

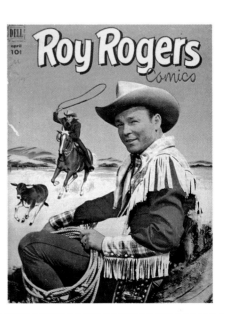

HARVEY KURTZMAN

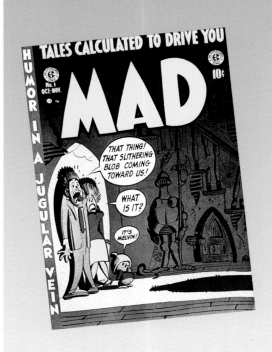

The 1950s brought a quartet of new American magazines that became enormously successful. *Sports Illustrated*, *TV Guide*, and *Playboy* were three of them; the fourth was Harvey Kurtzman's Mad (left). Wally Wood's interpretation of Kurtzman's "Little Orphan Melvin" *(Mad #9)* is at right.

©1952, 1953 by Educational Comics, Inc.

Among the several awards given out by fans each year for achievement in the comic book field are the Harvey Awards. These are named in honor of Harvey Kurtzman, and place him in the comic book pantheon with Will Eisner and Jack Kirby, who also enjoy the distinction of having had annual awards named after them. While not as prolific or as committed to the medium as other important artists, Kurtzman has been tremendously influential.

He was born in New York in 1924 and began to draw professionally for comic books while still a teenager. Most of Kurtzman's early work was in the superhero genre. In the middle 1940s, after leaving the service, he established a commercial art studio. By this time his style had changed and his *Hey Look!* humor filler pages, which graced various Marvel titles, were done with the loose, bold brushwork that became his trademark.

Kurtzman went to work for William Gaines at EC in 1950. He did horror and suspense stories for a time, then created and edited EC's *Two-Fisted Tales* and *Frontline Combat*. "All our stories protested war," he has been quick to assert.

A very thorough writer-editor, Kurtzman usually provided page layouts for his artists, and encouraged them to do historical research in order to be as accurate as possible. The EC war stories were set not just during World War II and the Korean conflict, but during ancient Rome, the Crusades, the American Revolution, the Napoleonic era, the Civil War, World War I, and many other fascinating periods. These war stories, many of them drawn by Kurtzman himself, are the finest ever seen in comic books.

Following the success of the EC war titles, Kurtzman created *Mad*. A ten-cent, full-color comic book for its first twenty-three issues, it sold briskly and went on to become a cultural icon that inspired innumerable comic book and magazine-format imitations.

Kurtzman left EC shortly after *Mad* converted to magazine format in 1955. He went on to edit and contribute to a trio of short-lived but worthy humor magazines—*Trump, Humbug,* and *Help!* He also created the saucy, long-running *Little Annie Fanny* strip for *Playboy*, bringing with him onetime *Mad* artist Will Elder. Although Kurtzman has slowed his activity in recent years, he remains highly popular.

Bill Elder's "Frank N. Stein" appeared in *Mad* #8 in 1953. Manic yet devoted to detail, Elder later worked with Harvey Kurtzman on *Little Annie Fanny*, a popular and long-running feature of *Playboy* magazine.

©1953 by Educational Comics, Inc.

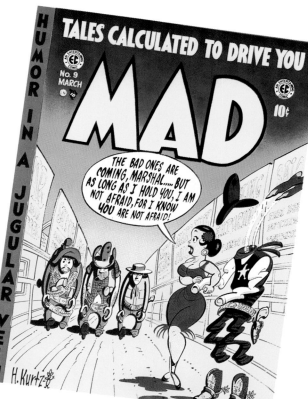

Harvey Kurtzman's wit and infallible sense of design illuminate this early *Mad* cover that spoofs the film *High Noon*.

©1953 by Educational Comics, Inc.

Kurtzman could get a fifty percent raise."

As Gaines remembered it, "*Mad* lost money for three issues. 'Superduperman' [Kurtzman's parody of Superman, drawn by Wally Wood] was in issue #4. *Mad* then became popular." So popular that other publishers quickly stepped in with imitations. "Martin Goodman had half a dozen," Gaines once said. "There were seventy titles, I understand; my printer counted them up because he used to keep a list of all comics published. And he told me there were seventy. I think he was wrong, but there were certainly thirty, forty or fifty imitations of *Mad*. You know, *Eek, Ecch, Oook* . . . I can't remember them all."

Well, there was no *Oook*, but included among the earliest actual imitations of *Mad* were EC's own *Panic* (edited by Al Feldstein) and many (short-lived) titles from other publishers—*Crazy, Riot, Eh!, Madhouse, Get Lost, Whack,* and *Nuts!* Most of the knockoffs aped *Mad*'s irreverence, but none came close to its sophistication and innate cleverness. Even EC's *Panic* seems labored.

Although not every comic book of the period was an artistic success, sales figures proved that the industry had met the postwar challenge, coming up with several successful alternatives to the declining superhero genre. Horror, war, jungle girls, cowboys, romance, humor—they all sold briskly. Millions of dollars were still being made. But, though few in the industry suspected it, bad times lay ahead.

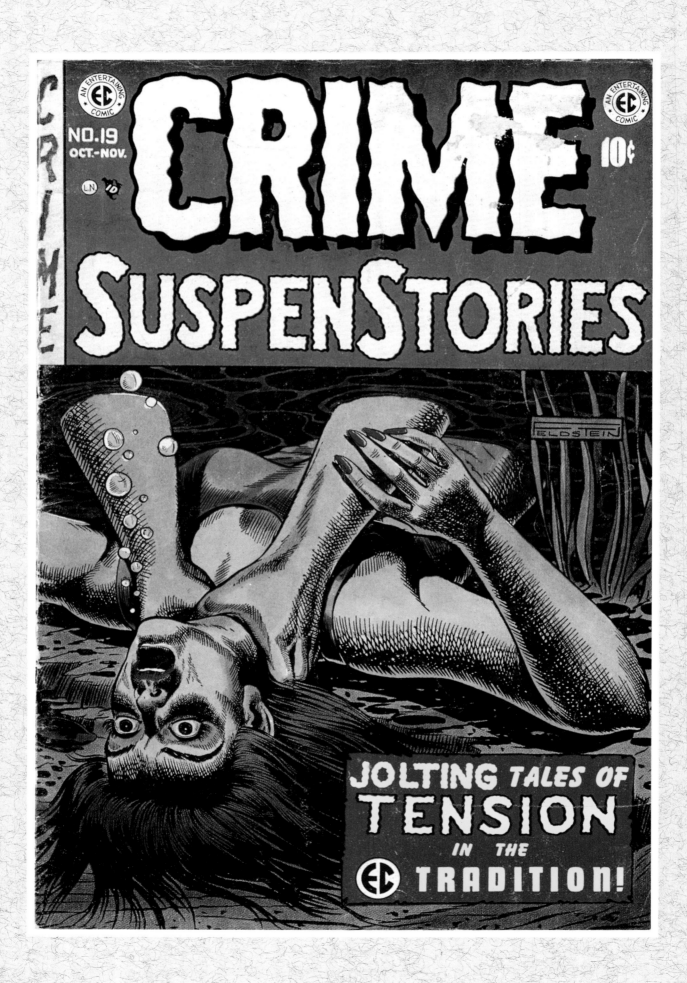

CHAPTER NINE

CRIME AND PUNISHMENT

Although stories of criminal life had been longtime staples of popular fiction, comic books were slow to aggressively exploit the genre. The first "true-crime" material (that is, stories that chronicled supposedly fact-based bank robberies, murders, and similarly violent crimes, and their perpetrators) to appear in comic book form was a four-page selection of the *War On Crime* newspaper strip, reprinted in *Famous Funnies* #27 (October 1936). The earliest all-new true crime material showed up in titles published by Whitman-Dell, a company that later was to specialize in animated cartoon animals, fairy tales, and magazines that were safe even for nursery-age tots. Issue #21 (June 1938) of the same company's *The Funnies* introduced *The Crime Busters*. This feature was fairly close in tone to the popular radio show devoted to true crime, *Gang Busters*, a Phillips H. Lord production that first aired in 1936. Dell's *Popular Comics* went to the source and started running *Gang Busters* in issue #38 (April 1939).

At MLJ, artist Jack Cole, obviously under the influence

Entertainingly lurid crime comics glutted America's newsstands in the late forties and early fifties. EC Comic's *Crime SuspenStories* was unflinching in its depictions of mayhem. This vivid 1953 cover was drawn by Al Feldstein.

of the *Gang Busters* radio show, introduced two short-lived true crime strips to that publisher's line late in 1939. *Blue Ribbon* carried his *Crime on the Run*, and *Top-Notch* featured *Man-Hunters*.

The earliest comic book devoted entirely to true crime was Dell's *Gang Busters*, issued irregularly from 1939 to 1943 and consisting mostly of reprints of the *Popular* material. Other publishers eventually got into crime comics. One of them was Arthur Bernhard, who had been involved in publishing magazines of all sorts in the 1930s. Late in 1939 he decided to venture into the comic book field with *Silver Streak Comics*. After a few issues, Bernhard hired Jack Cole to edit the magazine. Cole wrote and drew speedy Silver Streak's adventures with a great sense of fun, cramming the pages with action, violence, monsters, pretty girls, and humor. The magazine's other resident costumed hero was Daredevil and Cole drew him for a time, as well. In the summer of 1941 Daredevil graduated to a book of his own, the first issue of which was entitled *Daredevil Battles Hitler*. Bernhard has said that this comic was an expression of his own antifascist, anti-Hitler activities. His views were shared by publishing executive Lev Gleason, who became his partner at about this time.

The inside back cover of *Daredevil Battles Hitler* carried an ad for the upcoming *Daredevil Comics*. "BY POPULAR DEMAND—What you've all been waiting for—the DAREDEVIL'S OWN COMIC

Gang Busters (appearing here as issue #23 of *Four Color*) was one of the earliest crime comics.

©1941 by Phillips H. Lord, Inc.

Phillips H. Lord's popular radio program inspired a *Gang Busters* feature in *Popular Comics*.

©1940 by Phillips H. Lord, Inc.

BOOK." Bernhard and Gleason brought in Charles Biro and Bob Wood to edit and produce the new titles. Biro and Wood had met when they were both artists at the shop run by Harry "A" Chesler; both men had worked for MLJ in 1939. Biro, in fact, had helped to run things at that company, turning out *Pep Comics*, *Zip Comics*, and other titles. It was while there that Biro, as artist, writer, and editor, abandoned his interest in cute, "bigfoot" cartooning and gravitated instead to a potent blend of action, violence, bloodshed, and slinky sex. It was a powerful formula that Biro would refine later in the 1940s.

Besides exploiting the combination of sex and violence that would become a Lev Gleason hallmark, Biro added packaging tricks that eventually became industry standards. From its first issue, *Daredevil* bore an aggressive slogan—"The Greatest Name in Comics." Covers were littered with boxes of copy and multicolored headlines that promised all sorts of delights, including money—"$100 CASH PRIZES You May WIN" was a typical Biro come-on. Banners above the titles of a few early issues of *Daredevil* indulged in that popular new pastime, wartime xenophobia, promising an "Exciting New Game called Slap the Jap."

Biro wrote and drew the Daredevil yarns, developing the habit early on of addressing his readers directly, often hyping the story they were about to read. "None can rival the wild fantasy that will unfold within these pages! . . . So dim the lights and lock your doors as well, for this monster might strike at even YOU!"

When asked who had come up with the idea for Bernhard-Gleason's most successful comic book, *Crime Does Not Pay*, Bernhard replied that "Lev conceived the whole thing" and then turned it over to Biro. The new magazine was launched in 1942 with typical Biro enthusiasm. Teaser ads proclaimed, "IT'S COMING! The most sensational comic magazine ever created!!! This spectacular masterpiece is in production NOW! Get it on your newsstand soon!" Once *Crime Does Not Pay* appeared, full-page ads for it began running in the company's other titles. The copy proclaimed, "THE MOST SENSATIONAL COMIC IDEA ever is sweeping the country! Crime comics give you the REAL FACTS!! SEE why 'Crime Does Not Pay'! SEE for the first time how real criminals lived, stole, killed and then—" A line of copy below this particular ad, indicating that the company had a larger audience in mind, read, "Get 'Crime Does Not Pay'! Show it to Dad, he'll love it!"

Major influences on the genesis and evolution of *Crime Does Not Pay* were hardboiled periodicals such as *Master Detective*, *True Detective*, and *Official Detective*. Printed on somewhat better paper than the pulp fiction magazines and illustrated with grainy photos of vicious criminals, blowzy gun molls, and bloody corpses, they offered breathless nonfiction accounts of daring bank

A gun moll makes a fatal mistake in a story from *Crime Does Not Pay*. Art is by George Tuska, whose comic book career has spanned six decades.

©by Lev Gleason

193

robberies, brutal murders, and violent crimes of passion. *Crime Does Not Pay* came closer than any comic book had before to emulating this particular blend of gritty reality, shoot 'em up action, and titillation. (Ironically, co-editor Bob Wood was a violent man who went to prison in the early 1950s for beating his girlfriend to death.)

Crime Does Not Pay replaced *Silver Streak*, and assumed that title's numbering; the first issue was #22 (July 1942). The cover copy assured readers that *Crime Does not Pay* was "The First Magazine of Its Kind!" Inside, readers found true crime cases of Louis "Lepke" Buchalter of Murder, Inc. fame; the Mad Dog Esposito Brothers; and Wild Bill Hickok. The left margin of the cover featured photos of some of the showcased hoodlums but the real grabber was Biro's artwork, an impossibly kinetic depiction of a vicious brawl in an underworld dive. Gambling, gunplay, a redheaded gun moll in a tight crimson dress, a falling body, and a hand pierced with a knife figured in the action. All in all, a splendid example of effective packaging and of the tone of the day.

Crime Does Not Pay #24 introduced Mr. Crime, a ghostly, all-knowing wiseguy who was a cross between the nasty Mr. Coffee Nerves of the Postum coffee ads and the sardonic hosts of radio mystery shows like *Inner Sanctum*. He hosted each issue's leadoff story and inevitably offered a pithy remark in the final panel—"The law got ALL of them! Ralph Fleagle, Royston and Absher were all

hanged in Colorado State Penitentiary at Canon City! Good pupils, too, tsk, tsk!"

Crime Does Not Pay chronicled crooks of recent vintage, such as "Legs" Diamond, and older heavies like Billy the Kid. For those who favored the more intellectual sort of mystery, there was a monthly Who-Dunnit? story—"Test your wits—How good a detective are YOU?" Most of the comic's fact-based cases were packed with shooting, violence, and action, but little actual bloodshed was depicted. Mild sexual activity was typical, and was usually provided by the lady friends of the various crooks and killers.

Many of Biro's covers were as action-packed and gory as the stories, but some of his most effective covers were successful because they dealt in giddy *anticipation* of a violent act, rather than in a depiction of the act itself. He showed the moment just before the pool hustler gets his throat cut, the moment just before the hapless gas station attendants are buried alive, the moment just before the bootlegger is dropped into the lime pit. The social ramifications of this sort of work are certainly debatable, but Biro's covers did sell a lot of comic books. After leaving comics following the great industry shakeout of the mid-fifties, Biro took his talents to NBC's graphic arts department in 1962. He remained with the network for ten years until his death in 1972.

The three Bernhard-Gleason titles—*Daredevil*, *Boy*, and *Crime Does Not Pay*—had a combined sale of nearly one million copies

Charles Biro was the creative force behind *Crime Does Not Pay*, the most popular of all crime comic books, and one of the most notorious as well. A triple-threat man who wrote, drew, and edited, Biro knew how to snare buyers. The implications of this 1943 cover are pretty horrible, but the illustration is actually one of Biro's more restrained.

©1943 by Comic House, Inc.

a month in 1943. By 1945 the figure had climbed to more than 1,500,000 and by 1947 it was over two million. Late in 1947 the covers of *Crime Does Not Pay* boasted, "More Than 6,000,000 Readers Monthly!" (The hard-selling Biro was fudging some and assuming that more than one reader looked at each copy.)

Artwork in the early issues of *Crime Does Not Pay* had been drawn by such notable talents as Creig Flessel, Harry Lucey, Dick Breifer, and the creator of Archie, Bob Montana. As the war progressed, some lesser artists worked on the magazine, but in the middle and late 1940s George Tuska (who has been called "the premier crime comic artist"), Bob Fujitani, Dan Barry, and Fred Kida were among those who improved the comic's looks.

Crime Does Not Pay, despite its impressive sales, had the field pretty much to itself for several years. But because of the uncertain economics of the postwar period, other publishers decided to turn to crime. In the forefront of those who stepped into the genre were Joe Simon and Jack Kirby—longtime superhero specialists and inventors of the love-comic format. The team renovated Prize Publication's *Headline Comics* early in 1947, changing it from a comic book full of clean-cut boy heroes to one packed with gangsters and murderers. Joe Simon once explained that although *Headline* was inspired by *Crime Does Not Pay*, "we had our own style, we didn't copy them. We didn't agree with certain things they did. We didn't care for violence and sex."

Simon and Kirby also contributed true crime stories to *Clue Comics*, a Hillman magazine that became *Real Clue* with the June 1947 issue. This comic had a somewhat more erudite cover slogan than its competitors, using Ralph Waldo Emerson's line, "Commit a crime and the world is made of glass."

Marvel, always quick to capitalize on trends, took to a life of crime with great enthusiasm. Sub-Mariner's magazine was converted into *Official True Crime Cases* in the autumn of 1947, and over the next three years more titles were added to the Marvel/Atlas lineup— *Lawbreakers Always Lose*, *Crime Can't Win*, *Crime Must Lose*, *All-True Crime Cases*, *Crime Case Comics*, and many others.

The more conservative DC went along with the crime wave, but more cautiously than other, smaller publishers. DC's only "true crime" title was *Gang Busters*, which had been assumed from Dell in late 1947. While the title built stories around violent crime, the depictions of them were relatively bloodless and sedate. For crime fans who didn't insist on gospel truth, DC also offered *Mr. District Attorney* and *Big Town*, both based on radio—and later TV—crime shows.

The irrepressible Victor Fox went along with the trend, too. His *Phantom Lady*, that paragon of "good girl" art, managed to include one true crime story in most of its steamy issues. That was just good business, but Fox, sensing what at least a segment of the audience wanted, came up with an all-new title called *Crimes*

Crime comics usually went out of their way to demonstrate that, deep down, criminals were gutless. Of course, this message often came at the end of a story filled with invigorating violence and high living. Here, a punk turns yellow when the chips are down.

©1950 by Hillman Periodicals

INSIDE TRUTH ABOUT CRIME!!

REAL CLUE CRIME STORIES

NOV • 1950 10¢
A HILLMAN PUBLICATION

WHAT WENT WRONG ??— I THOUGHT WE FIGURED ON EVERYTHING...

...AND SO DID THE COPS...

POLICE FACTS!

The weed of crime bears bitter fruit—and makes for dirty, soiled suits, too. Two more bright guys learn that crime doesn't pay, on an unnumbered issue of *Real Clue Crime* Stories.

©1950 by Hillman Periodicals, Inc.

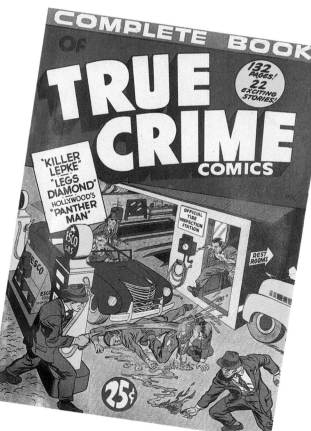

COMPLETE BOOK of **TRUE CRIME** COMICS

132 PAGES! 22 EXCITING STORIES!

"KILLER LEPKE" "LEGS DIAMOND" HOLLYWOOD'S "PANTHER MAN"

25¢

The Complete Book of True Crime Comics was an undated collection of issues of Crime Does Not Pay, stapled together beneath a new cover drawn by Charles Biro. The comic appeared about 1945.

©by William H. Wise & Co.

By Women. The first issue, dated June 1948, featured "the True Story of Bonnie Parker, Queen of the Gun Molls!" Less restrained than some of his competitors, Fox allowed the pages to be filled with scantily clad molls, sluts, and murderesses. "Catfight" fans doubtless appreciated the fact that women regularly fought and wrestled with each other within the comic's pages; sometimes they even threw acid into the faces of their rivals.

Fox was responsible for several similar titles, including *Crimes, Incorporated*; *Inside Crime*, and various issues of the *Fox Giants* series, which offered "Over 100 Pages" of true-crime stories by binding four coverless, remaindered (unsold) Fox comics under a new cover. The crime-oriented examples of these twenty-five-cent comic book collections were sold under a variety of titles, including *Album of Crime*, *All-Famous Crime Stories*, *All Great Crime Stories*, and *Almanac of Crime*. Covers were lurid and inventive, as evidenced by the first of three issues of *March of Crime* (*Fox Giants* #24; 1948)—a raven-haired beauty cuts loose with a tommy gun while falling out of her fur-trimmed kimono. A later issue of *March of Crime* (*Fox Giants* #26; 1950) features more tommy gun action on the cover, as a supposedly dead mobster bolts upright in his coffin and blasts the rats who had set him up for murder. Primitive and vibrant, these covers taught Fox, as similar covers had taught other crime comic publishers, that lurid images meant healthy sales.

At Toytown/Orbit Publications, meanwhile, a lady named named Ray Hermann was publishing and editing *Wanted*, a moderately bloody comic that advised its readers, "Crime Can't Win." This comic specialized in cautionary tales about contemporary crooks and criminals who were wanted by the law. Each story ended with a similar warning—"Joseph Anthony Cacciola is still at large! Watch for him, but remember—he is always heavily armed and dangerous!" Covers and most of the interior art were by Mort Leav and Mort Lawrence.

Among the other crime comics to be found on the stands from the late 1940s to the middle 1950s were EC's grimly realistic *Crime SuspenStories*, St. John's *Authentic Police Cases*, Charlton's *Crime and Justice*, D.S.'s astonishingly violent *Underworld*, Ace's *Crime Must Pay The Penalty*, Star's *All-Famous Crimes*, Ziff-Davis's *Crime Clinic*, Cross's *The Perfect Crime*, Hillman's *Crime Detective*, and Fox's lurid *Famous Crimes*.

Arthur Bernhard, parted from Lev Gleason in the mid-forties, now formed a new company, Magazine Village, and published *True Crime Comics*. He hired a single employee, Jack Cole, to package the book. Cole brought in the gifted artist Alex Kotzky (who later created the long-running newspaper strip, *Apartment 3-G*). Kotzky and Cole put in many all-nighters in order to get the artwork turned out on time. For the first issue (identified inside as issue #2), Cole produced a violent *film noir* leadoff story entitled "Murder,

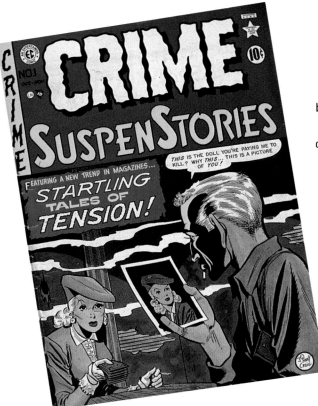

EC Comics introduced *Crime SuspenStories* in 1950, and the title soon became the best and most dramatic of all crime comics. Cover art for issue #1 is by Johnny Craig.

©1950 by L. L. Publishing Co., Inc.

Socks Lazia, the King of Kansas City, comes to a bad end on what was to have been a day of celebration. Typical of crime comics, Lazia's good-looking girlfriend pays the ultimate penalty, too. This story appeared in *Crime Must Pay the Penalty* #3.

©1948 by Junior Books, Inc.

THERE IS ONLY ONE TRUE CRIME COMICS — THIS IS IT!

The first issue of *True Crime Comics* was packaged by artist/writer Jack Cole, and featured one of the most remarkable stories ever to appear in a comic book: "Murder, Morphine and Me!" Sexy, fevered, and violent in the extreme, the story still has the capacity to shock.

Morphine and Me!" A remarkable achievement, the story is at once impressively drawn and vaguely repellent. "This flashback narrative begins with a crazed drug addict jabbing blonde Mary in the eyeball with a hypodermic," recounts a stunned Denis Gifford in his *International Book of Comics*, "continues with a montage of human dregs she acts as 'hostess' to, and goes rapidly down gutter from there." Actually the needle never goes *into* poor Mary's eye, but only threatens to. Regardless, Cole's artwork is frenzied and kinetic; characters sweat, grimace, and gesticulate with wild abandon. Violence and fear radiate from nearly every panel.

Kotzky's chief contribution to the debut issue of *True Crime* was "Demon Dance on Galloway Moor," an historical yarn about Sawney Bean and his family of marauding cannibals. Another story, drawn by Creig Flessel, opens with a memorable scene of two live crooks who are being dragged face-down along a gravel road after being tied by their ankles to the back bumper of a speeding car. In all, the first issue of *True Crime* is as much an aberration as a creative achievement; it quickly became a rallying point for anti-comic book crusaders, and selected panels from the issue's stories found their way into more than one exhibit of the excesses of crime comics.

Despite the creative innovations of other crime-comic pubishers, Lev Gleason's *Crime Does Not Pay* continued to lead the field in sales. Eventually, because so many other publishers were imitating his best-selling title, Gleason decided to introduce a knockoff of his own early in 1948. This was *Crime and Punishment*—"A FORCE FOR GOOD IN THE COMMUNITY!" The new title was a dead ringer for *Crime Does Not Pay*, right down to the wordy scripts that had become a Biro trademark.

Now thoroughly annoyed with imitations published by others, Gleason ran full-page attacks against them in the pages of his magazines—"Imitation is the highest form of flattery! Every time we bring out a new idea, imitators swarm around the newsstands like bees around honeysuckle! Some of these imitations are fair! But we warn our readers against the flood of cheap and shoddy magazines which are trying to latch on to the enormous popularity."

Lev Gleason had a legitimate gripe, but his was not the only critical voice to be heard. As soon as comic books had established themselves as a successful magazine category, in fact, outside criticism of comics had begun. In May of 1940, for example, an editorial in the *Chicago Daily News* labeled comic books a "national disgrace." Written by Sterling North, the piece was not a critique but a call to arms. Charged North, "Badly drawn, badly written and badly printed—a strain on young eyes and young nervous systems—the effect of these pulp-paper nightmares is that of a violent stimulant. Their crude blacks and reds spoil the child's natural sense of color; their

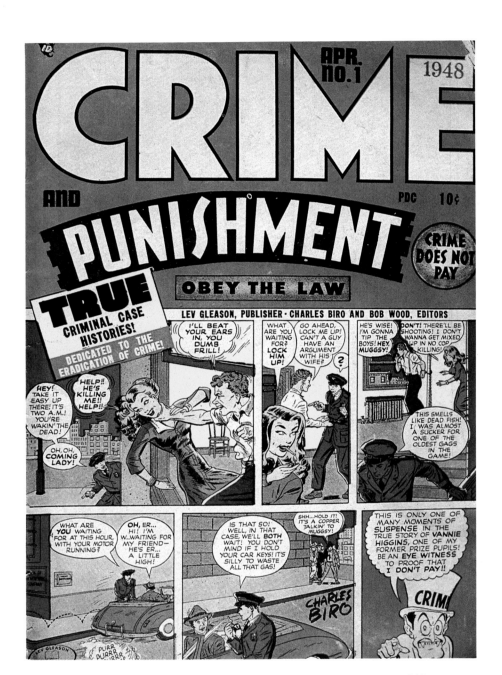

Publisher Lev Gleason struck back against the imitators of his *Crime Does Not Pay* by introducing a companion title, *Crime and Punishment*. Cover art, as usual, was handled by editor Charles Biro.

©1947 by Lev Gleason Publications, Inc.

hypodermic injection of sex and murder make the child impatient with better, though quieter, stories. Unless we want a coming generation even more ferocious than the present one, parents and teachers throughout America must band together to break the 'comic magazine.'"

North's recommended cure for this blight was good books. "There is nothing dull about *Westward Ho* or *Treasure Island,*" he declared optimistically. North concluded, "The shame lies largely with parents who don't know and don't care what their children are reading. It lies with unimaginative teachers who force stupid twaddle down eager young throats, and, of course, it lies with the completely immoral publishers of the 'comic'—guilty of a cultural slaughter of the innocents. But the antidote to the 'comic' magazine poison can be found in any library or good book store. The parent who does not acquire that antidote for his child is guilty of criminal negligence."

Teachers and librarians quickly took up the fight. As early as the spring of 1941, magazines aimed at people in those professions were running pieces with titles like "The Comic Menace" and "Librarians, To Arms!" The most frequently suggested technique was simply to wean bleary-eyed comics addicts off the funnies and onto good books. If a child asked a librarian if she had *Superman*, she was advised to reply, "No, but what do you think of Robin Hood and Baron Munchausen and Paul Bunyan? Aren't they supermen?"

Another technique was to fight fire with fire—to jump into the trenches and publish "quality" comic books. Early in 1941 George Hecht, the publisher of *Parents' Magazine*, released *True Comics*. The new title was edited by a "young historian" named David Marke. For its artwork and scripts, however, *True* went to Funnies, Inc., the same shop that had put together *Marvel Mystery Comics*, *Blue Bolt*, and many other titles. An article in *Parents'* by that magazine's editor, Clara Savage Littledale, heralded the coming of *True*. Littledale explained to concerned parents that while *True* might look like just one more comic, it was actually "attractive, interesting and worthwhile" and that the big "difference is in the subject matter, which deals with past and present history." In addition to having a young historian acting as editor, the magazine boasted a group of senior advisory editors that included George Gallup, Dr. Arthur Jersild, Hendrik Willem van Loon, and Mrs. Littledale. For good measure, there were several junior advisory editors, including film stars Shirley Temple and Mickey Rooney.

The first issue of *True Comics* (April 1941) started off with "World Hero No. 1," a seventeen-page story devoted to the life of Winston Churchill. There were also stories about malaria, the Marathon Run, and Simon Bolivar. Despite the elevated subject matter, Funnies, Inc. hadn't sent in its first team and relied instead on Harold Delary, Mike Roy, John Daly, and other second-echelon artists.

Subsequent issues of *True Comics* offered factual accounts of Richard Harding Davis, Marine paratroopers, Chinese guerrillas, General Charles de Gaulle, dog heroes, Harry Houdini, and ventriloquist's dummy Charlie McCarthy. The editor's job turned over frequently and was eventually filled by Elliot Caplin, brother of *Li'l Abner* creator Al Capp and scriptwriter on several newspaper strips. Even the celebrity-adviser roster underwent changes: By the summer of 1942, Roddy McDowall had replaced Mickey Rooney (who was probably too wrapped up in his stormy marriage to Ava Gardner to bother with a comic book).

Although a bland and deliberately unexciting publication, *True* posted exceptional sales figures. A news item in *Publishers Weekly* announced, "*True Comics*, the cartoon magazine for children which is based on carefully verified scientific and historical facts, has had a smashing success with its first issue, which sold out 300,000 copies in the United States within 10 days after publication early in March. . . . Originally planned for publication every two months, the magazine will now be a monthly. Meanwhile 10,000 extra copies of the first number are being printed."

Before 1941 was out, Hecht had added two more titles, *Real Heroes*, which had the same slant as *True*, and *Calling All Girls*. The latter was half comic, half slick magazine and was "published exclusively for girls

George Hecht's *True Comics* told exciting, real-life stories of courageous men and women. Issue #17 told the story of World War II Pacific hero "Uncle Joe" Stilwell.

©1942 by Parents' Magazine Press

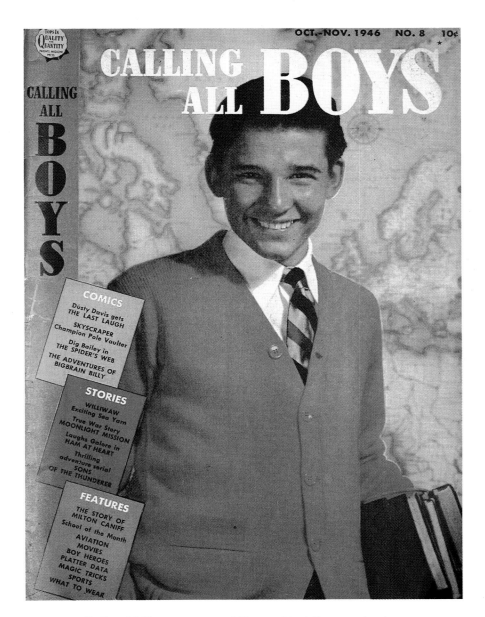

CALLING **BOYS**
ALL

CALLING
ALL
BOYS

Tops In
QUALITY
and
QUANTITY
PARENTS MAGAZINE
METAL

COMICS
Dusty Davis gets
THE LAST LAUGH
SKYSCRAPER
Champion Pole Vaulter
Dig Bailey in
THE SPIDER'S WEB
THE ADVENTURES OF
BIGBRAIN BILLY

STORIES
WILLIWAW
Exciting Sea Yarn
True War Story
MOONLIGHT MISSION
Laughs Galore in
HAM AT HEART
Thrilling
adventure serial
SONS
OF THE THUNDERER

FEATURES
THE STORY OF
MILTON CANIFF
School of the Month
AVIATION
MOVIES
BOY HEROES
PLATTER DATA
MAGIC TRICKS
SPORTS
WHAT TO WEAR

Calling All Boys was one of George Hecht's squeaky-clean
(and commercially successful) comic books.

©1946 by Parents Magazine, Inc.

and sub-debs," an audience that few publishers had as yet considered. Besides thirty-two pages of comics, *Calling All Girls* contained "up-to-the-minute departments on good looks, good manners, 'date' fashions, recommended movies, beginner's cooking, articles . . . and three smart fiction stories that are tops!"

Hecht did well with his innocuous, virtuous comic books; a report in the April 18, 1942 issue of *Business Week* stated that "a combined circulation of 750,000 is claimed for the three magazines." That meant a monthly gross of $75,000 and a yearly gross of nearly one million dollars.

That truth might sell nearly as well as fiction did not go unnoticed by the comics industry. Ned Pines, who was already publishing *Thrilling* and *Exciting*, launched *Real Life Comics* in the summer of 1941. *It Really Happened*, a second fact-based Pines comic, appeared in 1944. Street & Smith's entries were *Pioneer Picture Stories* and *Trail Blazers*, both debuting in 1941. Between 1942 and 1947, Hecht added *True Aviation*, *Calling All Boys*, *Calling All Kids*, and *True Animal Picture Stories*. Even DC tried a true comic, a 1946 title called *Real Fact*.

Another attempt to uplift comics, and make a buck at the same time, was *Classic Comics*. Begun in 1941 by Albert Kanter, who was doing business as Gilberton Publications, the magazines offered hastily drawn and badly adapted comic book versions of *The Three Musketeers*, *Ivanhoe*, *A Tale of Two Cities*, ▶

LEV GLEASON, PUBLISHER

The cover of *Daredevil* #24 (May 1944) shows Daredevil and the Little Wise Guys bursting in on a renegade Punch and Judy show. The Punch puppet is firing a blunderbuss into an audience of children. Among the frightened children sit a pair of adult hoodlums. One has already been shot and, writhing in agony, is clutching a bloody wound in his chest. The other thug is in the process of being shot by Punch and blood is spurting out of his chest, too. A crying little boy is hugging him. A circle of copy proclaims, "Here for the first time you can be an eyewitness to the most cruel and treacherous of all crimes—'The Punch and Judy Murders'!" Next to this breathless sell copy is the publisher's logo. It reads "Lev Gleason Publications. Integrity."

Leverett S. Gleason had been in publishing for several years before starting his own company. He'd worked in the advertising department at Eastern Color and then had gone over to United Features to edit *Tip Top Comics* and *Comics On Parade*. In 1940 he joined publisher Arthur Bernhard as an editor and later became a partner. In addition to such comic books as *Silver Streak* and *Daredevil*, Gleason worked on a magazine called *Friday*, a short-lived knockoff of *Life*. By the middle 1940s he and Bernhard had parted and Gleason headed the company alone.

A man of liberal social and political beliefs, Gleason got in trouble in the conservative postwar years. In 1946, while briefly serving as publisher of a veterans' magazine called *Salute*, he was accused of being "Communist party influenced." That same year he was charged with contempt of Congress, along with a group

Lev Gleason was a canny publisher who gave free reign to his gifted artist/writer/editor, Charles Biro. This 1941 Biro splash page from *Daredevil* #2 shows the action and vigor that characterized Gleason's titles.

©1941 by Your Guide

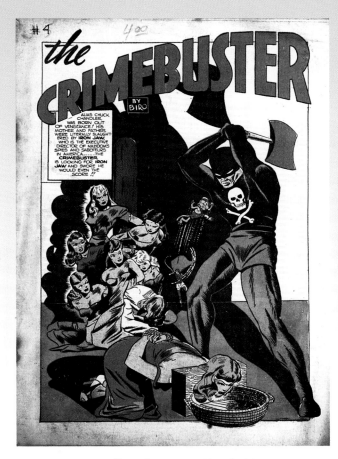

Fans knew exactly what to expect from a Lev Gleason comic. This striking Charles Biro splash page from *Boy Comics* #4 demonstrates the Gleason penchant for grotesque violence.

©1942 by Comic House, Inc.

of sixteen others that included author Howard Fast. The charge rose out of a House Un-American Activities Committee investigation into the Joint Anti-Fascist Refugee Committee of New York City. The House group was investigating charges that the antifascist organization had "Communist connections." When the chairman of the antifascist group refused to turn over subpoenaed records, a contempt citation was issued. By the time his comic books were under investigation years later, Gleason was well acquainted with the techniques of political browbeating.

Gleason was an articulate champion of comics who wrote articles and letters that spoke out against censorship. In a February 1949 letter to the *New York Times* Gleason said, "I believe that the control of children's reading material properly lies with the parent." He went on to point out that "between 40 percent and 60 percent of the 100,000,000 comic magazines sold each month are bought by adults for their own reading pleasure." He pointed out that any regulation of comics would dictate to adults as well as children.

Gleason attempted to appeal to this adult comic book readership later in 1949 by publishing *Tops*, a tabloid-size comic that offered slicker, more sophisticated material than Gleason's other titles. *Tops* didn't succeed and Gleason's attempts at unobjectionable kiddie comics, *Uncle Charlies' Fables* (1952) and *Adventures in Wonderland* (1955), didn't make it, either. Both *Crime Does Not Pay* and *Crime and Punishment* folded in the summer of 1955. *Boy* ceased publication early in 1956 and *Daredevil* was canceled in the summer of that year. Lev Gleason's days as the leader of a comic book empire were over.

Moby Dick, and other classic novels. The line caught on, possibly because kids discovered that the adaptations—as bad as they were—could be used as the basis for time-saving school book reports. The line's name was changed in 1947 to *Classics Illustrated* and continued to issue new adaptations and reprints until 1962. In all, 169 issues were produced. Art quality was variable but the most desirable issues were drawn by talents such as Matt Baker, Lou Cameron, Kurt Shaffenberger, Graham Ingels, George Evans, L. B. Cole, Gray Morrow, and Reed Crandall.

Kanter's *Classics* line never had much competition, although Dell tried its own line of adaptations in 1942. Called *Famous Stories*, the series lasted only two issues—*Treasure Island* followed by *Tom Sawyer*. In the early 1950s Seaboard's *Fast Fiction* (later called the more stately *Stories by Famous Authors Illustrated*) made its way through thirteen issues, adapting such works as *Scaramouche*, *Beau Geste*, and *Hamlet*.

Despite the above-mentioned efforts at uplift, criticism of comic books accelerated in the years following World War II. The Cold War era seemed to encourage the hunting of scapegoats, and comics—the good, the bad, and the ugly— found themselves being blamed for the alarming increase in juvenile delinquency and sundry other American social ills.

Negative public reaction to comic books reached a new plateau in 1948. That was the year that kids in several cities

Two generations of American schoolchildren relied on *Classics Illustrated* comics for quick relief when the deadline doom of book reports drew near. This page is from the 1945 *Classics* adaptation of *Frankenstein*, with art by Robert H. Webb and Ann Brewster.

©1967 by Gilberton Co., Inc.

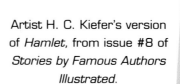

Artist H. C. Kiefer's version of *Hamlet*, from issue #8 of *Stories by Famous Authors Illustrated*.

©1950 by Seaboard Publications

Anti-comic book hysteria reached alarming proportions by 1954, when scenes such as this were enacted in communities across America.

around the country piled their comic books up in schoolyards and, encouraged by teachers, parents, and priests, turned them into blazing bonfires—never mind that this was the sort of mentality that millions of people had died fighting against during World War II. Nineteen forty-eight was also the year that the mass media really started kicking the comics around. On March 2 ABC-radio's *Town*

Meeting of the Air devoted itself to the biased-sounding inquiry, "What's wrong with the comics?" Cartoonist Al Capp and *True Comics* publisher George Hecht handled the defense. Taking care of the attack were John Mason Brown, of the *Saturday Review of Literature*, and Marya Mannes, a freelance critic and former editor of *Vogue* whose anti-comics piece, "Junior Has a Craving," had been published in the February 1947

issue of *New Republic*. What apparently impressed the listening public most were the arguments of Brown and Mannes. Brown was especially eloquent, deploring comics' "tiresome toughness, their cheap thrills, their imbecile laughter." And, in a widely quoted remark, he said that all comic books were "the marijuana of the nursery; the bane of the bassinet; the horror of the house; the curse of

kids, and a threat to the future."
Zany cartoonist Basil Wolverton
might have relished Brown's
alliteration, but the comic book
industry didn't laugh when the
broadcast drew six thousand
letters, most of which supported
the anti-comic book position.

March of 1948 also brought
another event, one that would
eventually have a critical impact
upon comic books. The event
was a symposium moderated by
Dr. Fredric Wertham, senior
psychiatrist of the New York
Department of Hospitals and
director of the Lafargue Clinic,
the first psychiatric clinic to be
established in Harlem. The
symposium was sponsored by
the Association for the
Advancement of Psychotherapy,
of which Wertham was president,
and had the ominous title "The
Psycho-pathology of Comic
Books." While the industry's
Charles Biro and Harvey
Kurtzman took part, it was
Wertham's remarks concerning
his two-year study of comic
books that got the attention of
the popular press and of national
magazines like *Collier's* and
Saturday Review. Wertham
charged that comic books
undermined morals, glorified
violence, and were "sexually
aggressive in an abnormal way."
Steve Mitchell remarked in a
detailed series of articles for *The
Comics Buyer's Guide* that "[t]he
most sweeping indictment was
[Wertham's] assertion that
'comic book reading was a
distinct influencing factor in the
case of every single delinquent
or disturbed child we studied.'"
Many parents and educators
absorbed this dubious piece of

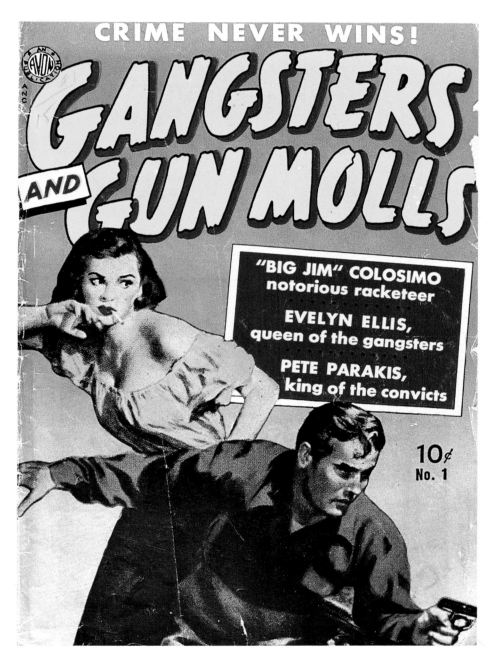

Avon Periodicals was an early player in the paperback-book market, so it's not surprising that many Avon Comics covers have an illustrative look reminiscent of paperback covers. Although *Gangsters and Gun Molls* proclaims that "Crime Never Wins," a life of crime does seem to have its compensations.

©1951 by Avon Periodicals, Inc.

news and concluded that it was comic book reading, not other factors, that was causing delinquency.

The attacks on comic books continued. Titles considered objectionable by various newsdealers and civic officials across the nation were banned, legal action was threatened against newsstands by police departments, and citizen's committees were set up to evaluate and control comic books. In his *Buyer's Guide* article Mitchell cites a study undertaken in St. Paul, Minnesota that resulted in the issuing of twelve standards of evaluation. "Among other provisions, comic books judged acceptable by [the St. Paul] standards portrayed home life as stable and permanent; [portrayed] policemen in a respectful manner; did not glorify criminals and their deeds; upheld the principles of democracy and the moral laws of God; and avoided gruesome scenes."

A forty-nine-page report prepared for the mayor of New Orleans by that city's public relations director noted that in many comic books "public officials repeatedly take it on the chin." The irreverence toward officials, bankers, and other businessmen was considered just as threatening as comics' frequent emphasis on sex and bloodshed.

The purported link between comic books and real-life delinquency was promoted by an increasing number of national magazines. In its October 4, 1948 issue *Time*, after referring to comic books as "the bastard

Joe Simon and Jack Kirby were at home with nearly all comic book genres: superhero, romance, adventure. In the late forties, they turned their talents to crime comics. This typically exciting S & K page is from a 1947 issue of *Real Clue*.

offspring of newspaper comics," reported, "The Los Angeles County sheriff had in custody a 14-year-old boy who had poisoned a 50-year-old woman. He got the idea, and the poison recipe, he said, from a comic book. There were other alarming cases, too. A 10-year-old boy's parents came home from the movies to find his body hanging in the garage. At his feet was a crime comic book depicting a hanging body. Two boys, 14 and 15, were caught committing a burglary. The crime comics they had with them had inspired the crime and shown them how to do it."

In an effort to counter the accelerating attacks in the late forties, the comic book industry formed the Association of Comics Magazine Publishers (ACMP). *Newsweek*, in its December 20, 1948 issue, reported that the group had selected "as director Henry Schultz, a strapping, darkly handsome attorney who is a member of the New York City Board of Higher Education." His task was, in his capacity as "comic-book czar," to get the magazines to police themselves. Schultz did not, however, have the cooperation of the entire industry, since not all publishers were willing to join the ACMP, and many of those who did exercised little restraint over the content of their titles. Worse, some of those publishers who spoke out publicly only hurt themselves. Victor Fox, for instance, made the mistake of attempting to defend sex and sadism in comics and was quoted in *Time* as cynically remarking,

The forceful cover of *Crime Exposed* #1 is a textbook example of how to entice a reader.

©1948 by Postar Publications, Inc.

Fight Against Crime, mindful of reader interest in horror comics, prominently featured the word "horror" on many of its covers. For good measure, our hero has been tossed into a snakepit.

©1952 by Story Comics, Inc.

"There are more morons than people, you know."

Damage was being inflicted on the industry from within and without. Amazingly, however, despite the comic book burnings and the increasing number of committees and attempts at censorship, the number of crime and horror comics continued to increase. Publishers may have seen the edge of the cliff as they raced toward it, but were compelled by the lure of easy money to keep going.

A certain solace was provided by the fact that not all educators agreed with the critics. Frederic M. Thrasher was a professor of education at New York University as well as a member of the Attorney General's Conference of Juvenile Delinquency. He wrote a piece titled "The Comics and Delinquency: Cause or Scapegoat?" for the December 1949 issue of the *Journal of Educational Sociology*. In it, he stated that many experts on delinquency "have been guilty of a long series of erroneous attempts to attribute crime and delinquency to some one human trait or environmental condition." He went on to say, "The most recent error of this type is that of psychiatrist Fredric Wertham, who claims in effect that the comics are an important factor in causing juvenile delinquency. This extreme position, which is not substantiated by any valid research, is not only contrary to considerable current psychiatric thinking, but also disregards tested research procedures which have discredited numerous previous monistic

theories of delinquency causation. Wertham's dark picture of the influence of comics is more forensic than it is scientific and illustrates a dangerous habit of projecting our social frustrations upon some specific trait in our culture, which becomes a sort of 'whipping boy' for our failure to control the whole gamut of social breakdown."

Thrasher concluded his bill of particulars against Dr. Wertham by saying, "No acceptable evidence has been produced by Wertham or anyone else for the conclusion that the reading of comic magazines has or has not a significant relation to delinquent behavior. Even the editors of *Collier's*, in which Wertham's results were first presented, are doubtful of his conclusions, as is indicated by a later editorial appearing in the magazine in which they say: 'Juvenile delinquency is the product of pent-up frustration, stored up resentments and bottled up fears. It is not the product of cartoons or captions. But the comics are a handy, obvious scapegoat. If the adults who crusade against them would only get as steamed up over such basic causes of delinquency as parental ignorance, indifference and cruelty, they might discover that the comics are no more a menace than Treasure Island or Jack the Giant Killer!'"

Neither the common sense of Thrasher's article in a journal of small circulation nor the second thoughts of *Collier's* did anything to halt the growing anxiety over the comic book "menace." Much of the blame for this is

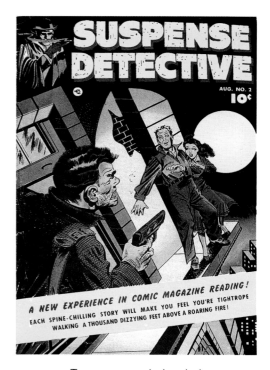

Terror on a window ledge—
a classic thriller situation.
Does the young couple
deserve to die? Ten cents
would have bought you the
answer back in 1952.

©1952 by Fawcett Publications, Inc.

attributable to the industry's failure to maintain its defenses. The members of the Association of Comics Magazine Publishers, apparently oblivious to the threat to their livelihood, soon lost interest in their protective organization and allowed it to fade away in 1950; the industry's (halfhearted) attempt at self-regulation had failed, and publishers were free to produce a steady stream of numbing violence and horror. By the middle 1950s an editor of the *Christian Science Monitor* would say about comic books, "Objection to censorship which can be, and has been, abused has been raised, but the conviction remains that the restriction of so-called personal liberty in an effort to protect the best interests of the public is not nearly as unconstitutional as the violation of decency by the money-making interests, and cannot be used as a reason for no regulations."

Several significant things happened in 1954. Dr. Wertham's crusading book, *Seduction of the Innocent*, was published; the U.S. Senate Subcommittee on the Judiciary held hearings in Manhattan on comic books; and the self-regulatory Comics Code Authority was established. The Wertham book, expanding on topics he'd been writing and lecturing about for several years, contended that "the bad effects of crime comic books exist potentially for all children." Among the bad effects cited by Wertham were the atmosphere of cruelty and deceit that the crime books created, the suggesting of criminal and

Dr. Fredric Wertham was a New York City psychiatrist whose practice brought him in contact with many troubled, violent children who were readers of comic books.

Wide World Photos

Wertham's 1954 book, *Seduction of the Innocent*, was brutally critical of comic books, and ignited a firestorm of controversy.

©1954 by Fredric Wertham

Some crime comics were probably more detailed than they needed to be. This helpful primer on how to rig a death trap is from *Clue Comics* #15. *Clue* began in 1943 as a superhero title, but made the transition to crime stories three years later.

©1947 by Hillman Periodicals, Inc.

War comics also came under the scrutiny of Dr. Wertham. Here, a pair of Red Chinese sappers are about to buy the farm, courtesy of a typically gung-ho American GI. Cover art is by Bill Everett.

©1952 by Newsstand Publications, Inc.

sexually abnormal ideas, and the means by which they could be rationalized. These magazines, Wertham asserted, also suggested the forms a delinquent impulse might take, supplied details of technique, and might well tip the scales toward maladjustment or delinquency. To the suggestion that there had always been a certain amount of violence in children's books and entertainments, Wertham answered, "The atmosphere of crime comic books is unparalleled in the history of children's literature of any time or any nation. It is a distillation of viciousness. The world of comic books is the world of the strong, the ruthless, the bluffer, the shrewd deceiver, the torturer, and the thief. All the emphasis is on exploits where somebody takes advantage of somebody else, violently, sexually, or threateningly."

Lacking in specific details of the backgrounds of problem children he had studied and vague even as to where the worst examples of comic books were to be found, Dr. Wertham's *Seduction of the Innocent* really didn't succeed in proving anything except that the author was deeply concerned about children. While there is no denying that many of the crime and horror comics of the period were deplorable and tasteless, the claim by Wertham that they were a direct cause of juvenile crimes of violence is highly debatable. Obviously, relatively few children of the postwar generation grew up to be stickup artists, cat burglars, and axe murderers.

Twenty years after the publication of *Seduction of the Innocent*, in an unusual interview with Jay Maeder, then of the *Miami Herald*, Dr. Wertham said, "I never spoke of comic books, I only spoke of crime comic books. That is important because there are of course good comic books, but a crime is a crime." But to the doctor, the term "crime comic" could be broadly applied; in 1954 Wertham had labeled *Detective, Superman*, and other mild-mannered titles as crime comics.

The section of Wertham's book that made a deep impression on many readers was a fourteen-page portfolio of panels and covers culled from the comic books themselves. There were scenes of murder, torture, and sexual titillation that came, interestingly enough, from all levels of the comic book business and not, as one reviewer assumed, from "the underworld of publishing." William Gaines's EC line was represented by the work of Johnny Craig, Bill Elder, and Jack Davis. Matt Baker's startling cover for *Phantom Lady* #17 was reprinted with the notation, "Sexual stimulation by combining 'headlights' with the sadist's dream of tying up a woman." Wertham also found the Jack Cole panel from the story in *True Crime* wherein the young woman drug addict dreams she's being attacked by a man wielding a hypodermic; Wertham cited this scene as "a sample of the injury-to-the-eye motif." The most widely discussed art sample consisted of two panels from "Foul Play" (see Chapter

In the world according to comic books, even the north woods were rife with violent crime. This 1948 *Manhunt* cover is by Ogden Whitney.

©1948 by Magazine Enterprises, Inc.

Artist Johnny Craig outdid himself with the cover for EC's *Crime SuspenStories #22*, perhaps the most notorious comic book illustration of all time. Undeniably compelling, the cover caught the eye of Senator Estes Kefauver, who lured EC publisher William Gaines into a debate about horror-comic aesthetics.

Eight) the infamous baseball story drawn by Jack Davis for EC's *Haunt of Fear.* As the perceptive cultural critic Robert Warshow remarked in *Commentary,* " I don't suppose I shall easily forget that baseball game."

In the 1974 interview with Jay Maeder, Dr. Wertham explained that "in psychological life, it isn't so that you can say one factor has a clear causal effect on anything." He added, "I never said, and I don't think so, that a child reads a comic book and then goes out and beats up his sister or commits a holdup." In 1954, though, that was exactly what a great many people who read *Seduction* did think.

The 1954 Senate hearings were held at the Federal Courthouse in New York City and presided over by senators Thomas Hennings and Estes Kefauver. Among those testifying were Dr. Wertham, Milton Caniff, Walt Kelly, and William Gaines. In a statement he'd sat up all night preparing, Gaines said, "It would be just as difficult to explain the harmless thrill of a horror story to Dr. Wertham as it would be to explain the sublimity of love to a frigid old maid." He concluded with, "[New York City mayor] Jimmy Walker once remarked that he never knew a girl ruined by a book. Nobody was ever ruined by a comic."

Things might have gone moderately well and Gaines might not have achieved nationwide notoriety had he not been lured into a discussion of good and bad taste with Senator Kefauver. Holding up the cover of *Crime SuspenStories #22,*

Kefauver inquired, "Here is your May issue. This seems to be a man with a bloody axe holding a woman's head up, which has been severed from her body. Do you think that's in good taste?"

Gaines replied, "Yes, sir, I do—for the cover of a horror comic. A cover in bad taste, for example, might be defined as holding the head a little higher so that the blood could be seen dripping from it, and moving the body over a little further so that the neck of the body could be seen to be bloody."

"You've got blood coming out of her mouth."

"A little," admitted Gaines.

But a little was finally perceived as being too much. In September of 1954 the comic book publishers formed a new organization, the Comics Magazine Association of America, and named Judge Charles Murphy to be the first administrator of the Comics Code. Gaines didn't join the association and announced that he was killing his horror and crime line "because of a premise, that has never been proved, that they stimulate juvenile delinquency. We are not doing it so much for business reasons as because this seems to be what American parents want—and the parents should be served." Actually, as Gaines said much later, "I'd been told that if I continued publishing my magazines, no [wholesaler or retailer] would handle them. I had no choice." He introduced a series of "New Direction" comics—*Impact, Valor, Aces High, Piracy,* even an oddity called *Psychoanalysis*—but the

EC was just one of many publishers to be crippled by the Comics Code. After killing the company's horror and science fiction titles, EC publisher William Gaines introduced a short-lived series of "New Direction" comics. *Extra,* with covers by Johnny Craig, was one of them.

The seal of the Comics Code Authority. To millions of parents and educators it meant peace of mind, but to comic book fans it stood for little except blandly "safe" entertainment.

new titles quickly died. "I later found out that this was because the word was passed by the wholesalers, 'Git 'im! So they got me. As soon as I heard this I joined the association." Even that was not enough to save Gaines's four-color comics, and he prospered only because he transformed the ten-cent, full-color *Mad* into a twenty-five-cent, black-and-white magazine that was not regarded as a comic book.

A great many other publishers either folded or drastically cut back their lines. The stipulations of the Code made it difficult, if not downright impossible, for most crime and horror comics to continue, since any that didn't abide by the Code's guidelines could probably not get distributed. The Code suggested, "No comics shall explicitly present the unique details and methods of crime . . . Scenes of excessive violence shall be prohibited. Scenes of brutal torture, excessive and unnecessary knife and gun play, physical agony, gory and gruesome crime shall be eliminated." And furthermore, "No comic magazine shall use the word horror or terror in its title . . . All scenes of horror, excessive bloodshed, gory or gruesome crimes, depravity, lust, sadism, masochism shall not be permitted. . . . Scenes dealing with, or instruments associated with walking dead, or torture shall not be used."

Leonard Darvin, who served as administrator of the Code for many years, once said, "The Wertham thing was completely biased because, although I don't condone some of the comics that were put out at the time, I think they were pushing it way out. They were combining sex and crime and horror in one book, and that was a little too much. But they only represented, even then, not more than 20 percent of the output. But they were the ones that gave comics as a whole a bad name."

In 1952 about five hundred comic book titles fought for attention on America's newsstands. By 1955 the number had dropped to around three hundred. The monthly sales of Lev Gleason's titles fell from 2,700,000 in 1952 to around 800,000 in 1956. DC went from combined monthly sales of 10,500,000 in 1955 to 6,200,000 in 1957 and Marvel plunged from 15,000,000 in 1953 to 4,600,000 in 1958. The boom times were definitely over and the anti-comic book crusaders had certainly played a part.

Years later Dr. Wertham said, "I had no idea at that time that I was doing any harm to any industry." But he had, and was branded by many comic book aficionados as the villain responsible for the comic book industry's collapse and the sole reason for years of fewer titles, duller titles, and lower sales. This theory overlooks something else that happened in the 1950s—the tremendous growth of television. Free, easily accessible, and far livelier than comic books, TV seduced millions of kids and was a major reason for the waning of comic books' Golden Age. The *Electronic* Age had begun, and the comic book industry would struggle to compete.

SURVIVING THE FIFTIES

uring the 1950s the comic book industry had plenty to fret about. The changing tastes of the postwar years had sidelined most of the superheroes. The advent of the Comics Code Authority in the middle of the decade made such previously salable elements as sex, crime, and gore virtually impossible. Dozens of publishers simply gave up and opted to get out of the comic book business altogether. The publishers that survived—and finally prospered—did so with alternate kinds of titles. Superheroes would eventually make a comeback, but in the meantime new categories had to be tried and old, safer ones expanded.

Perhaps the biggest obstacle to the continued health of the comic book industry in the 1950s was television. At the end of World War II, TV sets could be found in only one percent of American homes. By 1953, though, fifty percent of the households in the country had sets and at the end of the decade the figure stood at a robust ninety percent. Suddenly, a good deal of everyone's leisure time was being taken up with TV-viewing; readership of books, magazines, and comics declined. Kids were especially enamored of the electronic eye, and increasingly looked to it for entertainment. Full of noise and action and able to offer a greater illusion of "reality" than comics, TV threatened to gain a monopoly on the attention of youngsters—the youngsters upon whom the comic book industry depended for survival.

Some of the publishers who remained in business following the Code-inspired shakeout adopted the time-honored policy of "if you can't beat 'em, join 'em," and began issuing comic book versions of popular TV shows. In fact, some of the companies even got into this sort of publishing early in the decade, positioning their books as alternatives to the crime and horror titles that crowded the newsstands at that time. Western-Dell, a company with considerable experience in creating and publishing licensed adventures of movie and animated cartoon characters, led the way. Commencing in 1950 with *Howdy Doody*, they went on to publish a wide range of television-based comics throughout the decade. These included *Tom Corbett, Space Cadet*; *I Love Lucy*; *Leave It To Beaver*; *Captain Kangaroo*; *Gunsmoke*; *Zorro*; and *Circus Boy*. Most of these were part of the Dell *Four Color* series and didn't come out on a regular basis. *Captain Kangaroo*, for example, appeared just three times, between 1956 and 1958. Other titles, like *Zorro* and *Gunsmoke*, graduated to regular bimonthly

The Dell Publishing Company prospered throughout the fifties by offering wholesome, well-done comic books aimed mainly at young children. Many of the titles were authorized adaptations of popular movies, or TV shows like *I Love Lucy*.

©1955 by Lucille Ball & Desi Arnaz

Zorro capitalized on the popularity of the Disney-produced TV series of the same name starring Guy Williams.

©1955 by Johnston McCulley

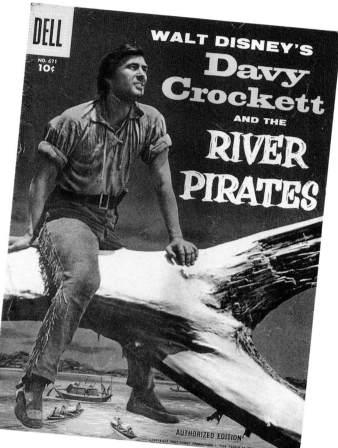

Fess Parker as Davy Crockett graces the cover of another Dell comic inspired by a Disney series.

©1955 by The Walt Disney Co.

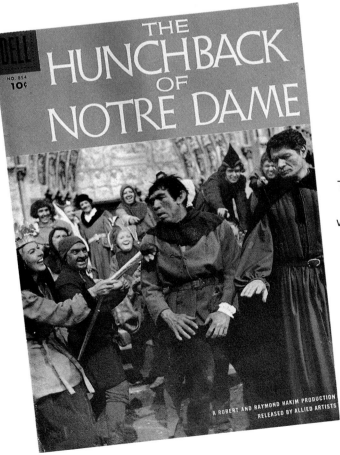

This comic was a spin off of the Anthony Quinn film version of the *Hunchback of Notre Dame*.

©1957 by Dell Publishing Co.

series of their own. Artwork for most of the Dell TV adaptations was done out of the publisher's Southern California offices by such capable illustrators as Dan Spiegle, Russ Manning, and Alex Toth. The clean, design-driven work of these and similar artists brought a laudable restraint and sophistication to comics.

In the early fifties Fawcett offered *Captain Video* and *Pinhead and Foodini*, the latter based on a popular TV puppet show, *Foodini the Great*. DC introduced *Sgt. Bilko*, adapted from *The Phil Silvers Show* (also known as *You'll Never Get Rich)*, in 1957. Other television personalities, including Jackie Gleason and Pinky Lee, also had comic books devoted to them. As one might imagine, TV-inspired comics were resolutely unsensational, and steered clear of sex and bloodshed.

Movies and movie stars were also the basis for many "safe" comic books in the 1950s. Included among the *Four Color* movie adaptation one-shots were *Ben Hur, Around the World in 80 Days, The Big Land, Moby Dick*, and *The Vikings*. The *Fawcett Movie Comic* series began late in 1949 and turned out twenty adaptations before closing up shop in 1952. Fawcett favored westerns, and adapted *Copper Canyon, The Last Outpost* (starring Ronald Reagan), *Montana*, and *Carbine Williams*. A companion series was *Motion Picture Comics*, which also concentrated on cowboy epics.

DC made an attempt to get into the act in 1950 with *Feature Films*. This title apparently. involved a licensing agreement with Paramount Pictures, since all four of the issues adapted movies from that studio: *Captain China*, *Riding High*, *The Eagle and the Hawk*, and a Bob Hope-Lucille Ball vehicle, *Fancy Pants*.

In addition, DC turned several Paramount stars into comic book characters. *The Adventures of Alan Ladd* was one such strip, and it debuted late in 1949 and lasted until early in 1951. Ladd's comic book adventures were far from fact-based, and characterized the popular actor as the sort of hardboiled action hero he often played on the screen. Dan Barry was the initial artist, followed by Ruben Moreira.

Not all of the movie comics were action-packed. Just for laughs, there was *The Adventures of Bob Hope*, introduced by DC in 1950; surprisingly durable, the title survived until early 1968. DC's *The Adventures of Dean Martin and Jerry Lewis* (surely one of the longest comic book titles ever) arrived in 1952. As in the highly successful Martin and Lewis movies, the comic book team ran into a variety of antagonists, including gorillas, gangsters, and assorted authority figures. Pretty girls (a specialty of the title's chief artist, Bob Oksner) were in abundance. In 1957, after Martin and Lewis split up, the magazine became simply *The Adventures of Jerry Lewis*, and continued on until 1971, with Oksner remaining as chief artist.

Movie cowboys remained popular comic book stars in the 1950s, and the most successful titles were offered by Dell. Rex Allen, Roy Rogers, Wild Bill

The characters of Spin and Marty were first introduced on Walt Disney's *Mickey Mouse Club* TV show.

©1956 by The Walt Disney Co.

This comic was based on a charming cartoon show about a boy named Beany whose best friend was Cecil—a lovable, if not too terribly intelligent, sea serpent.

©1955 by Bob Clampett

An animated series that recounted the adventures of the plucky Crusader Rabbit and his sidekick, Rags the Tiger, was the basis for this comic.

©1957 by Dell Publishing Co.

The Adventures of Bob Hope began a healthy eighteen-year run in 1950.

©1957 by National Comics Publications

Comedian Phil Silvers enjoyed great success as the scheming Sgt. Bilko on TV's *You'll Never Get Rich*; DC obliged him with a comic book spinoff.

©1958 by National Comics

Dean Martin and Jerry Lewis were movie box-office kings in the 1950s, and were featured in their own DC comic book. This 1955 cover is the work of the book's regular artist, Bob Oksner.

©1955 by National Periodical Publications, Inc.

Elliott, and Gene Autry were some who were featured in comic book adventures from that company. Western films like *The Searchers*, *Drum Beat*, and *The Horse Soldiers* also were adapted by Dell's *Four Color*.

Because Dell had ignored the boom in comic book crime, horror, and sex, the publisher weathered the 1950s much better than any of its competitors. For years the company had been aiming its titles at a very young audience, offering pleasantly innocuous fare such as *Walt Disney's Comics & Stories*, *Looney Tunes*, *Little Lulu*, *New Funnies*, *Tom and Jerry*, as well as *Tarzan*, *The Lone Ranger* and plenty of movie cowboys. So spotless was Dell's output, in fact, that the company never bothered to join the Comic Magazines Association and didn't submit any of its titles to the Comics Code Authority. In practice, Dell's standards were even higher than those laid down by the Code.

The numbers showed that Dell's insistence on being squeaky clean had paid off: In 1956, when Marvel had combined monthly sales of about four million and DC was doing about 6,200,000, Dell was averaging nine million. Dell reached a peak of over fourteen million copies sold a month in 1958. That was almost twice as much as what DC sales had climbed to and more than three times better than Marvel.

During the salad days of crime and horror, many publishing houses had ignored younger readers. But in the financially uncertain fifties young

children, especially in light of
Dell's strapping sales figures,
became an increasingly
important segment of the
audience and were once more
courted. This resulted in an
increase in humor comics,
especially those that featured kid
characters. When the boom got
lowered in the middle 1950s,
Harvey Comics (to name just
one publisher) had been earning
a good portion of its income from
titles like *Chamber of Chills*,
Tomb of Terror, and *Black Cat
Mystery*. But in 1949 Harvey had
added *Sad Sack* to its lineup,
cleaning up the character created
for GIs by George Baker during
World War II, and turning him
into a kid favorite.

In 1952 Harvey introduced a
pair of titles that had been taken
over from the St. John company,
Casper the Friendly Ghost and
Little Audrey. Both Casper and
Audrey had been adapted from
Paramount animated cartoons.
Baby Huey, a huge dimwitted
fowl, was another Paramount
character adapted by Harvey
beginning in 1956.

Harvey found impressive
success with its innocuous
humor titles, and quickly
capitalized on this good fortune
by creating numerous spinoffs
and variations. *Sad Sack's Funny
Friends* was added to the lineup
in 1955; *Sad Sack and Sarge*
showed up in 1957. *Spooky, the
Tuff Little Ghost*, featuring a
pugnacious character first seen
in *Casper*, was launched in
November of 1955. Other Harvey
humor books included *Little Dot*,
launched in 1953, and *Little
Lotta*, which came along in 1955.
Both Lotta, the voracious fat girl,

and Richie Rich, the likeable
little tycoon who would become
one of the major comic book
stars of the 1960s, first appeared
in Little Dot's magazine.

Harvey's combined monthly
sales in 1951 of nearly five
million copies was almost exactly
the same as it would sell in 1959.
For Harvey, then, the decision to
drop horror and add characters
with kid-appeal hadn't hurt
overall sales.

DC abandoned the funny
animal titles *Comic Cavalcade*
and *Funny Stuff* in 1954, but
stuck with *Fox and the Crow*.
They also kept the teen titles,
Buzzy and *Leave It To Binky*.
Then, in 1958, DC introduced
one of the undisputed classic kid
comics, Sheldon Mayer's *Sugar
& Spike*. The round-faced boy
and girl who were the book's
toddler stars weren't even able to
talk yet—or so it was surmised
by the unimaginative adults who
existed in the stories'
peripheries. Actually Sugar and
Spike communicated with each
other quite well in a special
babbling language that Mayer
has said he sometimes believed
to be real. Mayer had enormous
fun with the nearly one hundred
issues of the book that he wrote
and drew, alternating simple,
everyday-humor continuities
with slapstick and complex
fantasy adventures. Other than
Mayer's charming artwork,
perhaps the best qualities of
Sugar & Spike were its creator's
affinity for an inventive,
unmalicious sort of kid humor,
and his ability to look at the
world through toddlers' eyes.

Not every small child is
harmlessly cute, of course, and

One of Harvey Publications's
biggest successes was
Richie Rich, "The Poor Little
Rich Boy."

©1962 by Harvey Enterprises

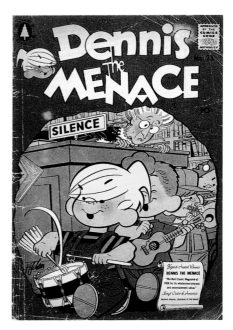

Pines Comics and, later,
Fawcett enjoyed
considerable success with
Dennis the Menace.

©1957 by Pines Comics

A latter-day example of Sheldon Mayer's *Sugar and Spike*.

the success of the "mean little kid" comic book subgenre that flourished in the fifties proves it. Leading the (brat) pack was *Dennis the Menace*, begun in 1953 by the Pines outfit and taken over by Fawcett beginning with issue #32. The comic book was based on Hank Ketcham's spectacularly successful newspaper panel and offered original stories about Dennis, the tow-headed terror whose mischief is the bane of his parents and the family's long-suffering next-door neighbor, Mr. Wilson. Al Wiseman was the chief artist, Fred Toole the head writer. A hit, the book enjoyed a run of more than twenty years.

None of the numerous *Dennis* imitators did nearly as well. Archie's *Pat the Brat* managed to hang on from 1953 to 1959, but three attempts by Atlas (Marvel) to cash in turned into train wrecks: *Melvin the Monster* appeared in 1956 and vanished in 1957 after six issues, while *Dexter the Demon* and *Willie the Wise-Guy* each lasted for just a single issue in '57. Fago Magazine's luck was no better, as that company's *Li'l Menace* saw just two issues in 1958. Reston's *Little Groucho* ("The Red-Headed Tornado") struggled through a pair of issues in 1955, while St. John's *Little Joe* was sent packing after just one 1953 issue.

Kid comics weren't the only survivors of the great comic book purge—science fiction and a watered-down sort of horror-fantasy also persevered. Although a great many of the superhero titles incorporated SF elements, there had been few comic books devoted exclusively

DC's *Strange Adventures*
was an entertaining science
fiction comic book that
avoided undue violence and
sensationalism.

Strange Adventures #9
introduced Captain Comet.

to that sort of subject matter in the thirties and forties. The only one that endured during comics' glory days was *Planet Comics*, which relied as much on female pulchritude as it did on "space opera." After the Second World War and the advent of the atomic bomb, America was swept by a renewed interest in science, along with a growing fascination with flying saucers. Hollywood's production of science fiction films reached an all-time high in the fifties, and the number of SF pulps increased.

EC Comics had introduced *Weird Science* and *Weird Fantasy* in 1950. Despite their vaguely schlocky titles, both offered fairly sophisticated stories and shied away from zap guns, space wars, and similar juvenilia. That same year Ziff-Davis, the publisher of *Amazing Stories*, *Fantastic Adventures*, and other pulps, introduced a comic book called *Amazing Adventures*. Promising "Thrilling Science-Fiction Tales!," it was slickly produced and boasted painted covers by such established pulp artists as Norman Saunders (who did the notoriously uninhibited paintings for Topps's gruesome *Mars Attacks!* bubblegum cards in the early 1960s).

More fanciful SF entries from 1950 included Fawcett's *Vic Tory and His Flying Saucer*, with artwork by Bob Powell, and Avon's *Flying Saucers*, illustrated by Wally Wood. That same year, under the editorship of Julius Schwartz, DC introduced its first science fiction title, *Strange Adventures*. The initial issue included an adaptation of the

Robert A. Heinlein movie *Destination Moon* and introduced Kris KL-99, a space explorer created by long-established SF author Edmond Hamilton and artist Howard Sherman.

Among the SF titles introduced by other publishers in the fifties were *Weird Thrillers*, *Fantastic Worlds*, *Lars of Mars*, *Man O'Mars*, *Crusader From Mars*, *Space Adventures*, and DC's long-running *Mystery in Space*.

Marvel, still doing business as Atlas at that point, branched out into science fiction, too. They introduced *Journey Into Unknown Worlds* in 1950, followed by *Strange Tales* in 1952. The early issues of *Journey* were straight SF, offering such tales as "End of the Earth," "Planet of Death," and "Trapped in Space." Within a year, however, the magazine made a shift, or possibly a lurch, to horror. Covers were suddenly dominated by corpses and skeletons, and all sorts of foul creatures prowled the comic's interior. *Journey Into Unknown Worlds* continued to be published after the advent of the Code, but with its contents toned down considerably.

"Toned down" is an apt description of what happened to horror comics after the Comics Code. The American Comics Group, an early purveyor of horror, managed to carry on with the genre and still follow Code guidelines. As noted in Chapter Eight, ACG introduced *Adventures Into the Unknown* in the autumn of 1948. That title was followed in 1951 by *Forbidden Worlds*. Like all ACG titles, the horror duo was edited by Richard Hughes. He also did much of the scriptwriting, with contributions in the early years from Manly Wade Wellman and Al Feldstein. Compared to the output of EC and Marvel, and of the lesser houses, the ACG stories were restrained. Monsters, demons, and skeletons were regularly seen on the covers but readers rarely saw a lethal weapon and never spied a drop of blood. In the immediate pre-Code years the company tried, briefly, three other horror titles—*Out of the Night*, *Skeleton Hand*, and *The Clutching Hand*—but dumped them when it appeared as though horror comics were on the verge of running into big trouble.

Hughes was able to keep *Adventures Into the Unknown* and *Forbidden Worlds* going in the post-Code years by modifying them. "The key to this," Edwin Murray has pointed out in *The Comic World*, "was the shift in story line to more human interest and adventure and the addition of science fiction in larger amounts." Both titles made it through the decade with stories that were more inoffensive than terrifying.

DC had ventured into the horror field late in 1951 with *House of Mystery*, which offered a polite brand of weird tale that eschewed corpses, skeletons, and the bloodshed produced by knives, axes, and blunt instruments. Instead, the emphasis was on ghosts, demons, ancient sorceries, black magic, and family curses. Suspense and mild fright, rather than physical horror, were

emphasized. Among the artists employed in the magazine's early years were Mort Meskin, Ruben Moreira, and Leonard Starr. Virtually unaffected by the stipulations of the Comics Code, *House of Mystery* continued on until the early 1980s. A similar DC book, *House of Secrets*, was introduced in 1956. Jack Schiff, who had come to DC from the Pines pulps in 1942, spent time as editor of both titles.

DC's *My Greatest Adventure* first appeared early in 1955 and was joined a year later by *Tales of the Unexpected*. The former book began as a fairly realistic anthology of daring adventures set in locales across the globe, and featuring big-game hunters, nitroglycerine-truck drivers, high-wire artists, and similarly stalwart protagonists. Fairly soon, however, the stories shifted to science fiction, fantasy, and mild horror. The book picked up an identifying trademark of wacky, first-person story titles like "I Sealed Earth's Doom," "I Wore the Faces of Doom," and "A Beast Was My Judge."

Only a few of Marvel's horror-fantasy titles carried on after the Code. One of these was *Journey Into Mystery*, which had been introduced in the anything-goes year of 1952—"As you turn these pages," proclaimed an early blurb, "you will read the world's WEIRDEST MYSTERY tales!" Until the Code went into effect, skeletons and freshly risen corpses were frequent guest stars, but from 1955 onward all of that ceased and haunted houses, mystic rings, parallel worlds, and dopplegangers were the

Penal science meets science fiction on the cover of *Mystery in Space* #18; art is by Murphy Anderson.

©1954 by DC Comics, Inc.

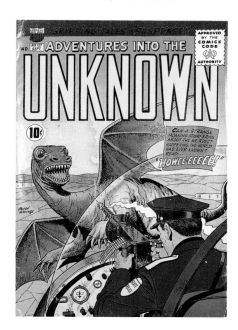

Just another day on the job with the state police. *Adventures Into the Unknown* #127, with cover art by Ogden Whitney.

©1961 by Best Syndicated Features, Inc.

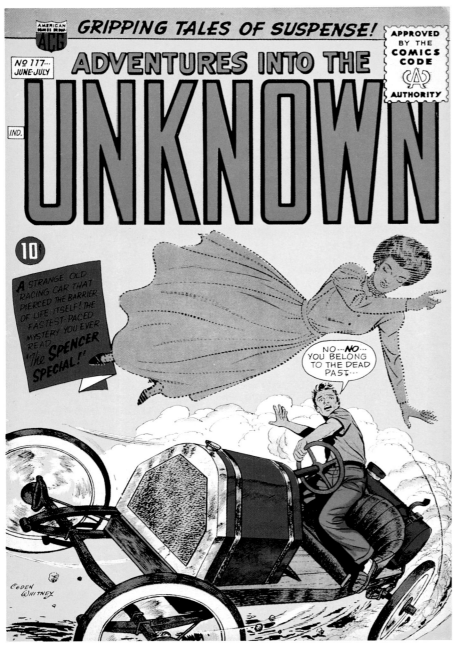

ACG's *Adventures Into the Unknown* survived the Comics Code by softening what had already been a rather innocuous title. Cover art is by Ogden Whitney.

dominant themes. A typical issue in the post-Code era might offer five short yarns, the longest running six pages and the shortest just three. As in the heyday of comic book horror, the twist ending was *de rigeuer*, but the worst horrors were only hinted at. Thankfully, these lackluster stories were graced by some very good art by such notable talents as Bill Everett, Bernard Krigstein, Russ Heath, Steve Ditko, and the ubiquitous Jack Kirby. Marvel's *Uncanny Tales*, which started in 1952, was another title that survived until 1957 by going soft under the Code. Marvel tried three comparable books in 1956— *World of Fantasy*, *World of Mystery*, and *World of Suspense*— but each was short-lived.

Another company that squeaked by with lukewarm horror was Charlton, a cost-conscious, Connecticut-based outfit that had entered the comics field in 1946. Charlton's first attempt at horror came early in 1954, with the amusingly titled *This Magazine Is Haunted*, a comic that had been taken over from Fawcett. The magazine shut down late that same year but was resurrected in 1957 with Steve Ditko as the star artist. Ditko—a prolific talent with a compellingly simple, almost diagrammatical art style—was also much in evidence in Charlton's *Unusual Tales*, started in 1955, and in *Out of This World* and *Tales of the Mysterious Traveler*, both inaugurated in 1956. The (inevitably) sardonic narrator of the last-mentioned comic was taken over from a radio show.

To tiptoe around the acceptable edges of the horror genre was one way to make a few dollars, but the fifties also brought an interesting, short-lived phenomenon that was more novel: the three-dimensional comic book. The term 3-D had been implanted in the public mind in 1952 when Hollywood producer-director Arch Oboler released a 3-D jungle adventure called *Bwana Devil*. Cheaply produced and none too exciting, the picture needed all of the appeal that stars Robert Stack, Barbara Britton, and Nigel Bruce could muster. It was the 3-D effects, though, that proved irresistible to audiences—never mind that to view the movie one had to wear special cardboard glasses designed to aid the illusion of hurled spears and leaping lions.

Bwana Devil earned a healthy profit, and before the novelty wore off several other successful 3-D epics were produced, including *It Came From Outer Space* and *House of Wax*. The first 3-D comic book appeared in 1953 and for a brief period stereoscopic comics flourished.

"All of the 3-D comic books made use of a 3-D device known as the anlglyph," stereoscopy expert Ray Zone has explained. "The system requires that the left image be dyed red and the right image be dyed green (or vice versa). The two images are then printed superimposed on the page slightly off-register. The red and green lenses [of the 3-D glasses] allow each eye to view the page separately and give the effect of depth."

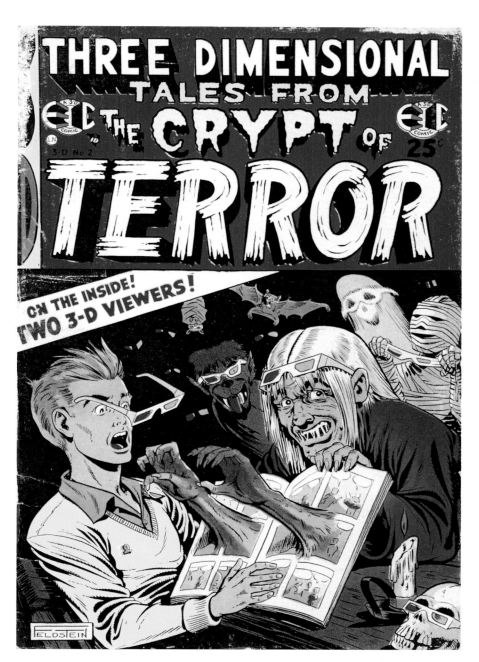

Just as Hollywood was swept by a 3-D craze in the early 1950s, so too did the comic book industry scramble to offer three-dimensional thrills. *Three Dimensional Tales From the Crypt of Terror* was a handsome attempt by EC Comics. Cover art is by Al Feldstein.

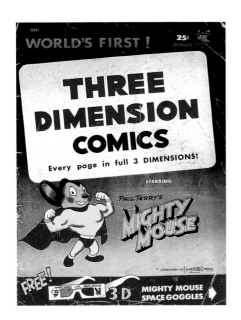

St. John's *Three Dimension Comics*, featuring super-rodent Mighty Mouse, was the first 3-D comic, arriving in 1953.

©1953 by St. John Publishing Co.

St. John was fortunate to have the services of artists Joe Kubert and Norman Maurer, who created *1,000,000 Years Ago*.

©1953 by St. John Publishing Co.

Archer St. John's company introduced *Three Dimension Comics* in the summer of 1953. The first issue starred Mighty Mouse, consisted of thirty-two off-register, red and green pages and sold for twenty-five cents (regular comics were usually forty-eight pages at the time and still sold for a dime). The slogan "WORLD'S FIRST!" was emblazoned across the top of the cover and a pair of 3-D glasses, made of cardboard and colored cellophane, were included inside. The three Mighty Mouse stories—"Men of Sola," "Jupiter Saboteurs," and "Jungle Dangers"—were loaded with in-depth depictions of whizzing space ships, crashing meteors, layered tropical foliage, and massive lost cities. The issue also included an ad for St. John's next 3-D titles, *The Three Stooges*, *Tor*, and *Whack*—"Everyone wants these great 3-D hits!"

The man behind the St. John projects was artist Joe Kubert. "The 3-D effect was put together by Norman Maurer, his brother Lenny and myself," Kubert once recalled. "I had been in the Army in 1950 and 1951 and while in Germany I had come across some magazines with photos in 3-D. I thought it would be terrific to use the effect in comic books . . . Norm, Lenny and myself sat down and we finally came up with a procedure to produce 3-D comic books and eventually gave it to St. John."

The group called their process 3-D Illustereo and applied for a patent. The Mighty Mouse issue sold well over a million copies and went into a second printing. St. John

followed it with four more 3-D titles, all of them cover-dated October 1953. The Stooges book and *Whack*, a *Mad* imitator, offered humor. *Tor* showcased Kubert's caveman adventure hero and *House of Terror* provided three-dimensional weird tales.

Not surprisingly, considering the fact that *Mighty Mouse* grossed over a quarter of a million dollars, other publishers decided to dabble in dimensional effects. The Harvey brothers rushed into the field, informing readers that "after many years of research and experiment, we now bring you the most startling magazine produced in three-dimensional illustrations in our own exclusive process." Harvey's initial title was *Adventures in 3-D*, cover-dated November 1953. Whereas St. John called their 3-D glasses Super-Sight Goggles, the Harvey brand was known as Magic Specs. Harvey's other stereoscopic titles included *True 3-D*, *Funny 3-D*, and the omnipresent *Sad Sack*.

Harvey also introduced a three-dimensional superhero in *Captain 3-D*, drawn by Jack Kirby. This inspired a flood of 3-D adventures featuring long-established heroes. DC, using a process of their own invention, published *3-D Superman* and *3-D Batman* late in 1953. Fans of "good girl" art were not ignored— the dependable Fiction House produced a *3-D Sheena, Jungle Queen*, promising both jungle beauties and jungle beasts (or is that *breasts*?) in three dimensions.

EC joined the parade early in 1954 with *Three Dimensional EC*

Classics and *Three Dimensional Tales from the Crypt*. EC's entries were superior, but by that late date the novelty of 3-D had definitely worn off. Even the pioneering St. John was in trouble. "By the tenth or eleventh 3-D book," recalled Kubert, "the sales were down about nineteen percent, so we had to stop publication."

The fact that Superman and Batman tested the 3-D waters indicates that comic book superheroes did not fade away completely during the 1950s. DC, for instance, had stuck with its sturdier superstars—Superman, Batman, and Wonder Woman. Although the trio weathered many a storm, they'd become rather stodgy. Superman, in particular, had become a dull, though still fairly popular, fellow. His condition was due chiefly to the ministrations of an editor named Mort Weisinger. Born in New York City in 1915, Weisinger had been a science fiction fan since his youth. In partnership with Julius Schwartz, he'd put out fanzines and operated the impressively named Solar Sales Service, a literary agency that specialized in selling stories to the growing number of SF pulps in the 1930s. He went to work for the Pines outfit in the middle thirties, becoming editor of *Thrilling Wonder Stories* and, later, *Startling Stories*. In 1941 Weisinger was hired as an editor at DC and given the responsibility of overseeing Superman's career. An awesome task, but at least through his earlier activities in the science fiction field, Weisinger had become friends with Superman's

creators, Siegel and Shuster.

After World War II, Superman's popularity had begun to slip. DC's "answer to that was Mort Weisinger," SF authority Sam Moskowitz has said in his profile of the editor in *Seekers of Tomorrow*. "Rallying his vast background in science-fiction plotting, he began to reshape the history of Superman to make it possible for new, more fascinating adventures to occur. . . . A new generation of readers was indoctrinated with a background that lent itself to greater thrills. Ancient evildoers of Krypton, men with powers approaching that of Superman, readers now learned, had been banished to 'The Phantom Zone' from which they could be released as needed to add zest to the continuities. The 'worlds of if' device was introduced. This featured things that Superman *might* have done and what would have happened if he had followed that course."

Weisinger also introduced several spinoff titles, giving books to Jimmy Olsen, a *Daily Planet* cub reporter, and to unceasingly snoopy *Planet* reporter Lois Lane, "Superman's Girl Friend." Weisinger even came up with Krypto the Super Dog. He saw his job as striving "to keep Superman popular. If he dies, I'd be out of a job. I think of practically all the plots, but I only write in an emergency." Despite his anxiety over the Man of Steel's welfare, Weisinger was able to state, "He's invulnerable, he's immortal. Even bad scripts can't hurt him."

One of the most imaginative Weisinger innovations was red ▶

The opening page of *Captain Flash* #1. The book was a short-lived attempt to wring excitement from the superhero genre in the mid-fifties. The feature was drawn by Mike Sekowsky.

©1954 by Sterling Comics

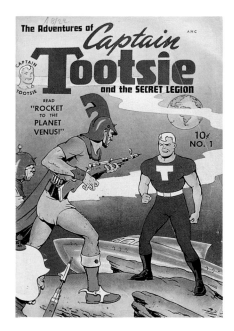

By 1950, a costumed hero as innocuous as Captain Tootsie seemed woefully behind the times.

©1950 by Toby Press, Inc.

THE SUPERMAN FAMILY

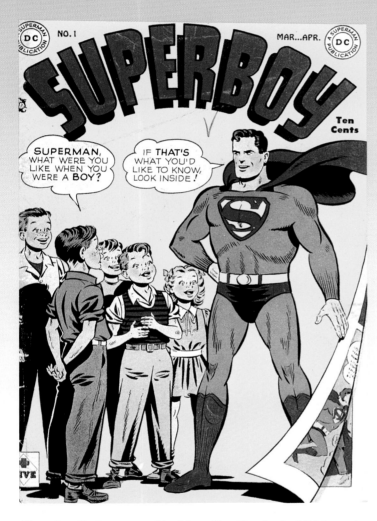

Superboy first appeared in *More Fun Comics* in 1944, and graduated to his own book five years later. The cover of his debut issue was penciled by Wayne Boring and inked by Stan Kaye.

©1949 by DC Comics, Inc.

The first family of comic books was the one that had the superhero fondly known as the Big Red Cheese as its nucleus. This was Fawcett's Captain Marvel family, which flourished in the 1940s and early 1950s. Besides Cap, the group included the three Lt. Marvels; Captain Marvel, Jr.; Mary Marvel; Uncle Marvel; and Hoppy the Marvel Bunny. DC needed a bit longer than arch-rival Fawcett to get around to exploiting the commercial possibilities of kinship. It wasn't until late in 1944, when Superboy was introduced as a backup feature in *More Fun Comics*, that DC started adding branches to the Superman family tree. Slow or not, it was no accident: According to DC historian Richard Morrissey, DC had trademarked the names "Superwoman" and "Superboy" in 1941, and "Supergirl" in 1944.

Initially Superboy was a little boy, no more than nine or ten, but he soon turned into a teenager and remained at that stage of development. The feature named Smallville, the quintessential Midwestern town, as the spot where the tiny rocketship from Krypton had landed. Soon, the Superboy stories filled in numerous details about Smallville's citizenry and geography. Occasional stories revolved around Superboy's adoptive parents, Ma and Pa Kent, or around his best friend, Pete Ross. It was in Smallville that young Clark Kent first met Lana Lang, a vivacious redhead who was destined to be an important woman in Superman's life.

Superboy moved to *Adventure Comics* in 1946 and was given his own title in 1949. Artists who drew his adventures included Stan Kaye, John Sikela, George Papp, and Curt Swan.

Supergirl was introduced in a story of her own in *Action Comics* #252 (May 1959). A pretty, blonde teenager, she arrived on Earth by way of a small rocketship similar to the one used by the Man of Steel two decades earlier. Superman happens to be on hand at her arrival, and is understandably perplexed when the girl, clad in a costume very much like his own, pops from the wreckage. "Great guns!" he exclaims. "I seem to see a youngster flying, dressed in a super-costume! I . . . uh . . . must be an illusion!" But no, the girl was no hallucination—just Superman's long-lost cousin, Kara. After adopting a mousy secret identity and the name Linda Lee, she goes to live in an orphanage in a town called Midvale.

Supergirl proved moderately popular, and continued as a backup feature in *Action* for the next ten years. She also appeared in *Adventure* and in a *Supergirl* title of her own. By the 1980s, however, readers (or maybe DC) had had just about enough, and the character was killed off—literally.

The scripter and co-creator of Supergirl was Otto Binder, a longtime science fiction and comic book writer who had devised the earlier Mary Marvel adventures. Editor Mort Weisinger suggested the idea to Binder, but never mentioned Captain Marvel's kid sister as his source of inspiration. "It was kind of weird in a way," Binder once remarked. "Like reliving the past." The chief artists throughout Supergirl's run were Jim Mooney, Kurt Schaffenberger (who'd drawn all the members of the Marvel Family), and Bob Oksner.

The fertile mind of Mort Weisinger also added a few non-human members to the Superman family. Foremost among the several he concocted was Krypto the Superdog. White, loyal, and appealing in a dimwitted sort of way, Krypto served as a pet to Clark and Superman. Like his master, he could fly, and when he did his cape fluttered impressively. Supergirl had a *pair* of animal sidekicks—Comet the Super-Horse and Streaky the Super-Cat. Both of them wore capes, too. Even Beppo the Super-Monkey got to wear a cape. The mind boggles.

Superheroine as debutante: Supergirl met her public in 1961. Cover art by Curt Swan and George Klein.

Superman's sweetie, Lois Lane, had a title of her own for many years. Though entertaining, the comic didn't exactly elevate the image of the female sex; jealousy and catfights were familiar story elements. This 1960 cover (left) was penciled by Curt Swan and inked by Stan Kaye; Lois's head was drawn by Kurt Schaffenberger. Swan and George Klein drew the silver kryptonite cover of *Jimmy Olsen #70* (right).

©1960 by Superman, Inc.

©1963 by National Periodical Publications, Inc.

kryptonite. "This aberration of the notorious green kryptonite, the only substance in the universe capable of weakening Superman, had the ability to work weird transformations in Kryptonian minds and bodies for up to forty-eight hours," explained Will Jacobs and Gerard Jones in *The Comic Book Heroes*. "This gives Superman's writers an open field for bizarre story angles, turning him into a fire-breathing dragon, making him a giant or a midget, giving him a third eye in the back of his head, even splitting him into two beings, one good and one evil. Red K also induced nightmares, such as the one in which Superman and Supergirl imagine they have destroyed the earth."

The trouble with any gimmick is that it can be overused. "The [red kryptonite] novelty was fairly interesting at first," observed Mark Waid in *Amazing Heroes*. "Bizarre things happened to the members of the Superman family that were truly menacing, like amnesia, or loss of certain superpowers at crucial times. Twelve years later, at the end of the Mort Weisinger era, what was once a clever plot idea had become hackneyed and, ultimately, laughable." It's no surprise that, when Weisinger left DC in 1970, the company decided to get back to basics in regard to Superman.

The chief Superman artist in the 1950s was Wayne Boring. A longtime assistant and ghost on

the feature, he stayed on after Siegel and Shuster were dumped by DC in 1947. Never a close imitator of Joe Shuster, Boring eventually worked out a drawing style that was recognizably his own. By the late 1940s he had changed the look of Superman entirely. "Boring salvaged the Man of Steel by transforming him into a massive, muscled version of virile exuberance," comics artist and historian Jim Steranko has observed. "[Boring's] expressive faces and tight, incisive rendering breathed new life into Superman's tired hulk. Cities became skyscrapered stylizations of vertical lines. . . . Boring's classic figure remains as the model for today's

Of the many conceptions of Superman that have been drawn over the last fifty-plus years, Wayne Boring's is arguably the best. This 1954 panel (probably inked by Stan Kaye) shows the drama and heroism that Boring brought to the character. DC editor Jack Schiff introduced peculiar science fiction elements to *Batman* (right).

©1954 by National Comics Publications, Inc.

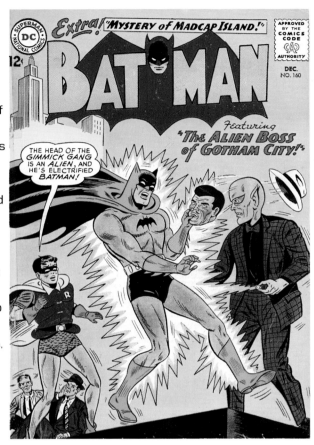

Superman." Indeed, all subsequent versions of the hero owe more to Boring than they do to Shuster. Boring stayed with Superman until the day in the late 1960s when Weisinger simply called him into his office and fired him. (Later, after Weisinger's tenure at DC, Boring was invited back to do occasional special issues.)

Other artists who drew Superman adventures throughout the fifties were Al Plastino (who modeled his approach closely on Boring's) and, more notably, Curt Swan, a talented draftsman (if rather sedate storyteller) who would become the preeminent Superman artist of the 1960s and 1970s.

Batman and Robin spent the 1950s in bland recyclings of the sort of adventures they'd had in the 1940s and, in Batman's case, in oddball science fiction tales. By the late fifties *Batman* and *Detective Comics* had come under the stewardship of editor Jack Schiff, and featured the caped crusader in wild (and wholly incongruous) SF adventures; some of the most memorable were "The Interplanetary Batman" (*Batman* #128), "The Eighth Wonder of Space" (*Batman* #140, in which Batman and Robin become little green men with barrel chests and spindly legs), and "The Alien Batman" (*Detective* #251).

Keenly interested in getting more mileage out of their superstar superheroes, DC revamped *World's Finest* with issue #71 (August 1954) so that each issue's leadoff story was a Superman-Batman team-up, rather than the independent adventures that had been seen before. Robin was also involved in the revamp, and ad copy described the trio as "the mightiest team in the world!"

Although they'd put their superheroes out to pasture at the end of 1949, Marvel/Atlas and writer-editor Stan Lee never gave up on them completely. Late in 1953 an effort was made to revive the three best known. *Young Men*, which had previously been both a war book and an adventure comic, became the home of the Human Torch, ▶

DICK SPRANG

During the nearly twenty years that he drew the comic book adventures of Batman, Dick Sprang was never allowed to sign his work. When asked years later if the anonymity had bothered him, he replied, "The only place where I wanted to see my name was on a check." Despite this cavalier attitude, Sprang turned out a great many handsome Batman stories in *Batman*, *Detective*, and *World's Finest*. In recent years his work, with full credit given, has been reprinted in several DC compilations, and the artist has finally received the recognition he has long deserved.

Sprang first drew the caped crusader in 1943. A freelance pulp, comic, and advertising artist since the 1930s, Sprang worked directly for editor Whitney Ellsworth and had no contact with Bob Kane; "I only met him once," Sprang has recalled. According to Sprang, he merely walked into DC, showed his work to Ellsworth, and was offered the job. For a sample he had drawn "a one-page *Terry and the Pirates* type story. I managed to drag about everything possible into one page." After looking at the sample, Ellsworth asked Sprang to do three Batman audition pages. Ellsworth liked those and Sprang commenced an association with DC that would continue for almost two decades. His first stories and covers were for the *Batman* bimonthly and from 1944 on he was providing most of the Batman stories for *Detective Comics*, too. He quickly made *Batman* his own.

Much influenced by the visual storytelling techniques of movies, Sprang worked in a cin-

ematic style that blended cartoon and illustration elements. He was especially skilled at rendering complex machines and intricate cityscapes. His interpretation of Gotham City is startling even today—a landscape of shadowed alleys, oddly tilted buildings, and sleek autombiles that race around corners on two wheels. Sprang's villains were equally memorable, characterized by square jaws and beady eyes, and decked out in pin-striped suits with aggressively padded shoulders. Sprang's conception of the Joker— laughing, psychotic, wholly intimidating—is particularly powerful.

Like Sprang's villains, his version of Batman is aggressive and very physical. Of all the many interpretations of the character, Sprang's is probably the most kinetic, and is certainly the one with the most honest echoes of the Hollywood *film noir* style.

Urban settings were just one of Sprang's specialties; he was a versatile artist who obviously enjoyed the outlandishly entertaining time-travel yarns that took Batman and Robin to Ancient Rome, the Old West, and the France of the Three Musketeers. His favorite writer was Bill Finger, who "would come up with scripts that were obviously tailored to what I like to do."

While still working for DC, Sprang resettled in Arizona. He retired from comics in 1962 and has been lured back only once or twice since then, for special, commemorative illustrations. Besides these, the only comic book work Sprang has ever signed were a few nonfiction stories he drew for *Real Fact comics* in the middle 1940s.

Sub-Mariner, and Captain America with issue #24 (December 1953). The cover showed the Torch flying over the night city and hurling great balls of fire while one of the startled citizens below exclaims, "Look! He's back from the dead! It's the HUMAN TORCH!" Other Marvel heroes came back from the dead in the spring of 1954, when the company resurrected three once popular titles, *The Human Torch*, *Captain America*, and *Sub-Mariner*. Adapting to the political climate of the Cold War years, all three of the revived heroes now specialized in battling Russian villains; the dreaded hammer and sickle of the Soviet Union was a frequently seen symbol. Cap was even billed on the covers as "Captain America . . . Commie Smasher!!"

The resurrected *Young Men* lasted only five issues, and *Captain America* and *The Human Torch* lasted just three apiece. The Sub-Mariner, with Bill Everett once again drawing his aquatic creation, fared better than his colleagues and managed to appear in ten issues of his magazine before going under. He battles commies on nine of those covers, declaring on one, "You Reds'll never trap that destroyer between these icebergs while I'm here!" Well, it wasn't the Reds that sank Subbie—just plots that struck readers as stale and worn-out.

At just about the same time that Captain America and Bucky were returning in their own magazine, their creators, Joe Simon and Jack Kirby, were introducing a brand new

superpatriotic team. The first issue of *Fighting American*, published by the Prize Group, had a cover date of April-May 1954. Partnered with a kid hero named Speedboy, Fighting American (perhaps the most obvious of all the Captain America imitators) rounded up gangsters, ghouls, and, of course, Communist spies. As the feature progressed, its tone lightened and became almost self-spoofing, introducing Communist villains like Poison Ivan and Rhode Island Red. "The first stories were deadly serious," Simon has said. But as he and Kirby grew increasingly uneasy about the hysterical Red-baiting perpetrated by Senator Joe McCarthy and his cohorts in the U.S. House and Senate, Simon and Kirby decided to poke a little fun at the idea of a Red Menace. Unfortunately, the times were not right for either a serious or satirical new superhero, and *Fighting American* expired after seven issues.

Vincent Sullivan, the editor who'd purchased both Superman and Batman in the late thirties, continued to have faith in superheroes two decades later. Late in 1954 his Magazine Enterprises (ME) published the first issue of *The Avenger* and followed it a year later with *Strong Man*. The titles appeared in alternate months and each lasted only four issues. The Avenger wore a red costume and devoted some of his time to bashing the prime threat of the decade, "the Red Menace." Dick Ayers drew the first issue, Bob Powell the rest. The prolific Powell also drew Strong Man, a

Marvel, under its Atlas imprint, used the Cold War as an excuse to resurrect Captain America in 1954. The comeback failed.

©1954 by Prime Publications

Although vigorous in his war against communism, the Human Torch was not embraced by readers this time around.

©1953 by Interstate Publishing Corp.

Fighting American, seen here in his one-shot revival in 1966, was Simon & Kirby's immensely appealing but commercially unsuccessful takeoff of their own Captain America.

©1966 by Harvey Features Syndicate

blond muscleman who wore a leopard skin and who made his living by running a gym. Copy pointed out that while Strong Man was "the strongest human being alive today . . . he has no SUPERHUMAN powers." Regardless, Strong Man didn't hesitate to take an occasional stand against "the grim threat of COMMUNIST attack."

This sort of transparent patriotism didn't fool anybody, and after this last fling with serious costumed crimefighters, ME turned to such comedy titles as *Mighty Atom* and *The Brain*. By the end of the decade the company was out of business.

Other publishers fared no better with supermen. One of Robert Farrell's companies, Sterling Comics, tried to buck the odds late in 1954 by introducing *Captain Flash*. Drawn by Mike Sekowsky, the character was a traditional superhero in a red and blue costume. *Captain Flash* was also a flash in the pan, and was gone after four issues. Early in 1955 Charlton brought back *Blue Beetle*, managing to put out four issues of reprint and new material before folding the title.

Not only were the superheroes worn-out, but the readers of the 1950s were tired of reading about them. The right combination of a fresh approach and audience receptiveness had not been discovered. The times were still not quite right for a large-scale superhero revival. In the meantime, comic books soldiered on as bravely as they could, neither as excitingly nor as profitably as in the industry's glory years.

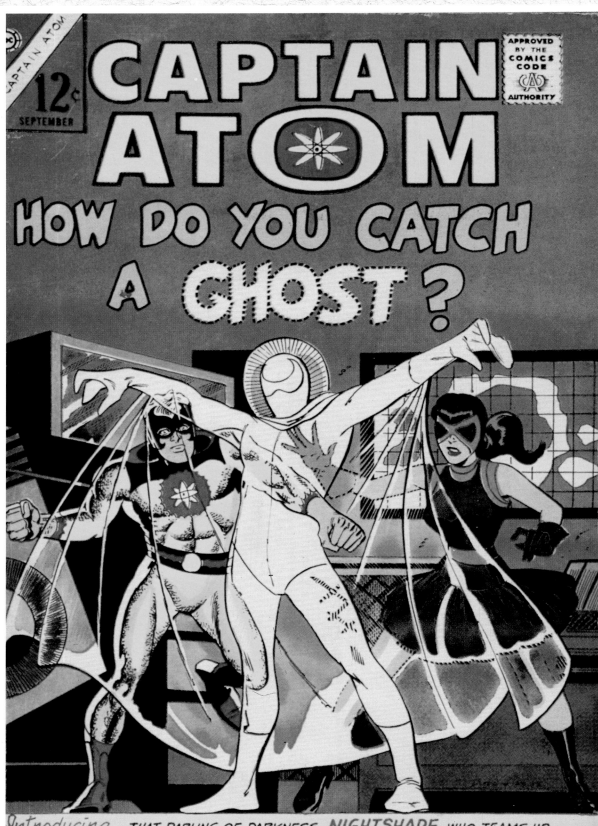

THE GREAT SUPERHERO REVIVAL

Superman remained the cornerstone of the DC empire in the late 1950s, and the most important of all comic book characters. Regrettably, his adventures had become predictable and occasionally even silly. Comic books were ripe for new ideas, and it was a DC editor who came up with them.

The man who served as the godfather to what fans call the Silver Age of comic books went to work for DC Comics as an editor in 1944. Although his influence on comic books would turn out to be great, Julius Schwartz was a science fiction enthusiast long before he had anything to do with comics. In 1932 he and another science fiction fan who would one day become a DC editor, Mort Weisinger, had founded *The Time Traveler*, the first nationally distributed science fiction fanzine. Schwartz also had served as literary agent for Edmond Hamilton, Ray Bradbury, Alfred Bester, Otto Binder, Stanley Weinbaum, Robert Bloch, and several other well-known fantasy-science fiction authors.

During the Second World War, Schwartz applied for a

job as an associate editor with the All-American branch of DC—reading his first comic book, he's claimed, on the subway ride to the interview. Sheldon Mayer was impressed with Schwartz, despite the young man's obvious lack of knowledge about the funny book business. "He had a few things going for him," Mayer has said. "He had a quick intelligence. His responses to my comments were sharp and discerning. And above all, there was that patient look to him. I think that's finally what sold me."

Schwartz rose quickly in the DC organization, editing *All Star*, *Western Comics* and, as we've seen, *Strange Adventures*, the company's first out-and-out science fiction title. *Mystery in Space*, the eventual home of galaxy-spanning hero Adam Strange, was soon added to Schwartz's title lineup. By 1956, while other comic book editors were contemplating wholly new genres, Schwartz's thoughts were turning again to superheroes. He wanted to resurrect some of the costumed stars of the past, and he began with ones who had originally been featured in Mayer's All-American titles.

Schwartz once recalled, "Someone, I don't know who, said, 'The Flash was always one of my favorites and maybe we ought to take a crack at putting him out again.' All eyes turned to me. So I said, 'OK, I'm stuck.'" Thus, the Flash became the first Golden Age superhero that DC Comics took out of mothballs.

"For some reason I decided not to revive the original Flash," Schwartz remembered, "but do a

new Flash with the same power, super-speed. I think I wanted to do an origin [story], which I always found fascinating, and I didn't like the original. I worked out a story with [writer] Bob Kanigher—new costume, new secret identity, new origin. The Flash's name, Barry Allen, came from two show business personalities, Steve Allen and Barry Gray. The thing I like best about what we did is that the [new] Flash got his inspiration of naming himself for a comic book character he read as a kid after he got doused with that lightning bolt and realized he has super-speed himself."

The revamped "fastest man alive" debuted in *Showcase* #4 (September-October 1956), a magazine that lived up to its name by giving characters, new and old, a place to try out. The first adventure of the new Flash was pencilled by Carmine Infantino and inked by Joe Kubert—talented artists who had taken turns drawing the original Flash in the 1940s.

By the 1950s the notion of an anthology magazine, such as the original *Flash Comics*, had lost favor. A typical comic had fewer pages now—usually forty-eight or thirty-two instead of sixty-four—and it was felt that a strong character should be able to carry an entire book without having to be backed up by any second bananas. The new Flash, therefore, had that whole issue of *Showcase* to himself. He streaked through his first story wearing a bright red costume that offered less wind resistance than that of his predecessor (mainly because he'd abandoned

A popular non-super group, the Challengers of the Unknown first appeared in *Showcase* #6 in 1957. Jack Kirby drew the cover.

DC editor Julius Schwartz instigated comic books' "Silver Age" when he brought back the Flash in 1956. Reader enthusiasm left no doubt that the time was ripe for a full-scale superhero revival. Cover art for this, the new Flash's second appearance, is by Carmine Infantino.

©1957 by National Periodical Publications, Inc.

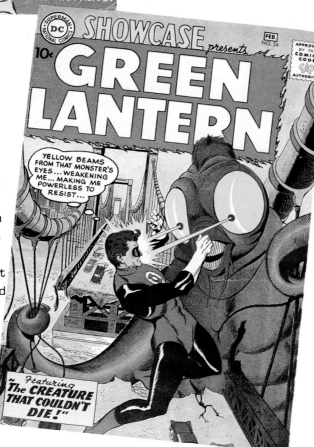

Thanks to editor Julius Schwartz, another great hero of DC history, the Green Lantern, enjoyed a comeback. Following this 1960 appearance in *Showcase #24*, (cover art by Gil Kane), GL graduated to his own book.

©1960 by National Periodical Publications, Inc.

the winged, doughboy-style tin hat worn by the original Flash). The new Flash's first adventure came off nicely, and he zoomed through *Showcase* #8, 13, and 14. Early in 1959, after proving he was a salable commodity, the Flash was granted a magazine of his own. Infantino remained the artist and John Broome became the scriptwriter; the Silver Age of comic books was underway.

Schwartz next turned his attention to a hero who had been the star of *All-American Comics*, the Green Lantern. After being given a new identity, origin, and costume, the updated GL bowed in *Showcase* #22 (October 1959). He auditioned again in the next two issues, then moved into a book of his own in the spring of 1960. "When the returns started coming in on the Flash and we saw we had a hit, the natural instinct was to do something similar," Schwartz has said. "That's how we decided to go ahead with Green Lantern, and I worked out the same theory of giving him a new personality, a new costume, a new everything. I have a theory that, when you revive a hero, you can base it on the original but go off on a different track. We decided to come up with a new type of Green Lantern where he could expand his activities. With John Broome, I worked out the idea of a whole universe full of Green Lanterns."

The new GL was Hal Jordan, who "had a fine reputation as an ace test pilot." In the desert in the American Southwest, Jordan has a strange encounter with a red-complected alien named Abin Sur, who has crash-landed.

The alien is dying, and the meeting concludes with Jordan inheriting Abin Sur's green lantern, power ring, and snappy black-and-green costume. At the end of the origin story, as Jordan charges himself up with superpowers by touching the power ring to the lantern, he says, "And I hope to make GREEN LANTERN a name to be feared by evildoers everywhere!"

The new feature's initial artist was Gil Kane, a skilled draftsman and highly talented storyteller who could choreograph fight scenes so that they looked like ballet. Kane, who had entered comics in the early 1940s while still in his teens, designed the new Lantern's capeless costume to be slicker and more functional than the blousy outfit of the character's predecessor. "I was trying for a balance between power and lyricism," Kane has said. "A cape would have gotten in the way of the figure."

The pair of superhero revivals proved to be more popular than anyone at DC, except possibly Schwartz himself, had anticipated. "A straw poll of readers, published in *Green Lantern* #3, showed him to be for the moment DC's most popular hero, with 888 votes to Superman's 600," reported Will Jacobs and Gerard Jones in *The Comic Book Heroes*. "Flash followed with 521, Batman with 512."

Inspired by his success, Schwartz resolved to bring back a whole *team* of superheroes by taking the Justice Society from *All Star* and rechristening it the Justice League. The membership

Editor Julius Schwartz updated the Justice Society idea in 1960, when he masterminded a new super-group called the Justice League of America. The feature made its debut in *The Brave and the Bold* #28. Clockwise from top left, the heroes are Green Lantern, Aquaman, Wonder Woman, the Flash, and J'onn J'onzz.

©1960 by National Periodical Publications, Inc.

A refurbished Green Arrow joined the Justice League in the fourth issue.

©1961 by National Periodical Publications, Inc.

Writer Gardner Fox, who had scripted Hawkman's adventures in the 1940s, returned to the feature when Hawkman was revived in 1961. Another comic book veteran, Joe Kubert, contributed the cover art.

©1961 by National Periodical Publications, Inc.

roster now included the Flash, Green Lantern, Superman, Batman, Aquaman, Wonder Woman, and Martian Manhunter; Green Arrow was added shortly thereafter. Gardner Fox, writer of the original gang's adventures, was brought back to write the book-length adventures of the new group. The team was introduced in *The Brave and the Bold* #28 (March 1960) and got its own title, *Justice League of America*, in the fall of that year. Mike Sekowsky, a disciple of the design-conscious artist Alex Toth, was the illustrator.

"It was a thrilling moment for DC's older fans," assert Jacobs and Jones. "And there were signs—letters from grateful adults scattered throughout the country—that the number of fans was steadily growing. With his intelligent sense of fun, Schwartz was beginning to reach an audience who would normally have put comic books behind them."

Turning again to the old *Flash Comics* for inspiration, Schwartz and DC next brought back Hawkman. Hawkgirl returned, too, and the revived, revamped team first reappeared in *The Brave and the Bold* #34 (March 1961). The prolific Gardner Fox, creator of the original feathery duo, wrote the scripts and Joe Kubert, the premier illustrator of the feature during the Golden Age, was once again the artist. However, this time Carter Hall and Shierra (the pair's alter-egos) were married and not just good friends. Furthermore, they were aliens "of the star system Polaris"

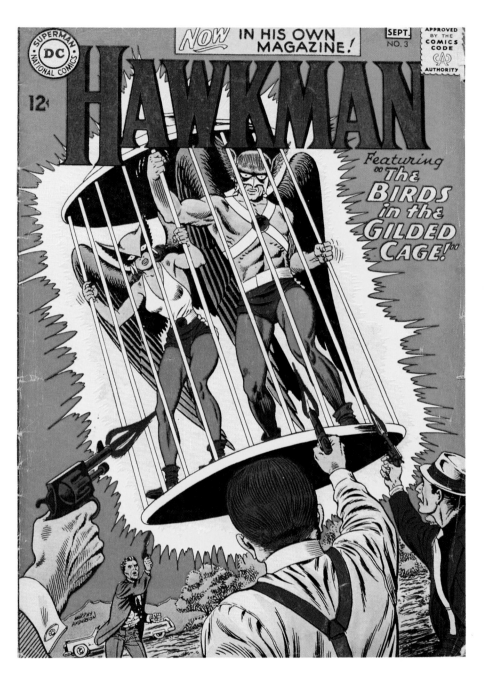

Hawkman's *Brave and the Bold* tryout was successful, and the character graduated to his own book in 1964. Cover art is by Murphy Anderson.

©1964 by National Periodical Publications, Inc.

visiting Earth. Their costumes, nearly identical to the striking outfits they'd worn in the 1940s, were now referred to as their "alien garments." Eventually they settled on Earth, adopted local identities, and took up residence in Midway City. Numerous fans took the new winged wonders to their heart at once; writing in the twentieth edition of *The Official Overstreet Comic Book Price Guide*, Gary M. Carter describes *The Brave and the Bold* #34 as "one of the greatest, most imaginative superhero comebacks of the Silver Age."

Hawkman and his missus also were featured in *B & B* #35 and 36. Apparently not as immediately popular as the other revitalized characters, the couple had to try out all over again in 1962, when they appeared in *The Brave and the Bold* #42, 43, and 44. Early in 1964 a regular *Hawkman* bimonthly was at last introduced.

The Atom, once a backup in *All-American Comics*, was given a turn at a comeback in *Showcase* #34 (October 1961). Borrowing a bit from Quality Comics's Doll Man, Schwartz and Gardner Fox converted the mighty mite into a chap who could shrink at will. "I always felt the Atom of the 1940s was misnamed," Schwartz has said. "He was simply called the Atom because he was a short fellow. I got the idea of having him a regular six-footer able to reduce himself to any size he wanted to. It just struck us as we were groping around for a theme that wasn't being done by any superheroes." Gil Kane, a longtime admirer of Doll Man's original artist Lou Fine, got the

job of drawing DC's minuscule hero.

Suddenly, DC was flying high, enjoying healthy sales and gaining a whole new generation of fans. Marvel, never a company content to remain on the outside looking in, eventually geared up to duplicate DC's success. For a while, though, things were tough. Marvel/Timely/Atlas writer-editor Stan Lee once described how the company functioned in the years between the superhero booms. "If cowboy films were the rage, we produced a lot of westerns," he explained. "If cops and robbers were in vogue, we'd grind out a profusion of crime titles. If the trend turned to love stories, Timely (as well as the competition) became big in romance mags. We simply gave the public what it wanted—or so we thought."

One of the things the public seemed to want in the 1950s was monsters. Hollywood and Japan's Toho Studios cranked 'em out in all shapes and sizes, in box-office hits like *Godzilla*, *The Fly*, *The Thing*, and *Creature from the Black Lagoon*. While the Comics Code wouldn't allow zombies, vampires and werewolves, it didn't say anything about giant lizards and similar huge creatures. So Marvel gave its readers a steady diet of monsters in the late 1950s and early 1960s, in *Tales to Astonish*, *Strange Tales*, *Journey into Mystery*, *Tales of Suspense*, and other titles.

Artist Jack Kirby had come back to work for Marvel during that period, and teamed with Stan Lee, who was the creative director of the whole Marvel operation. According to Lee, the

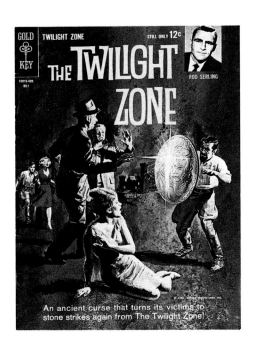

TV-based comic books had reached their peak in the fifties, but carried on into the 1960s. One of the better examples was Gold Key's *The Twilight Zone*, based on the hit CBS series.

©1964 by Cayuga Productions, Inc.

Before seguing into superheroes, Marvel cranked out innumerable stories about giant monsters who had names like "Groot," "Krang," and "Vandoom." *Tales to Astonish* #23 featured a critter called "Moomba." Cover art is by Jack Kirby and Dick Ayers.

©1961 by Vista Publications, Inc.

two of them began "having a ball turning out monster stories with such imperishable titles as 'Xom, the Creature Who Swallowed the Earth,' 'Grottu, the Giant Ant-Eater,' 'Thomgorr, the Anti-Social Alien,' 'Fin Fang Foom' . . . and others of equally redeeming artistic and literary value."

Lee's recollection is only half in jest. The monster formula was absurd, but it was followed faithfully, story after story. "Each issue stabilized roughly into this lineup," comic book historian Will Murray has commented. "Jack Kirby, usually inked by Dick Ayers, led off with a monster epic of anywhere from seven to thirteen pages; next would be a moody five-pager by Don Heck (or, occasionally Paul Reinman or Joe Sinnott), and Steve Ditko usually closed out the book with a gentle thought-provoker of the same length. For slightly more than three years, this tight little team wove their dreams and birthed their monsters."

And it was in this small Marvel bullpen that the superhero virus finally struck. As noted above, Jack Kirby had come back to the fold in the late 1950s. "It was a sad day," Kirby has recalled. "I came back the afternoon they were going to close. I remember telling Stan Lee not to close. What had been done before, I felt could be done again. I think it was the time when I really began to grow."

Late in 1961, according to Lee, "[Publisher] Martin Goodman mentioned that he had noticed one of the titles published by National Comics [DC's name at the time] seemed to be selling better than most. It was a book called *The Justice League of America* and was composed of a team of superheroes. Well, we didn't need a house to fall on us. 'If *The Justice League* is selling,' spake he, 'why don't we put out a comic book that features a team of superheroes?'

"I would create a team of superheroes if that was what the marketplace required," Lee said. "But it would be a team such as comicdom had never known. For just this once, I would do the type of story I myself would enjoy reading . . . and the characters would be the kind of characters I could personally relate to; they'd be flesh and blood, they'd have faults and foibles, they'd be fallible and feisty, and—most important of all—inside their colorful, costumed booties they'd still have feet of clay."

Lee, naturally enough, picked Kirby to work on the new project—the Fantastic Four, composed of Mr. Fantastic, Human Torch, Invisible Girl, and the Thing. Or, at first glance, variations on Plastic Man, the original Torch, Invisible Scarlet O'Neil of the funny papers, and one more *Tales to Astonish* monster, respectively. But what excited Stan Lee was his discovery of "the in-depth characterization that was to become a Marvel trademark." He didn't have it all worked out yet, but he suspected that superheroes struggling not only with supervillians but with the sort of personal problems that plagued ordinary mortals ought to be interesting.

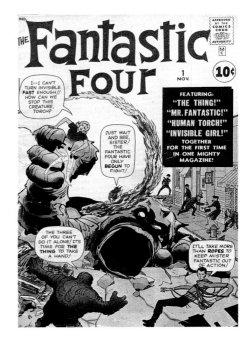

Marvel's first shot in the superhero wars of the 1960s—and its greatest super-group—was the Fantastic Four. Perhaps hedging his bets, writer/editor Stan Lee made sure that the cover of *The Fantastic Four* #1 included an enormous monster of the sort that had sustained Marvel during the late 1950s. Art is by Jack Kirby and Dick Ayers.

©1961 by Marvel Comics Group

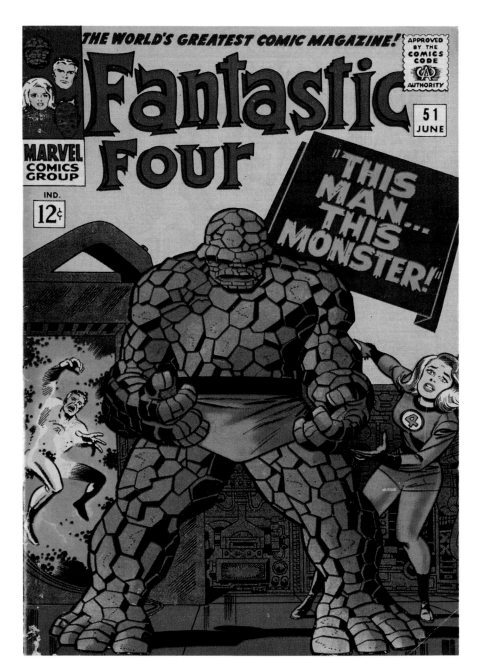

THE WORLD'S GREATEST COMIC MAGAZINE!

APPROVED BY THE COMICS CODE
CA
AUTHORITY

Fantastic Four

51
JUNE

MARVEL
COMICS
GROUP

IND.
12¢

"THIS MAN... THIS MONSTER!"

By the mid-sixties, Lee and Kirby had turned *The Fantastic Four* into a sophisticated title that was almost operatic in its splendor. The orange-skinned Thing was one of the most popular comic book characters of the period. Cover art of this 1966 issue is by Jack Kirby and inker Joe Sinnott.

The early response to the FF was, according to Lee, "one of the most exciting things that ever happened to us. We found out that there were actually live readers out there—readers who took the trouble to contact us, readers who wanted to talk to us about our characters." The most frequently asked question was, "When will you bring out another new superhero book?"

It wasn't long at all. Marvel's next superhero was the green, distinctly antisocial Hulk, whose tormented alter-ego is a mild man named Bruce Banner. While the Hulk's co-creators agree as to the original source of inspiration, they don't see eye to eye on who did what. "I decided I might as well borrow from Dr. Jekyll and Mr. Hyde," remembers Stan Lee. "Our protagonist would constantly change from his normal identity to his superhuman alter ego and back again." Jack Kirby has contended, "I began with the classics that were very powerful. What comics were doing all the time was updating the classics. So I borrowed Dr. Jekyll and Mr. Hyde. I felt there was a Mr. Hyde in all of us, and that was a character I wanted, and I called him the Hulk."

Whatever the character's exact parentage, *The Incredible Hulk* arrived on the newsstands in the spring of 1962. "Half man, half-monster, the Mighty Hulk thunders out of the night to take his place among the most amazing characters of all time!" Readers responded to the Hulk immediately. Lee and Kirby's variation on the Jekyll/Hyde premise—in which a quiet,

Although Stan Lee and Jack Kirby differ as to the precise origin of Spider-Man, no one can deny the appeal and terrific impact of this great character. Spidey made his debut in *Amazing Fantasy* #15; cover art is by Jack Kirby.

©1962 by Atlas Magazines, Inc.

decent man is physically and psychologically tortured by suddden transformations into a brutal, unreasoning beast—proved irresistible.

Heroes continued to pour forth from Marvel. The most important of them all was Spider-Man. Again, those who were involved in the creation of this great character differ as to how everybody's favorite web-spinner came to be invented. "Just for kicks I wanted to try something different," Lee has recalled. "For quite awhile I'd been toying with the idea of doing a strip that would violate all the conventions—break all the rules. A strip that would actually feature a teenager as the star. . . . A strip in which the main character would lose out as often as he'd win—in fact, more often. A strip in which nothing would progress according to formula—the situations, the cast of characters, and their relationship to each other would all be unusual and unexpected. Yep, I knew what I wanted all right, but where would I ever get a chance to try it? Where, except in a magazine that we were planning to kill anyway? You guessed it. I figured there was nothing to lose. *Amazing Fantasy* #15 would be the last issue before its preordained demise."

A fictional figure from the 1930s provided Lee with the inspiration for the name of his character. "One of my favorite pulp magazine heroes was a stalwart named the Spider."

Jack Kirby has offered a different version of what went on. "Spider-Man was not a product of Marvel," he has said.

"It was the last thing Joe Simon and I had discussed. We had a . . . script called *The Silver Spider*. *The Silver Spider* was going into a magazine called *Black Magic*. *Black Magic* folded with [its publisher,] Crestwood, and we were left with the script. I believe I said this could become a thing called *Spider-Man*, see, a superhero character. I had a lot of faith in the superhero character, that they could be brought back, very, very vigorously. . . . So the idea was already there when I talked to Stan."

What is uncontestable is that Spider-Man made his debut in that fifteenth and final issue of *Amazing Fantasy* (August 1962). Kirby drew the cover, Steve Ditko drew the eleven-page origin story and made some contributions to the character's origin, and Lee got the script credit. The *Official Marvel Index* to Spidey's exploits sums up the initial adventure this way: "During a demonstration at General Techtronics Laboratories, a spider is exposed to a lethal dose of radiation. Just before dying it bites Peter Parker, a brilliant science student from Midtown High School, who was invited to the demonstration. As a result, Peter Parker gains various 'spider powers': superhuman strength and agility, and the ability cling to any surface. His newly acquired powers suggest a way that Peter Parker can repay his Uncle Ben and Aunt May for the unselfish devotion to him as they raised him from childhood. He designs a costume and a pair of web-shooters, and accepts an offer to

Although just a teenager, Spider-Man had to deal with some formidable foes early in his crimefighting career. Perhaps the most intimidating of all was Doctor Doom, the mad genius who was the chief antagonist of the Fantastic Four. Cover art is by Steve Ditko.

appear on television as the Amazing Spider-Man. He keeps his true identity secret from everyone. . . . Several days later, Peter Parker arrives home to discover that his Uncle Ben has been killed during a burglary, leaving his Aunt May a widow. Using his spider powers, he tracks the killer."

The simplicity and power of Spider-Man's origin story were perceived by readers as a breath of fresh air. In particular, readers empathized with Peter's adolescent angst, his desire to do the right thing even as the circumstances of his life seemed to go wrong. The first issue of the character's own magazine, *The Amazing Spider-Man*, appeared early in 1963 and soon became a monthly title.

In addition to Spider-Man, 1962 saw the introduction of Marvel's Thor and Ant-Man. The Mighty Thor, described in cover copy as "the most exciting superhero of all time!!," debuted in *Journey into Mystery* #83 (August 1962). Written by Lee and drawn by Kirby, the origin story told how frail Dr. Blake, while vacationing in Norway, finds the hammer of the god Thor in a secret cave. Once he clutches the legendary implement, the spindly doctor is miraculously transformed into a muscular superman with shoulder-length blond hair and a form-fitting Norse costume. In subsequent stories the amount of Norse mythology increased considerably, even encompassing Thor's traditional nemesis, Loki.

Ant-Man, yet another hero who could shrink, was introduced in *Tales to Astonish*

#35 (September 1962). He, too, was initially a joint effort of Kirby and Lee.

The next year Iron Man was introduced in *Tales of Suspense* #39 (March 1963) and Dr. Strange was added to *Strange Tales* with issue #110 (July 1963). The latter character, who was written by Lee and drawn by Steve Ditko, was a "master of black magic." He seems to owe something not to the Dr. Strange of the 1940s but to DC's mystical Dr. Fate.

Daredevil, the Man Without Fear, was launched in his own magazine early in 1964. Notable for the humanizing affliction of blindness, Daredevil is really attorney Matt Murdock. Because he lost his sight after being struck by a truck hauling radioactive materials, he has acquired "incredible powers" that allow him to navigate the city's rooftops with an uncanny sixth sense that is rather like radar. Daredevil headed out for his first adventures garbed in a red, yellow, and black costume that he sewed himself; by the seventh issue, his outfit was a deep red. Bill Everett illustrated Daredevil's first adventure, and was followed by Joe Orlando and Wally Wood.

Daredevil was another script credit for Stan Lee, who, anticipating comics collectors and price guides to come, told readers right on the first page of DD's first story that "this magazine is certain to be one of your most valued comic mag possessions in the months to come!" He was right, for twenty-six years later a copy in mint condition would be valued in the

Marvel editor Stan Lee found inspiration for the Mighty Thor in Norse mythology. The character first appeared in *Journey Into Mystery* #83 and went on to become one of the most enduring Marvel stars.

©1961 by Marvel Comics Group

The Avengers—Marvel's response to DC's Justice League—was energized in its fourth issue by the addition of Captain America to the roster.

©1964 by Marvel Comics Group

Marvel's clever variations on the superhero formula during the 1960s seemed endless. Daredevil may have been the most ingenious creation of all—he was totally blind, but aided in his crimefighting career by an infallible "radar sense." Cover art is by Wally Wood.

Overstreet Comic Book Price Guide at $525.

Marvel eventually realized that its new heroes were reaching more than just the kid audience. "My characters were more mature, and that made them different," Jack Kirby once said. "I didn't realize I was building a college audience. When I created the Hulk, [Marvel] wanted to discontinue it after three issues. What saved me was the fact that some Columbia students came up to Marvel, and they had along a whole list of names. They said the Hulk was the mascot of their dormitory. It was the first time I realized we have a college audience." That college audience would account for the increasing success of Marvel throughout the 1960s.

The Kirby-Lee team continued to come up with new heroes—whole mobs of them. Where Jack Kirby had once invented kid gangs—the Young Allies, the Boy Commandos, The Newsboy Legion—he now gave himself over to creating groups of grownups. The summer of 1963 brought two of the company's most enduring, the Avengers and the X-Men. The Avengers were in the Justice League tradition and consisted initially of Iron Man, Thor, the Hulk, Ant-Man, and the Wasp. *The Avengers* #4 (March 1964) was capped by a big event— Captain America's joining of the group. "Captain America Lives Again!" proclaimed the cover headline above the charging figure of Kirby's star-spangled hero. America's number-one superpatriot had been gone a long time; readers were informed that Cap had been frozen inside an iceberg since the waning days of World War II.

The X-Men was to be an even more important title than *The Avengers*. Its significance lies chiefly in that fact that it introduced mutants into the Marvel universe. As is explained in the *Official Handbook of the Marvel Universe*, the X-Men were founded by a wheelchair-bound gentleman named Professor Charles Xavier, "the mutant son of nuclear researcher Brian Xavier and his wife Sharon. Even as a pre-adolescent, Xavier could use his powers to sense other people's intentions and emotions. Upon reaching puberty, Xavier's telepathic powers began to fully emerge. As a side effect, he began losing his hair until by high school graduation he was completely bald." Professor X also "possesses numerous psionic powers, making him the world's most powerful telepath." Among his talents are the abilities to read minds and project his own thoughts within a radius of 250 miles. He can make others think he's invisible, can sense the presence of another mutant "within a small but as yet undetermined radius," can project his astral body, and can control matter psychokinetically. For good measure he is "a genius in genetics and other sciences."

The original X-Men, recruited by Xavier, were even bigger misfits than Spider-Man's alter-ego, Peter Parker. They consisted of, to quote the *World Encyclopedia of Comics*, "Cyclops, whose eyes emitted a powerful

Marvel's *X-Men* introduced the idea of mutant heroes to comic books. Much of the energy and power of the Marvel style is summed up by this Jack Kirby cover.
©1965 by Canam Publishers Sales Corp.

Joe Simon and Jack Kirby created a new superhero, Private Strong, for the Archie Comics group in 1959. Strong's alter ego was the Shield.

©1959 by Radio Comics, Inc.

Adventures of the Fly #1: Simon & Kirby's the Fly meets Spider Spry.

©1959 by Radio Comics, Inc.

blasting beam; The Angel, born with operative wings; Iceman, a reverse Human Torch, able to hurl snow and ice bombs; The Beast, an apelike being whose erudite speech was in marked contrast to his bestial appearance; and Marvel Girl, able to levitate objects and command a force-field." As with the Fantastic Four and Marvel's other super-groups, the X-Men were distinguished as much by their fascinating character interplay as by the *sturm und drang* of their adventures.

By combining old-fashioned superhero adventure with meaty characterizations, Marvel and DC had hit upon something very big; other publishers were sharp enough to perceive the coming boom in superheroes. Sensing a trend, Archie Comics (formerly MLJ) had started experimenting with superheroes again in the late 1950s. Joe Simon and Jack Kirby, who were still in partnership at the time, were hired to help create an adventure line. The first Archie title created by S & K was *The Double Life of Private Strong*, which appeared in the spring of 1959. Private Strong's other self was the Shield. This updated version of the 1940s MLJ superpatriot, even though it also made use of elements from Captain America, was not a success and the title ended with its second issue. Simon and Kirby's other creation, *The Adventures of the Fly*, debuted in the summer of 1959, and fared somewhat better—it didn't fold until 1964. Two artists, John Giunta and John Rosenberger, later took care of the art chores.

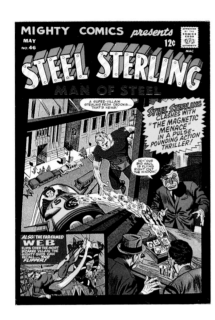

Archie Comics was determined to carve itself a piece of the pie during the superhero boom of the mid-sixties, but failed.

©1967 by Radio Comics, Inc.

The robot called Platinum attempts to save the life of her creator on the cover of *Metal Men* #1. Art is by Ross Andru and Mike Esposito.

©1963 by National Periodical Publications, Inc.

Comics historian Lou Mougin, writing in *The Comic Reader*, ably summed up the origin of the Fly. "The Fly was in reality Thomas Troy, originally a youth beset by evil step-parents straight out of the Brothers Grimm. He was befriended by the Shazam-like Turan, a humanoid whose people had evolved from the common housefly. . . . Turan gives Tommy a magic Fly Ring, which, when rubbed and encouraged by Tommy's saying, 'I wish I were the Fly!' turns him into an insect powered superhero in yellow and grey. Tommy, with ant-like strength, flight power, firefly heat-radiance and numerous other powers, is sent to combat Evil in All Its Forms." And so he did, buzzing off with his partner, Fly Girl (who joined the cast in 1961), to do battle with bad guys.

Archie was nothing if not optimistic, and introduced *The Adventures of the Jaguar* in the summer of 1961. Another in a long line of heroes costumed in red, the Jaguar was handled by artist John Rosenberger. Essentially uninspired, the book lasted fifteen issues. Archie tried again in 1964, when the mysterious Shadow of radio fame made an odd comeback as a costumed superhero. Readers didn't go for this idea, either, and *The Shadow* faded after eight issues.

Archie still wasn't ready to call it quits, so in the spring of 1965 the Fly returned, this time as Fly Man. No longer a solo hero, Fly Man was now part of a group that included a clutch of resurrected MLJ heroes: the Black Hood, the Comet, and the Shield. Superman's co-creator, Jerry Siegel, wrote the feature and Paul Reinman, a second-rate talent, drew it. The same group, sans Fly Man, starred in *The Mighty Crusaders*, which appeared late in 1965. Siegel and Reinman were again the creative team. Alas, Archie struck out again: *Fly Man* lasted eight issues, *The Mighty Crusaders* only seven.

When Dell and Western parted company in 1962, the latter organization continued to publish comics under the Gold Key imprint. As Mike Benton points out in *The Comic Book in America*, "Western took the lion's share of the titles," including all the Disney and Warner cartoon character books. Gold Key also tried superheroes, the first of which was *Doctor Solar, Man of the Atom*. While the magazine sported handsome painted covers, the good doctor's adventures were bland stuff.

Dell's attempt at a superhero was *Nukla*, introduced in 1965. Despite being dubbed "the Greatest SUPER HERO on Earth!," Nukla vanished after just four issues.

The American Comics Group took a stab at superheroes late in 1964 by adding a turbaned, masked superhero named Magicman to *Forbidden Worlds*. Early the next year *Adventures Into the Unknown* began to feature the spectral Nemesis. The adventures of both characters were written bu ACG editor Richard Hughes. Much of the drawing was by Pete Costanza, who'd apparently forgotten just about everything he'd learned while working with

C. C. Beck on *Captain Marvel*. Uninspired artwork was obstacle enough to the characters' success, but even the basic ideas didn't fly with the titles' regular fans, many of whom didn't take kindly to the intrusion of supermen into the realm of horror and fantasy. In the end, after about fifteen issues of each character's adventures, Robert Hughes was forced to admit in an editorial that there was "a large and fast-growing group that prefers our established formula of the supernatural and science fiction to the big muscle guys."

In the meantime DC, the publisher that had instigated the superhero revival, continued to successfully update heroes who'd been benched back in the forties, including Green Arrow and the Spectre. DC introduced all-new teams of heroes, as well. One of the more novel super-groups was the Metal Men, who were first seen in *Showcase* #37 (April 1962). As their collective name implied, this group was made up of six robots—Iron, Gold, Mercury, Tin, Platinum, and Lead. All the robots were "male" except for the shapely Platinum; comic relief was provided by the skinny, chronically insecure Tin. The group had been built and was led by Will Magnus, a young scientist. Lively as well as vaguely eccentric, the feature was written by Robert Kanigher and nicely illustrated by Ross Andru and Mike Esposito. The group's own title, *Metal Men*, began in the spring of 1963 and continued for forty-one issues. The title was briefly revived in 1973 and again in 1976.

The Spectre had been a spooky mainstay of DC's superhero lineup in the forties. Like the Flash, Hawkman, and other Golden Age heroes, he was resurrected in the 1960s. Neal Adams drew this vivid cover image.

©1967 by National Periodical Publications

Archie Comics's Jaguar ("the master of all animals") was an uninspired character whose adventures were competently drawn by John Rosenberger.

©1963 by Radio Comics, Inc.

DC's Doom Patrol, who first set up shop in *My Greatest Adventure* #80 (June 1963), was, like Marvel's X-Men, a gang of misfits presided over by a genius in a wheelchair. They were Robot Man; Elasti-Girl, who was afflicted with Plastic Man Syndrome; and Negative Man, who had the dubious ability of being able to send out a negative-energy duplicate of himself. Arnold Drake wrote the series and it was drawn by Bruno Premiani, an Italian-born, Argentinian-raised artist who brought an agreeable realism to Drake's entertaining, often peculiar stories. Although clearly inspired by the needling character interplay that had turned Marvel's Fantastic Four into a big hit, the Doom Patrol rose to a special weirdness by emphasizing story elements such as dangerously sentient gorillas, disembodied brains, and a whole catalog of villains with physical deformities. Because readers responded positively to the group, *My Greatest Adventure* was retitled *The Doom Patrol* with #86 and stayed in business until the fall of 1968; the team was brought back for all-new adventures in 1987.

DC's supply of superheroes seemed inexhaustible. Aquaman resurfaced in 1961, accompanied this time around by a new character, Aqualad. In 1964 Aqualad joined Robin and Kid Flash to form the first incarnation of the Teen Titans (a group that, in altered form, would enjoy enormous popular success in the 1980s). These traditional-style superheroes were good fun, but DC found

Although inspired by Marvel's Fantastic Four, DC's Doom Patrol had a personality of its own. This 1965 page was written by Arnold Drake and illustrated by Bruno Premiani.

©1965 by National Periodical Publications, Inc.

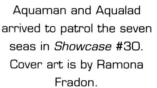

Aquaman and Aqualad arrived to patrol the seven seas in *Showcase* #30. Cover art is by Ramona Fradon.

©1961 by National Periodical Publications, Inc.

Metamorpho was one of the more imaginative DC superheroes of the sixties. A wisecracking shape-changer, he starred in adventures that were well illustrated by Ramona Fradon.

©1964 by National Periodical Publications, Inc.

"Planeteer" Tommy Tomorrow had appeared as a backup feature in *Action Comics* in the 1940s. In 1962, he graduated to solo-star status in *Showcase* #41 and 42. Lee Elias handled the cover art for issue #41, seen here.

©1962 by National Periuodical Publications, Inc.

A trio of Golden Age superheroes and a memorable villain were reunited in this 1965 issue of *Showcase*. Murphy Anderson created the cover art.

©1965 by National Periodical Publications, Inc.

Perhaps inspired by the campy tone of the *Batman* television series, DC introduced the Inferior Five, a group that parodied the whole idea of superheroes. The feature was introduced in *Showcase* #62 and illustrated by onetime EC Comics artist Joe Orlando.

©1966 by National Periodical Publications, Inc.

equal entertainment value in new characters who had no superpowers at all. In 1957 the company had introduced the Challengers of the Unknown, an all-male group of macho do-gooders who had a wide variety of adventures, many of them science-fictional. After tryout appearances in *Showcase* #6, 7, 11, and 12, the group won its own title in the spring of 1958; early issues, drawn by Jack Kirby with occasional inking assists by Wally Wood, are particularly attractive.

DC introduced *Rip Hunter, Time Master* in 1959 and followed up a year later with the scuba-diving *Sea Devils*, a feature that was nicely rendered by the highly talented Russ Heath, one of comic books' most dependable "realist" artists. Science fiction hero Adam Strange (whose best adventures were beautifully drawn by Carmine Infantino) was first seen in 1958 and Tommy Tomorrow, who'd begun life as a backup character in the middle 1940s, graduated to a book of his own in 1962.

Marvel, too, offered non-super heroes. Rugged Nick Fury began his career as an Army sergeant, leading a band of stereotypical misfits (a ladies' man, a strong man, a country boy, etc.) against the Nazis in World War II. "Keep movin', you lunkheads!" Fury urges his men on the cover of the first issue of *Sgt. Fury and His Howling Commandos* (May 1963). "Nobody lives forever! So git the lead out and follow me! We got us a WAR to win!" Yet another creation of Lee and Kirby, the book was later successfully handled by writer Gary Friedrich and artist John Severin. The commandos fought the Second World War (almost singlehandedly, it seemed) in their own title until the early 1980s.

Meanwhile, over in *Strange Tales* #135 (August 1965) the sarge began to live a second, postwar life as Nick Fury, Agent of S.H.I.E.L.D. The acronym, inspired by television's *The Man from U.N.C.L.E.*, stood for **S**upreme **H**eadquarters, **I**ntelligence **E**spionage **L**aw-enforcement **D**ivision, and in this incarnation the cigar-chomping, rough-mouthed Fury, complete with eyepatch picked up in combat, was a superspy. A young artist-writer named Jim Steranko (see sidebar) eventually turned *Nick Fury* into one of the best and most innovative comic book series of the 1960s.

Comic books' Silver Age, heralded by the tentative re-introduction of characters that had been written off years before, and confirmed by the appearance of a host of novel, all-new characters, may have reached its fullest flower with the work of Jim Steranko. The whole panoply of characters and epic adventures offered by Marvel, and the only slightly less exciting offerings from DC, had restored vigor and confidence to the medium. Pardoxically, then, the most successful comic book phenomenon of the 1960s also created a climate in which comics were regarded as laughable kitsch.

The American Broadcasting Company aired the first episode of *Batman* on the evening of

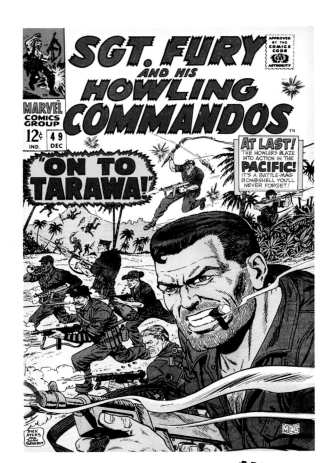

Marvel Comics relives World War II, with the invincible Nick Fury and his go-anywhere commandos. Cover art is by Dick Ayers and John Severin.

©1967 by Bard Publishing Group

Batman goes to camp on this 1966 cover; pencils by Carmine Infantino, inks by Murphy Anderson.

©1966 by National Periodical Publications, Inc.

The Shield was another short-lived superhero for the Archie Comics group. Paul Reinman drew the cover.

©1966 by Radio Comics, Inc.

Jim Steranko's sense of drama and design shook up the comic book industry, and impressed thousands of fans. This striking page from *Nick Fury* #1 was slickly inked by Joe Sinnott.

©1968 by Olympia Publications, Inc.

A nicely designed *Peacemaker* cover by artist Pat Boyette.

©1967 by Charlton Comics Group

Wednesday, January 12, 1966. The show was slow to catch on, but once it did, it was a sensation. Its enormous (if relatively short-lived) popularity led to a new phase of comic book publishing—a phase that, depending on how one looks at it, either enhanced or destroyed the euphoric era that fans like to call the Silver Age. Essentially, the television show treated the comic book notion of crime fighting in a less than serious manner. "'Batman' was the ultimate 'camp' show of the 1960s and was definitely not to be taken seriously even by those who acted in it," explained *The Complete Directory To Prime Time Network TV Shows*. "The fight scenes were punctuated by animated 'Pows,' 'Bops,' and 'Thuds' that flashed on the screen when a blow was struck, obliterating the actors. The situations were intentionally contrived and the acting was intentionally overdone by everyone except [star] Adam West, who was so wooden that he was hilarious."

Campy or not, the *Batman* TV series inspired merchandising spinoffs—toys, games, peanut butter, clothes, costumes, and more—that grossed $150,000,000 in 1966. The show's financial success was so enormous, and its impact on great masses of people so obvious, that a host of small (or unlikely) publishers hastened to grab for a share of the riches.

Tower, heretofore a paperback house, had actually entered comics in 1965, a few months before the *Batman* boom. Although leavened with a ▶

STERANKO

By the time he was thirty years old, Jim Steranko (born 1938) had brought a remarkable freshness and vigor to comic books. Intensely creative, Steranko got into comics after professional experience as a graphic artist, ad man, musician, and escape artist. His first published comic book work was interior art in the first issue of Harvey Comics's *Spyman*, cover-dated September 1966. He went to Marvel later that same year and worked as an inker of pencil art by Jack Kirby. After assisting Kirby on a few issues of *Strange Tales* adventures starring super-spy Nick Fury, Steranko assumed responsibility for the feature's scripts and art. In short order, he impressed readers with his fertile imagination and sophisticated approach to storytelling.

Fury graduated to a comic book of his own in 1968, and Steranko went with him, bringing a diversity of influences to the feature: "Everything from films, radio, pulps, business, everything I could possibly apply from my background," Steranko once explained, "including the magic I've done, the gigs I've played—everything goes into every comic story. Nick Fury became Steranko."

In 1969 Steranko was handed *Captain America*, and proceeded to energize the character as no artist had since Jack Kirby. He wrote and pencilled three memorable issues, #110, 111, and 113. (The first two stories were inked by Joe Sinnott, the third by Tom Palmer.) Muscular and every bit as heroically emblematic as his name implied, Steranko's Captain America became a character of epic proportions.

Captain America had always cut a dramatic figure since his first appearance in 1941, but may never have looked more emblematically heroic than when interpreted by Jim Steranko. Inks on this art were provided by Tom Palmer.

©1969 by Marvel Comics Group

The look of futurist technology and a fanciful notion of human anatomy were trademarks of Jim Steranko's work. This art is from *Nick Fury* #1, and was inked by Joe Sinnott.

Steranko, too, assumed heroic proportions in the eyes of fans, who eventually referred to him simply as "Steranko"—nothing so mundane as a first name was necessary.

Steranko's eclectic interests and professional experiences allowed him to bring a marvelous texture and variety to his work. Visually, he blended the Marvel house style of muscular heroes and fast action with the sophisticated storytelling techniques of Spirit creator Will Eisner and noted EC artist Bernard Krigstein. He added the flash and dazzle of pop art posters to his work and created splash (opening) panels that were—except for Eisner's—unprecedented in their imagination and cleverness of design. A tattered poster plastered to a fence might announce the story's title, or the title might be constructed of enormous, three-dimensional letters across which characters play out deadly games of pursuit. Spatial relationships fascinated Steranko, as did time, which he compressed and expanded to suit the requirements of his stories. Like Krigstein before him, he might break a row of panels into as many as eight in order to accelerate or slow down the action. And typical of many accomplished comic book artists, Steranko was adept at drawing beautiful women. Of all of Steranko's attributes, though, perhaps the most important were his obvious respect for the comic book art form, and his belief in its storytelling potential. Steranko eventually moved on to painting and a successful career as a magazine publisher; his career in comics was short but response to it was, and still is, enormously enthusiastic.

cheeky sort of humor, the company's comics emphasized adventure rather than self-parody. Harry Shorten, who had been an editor and writer at MLJ in the forties, headed up Tower's comic book project. The keystone title was *T.H.U.N.D.E.R. Agents*, a well-done book that featured some appealing new superheroes: Noman, Lightning, Menthor, and Dynamo. Several first-rate artists, including Wally Wood, Gil Kane, Reed Crandall, Steve Ditko, and Ogden Whitney, drew for the Tower line. In time, the company's titles included *Dynamo* and *Noman*; a pair of war books, *Undersea Agent* and *Fight the Enemy*; and a teen comic, *Tippy Teen*. Although of high quality, the Tower line was undone by distribution problems, and folded in 1970.

Charlton, the weakest and least innovative of the established publishers that had survived the Comics Code, introduced *Captain Atom*, *Thunderbolt*, *Judomaster*, and *Peacemaker* in 1966-67. This last character was right in tune with America's schizophrenic foreign policy at the time and was described as a "man who loves peace . . . so much that he is willing to fight for it!"

Harvey Comics, an outfit that was still doing well with funny stuff like *Sad Sack*, *Casper*, and *Richie Rich*, came into the hero field in the summer of 1966 with *Spyman*, *Thrill-O-Rama* (featuring Pirana), *Double-Dare Adventures* (featuring Bee-Man, Glowing Gladiator, and Magic-Master), and *Jigsaw*. The Harvey titles were minor and doomed to

Although plagued by problems with distribution, Tower Comics hung on long enough to produce some of the best superhero comics of the late sixties. A top-notch art staff led by Wally Wood was one of the reasons. Wood inked Al Williamson's dynamic pencils on this *T.H.U.N.D.E.R. Agents* cover.

©1966 by Tower Comics, Inc.

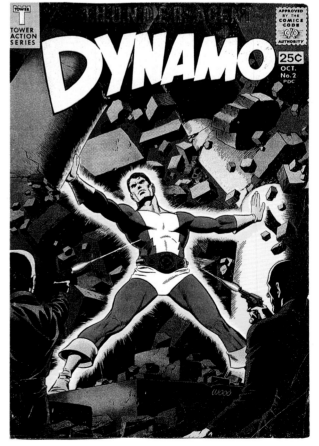

Wally Wood penciled and inked the beautiful *Dynamo* cover seen here.

©1966 by Tower Comics, Inc.

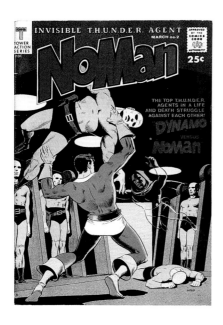

This issue of *NoMan* has yet another cover penciled and inked by Tower Comics' Wally Wood.

©1966 by Tower Comics, Inc.

So great was the Batman-inspired superhero craze that even Archie Andrews donned long underwear and strode forth to battle crime as Captain Pureheart. Following a tryout in *Life with Archie*, Pureheart gained a title of his own. Mercifully, Archie's superhero career was short-lived.

©1965 by Archie Comic Publications, Inc.

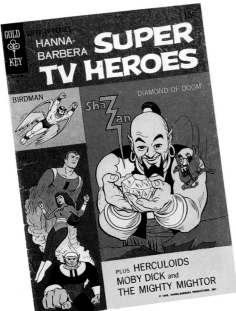

Saturday-morning animated cartoons also inspired comic book titles. *Super TV Heroes* featured characters from the Hanna-Barbera lineup.

©1968 by Hanna-Barbera Productions, Inc.

quick extinction. Ditto Milson Publishing's *Super Green Beret*, an absurd war/superhero pastiche that, mercifully, lasted just two issues in 1967. Milson's other attempt at a superhero was C. C. Beck and Otto Binder's *Fatman, the Human Flying Saucer*, a whimsical, three-issue spoof that never found the audience it deserved.

Archie Comics, which had stumbled earlier in the decade with *The Mighty Crusaders* and *Fly Man*, went campy in 1967 by introducing *Archie as Captain Pureheart*, a harmless but completely unnecessary comic book that cast carrot-topped teenager Archie Andrews as a red-suited superhero. The captain may have been pure of heart but he was also weak in sales; this nonsensical aberration came to an end after six issues.

Despite the failures described above, the 1960s were a period of great commercial success for the superhero genre, with 1966 and '67 the years of peak industry earnings. Unfortunately, the *Batman* TV fad fizzled nearly as quickly as it had developed; the show was canceled in 1968 and the public—even kids—lost interest in the whole idea of campy supermen. By the end of the decade the quick-buck outfits had faded away or abandoned their superheroes. The genre would survive into the 1970s, but the new decade would bring some interesting new genres, too. The industry would be dominated by just two companies, Marvel and DC. As the seventies dawned, the two giants prepared to slug it out.

CHAPTER TWELVE

"IT'S GOOD, BUT IS IT RELEVANT?"

An odd assortment of comic book genres and characters turned out to be commercial in the 1970s. Among the topics and themes comic book publishers offered to readers were barbarians, the environment, vampires, drug abuse, werewolves, mythology, and Oriental martial arts. A peculiar mix, but a moneymaking one, too. For Marvel, the 1970s would be the most profitable decade thus far, with sales jumping over five million copies per month from 1970 to 1979. DC's sales rose, as well, by a little less than two million copies a month in these years. By 1979, with monthly sales at around 7,200,000, DC was almost exactly where Marvel had been ten years earlier.

Each of the three other major companies (Harvey, Archie, and Gold Key), all of whom aimed at a younger audience, showed losses for the decade. In 1979 Harvey's sales were down over two million from a 1970 high of about 5,500,000. Archie's monthly sales dropped from 6,200,000 to 3,500,000 in the 1970s and Gold Key dropped from nearly 4,500,000 to about three million. It had become clear that

Comic books gained a remarkable sophistication in the seventies. Seemingly overnight, once taboo subjects like drug abuse became the basis of stories. Leading the way in this rush to relevance were issues of *Green Lantern* written by Denny O'Neil and illustrated by Neal Adams. Superheroes had entered the real world to face real problems.

©1970 by National Periodical Publications, Inc.

to maintain the top position in the comics industry now depended on reaching and holding an older audience.

Comic books had risen in price and dwindled in thickness throughout the 1960s, the decade that saw the ten-cent comic book go the way of the five-cent soft drink. By the early 1970s comics were selling for twenty cents and contained thirty-two pages. They would grow no thinner over the next decade or so, although more pages would be devoted to ads and fewer to story and art. But the per-copy price would keep climbing, inching ever closer to one dollar.

Because so much of the comic book product of the 1970s was interesting, readers seemed to take the price increases in stride. One of the most successful, and influential, new comic book stars of the decade was Conan the Barbarian, a pulp-fiction character who first appeared in the December 1932 issue of *Weird Tales*. He was the creation of Robert E. Howard, a young Texan who had begun turning out large quantities of pulp stories while still in his teens. Howard sold stories not just to the weird and fantasy markets, but to many of the action and adventure magazines as well. When he wasn't writing for the pulps, he was reading them attentively; the "sword-and-sorcery" facet of his work was much influenced by such writers as Talbot Mundy and Harold Lamb. Howard borrowed what he could from both, though he was never able to imitate their restraint.

"As nearly as such things can be calculated, Conan flourished about 12,000 years ago," explained writer L. Sprague deCamp, who revised and refurbished much of the Conan pulp material for book publications. "In this time (according to Howard), the western parts of the main continent were occupied by the Hyborian kingdoms. . . . Conan, a gigantic adventurer from Cimmeria, arrived as a youth in the kingdom of Zamora. For two or three years he made his living as a thief in Zamora, Corinthia and Nemedia. Growing tired of this starveling existence, he enlisted as a mercenary in the armies of Turan. For the next two years he traveled widely and refined his knowledge of archery and horsemanship."

Brooding, truculent, and heavily muscled enough to split skulls with single blows from his broadsword, Conan was fond of spending his days with lovely princesses and slave girls. Against his will, he struggled against malignant magic and sorcery. The rest of the time he got into violent fights—"A snarl of bloodthirsty gratification hummed in his bull-throat as he leaped, and the first attacker, his short sword over-reached by the whistling saber, went down with his brains gushing from his split skull. Wheeling like a cat, Conan caught the descending wrist on his edge, and the hand gripping the short sword flew into the air, scattering a shower of red drops."

In 1936 Howard, just thirty years old, killed himself. His stories of Conan, epics of

Marvel's Conan—based on the brooding barbarian character created by pulp writer Robert E. Howard—proved to be an enormous commercial and critical success. Roy Thomas's scripts were exciting and literate, and Barry Smith's art was both dynamic and subtle. Cover art on this 1971 issue is by Smith.

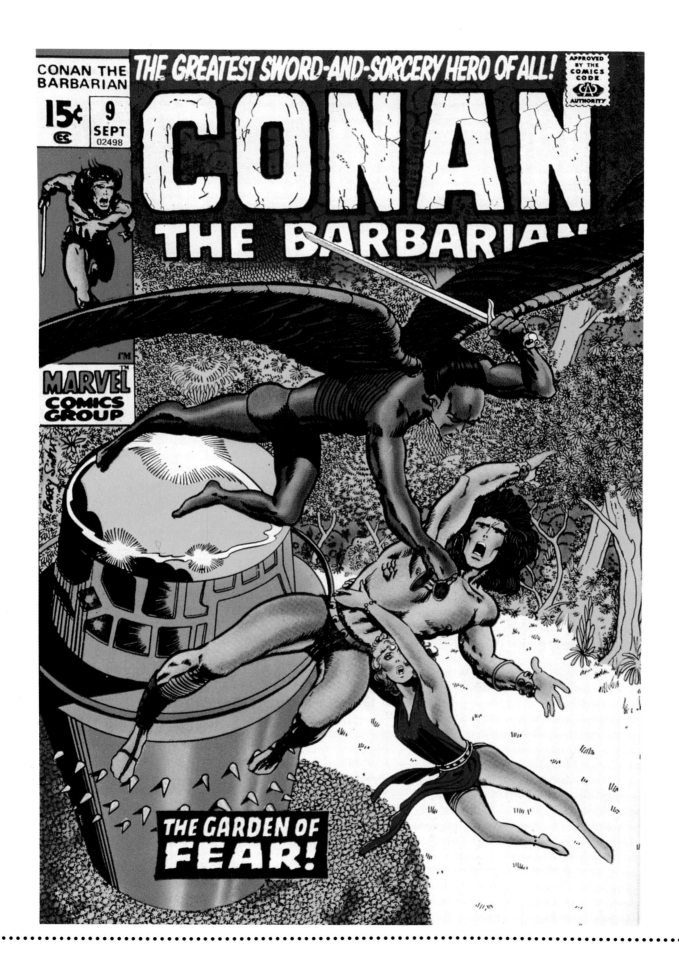

adolescent fantasies and fears, were forgotten for nearly two decades. Then they gradually began coming back into print, first in hardcover then, in the 1960s, in paperbacks adorned with striking cover paintings by Frank Frazetta.

Conan found his widest and most enthusiastic audience in the 1970s, thanks to Marvel Comics and a young writer named Roy Thomas. Thomas has said, "I guess you could say I was the first [comic book] fan to break into the business." After working on the fanzine *Alter Ego*, the onetime Missouri high school teacher entered comics' professional ranks by writing scripts for DC. By 1970 he was an editor and writer at Marvel, concentrating on superheroes. Although Thomas is usually given credit for deciding to adapt Howard's barbarian to the comic book format, artist Gil Kane has said that he was the one who originally got Thomas and Marvel interested in experimenting with the character. At any rate, *Conan* burst onto America's newsstands in the autumn of 1970. Scripts were by Thomas and the art was handled by a young, transplanted British artist, Barry Smith. Originally working in a Kirby-inspired variation of the Marvel house style, Smith soon developed his own, intricately personal approach, one that was eventually more akin to 19th-century book illustration than to traditional comic book art.

Thomas's adaptations of Robert E. Howard's original Conan tales drew considerable praise at the time. "In fleshing out these tales, Thomas produced without question the finest scripting of his career," comments *The Comic Book Heroes*. "Not bound to emulate [Stan] Lee's quasi-realism, he wrote vivid descriptions and stylized dialogue with elegance and distinction." Smith, too, attracted attention and was soon winning awards from both his peers and fans. He left Conan in 1973 and was followed on the feature by several other artists, among them Gil Kane. The success of the *Conan* title sparked a small boom in sword-and-sorcery. Marvel led the way, with Thongor, Kull, and Red Sonja.

Justifiably dubbed the "She-Devil with a Sword", the comic book incarnation of Red Sonja first appeared in late 1972, in *Conan* #23. Thomas took the character from another Howard pulp tale and, changing her name slightly, let her loose in the Hyborean Age. She was the guest star in two issues of *Conan* and returned in 1974 for a single appearance in a black-and-white magazine, *The Savage Sword of Conan*. She fought her way through two issues of *Kull and the Barbarians* in 1975, with Howard Chaykin drawing her sword-wielding escapades. Sonja then became the star of *Marvel Feature*, with Frank Thorne handling the art chores from the second issue onward. With her bright orange hair and chain-mail bikini, Thorne's version of Red Sonja attracted considerable interest. Late in 1976 the she-devil got a book of her own and it continued, with a hiatus or two, until the middle 1980s.

Shapely Red Sonja was the female equivalent of Conan. This pin-up by artist Frank Thorne appeared in *Red Sonja* #5.

©1976 by Marvel Comics Group

Marvel scored a bullseye with *Conan the Barbarian*, so DC countered with *Sword of Sorcery*. Fantasy specialist Mike Kaluta drew the cover for the first issue.

DC attempted three unsuccessful experiments with swords and sorcery in the middle 1970s. *Sword of Sorcery*, *Claw the Unconquered*, and *Beowulf* (based on the oldest barbarian property in Western literature) did not fare well. Only Mike Grell's *Warlord*, introduced late in 1975, survived.

There was a great deal of migration on the part of artists and writers in the 1970s, mostly consisting of moving back and forth between Marvel and DC. As far as superheroes and adventure material were concerned, the two publishing houses were just about the only outlets. Jack Kirby startled his fans by returning to DC in 1970, leaving behind at Marvel an impressive list of hot properties, including the highly popular *Fantastic Four*.

"I was living here in California," Kirby recalled. Carmine Infantino, then editorial director of DC, was visiting the state and got in touch with him. "To make it short, they wanted me to save *Superman*. I said, well, I wasn't too happy with what was happening at Marvel. I thought maybe this was the time to change. But, I said, 'I don't want to take work away from the guys who have been doing it for years.' I said, 'I'll take that book, *Jimmy Olsen*. I'll take the one that has no sales . . . and I'll do my own books, titles of my own.'. . . So I turned *Jimmy Olsen* into something different."

Kirby enlivened *Jimmy Olsen* by bringing back an old Simon and Kirby creation, the Newsboy Legion, which had first appeared in *Star Spangled Comics* in the

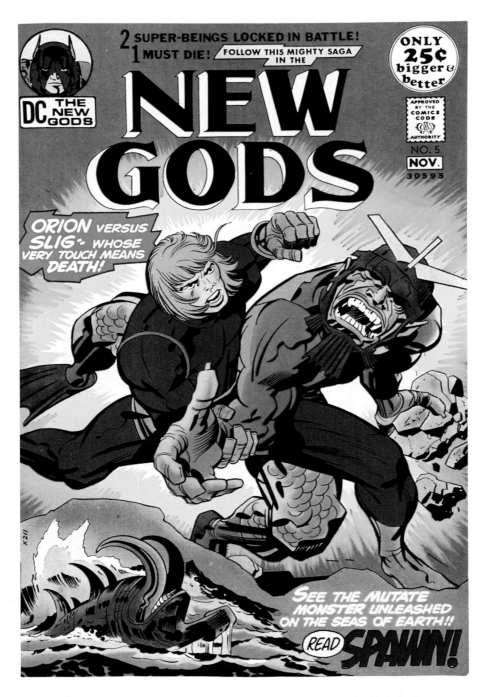

Jack Kirby created *New Gods* as part of a thematically linked group of titles that included *The Forever People* and *Mr. Miracle*. Concerned with an epic struggle between good and evil, the intertwined storylines were rich with mock-Shakespearean dialogue and apocalyptic visuals. This action-packed cover is the work of Kirby and inker Mike Royer.

©1971 by National Periodical Publications, Inc.

early 1940s. Kirby placed Jimmy and the Legion into weird and wild adventures with vampires, werewolves and, once, Don Rickles. Although DC had originally wanted Kirby to energize Superman, they apparently weren't happy with Kirby's rendering of the character—the Superman heads in all the Kirby *Jimmy Olsen* issues were redrawn by longtime Superman artist Al Plastino.

Kirby followed *Jimmy Olsen* with his complex New Gods/Fourth World concept, an epic drama that unfolded in no less than three separate titles—*Mister Miracle*, *Forever People*, and *New Gods*. With them, Kirby created an enormous mythology of his own, made up of bits and pieces of myths and popular culture that had influenced his work over the years. The saga involved new gods, New Genesis, the Astro-Force, and beings named Darkseid, Orion, Lightray, and Metron. Writing the book as well as drawing it, Kirby blended his wall-banger style—"Krak! Bam! Pow! Pow! Pow! Blaam!"—with dialogue worthy of an Elizabethan tragedy: "FIEND OF THE PITS! No being of New Genesis ever spawned one like YOU!! You're something OUT of any known realm!!" "HAHAHAH—I smell the seeds of FEAR sprouting in your stone heart, Kalibak!"

Kirby's grandiose new comic books had power and plenty of operatic splendor, but all were canceled within a couple years of their debuts. (Kirby maintained that "they were in DC's top 10.") Because Kirby had a five-year contract with DC, he came up with other comics. These included *The Demon*, which lasted from late 1972 to early 1974, and *Kamandi, the Last Boy on Earth*. In *The Comic Book Heroes* Will Jacobs and Gerard Jones describe the latter book as "a twist on *Planet of the Apes*, about a human boy in a post-nuclear-war future in which other animals have gained intelligence and reduced mankind to [slavery] . . . It was allowed to become repetitious when Kirby settled for a long series of different talking animals (including even talking snails)." *Kamandi* held on until 1978, but Kirby had long since left the title. He also came up with *OMAC*, another science fiction comic, about a One Man Army Corps in a futuristic setting. That failed, too.

For Kirby, the artist who had been dubbed the King of Comic Books in the 1960s, the seventies were years of decline. "Kirby's art took a slow but steady turn for the worse," comments *The Comic Book Heroes*. "At the same time, his scripting, always unusual, began to take a swing toward the oblique and confusing." His art, always heavily stylized, became almost a parody of the classic Kirby style. Human figures became impossibly musclebound and stiff, faces became uninvitingly harsh and angular. Even the artist's flair for movement and action became static and flat. When his contract ran out in 1975, Kirby left DC.

DC stumbled with Jack Kirby's overblown superheroes, but found considerable success

Much of the imagination had gone out of Jack Kirby's work by the time he created *Kamandi* in 1972. The title borrowed ideas from many sources, notably from the film *Planet of the Apes*. Cover art is by Kirby and inker Mike Royer.

with a clever variation on the horror genre—*Swamp Thing*, one of the key comic book titles of the early 1970s. Owing a great deal to Theodore Sturgeon's short story "It" and to a villain from 1940s comic books known as the Heap, this walking compost pile first appeared in DC's *House of Secrets* in 1971 and was promoted to a book of his own the following year. Writer Len Wein and artist Berni Wrightson wove peculiarly moving tales featuring a scientist who has been transformed into a muck-encrusted horror after being doused by chemicals when his bayou lab is destroyed by criminals. Wein's scripts were unexpectedly touching, even philosophical, but the real selling point of *Swamp Thing* was the spidery, vaguely disturbing artwork of Wrightson, a young man under the spell of fantasy illustrator Frank Frazetta and legendary EC horror artist Graham "Ghastly" Ingels.

Marvel, apparently by coincidence, had hit the stands with a similar protagonist, Man-Thing, only weeks earlier. The Comics Code relaxed somewhat in the early seventies, opening the door for Swamp Thing, Man-Thing, and other ooky monsters. Marvel featured a variety of such critters in *Werewolf by Night*, *Chamber of Chills*, and *Supernatural Thrillers*. These and similar efforts brought a certain liveliness to comic books, but the greatest comic book monster of the seventies was a fresh interpretation of Dracula, introduced by Marvel in 1972. *Tomb of Dracula*, drawn from the outset by Gene Colan and scripted after the first few issues

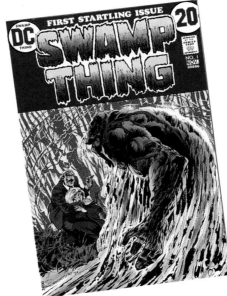

With *Swamp Thing*, writer Len Wein and artist Berni Wrightson brought an unexpected gothicism to the "ooky monster" genre. In time, the feature would inspire a pair of movies and a television series.

©1972 by National Periodical Publications, Inc.

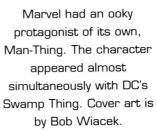

Marvel had an ooky protagonist of its own, Man-Thing. The character appeared almost simultaneously with DC's Swamp Thing. Cover art is by Bob Wiacek.

©1974 by Marvel Comics Group

Tomb of Dracula was not merely the best horror comic of the seventies and a success for Marvel, but one of the best comics of any type to be published during the decade. Writer Marv Wolfman and illustrators Gene Colan and inker Tom Palmer created stories of impressive scope and power. This glimpse of the undead count is from *Tomb of Dracula* #6.

©1972 by Magazine Management co. Inc., Marvel Comics Group

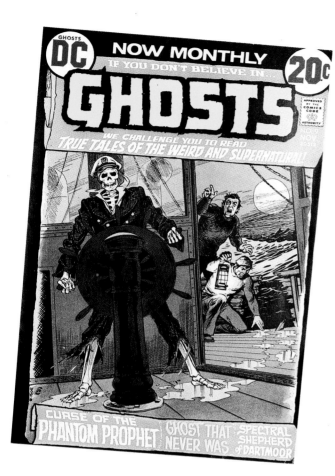

As in the fifties, DC's horror titles of the seventies were innocuous and faintly dull. Nick Cardy drew this handsome but cliched cover for *Ghosts*.

©1972 by National Periodical Publications, Inc.

EC Comics pioneered the idea of oversize, magazine-style comic books in the middle fifties, when the company was feeling the heat of educators and other critics of traditional comic books. The magazines were dubbed "Picto-Fiction," and had black-and-white or two-color interiors. This remarkably effective *Terror Illustrated* cover is by longtime industry star Reed Crandall.

©1955 by I. C. Publishing Co., Inc.

by Marv Wolfman, was not simply an effective spook comic, but one of the finest and most imaginative titles of the decade. "Wolfman was able," commented Jacobs and Jones, "to unite horror, mystery, humor, tragedy and warmth in—of all unexpected places—a vampire comic." Colan, a skilled draftsman with a talent for disjointed panel layout, brought an effective disquiet to the feature.

Horror also provided the entree for magazine-size, black-and-white comic books, publications with an ostensibly more adult content than that of traditional comics. EC Comics's text-heavy (and short-lived) "Picto-Fiction" magazines had pioneered the concept in the mid-fifties, but it was not until 1965 that the idea succeeded. At that time, James Warren, the publisher of *Famous Monsters of Filmland*, introduced *Creepy* and, soon after, *Eerie*, black-and-white comics that sold for thirty-five cents. Because of their size and price, the magazines were not classified as regular comic books and didn't fall under the jurisdiction of the Comics Code Authority. Warren was able, therefore, to emulate the style and tone of the EC horror comics without running afoul of anyone. When Warren added *Vampirella* in 1969, the kind of "good girl" art that had nearly vanished with the retirement of publisher Victor Fox made a comeback. Archie Goodwin and Bill Dubay contributed many scripts to Warren's titles, and stories were drawn by highly talented EC veterans such as

Publisher James Warren offered a variation on EC's Picto-Fiction idea when he introduced *Creepy* in 1964. Printed with black-and-white interiors and free of the scrutiny of the Comics Code, Creepy was free to give readers a good thrill ride. The early issues—written mainly by Archie Goodwin and illustrated by a number of original EC artists—were the most effective. The cover for Creepy #4 was painted by celebrated fantasy artist Frank Frazetta.

©1965 by Warren Publishing Co.

Creepy was a success and inspired a pair of companion *magazines—Eerie* and *Vampirella.* The overtly sexy tone of the latter title is amply suggested by the Frank Frazetta cover painting that adorned Vampi's first issue.

©1969 by Warren Publishing Co.

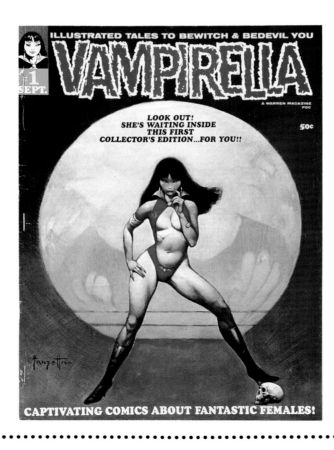

George Evans, Reed Crandall, Alex Toth, Al Williamson, Frank Frazetta, Johnny Craig, Angelo Torres, and Jack Davis.

Like Warren, Marvel used the monochrome format to offer material that would not have been possible under the strictures of the Code. The company initiated its own line of black-and-white comics in the early 1970s, with *Savage Tales, Savage Sword of Conan*, and others that exploited the popularity of the company's *Conan the Barbarian*. Horror titles followed in 1973—*Dracula Lives, Vampire Tales, Tales of the Zombie*, and *Monsters Unleashed*. Besides Marvel's version of Count Dracula, the horror titles featured Frankenstein's Monster and a curvy new villainess named Satana.

The jungle genre, another old standby from comics' glory days, was revived in the seventies. Unlike horror, though, jungle stories were tied to a cultural mindset that, by the seventies, seemed very dated. Indeed, the popularity of Tarzan, the greatest of all jungle heroes, had slipped badly by 1970. The character's moribund comic book sales contributed to a decision by Edgar Rice Burroughs, Inc. to end a long association with Western-Gold Key and license Tarzan and other Burroughs creations to DC. Artist Joe Kubert, a comics industry veteran and one of its top talents, headed up the resulting titles. *Tarzan #207*, carrying on the Gold Key numbering, was the first DC issue and appeared early in 1972. Kubert, who wrote and drew the jungleman's adventures, returned to the Tarzan of the early novels and even adapted several of them. He set the stories in the early years of this century, in a fantasyland jungle populated by black savages and citizens of lost cities and ancient empires. It was handsome, imaginative material that, like the original novels by Edgar Rice Burroughs, had little relation to life in the real Africa. Unfortunately comic book readers didn't seem particularly interested in Burroughs's jungle lord, so DC shut down their jungle operation in 1977. Marvel, who'd been doing a comic with their imitation Tarzan, Ka-Zar, dropped him and took over the real thing. The Marvel *Tarzan* was even less successful than DC's, lasting only two years.

While affiliated with ERB, Inc., DC also produced *Korak, Son of Tarzan*. Kubert edited and wrote the scripts for the adventures of the teenage character and Frank Thorne did an impressive job of drawing. *Carson of Venus*, scripted by Len Wein and drawn by Mike Kaluta, was the backup feature. The book expired in 1975. *The Tarzan Family* succeeded *Korak* and lasted only a year. *Weird Worlds* offered John Carter of Mars and David Innes, who hung out at the Earth's core. The magazine ended in 1974. Burroughs's Mars saga, like Tarzan, eventually moved to Marvel and, as *John Carter, Warlord of Mars*, made it through twenty-nine issues. Gil Kane was the initial artist.

Neither fantasy nor horror were the big stories of comic

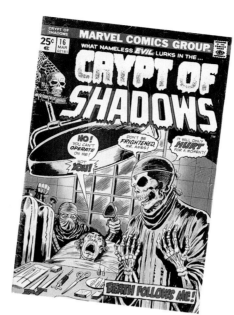

The relaxed standards of the Comics Code allowed horror comics to make a mild comeback in the 1970s. *Crypt of Shadows* was a competent but unremarkable entry from Marvel.

©1975 by Marvel Comics Group

DC took a stab at adapting Edgar Rice Burroughs's Tarzan in the early seventies. Although effectively written and beautifully drawn by Joe Kubert, the title failed to attract a large readership.

©1974 by Edgar Rice Burroughs, Inc.

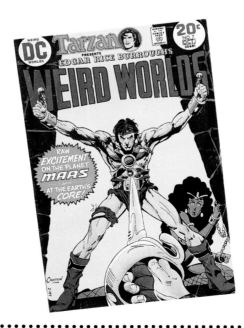

Another Burroughs title, *Weird Worlds,* adapted the adventures of David Innes and John Carter of Mars. Cover art on this 1973 issue is by Howard Chaykin.

©1973 by Edgar Rice Burroughs, Inc.

Comic book fans were rightly impressed by a series of hard-hitting issues of *Green Lantern* that were written by Denny O'Neil and illustrated by Neal Adams and Dick Giordano. Besides the obvious appeal of Adams' drafstmanship, the stories benefited from O'Neil's grasp of social problems; comic books were suddenly "relevant." These powerful panels are from *Green Lantern* #76.

©1970 by National Periodical Publications, Inc.

books in the seventies. The new byword—and source of some of the industry's most significant successes—was *relevance*. Comic books suddenly wanted to grow up and reflect the real world. This they did, and the architects of this movement were a creative team at DC, artist Neal Adams and writer Denny O'Neil.

Neal Adams had been something of a boy wonder. Working in a slick, "realist" style that had been influenced by the newspaper strip work of Stan Drake and the advertising art of onetime comic book artist Lou Fine, Adams was drawing the syndicated *Ben Casey* newspaper strip before his twenty-first birthday. Switching to comic books in the middle 1960s, Adams first won wide notice with DC's *Deadman*. In 1970, Adams was teamed with O'Neil and

given the job of revitalizing Batman. The two got rid of all traces of 1960s camp and made the caped crusader once again, to quote DC, "a grim avenger of the night, a shadowy crimefighter who stalked back alleys." That same year, working with editor Julius Schwartz, Adams and O'Neil spruced up the *Green Lantern* book and teamed him with the Green Arrow. This title ushered in the era of relevance at DC.

"I considered myself a combination journalist and fiction writer," O'Neil has said. "In the early sixties the 'new journalists'—Wolfe, Mailer, Breslin and Hamill—were combining fiction techniques with reporting. I wondered if comic book news journalism was possible." O'Neil wanted these new books to be, "Not fact, not

current events presented in panel art, but fantasy rooted in the issues of the day."

Among the issues that O'Neil eventually explored in his thoughtful *Green Lantern* stories were racism, overpopulation, pollution, and drug addiction. The drug abuse problem was dramatized in an unusual and unprecedented way when Green Arrow's boy companion Speedy was revealed as a heroin addict. This endeared DC to the dedicated college readers of the period and won awards for both artist and writer. Sales, however, weren't especially influenced by all the praise and by the middle 1970s this type of crusading had pretty much ceased.

Still, a barrier of sorts had been breached, and comics entered a new, franker era. Marvel dealt with a few social ▶

WHY A DUCK?

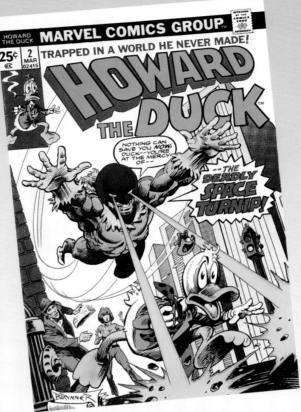

"Trapped in a world he never made!" That was the existential plight of Steve Gerber's unique creation, Howard the Duck. Cover art on Howard's second issue is by Frank Brunner.

©1975 by Marvel Comics

Of all the ducks who have flourished in comic books— Donald Duck, Daffy Duck, Super Duck, and Uncle Scrooge—the strangest of all must be the cigar-smoking fowl named Howard. Extraterrestrial in origin but looking for all the world like a funny-animal character come to life, Howard won his own comic book late in 1975, after appearing in Marvel's *Fear* and *Man-Thing*. An anomaly of comic book history, *Howard* wasn't exactly a funny animal comic, nor was it a superhero title. The world in which Howard had to function—a freely rendered version of Cleveland, Ohio—was the "realistic" one inhabited by most of Marvel's heroes and heroines. Confused and angry at being stranded on Earth, and (as cover blurbs reminded us) "trapped in a world he never made," Howard was more a figure of confrontation than humor.

Talkative and cynical, Howard was used by writer-creator Steve Gerber to comment on a wide variety of social issues. Gerber had scripted Marvel superhero titles like *The Defenders*, so Howard also poked fun at the fairly rigid Marvel superhero "formula." Critic Dale Luciano, writing in *The Comics Journal*, felt the Gerber stories had "an abrasive, zany, satirical clout without taking themselves too seriously."

Frank Brunner was the feature's original artist, and was succeeded by Gene Colan beginning with *Howard the Duck* #4. The title lasted for thirty-one issues, and was canceled in 1979; two additional issues that carried on the original numbering appeared in 1986, to coincide with the movie *Howard the Duck*, a big-budget flop. The sarcastic bird also appeared in the nine-issue run of the black-and-white *Howard the Duck Magazine*. Additionally, Gerber and Colan turned out the cryptic and short-lived *Howard the Duck* newspaper strip that was distributed by the Register and Tribune Syndicate.

topics in the early seventies, most noticeably in a three-issue drug abuse story in *Spider-Man* in 1971. At that point the Comics Code still did not allow drug stories, not even anti-drug stories. In an unprecedented move, Marvel boldly went ahead and brought out the issues without the Code seal on the covers. Amazingly enough, the world did not end and the issues reached the nation's newsstands without incident. Clearly, the Code no longer had the clout it had enjoyed in the 1950s.

"Forced into an awareness of the changing times," Jacobs and Jones pointed out in *The Comic Book Heroes*, "the Comics Code Authority granted more freedom to the industry." This is the true significance of the well-meaning but self-conscious shift to "relevant" stories.

Marvel's increased "social awareness" (which one might interpret as simply a casting about for new ways to boost sales) led to the introduction of black heroes. The first, a tough, urban mercenary named Luke Cage, was first seen in his own title, *Hero For Hire* #1 (June 1972). Archie Goodwin scripted, with art provided by penciller George Tuska and inker Billy Graham. A more fanciful hero, the Black Panther, was launched in 1973 in *Jungle Action* #6; the creative team on this superhero feature (which had no link or relationship to the Black Panther political movement of the 1960s) was writer Don McGregor and artist Billy Graham.

Along with a willingness to create characters and stories that mirrored contemporary

Spider-Man #96 was the first of a three-issue storyline that had a drug-abuse sub-plot. Because the Comics Code still prohibited "drug stories" at that time, approval of the issues was denied. Marvel put a big dent in the Code's power by successfully publishing the three issues without the Code seal. Cover art is by Gil Kane.

©1971 by Magazine Management Co., Inc., Marvel Comics Group

The action and streetwise sass of black-action films undoubtedly inspired Marvel to come up with the urban mercenary named Luke Cage. John Romita created the dynamic cover for Cage's debut issue.

©1972 by Magazine Management Co., Inc., Marvel Comics Group

Movies of all sorts inspired comic books in the seventies. The Bruce Lee/kung fu craze led to *Master of Kung Fu*, which debuted in the *Special Marvel Edition* tryout book. Cover art is by Jim Starlin.

©1973 by Marvel Comics Group

concerns, comics had learned to exploit fads. In 1972 a low-budget Chinese martial arts film called *Fists of Fury* was released in the United States. Audiences composed mainly of boys and young men were awed by the lightning-fast moves of the film's star, Bruce Lee. Nineteen seventy-two also brought *Kung Fu*, a philosophical action show starring David Carradine that was a moderate hit for ABC television. A subsequent Bruce Lee vehicle, the American-made *Enter the Dragon*, was a box-office smash in 1973, and led to a moderate karate and kung fu craze that inspired several comic books. The most successful, and certainly the oddest, was Marvel's *Master of Kung Fu*. The master was a young Asian man named Shang-Chi, who was the son of no less a personage than the insidious Dr. Fu Manchu. The comic book mixed elements from Sax Rohmer's overwrought novels and the movies and serials derived from them with the latest props, paraphernalia, and tone of the films churned out by Bruce Lee and his many imitators (who included Bruce Li, Bruce Le, and Bruce Lei). A cult favorite, *Master of Kung Fu* was originally the work of artist Jim Starlin and scripter Steve Englehart. Doug Moench eventually took over the scripting and Paul Gulacy and Mike Zeck took over the art chores. Marvel added a black-and-white version, *Deadly Hands of Kung Fu*, and another martial arts title, *Iron Fist*, before the craze subsided. DC—never quite as skilled as Marvel at exploiting trends—suffered a pair of kung

Marvel and scripters Len Wein and Chris Claremont had a huge hit with an all-new version of *X-Men*. This clever cover by penciller Dave Cockrum and inker Terry Austin features some of the new personnel (clockwise, from left): Storm, Colossus, Nightcrawler, and Wolverine.

©1978 by Marvel Comics Group

fu flops, *Richard Dragon, Kung Fu Fighter* and *Karate Kid*.

Marvel found still more success with mutants, a type of character that made a great leap forward in 1975. The original X-Men had been in limbo for several years, existing only in reprints. Then Marvel issued an annual titled *Giant-Size X-Men*, which introduced a new batch of teenage mutant heroes. This included Colossus, Nightcrawler, Thunderbird, Storm, Banshee, and a pathologically violent anti-hero named Wolverine. Len Wein was the writer, Dave Cockrum the artist. Starting with *X-Men* #94 (August 1975) the group began appearing in brand new adventures in their own, revived magazine. Very shortly Chris Claremont took over as writer and made the X-Men his own for the next several years. His intricate plots, stretching over many issues and mixing fantasy, science fiction, physical transmutation, adolescent anguish, identity crises, and topics of the day, won an increasing readership. The success of the new, improved bunch encouraged Marvel to add more mutant characters to their lineup over the years and inspired other publishers to do likewise.

As DC and Marvel battled for industry dominance, publisher Martin Goodman returned to comics in 1974. He had retired from Marvel, but later decided to reactivate his old Atlas trade name and start a new line that would rival DC and Marvel. His son Chip helped run the company with the help of Larry Lieber, Stan Lee's brother. "21

Action Packed Full Color Comics!" was what the reborn Atlas promised and the titles began appearing at the end of 1974. There was *Iron Jaw*, described as "a savage sword and sandal epic set in the far future," written by Michael Fleisher and drawn by Mike Sekowsky and Jack Abel; *Wulf the Barbarian*, featuring another fellow who practiced the sword and sandal trade, this time on "a planet the size of which is beyond mortal comprehension"; *Planet of Vampires*, "the story of six astronauts who return from a Mars mission to find Earth devastated by biological warfare . . . and a super-scientific race of vampires!" For hero enthusiasts, Atlas provided *Phoenix, Cougar*, and *Scorpion*. There was also *Targitt*, a Dirty Harry knockoff that was the "story of one man's vengeance against the mob," and *Police Action*. For those who yearned for the sort of thrills offered by the antics of the Hulk and the Thing, Atlas offered *The Brute*, "a CroMagnificent comic" about a frozen caveman who thaws out in the contemporary world.

Ambitious to a fault, Atlas promised a line of black-and-white books as well. Two of them, *Weird Tales of the Macabre* and *Thrilling Adventure*, actually reached the stands. *Tales of the Sorceress*, intended to star a horned, Vampirella type, never did.

Because Atlas was paying top dollar, it was able to recruit some talented people; contributors included artists Howard Chaykin, Steve Ditko, Alex Toth, Russ Heath, Frank Thorne, Neal

Neal Adams provided a gutsy cover for the first issue of *Ironjaw* but, as with all of the Atlas product, the title was undone by poor distribution and the readers' sense that they'd seen it all before.

©1975 by Seaboard Periodicals, Inc.

Targitt was the Atlas Comics knockoff of *Dirty Harry* and similarly violent cop thrillers that filled movie screens in the 1970s. Cover art is by Dick Giordano.

©1975 by Seaboard Periodicals, Inc.

San Francisco Comic Book was one of many undeground "comix" that simultaneously mocked and paid homage to traditional comic book formats. Cover art was provided by the redoubtable Robert Crumb, creator of *Zap Comix*.

©1970 by The Print Mint

Like Robert Crumb, *Bijou Funnies* cover artist Skip Williamson worked in a modern variation of the "bigfoot" cartoon style of the thirties.

©1970 by Bijou Publishing Empire, Inc.

Adams, Howard Nostrand, and John Severin, and writers Archie Goodwin and Rick Meyers.

As the descriptions of the Goodman titles suggest, there was very little that was fresh and original about any of the company's books. Theoretically, an entrepreneur should be able to set up a successful line of comics simply by imitating the industry's dominant players. But the Goodmans, plagued by problems within their office and by a weak distribution system, weren't able to bring it off. Before 1975 was over, the new Atlas line was gone.

Like other failed comic book publishers before them, the Goodmans learned that effective distribution is essential to broad-based, mainstream publishing success. But although comic books had become a very sophisticated business by the seventies, a place did exist for small publishers who put out esoteric or special-interest titles. This had first become apparent in the late sixties, when so-called underground "comix" produced mainly in San Francisco began to reach a select, enthusiastic audience. Not bothered by the Comics Code Authority or even the reproach of polite society, artist-writers like Robert Crumb, Rick Griffin, Gilbert Shelton, S. Clay Wilson, Jay Lynch, Spain Rodrigues, Greg Irons, Trina Robbins, Skip Williamson, and a host of others began turning out comic books that they published and distributed themselves.

The creators of underground comix rightly perceived themselves as purveyors of legitimate alternatives to the mass-produced product of DC and Marvel. An alarming proportion of the underground comic books were crude and peurile, but the best examples were vibrant, witty, and entertaining in an anarchic sort of way. Mainly satiric, underground comix poked fun not just at society's political foibles and sexual hang-ups, but at the whole idea of comic books themselves. *Young Lust*, for instance, was a hilarious takeoff of romance comics, while *Skull* was a sinister, darkly funny homage to EC's horror comics. Other notable underground titles—*Zap Comix, Gothic Blimp Works, Bijou Funnies, Snarf, Slow Death, Trashman, The Fabulous Furry Freak Brothers*—tickled readers with their irreverence and raunch. Mainstream comic book artists like Basil Wolverton and Harvey Kurtzman were among the idols of some of those involved in comix, and many of the early efforts resembled scruffy, psychedelic versions of Kurtzman's *Mad*.

Because of their unremitting (and quite unapologetic) interest in sex, drugs, and other taboo topics, the comix could not be distributed through normal channels and were sold instead in head shops and in a new sort of outlet—stores that specialized in regular comic books and science fiction. Finally, comic book fans could pick up their comics at shops where new titles were always in plentiful supply, where old issues were often available, and where the customers could meet other comic book fans. No longer ▶

Skull cover artist Greg Irons drew from the EC tradition established by artists like Jack Davis.

©1972 by Corben, Irons & Veitch

ROBERT CRUMB: GURU OF THE UNDERGROUND

Cartoonist Robert Crumb illustrated his frightening encounter with one of his ruder creations, Mr. Snoid. This self-portrait is from *Snoid Comics*.

©1980 by R. Crumb

One of the founding fathers of underground comix, Robert Crumb has remained stoutly independent. Better known than any of his comix colleagues, the iconoclastic Crumb popularized the phrase "Keep on truckin'," and has seen his style aped by advertising art directors and mainstream illustrators. But he himself has been steadfast in his desire to maintain the purity of his work, and remain out of the limelight.

Robert Crumb was born in Philadelphia in 1943. As a youngster, he was enamored of the Walt Disney comic book characters, particularly the Disney-duck stories by artist-writer Carl Barks. Throughout the fifties, Crumb wrote and drew homemade comic books with his older brother, Charles. The first of these, *Diffy in Shacktown*, was completed in 1950, when Crumb was seven years old.

By 1962, full of post-adolescent anxiety and eager to escape Philadelphia, Crumb moved to Cleveland, where he found work as a color separator and, later, illustrator at American Greetings, the nation's second-largest manufacturer of

greeting cards. One of Crumb's more notable efforts while with American Greetings was *Roberta Smith, Office Girl*, a comic strip he wrote and drew for the company newsletter. It was at this time also that Crumb created Fritz the Cat, the bourgeois, middle-class tomcat who yearns to be a political revolutionary and sexual athlete.

Crumb moved to New York City in 1965 and knocked around various comics-oriented art studios. He assisted on backgrounds for Harvey Kurtzman's *Little Annie Fanny* strip and did some work for the Topps gum card company. By early 1967, Crumb had moved to San Francisco. Caught up in the full flower of the hippie movement, he dropped LSD and did his first sketchbook renderings of some of the characters that would later make him world famous: Mr. Natural, Flakey Foont, the Snoid, Eggs Ackley, and others.

A self-styled loner, Crumb became a sort of graphic Boswell to the Haight-Ashbury scene. During this period he launched *Zap Comix*, described as "the first successful underground

Not all of Robert Crumb's work has been mischievous. The *Despair* cover is an example of the darker side of his nature. This issue of *Snoid Comics* provides an excellent example of Crumb's "bigfoot" cartoon style.

©R. Crumb (Despair); ©1980 by R. Crumb (Snoid Comics)

comic book," and also sold *Fritz the Cat* to the men's magazine *Cavalier*.

By the early seventies, underground comix had become a publishing phenomenon that could be found in head shops and "alternative" bookstores around the world. Crumb was amazingly prolific during this time, and created or contributed to many comix titles, including *Bijou Funnies*, *Bizarre Sex*, *Uneeda Comics*, *Head Comix*, *Slow Death*, and *Homegrown Funnies*.

Animator Ralph Bakshi produced a feature-length, X-rated cartoon, *Fritz the Cat*, in 1972, but Crumb has generally not been interested in "mainstream" success. Although courted at various times by ad agencies, film producers, merchandisers, and even *Playboy* magazine, he has chosen to produce highly personal—and hilariously funny—comics stories for publication in small-circulation magazines. Even while under siege by the IRS in the 1970s, Crumb remained true to his convictions, refusing to go for the easy buck. Since the eighties, his work has been seen most regularly in *Weirdo* magazine, which

is distributed mainly to comic book shops.

Crumb's drawing style is an intense blend of a multitude of influences. These include the funny animal comics he'd doted on as a child, the "bigfoot" newspaper-cartoon style of the twenties and thirties, 19th-century political cartoons, and the mainstream-comic book work of such fellow eccentrics as Basil Wolverton.

As a writer, Crumb is apt to fill his work with allusions to jazz and forgotten rural blues singers, and with highly critical references to less worthy aspects of American popular culture. His work is often controversial, as evidenced by local-community reaction to his "Joe Blow" story (*Zap* #4), an outrageous attempt to mine laughs from suburban incest.

Crumb is keenly devoted to his work, and has used it with increasing frequency to reveal his own obsessions with sex and death, and his distaste for an increasingly artificial, acquisitive culture. As *The Encyclopedia of American Comics* has observed, "His pen was merciless. He spared nothing and no one, including himself."

EC Comics artist Wally Wood served as the inspiration for this *Slow Death* cover by Rand Holmes.

©1973 by Last Gasp Eco-Funnies

Spain Rodriguez, creator of *Subvert Comics*, promoted leftist politics with a radicalized variation on the Marvel superhero style.

©1972 by Spain Rodriguez

would fans have to suffer the disinterest of poorly stocked drugstores or supermarkets. At last, comic books had retail outlets of their own.

"The independent publications were traditionally distributed to collector shops in . . . irregular patterns," explained *Publishers Weekly*, "usually by specialty-shop owners themselves. This became known as 'direct distribution.' Distinct from regular magazine distribution, there were no returns [of unsold copies], but discounts given to retailers were higher."

The new age of comic book distribution was pioneered by a pleasantly gruff, bear of a man named Phil Seuling, who went from being a high school teacher to a comic book entrepreneur. He started by selling old comics by mail in the middle 1960s, staged some of the earliest comic book conventions in the Manhattan area, and got the idea in the middle 1970s to distribute DC and Marvel comics, and others, directly to comic shops. By that time there were quite a few such shops around the country. Seuling negotiated with publishers and won the right to deal directly with them and the shops. Until that time, any retailer who wanted to sell mainstream comic books had to deal with a wholesaler. Most often, a retailer would have to agree to sell all sorts of other magazines, such as *Time*, *Playboy* and *TV Guide*, along with the comics. Seuling changed all of that.

A comics industry spokesman said that Seuling's

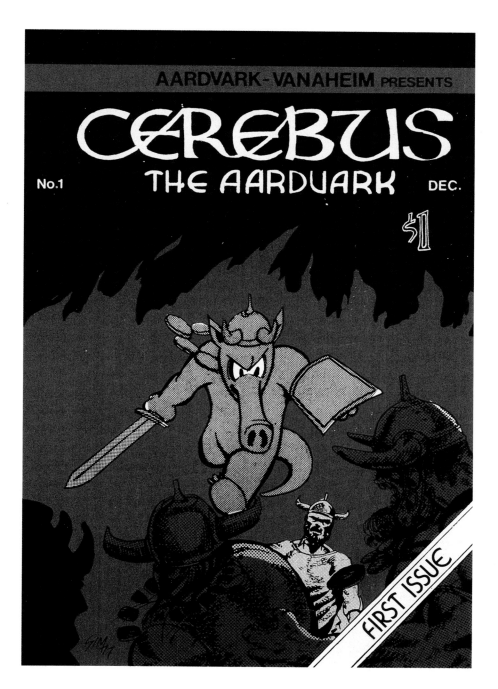

Dave Sim's *Cerebus the Aardvark* poked fun at the sword &
sorcery genre, and became one of the first independently
produced comic books to become commercially successful.

©1977 by Dave Sim

Seagate distributing outfit "grew very quickly from nothing into a multimillion dollar business, and may well have been the savior of the comics industry. We were looking at a decade of declining sales." The number of newsstands had been dwindling, the small grocery store had all but vanished, and many of the outlets that still existed no longer wanted to handle comic books because the profit margin was so small. Seuling's notion had come along at a good time and, implemented by people like Bud Plant on the West Coast, it soon took hold all over America.

The growth of comics shops encouraged the development of a new sort of comic book. Somewhat similar to underground comix, but far less explicitly "adult," the independent comic book emerged in the late 1970s. Initially produced on the cheap, with interiors printed in humble black and white, comics such as Dave Sim's *Cerebus the Aardvark* and Richard and Wendy Pini's *Elfquest* were among the earliest and most successful independents. Sim used his sword-wielding aardvark to make fun of society in general and comic books in particular, producing what *Amazing Heroes* has called "cutting satire." *Elfquest*, drawn by Wendy Pini, was a complex and personal fantasy in the tradition of J.R.R. Tolkein's epic adventures. Both *Cerebus* and *Elfquest* enjoyed vigorous sales and widespread poularity, and would have considerable influence on the shape of the comic book business of the 1980s.

CHAPTER THIRTEEN

STATE OF THE ART

F or certain comic book publishers the decade of the 1980s was the best of times and for others it was the worst of times. Some companies surged ahead and prospered. Others surged ahead, prospered briefly, and then collapsed. DC celebrated its fiftieth year in the business, Marvel its twenty-fifth under that name. Superman enjoyed a fiftieth birthday as well, and that was celebrated nationally. Batman also turned fifty and, though his birthday festivities weren't as impressive as Superman's, the movie based on his night life was a box office smash. New artists came to the fore in the eighties, and names like Frank Miller, John Byrne, and Steve Gibbons replaced those of Jack Kirby and Neal Adams on the fan-favorite lists. Black-and-white comics enjoyed another brief vogue, limited-issue "miniseries" and "maxiseries" blossomed, and book-length "graphic novels" of all sorts hit the bestseller lists. Most importantly, for the surviving publishers, the sales of comic books continued to rise; the final decade of the century promises to be, at least from a financial standpoint, the

Comic books headed into the nineties with savvy and sophistication. *Batman: The Killing Joke,* written by Alan Moore and superbly illustrated by Brian Bolland, was an off-kilter combination of familiar comic book thrills and brazenly adult situations.

© 1988 by DC Comics, Inc.

most successful so far.

From the late 1970s into the early 1980s, while the average price of a thirty-two-page comic book rose from forty cents to sixty cents, Marvel titles dominated the top of the sales lists. Each month *The Comic Reader* fanzine ran its list of the one hundred best-selling comics; in September of 1979, for example, Marvel's *X-Men*, *Amazing Spider-Man*, and *Micronauts* held the top three positions. The only DC title to place in the top twenty was *World of Krypton*, a miniseries title. The June 1980 list was headed by Marvel's *Epic*, *X-Men*, and *Star Trek*; DC didn't place in the top twenty at all. In January 1981 Marvel's *X-Men* and *Moon Knight* were at the top, but DC's *New Teen Titans* was in fifth place. By August of 1981 *Titans* was in third place and DC's *Tales of the Green Lantern Corps* was in fourth.

George Perez, who'd been lured from Marvel to DC, was the artist on the *New Teen Titans*, and it was Perez, along with writer Marv Wolfman, who revitalized the property and helped DC move up on the charts. As *Amazing Heroes* pointed out, "The *Titans* have gone on to achieve a place in the hearts of fans, enthusiasts and pros alike that had not been achieved by a new DC book for many, many years. . . . A far-reaching series whose simplicity and involvement have attracted new fans and rejuvenated the interest of old readers." Sales successes such as this one demonstrated that specific artists, writers, and combinations

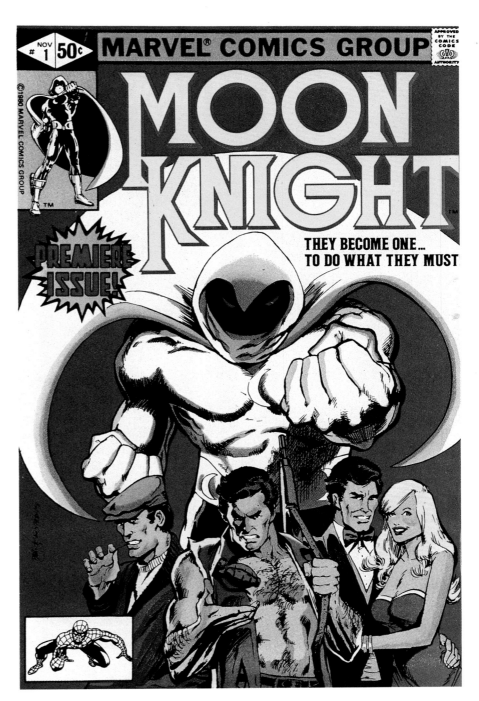

In the tradition of the Shadow, the Moon Knight operates with multiple secret identities. Bill Sienkiewicz provided the feature's handsome art.

New Teen Titans was a solid hit for DC in the early eighties. Cover artist George Perez also handled the interiors, and was a major reason for the title's success.

thereof would be increasingly important to comic book sales in the 1980s.

Every ten years or so a few young artists come along who shake up the comic book field by re-examining the established ways of telling a story. These outstanding artists in the eighties included Frank Miller, Bill Sienkiewicz, and Walt Simonson. All three developed new ways of presenting superhero material and all three bolstered the careers of established characters.

Miller was in his early twenties when he took over the drawing of Marvel's venerable Daredevil in 1979. He drew in a highly personal style that showed a variety of influences, including Will Eisner, Jim Steranko, Japanese prints, Bernard Krigstein, martial arts movies, and sophisticated European comic book artists such as Moebius and Guido Crepax. Miller was very much aware that page breakdowns can be used to control and manipulate time. As Bernie Krigstein had done at EC in the fifties, Miller experimented with multipaneled pages. He chopped them up horizontally, vertically, and sometimes sliced each tier into a half dozen or more frames. Readers soon noticed Miller's freshness of approach, and although *Daredevil* didn't shoot straight up to the lead position on the sales lists, it was very soon in the top twenty.

Late in 1980, Miller also assumed the scriptwriting of *Daredevil*. In that title, he introduced Elektra, an assassin for hire and one of the most formidable women ever seen in comics. She was Daredevil's most fascinating foe and the two of them carried on a complex love-hate relationship. "Coming in at the end of a decade of wordy, introspective, unimaginative fare, Miller distinguished himself not only as a good plotter but as a dazzlingly effective storyteller," observed Will Jacobs and Gerard Jones *The Comic Book Heroes*.

A noticeable element of Miller's storytelling was its graphicism. Censorship standards had relaxed considerably in the years since comic books had been tossed on bonfires by their critics, and Miller's *Daredevil* became increasingly bloody and violent. "Elektra was truly ruthless in her assaults, with an arsenal of Oriental death-devices," commented Jacobs and Jones. "In issue 181 (April 1982) this violence reached its culmination in the grittiest scene ever presented in a mainstream comic book. In a vicious fight between Bullseye and Elektra, Bullseye not only kills his opponent but, relishing every blow, breaks her jaw, slits her throat, and thrusts a knife through her body. Costumed heroes were clearly no longer just entertainment for children."

Another notable hero of the 1980s was Moon Knight, who had first shown up in the middle seventies in Marvel's *Werewolf By Night*. In the autumn of 1980, after appearing in other titles occasionally, he was promoted to a book of his own. Doug Moench was the scriptwriter and Bill Sienkiewicz, handling his first regular comic book assignment, was the artist. In reality the Knight was Marc Spector, "who holds three secret identities simultaneously—ruthless mercenary, rich playboy, and cab driver." In his costumed mode he battles zombies, werewolves, madmen, and sundry thieves, behaving all the while like a sort of rougher, tougher Batman. Sienkiewicz was very much under the influence of his early idol Neal Adams when he began his assignment, but gradually found an art style of his own. He favored unconventional layouts and perspectives, and figure exaggeration that was inspired by animated cartoons. In time, Sienkiewicz brought an almost lyric approach to the staging of violent scenes.

Walt Simonson had been active in comics since the early 1970s, first gaining attention for an updated version of the venerable character Manhunter in *Detective Comics*. Simonson moved to Marvel in the middle of the decade, working on *Master of Kung Fu*, *Battlestar Galactica*, *Fantastic Four*, *The Hulk*, and other top titles. In the summer of 1983, he took over both the drawing and writing of *Thor* and suddenly had a hit on his hands. The title rapidly turned hot, selling out in comic book shops across the country. The work Simonson did on *Thor* was impressive, but more subdued than his earlier output. He drew in a scratchy, cartoony manner and his layouts and page breakdowns were often eccentric. Although his stories were violent and accompanied by the usual sound effects—*krakk!*,

Wolverine first appeared in *X-Men* in the mid-seventies, and quickly became a reader favorite. As his gleeful expression might suggest, Wolverine enjoys violence. The cover art is by Klaus Janson

© 1982 by Marvell Comics Group

Walt Simonson's powerful sense of design and flair for action won him many fans, and turned *Thor* into a best-selling title.

©1983 by Marvel Comics Group

DC's violent man of action is Vigilante. The cover of his debut
issue was created by Keith Pollard.

©1983 by DC Comics, Inc.

thakk!, barrowham!—Simonson,
unlike many of his young
colleagues, did not dwell on
bloodshed.

Simonson's restraint aside,
there is no denying that violence
sells. It sells movie tickets and
football admissions, and it sells
comic books, too. From the late
1930s onward just about every
superhero and costumed
crimefighter in comic books
operated in a vigilante fashion.
Physical force has been depicted
as the best, and final, arbitor of
complex problems. But in the
1980s an even more violent
breed of comic book vigilantes
came to prominence. Notable
among this group is Marvel's
Wolverine, a frighteningly
aggressive anti-hero who sports
razor-keen, extendable claws of
forged adamtium. Others include
the Vigilante, DC's motorcycle-
riding killer of criminals; and,
most startling of all, the
Punisher, another one-man death
squad from Marvel.

The Punisher was first seen
in 1974, when he appeared as the
villain-of-the-month in *Amazing
Spider-Man* #129. *The Official
Handbook of the Marvel Universe*
explains how the Punisher, a
former Marine captain, got to be
the way his is: "While on leave,
he took his wife and two small
children to Central Park . . . the
family happened on the scene of
a mob killing . . . Fearing
witnesses, the mobsters
murdered the captain's family in
cold blood. The captain managed
to survive the attack but was
traumatized by the incident. He
decided not to return to Marine
duty, but instead, outfitted
himself with assorted weapons

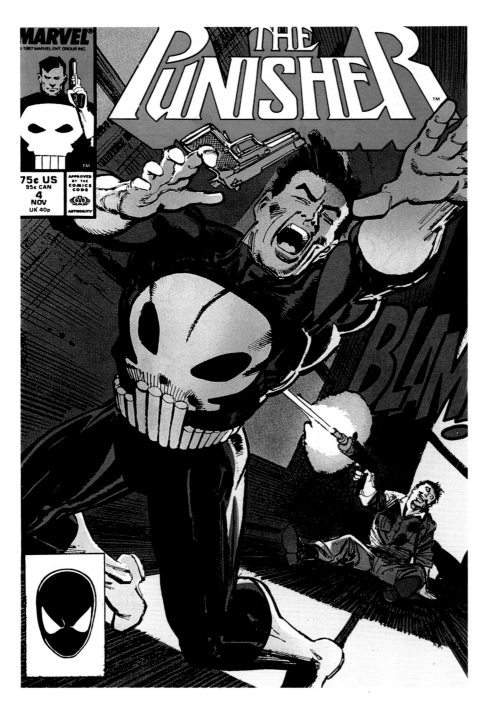

As the eighties progressed, superheroes became rougher and more violent. The roughest of all is the Punisher, a trigger-happy vigilante who stops at nothing to pursue his crusade against the underworld. Cover art is by Klaus Janson.

©1987 by Marvel Entertainment Group, Inc.

and a battle suit that displayed a large death's head on the chest, and embarked on a one-man anti-crime campaign throughout New York City."

A hero who relies not on superpowers but on his physical prowess and an arsenal of lethal weapons, the Punisher made a very successful comeback in the middle eighties. His adventures have the same grimness of tone that characterizes paperback avengers like Don Pendleton's Executioner, and Warren Murphy and Richard Sapir's Destroyer. The Punisher's origin owes something to that of Batman and something to the protagonist of Brian Garfield's 1972 novel, *Death Wish*, which inspired a series of bloodthirsty urban vigilante movies starring Charles Bronson. Punisher also has echoes of Rambo and other fictional action heroes. Many of the Punisher's best adventures have been illustrated by Klaus Janson. Mike Baron, who writes the feature's scripts, has said, "The Punisher is based on the Executioner, was inspired by him. But the Punisher, being of the world of comic books, gets to indulge in a lot more flamboyant behavior."

Like the muscular movie avengers, the Punisher is a man of action and his adventures are frequently punctuated by car chases, crashes, explosions, brawls, and, of course, shootouts. Gunshots abound—*Blam!Blam!*, *Brapp!*, *Zing!*, *Budda Budda Budda!* The Punisher's handgun also serves as a tool of interrogation—most effective when jammed into a thug's temple ("Who are you, and why do you rob banks?") or into a mouth ("Who owns this joint?"). Like other fictional heroes, Punisher never has to worry about funding for his crusade. As Baron explains, "He busts into the bad guy's place, he shoots everyone, he cracks open the wall safe and usually there's a couple of hundred thousand bucks sitting around. He has no problem getting financing whatsoever." Currently one of Marvel's more successful heroes, the Punisher's adventures can be found in three magazines. Significantly, the Code-approved title, *Punisher*, is hardly less violent than the others.

Macho heroes are perennially popular, but the late seventies and early eighties also brought some feisty women to comics. Unfortunately, the novelty of the aforementioned Elektra was not matched by Marvel's Spider-Woman, introduced in 1978 in *Marvel Spotlight* #32, or by a 1980 creation, the She-Hulk (introduced in her own title, *The Savage She-Hulk*). Competently produced in the kinetic Marvel manner, each character was nonetheless a transparent attempt to mix feminine pulchritude with the proven appeal of established comic book stars.

In 1981 Marvel introduced a far more significant female character. This was Dazzler, a beautiful mutant who worked as a disco singer. By any standard, Dazzler was just one more variation on a familiar theme, but in launching the *Dazzler* comic book, Marvel tried something

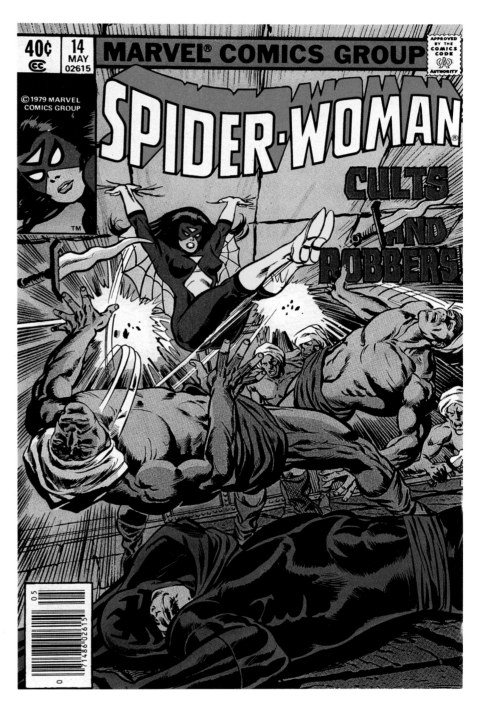

Derivative and minor, Spider-Woman nonetheless cut a pretty figure as she fought the forces of evil. Cover art is by John Romita and Tom Palmer.

that altered the nature of the comic book business. "Marvel was rapidly becoming aware that direct-sales comic shops were becoming a significant factor in comic sales," Richard Gagnon observed in *Amazing Heroes*. "The shops, at that time, were accounting for some 30 percent of Marvel comic sales. Marvel decided to give *Dazzler* a big send-off by making it Marvel's first direct-sales-only experimental comic. Expectations were high and dealers ordered 400,000 copies. . . . It was the first time that a major comic book company had intentionally bypassed the traditional method of selling a comic on the newsstands." Here, at last, was recognition from the industry's largest, most successsful publisher that direct-sales shops had the clout to make or break individual titles.

Independent publishers, selling their wares exclusively through the growing number of comic shops across the country, were also generating new heroes in the eighties. Unlike the underground publishing outfits of the sixties and seventies, most of the independents weren't interested in humor, satire, or social comment. Instead, they were out to beat Marvel and DC at their own game, namely the creation and marketing of salable heroic characters. In August of 1981, for instance, Pacific Comics introduced *Captain Victory and His Galactic Rangers*. The book marked the return to comics of Jack Kirby, the man, according to *The Comics Journal*, "many people consider the most important creative force in the

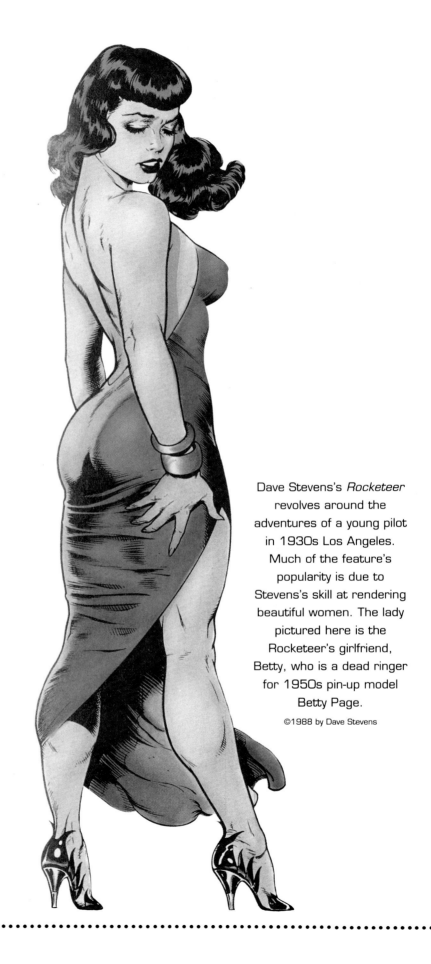

Dave Stevens's *Rocketeer* revolves around the adventures of a young pilot in 1930s Los Angeles. Much of the feature's popularity is due to Stevens's skill at rendering beautiful women. The lady pictured here is the Rocketeer's girlfriend, Betty, who is a dead ringer for 1950s pin-up model Betty Page.

©1988 by Dave Stevens

history of American comics."
The thematic territory explored
by *Captain Victory* had been well
covered by Kirby in the past, and
the title survived for only
thirteen issues. Its existence
indicated, though, that
independents were potential
outlets for established artists and
writers, and could provide an
alternate marketplace for their
work.

Other independents entered
the field, offering a variety of
superheroes and vigilante types.
Eclipse delighted readers with
Dave Stevens's *The Rocketeer*, a
whimsical, amusingly sexy series
set in the Los Angeles of the
1930s. Capital Comics found
success with *Nexus*, written by
Mike Baron and drawn by Steve
Rude, and *Badger*, another Baron
creation, "about a psychotic
costumed hero in partnership
with a fifth-century Druid." First
Comics was responsible for Mike
Grell's *Jon Sable, Freelance*;
Grimjack by writer John
Ostrander and artist Timothy
Truman; and Howard Chaykin's
American Flagg! Chaykin, a
young veteran of both Marvel
and DC, took advantage of the
fact that direct-sales books didn't
have to answer to the Comics
Code, or to any other board of
censorship or review. He
described the adventures of
Flagg, a futuristic lawman, as a
"wonderful combination of snotty
dialogue, nasty characters, venal
attitudes, petty motivations, and
sex and violence, with a bit of my
new-found prejudices."
According to historians Jacobs
and Jones, "*American Flagg!*
quickly became the most
critically acclaimed and, by most

Mike Baron and
Steve Rude's smartly
produced *Nexus* was one of
the better independent
superhero titles of the
eighties.

©1988 by First Comics, Inc.

Howard Chaykin's *American
Flagg!* poked fun at power
politics, sex, and other
human foibles, and became
one of the best-selling
independent comic books.

©1983 by First Comics, Inc. and Howard
Chaykin, Inc.

reckonings, the best-selling product of the independents, outselling some Marvel and DC titles. It has strengthened the standing of the entire [independent] movement and opened the door to sophisticated subject matter that adds a new dimension to the phrase 'adult comics.'"

Commencing in 1983 Eagle Comics began publishing magazines that recycled British material—*Judge Dredd*, *2000 A.D.*, and *Robo-Hunter*. These were grim and violent science fiction features, utilizing artists the caliber of Brian Bolland and Dave Gibbons and sophisticated writers such as Alan Moore. In an article on vigilantism in comics in a 1984 issue of *The Comics Journal* Dale Luciano said of *Judge Dredd*, "It is a jubilant, delirious *celebration* of the fascist underpinnings of most comic book adventure. . . . Dredd himself is such an amusing cartoon of bellicose, avenging justice ("*He is the LAW and you'd better believe it!*" trumpets the cover of the first issue) that I can't imagine anybody taking this stuff seriously as a symbolically earnest endorsement of vigilantism."

Bolland, a talented and meticulous artist well known in Great Britain from the late 1970s onward, began doing jobs for DC in 1980. The end of 1982 brought his *Camelot 3000*, a mix of science fiction and Arthurian lore that was written by Mike Barr and published as a twelve-part maxiseries. The title was a landmark in several ways. "It was DC's first comic book printed on high-quality paper, with

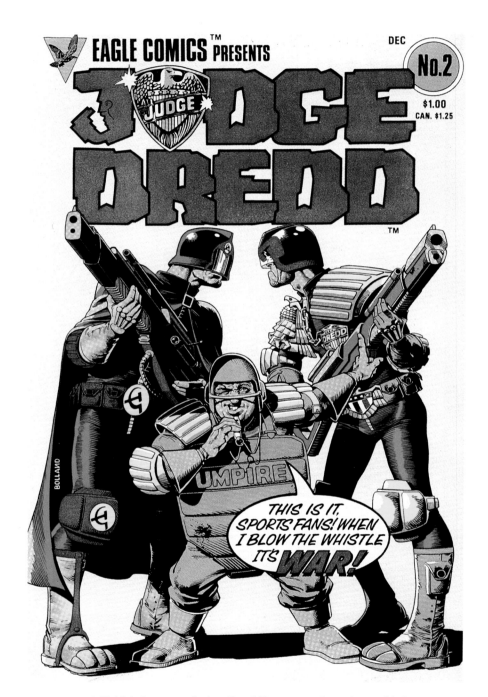

A British import, *Judge Dredd* impressed readers with its cynical humor and the splendid artwork of Brian Bolland.

©1983 by IPC Magazines Limited

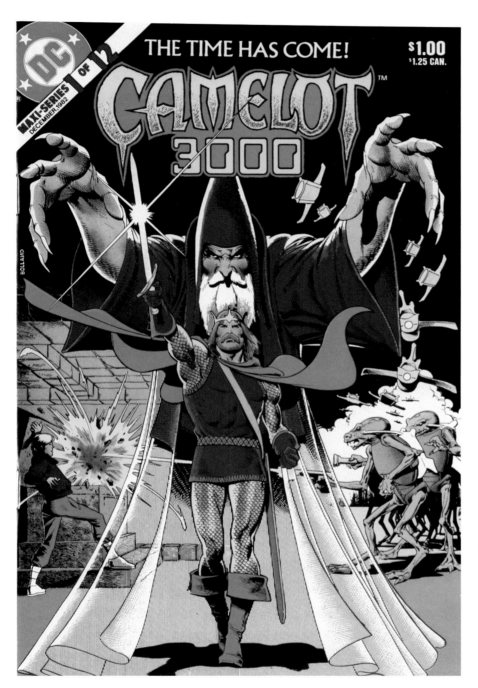

Arthurian legend was given an imaginative, futurist twist in *Camelot 3000,* a twelve-issue miniseries created by writer Mike Barr and artist Brian Bolland.

reproduction previously undreamed of for comic books," noted Don and Maggie Thompson, editors of the *Comics Buyer's Guide.* "It was one of the first DC comic books to be distributed solely through the nation's comic shops. . . . *Camelot 3000* was DC Comics' first comic book for mature readers."

Frank Miller, not to be outdone by any of comics' other young turks, had been forging ahead with interesting new projects of his own. *Ronin,* a six-part miniseries issued by DC in 1983, demonstrated Miller's fascination with Japanese culture (particularly the samurai ethic) and his admiration for some of the European comics artists—"I mean, who could look at *Valerian* or the work of [French artist] Moebius and not have it affect you some way," Miller wondered.

Miller made a tremendous splash early in 1986, when the first issue of his four-part deluxe miniseries *Batman: The Dark Knight Returns* appeared in comic shops. Written and drawn by Miller, with an inking assist by Klaus Janson, the series was an immediate and impressive success. Miller chose to portray an aging Batman, a girl Robin, and a Gotham City that was grim, shadowy, and infested with frightening crime and violence. The narrative is rife with gunfire, explosions, and bloodshed. Miller offered a gritty, almost surreal view of urban life and a realist's perspective on the implications of costumed crimefighting as a career. Horror novelist Stephen King called the *Dark Knight* series "probably the

The most notable of the new breed of comic book writer-artists is Frank Miller. The sophistication of his rendering and storytelling technique can be seen in this two-page spread from *Ronin* #1.

©1983 by Frank Miller

finest piece of comic art ever to be published in a popular edition."

Miniseries and graphic novels—rougher and tougher, higher priced, and aimed at an adult audience—remained a staple of the comic book business for the remainder of the 1980s, and will most probably continue to be so into the 1990s. Other notable examples of the form include Alan Moore and Dave Gibbons's *Watchmen*—a look at the plight of weary, aging superheroes in a corrupt world—and Moore and Brian Bolland's *Batman: The Killing Joke*, a grimly violent examination of the singular psychosis of the Joker. Both of these highly successful, critically acclaimed works were published by DC.

The graphic novel format, which has become increasingly popular in America, originated in Europe. Always more receptive to the whole idea of comics than Americans, European adults had enjoyed book-length comic book stories for decades. One of the pioneer creators was Belgian cartoonist Herge, whose first of many *Tintin* novels—fanciful, sophisticated adventures of the boy, Tintin, and his dog, Snowy—appeared in Europe in 1930. Says comics historian Richard Marschall, "Adults followed the series as avidly as did children, and were not embarrassed to be seen reading them. The books were full-length stories with subplots and twists. The Graphic Novel [sic] was established. The sophistication of expression liberated the European comic strip from its juvenile associations. Thematic preoccupations were to be as varied as the brilliant colors of the graphic novels: kids' ▶

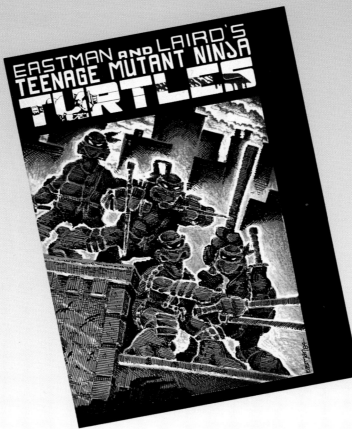

The Teenage Mutant Ninja Turtles turned into a marketing phenomenon in the late eighties. Toys, games, clothing, animated cartoons, even a live-action feature film sprang from the characters' humble beginnings in this independently published 1984 comic book.

©1984 by Mirage Studios U.S.A. Characters created by Kevin Eastman and Peter Laird.

Born in a sewer in 1984, the Teenage Mutant Ninja Turtles went on to become one of the most widely merchandised comic book properties in the world. The four of them—Donatello, Leonardo, Michelangelo, and Raphael—were created by writer Kevin Eastman and artist Peter Laird. The first issue of *Teenage Mutant Ninja Turtles*, published at the cost of $1,200 by the creators themselves, was intended as a burlesque of all the mutants, teenagers, and ninjas who flourished in mainstream comic books at the time. Transformed into superheroes by radioactive waste dumped into the sewer in which they happened to be residing, the Turtles went on to conquer not only villainy but the marketplace. Comics fans took a liking to them and, more importantly, people outside of the fan community eventually took notice. Not only did the Turtles have a catchy name, but they seemed to have special appeal to small children.

A hit television show and impressive toy sales followed.

By 1987 each of the partners was earning over $100,000 a year and today Laird and Eastman are multimillionaires. After succeeding in animated kid TV, the Turtles branched out into a variety of merchandising that included a full line of toys, costumes, video games, audio cassettes, and other products. The TMNT live-action movie released in the spring of 1990 was a box-office hit, and a sequel was rushed into production. In the meantime, young fans could enjoy arena shows featuring actors costumed as the Turtles. By early 1990, nearly two hundred companies and manufacturers worldwide were Turtle licensees—a satiric little comic book had become big, big business. It is success stories such as Laird and Eastman's that give struggling independent comic book creators the impetus to keep going, and reason to hope.

adventures; adult mysteries; science fiction; social satire; adaptations of classics; even the gamut from religious tales to pornographic stories."

The *Tintin* books have sold millions of copies, as have those featuring such latter-day European successes as Asterix, Lucky Luke, and the Schtroumpfs (known in North America as the Smurfs). European graphic novels that offer straight adventure fare have also done well, particularly the Lt. Blueberry western series by Jean Giraud (aka Moebius), Hugo Pratt's Corto Maltese tales, and Edgar Jacobs's Blake and Mortimer stories. For the past several years many of these European graphic novels, both in original foreign languages and in English translation, have been on sale in comic shops around the United States and Canada. Manhattan-based Catalan Communications has been a major publisher of English translations, and has reprinted the work of such gifted artists as Enki Bilal, Vittorio Giardino, and Milo Manera.

The existence of comic shops has also made possible several ambitious projects to reprint classic newspaper strips. Companies such as Flying Buttress, Eclipse, Eternity, Fantagraphics, and Kitchen Sink have produced high-quality volumes of *Terry and the Pirates, Thimble Theatre, Krazy Kat, Li'l Abner, Flash Gordon, Little Nemo, Wash Tubbs, Little Orphan Annie, Steve Canyon,* and *Buck Rogers.* Since larger publishing outfits, for the most part, have long ignored strip reprints, it has been

Fans of classic newspaper strips are well-served by a variety of high-quality reprint magazines. Kitchen Sink's *Steve Canyon,* which reprints Milton Caniff's impeccably done adventure strip, is one of the best.

©1985 by Milton Caniff

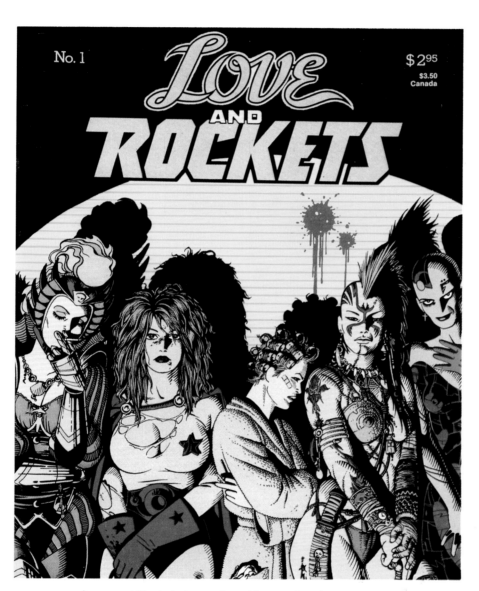

Love and Rockets is produced by two brothers, Jaime and Gilbert Hernandez. Sassy, insightful, and rich with the language and concerns of the street, the title suggests that the storytelling potential of comic books is almost limitless. The cover of the first issue was drawn by Jaime Hernandez.

©1982 by Gilbert and Jaime Hernandez

the independents who have carried on a comic book tradition that began nearly sixty years ago with *Famous Funnies*.

Independent comic books continued to multiply through the middle 1980s. Traditionally sized comics with black-and-white interiors, which were cheaper to produce, became especially plentiful. "As small publishers started to turn out more and more comic books of questionable to poor quality, collectors and comic-book-store retailers cut back drastically on their buying," reports *The Comic Book in America*. "At the same time that so many marginal titles were being printed, several comic-book distributors failed financially, which especially hurt the small publishers. Within a matter of months, the demand for independently produced comic books plummeted."

While many worthless titles were pruned from the stands during what came to be known as the Panic of '87, a few good ones, such as William Van Horn's satirical *Nervous Rex*, also went under. Stronger titles, like Paul Chadwick's *Concrete* and the Hernadez Brothers' *Love and Rockets*, managed to survive.

Pardoxically, perhaps, many of the long-neglected comic book genres were revived in the eighties. Even kid comics and funny animals made a comeback. In 1986 Bruce Hamilton and Russ Cochran, doing business as Gladstone Publications, Ltd., resurrected many of the Disney titles, including *Mickey Mouse*, *Uncle Scrooge*, and *Walt Disney's Comics & Stories*. Though Gladstone initially relied on reprints of the work of Carl Barks, Floyd Gottfredson, and other stalwarts of the past, the company eventually started using original material by Don Rosa, William Van Horn, and other contemporary writer-artists. The Walt Disney Company itself took over publication of the titles in 1990, installing longtime superhero scriptwriter and editor Len Wein as Editor-in-Chief.

Nineteen-ninety was also the year DC, somewhat cautiously, brought back *Bugs Bunny* as a comic book. The *Looney Tunes* title was also revived, but as a magazine that mixed comics with "puzzles, games, stories, jokes and fun galore!" Eclipse undertook to reprint Walt Kelly's *Pogo* comic book stories in a series of paperback books.

The Archie line of comics has continued to thrive, and in 1983 the company brought back *Katy Keene*, comics' most appealing clotheshorse. A new Harvey company appeared in 1986, and brought back *Richie Rich* and *Casper*. Marvel, using some former Harvey personnel, started a kid line called Star Comics in the middle 1980s. Star has tried original titles, such as *Planet Terry*, and adaptations of successful properties from elsewhere, such as *Count Duckula* and *Heathcliff*. Today many comics shops offer at least one rack or a whole section devoted to kid comics.

Adaptations of classic fiction made a comeback as well. In 1990, First Comics, in partnership with Berkley Books, launched a new series of *Classics Illustrated* comics. Forty-eight-

A glut of independent comic book titles prompted the Panic of '87, in which many worthwhile books—like William Van Horn's *Nervous Rex*—went under.

©1985 by William Van Horn

First Comics joined with Berkley Books in 1990 to launch an all-new series of *Classics Illustrated* comics. Kyle Baker's adaptation of *Through the Looking Glass* was one of the more ambitious titles.

©1990 by Berkley Publishing Group and First Publishing, Inc.

Reprint translations of Herge's marvelous *Tintin* have sold millions of copies worldwide. Their success encouraged the growth of the "graphic novel" comic book format.

©1947 by Editions Casterman, Paris, and Tournai

Below: Archie Comics rolled into the nineties in good shape. Riverdale's own femme fatale, Veronica, got a book of her own and went to Paris. Art is by Dan Parent and Dan DeCarlo. The "Inker of the Month" box at lower left suggests that Archie artists no longer labor in anonymity.

Above: The delightful Katy Keene had been an Archie Comics stalwart in the forties, when the company was known as MLJ. The beautiful fashion plate was brought back in 1983 and enjoyed modest success. Cover art on this comeback issue is by Katy's creator, Bill Woggon.

page, four-color comics in an oversized paperback format, they were sold in comic shops and bookstores for $3.75 each. Among the first titles were *Great Expectations*, illustrated by Rick Geary; *Moby Dick*, illustrated by Bill Sienkiewicz; *The Count of Monte Cristo*, illustrated by Dan Spiegle; and a selection of Poe's poems, illustrated by macabre cartoonist Gahan Wilson. Although much better drawn and printed than the *Classics Illustrated* of yesteryear, the new books served chiefly to prove that a novel is a novel and a comic book is a comic book, and that turning one into the other is usually impossible.

DC tried a different sort of classic in 1990 with a handsome four-part adaptation of *The Ring of the Nibelung*, by Roy Thomas and Gil Kane. That same year Eclipse brought out P. Craig Russell's adaptation of *The Magic Flute*.

War made a comeback in the eighties, though in grittier form than before. In 1986 Marvel began *The 'Nam*, written by Doug Murray, a wartime veteran of eighteen months in Vietnam. In 1987 Apple Comics introduced *Vietnam Journal*. Written and drawn by Don Lomax, another Vietnam vet, this black-and-white publication is undoubtedly the most realistic and downbeat war comic book to date.

The relaxed climate of the late eighties allowed the resurgence of an explicit kind of comic book horror. Not surprisingly, the content of much of the material equals or exceeds the gruesomeness of the most excessive work of the pre-Code ▶

SUPERMOVIES

Left: Weightlifting champion and movie-cowboy star Tom Tyler was perfectly cast in *The Adventures of Captain Marvel*. The 1941 serial was the first filmed adaptation of a comic book superhero. Right: Comic actor Michael Keaton put on a taciturn face and made box-office hay as the star of *Batman*.

©1941 by Republic Pictures;
©1989 by DC Comics, Inc.

There was a time when comic book heroes were not thought to have much movie box office appeal. In the 1940s, when a few of them were brought to the screen, it was in relatively low-budget serials clearly aimed at youngsters. Most moviegoers in those days were grown-ups, so few big-budget films were aimed exclusively at kids.

The first comic book superhero to turn up in movie houses was Captain Marvel, who was featured in a slick twelve-chapter serial, *The Adventures of Captain Marvel*. Released by Republic in 1941, the film featured weightlifting champion and cowboy star Tom Tyler in the title role. The following year Republic adapted another Fawcett hero, Spy Smasher, to the serial medium; Kane Richmond starred.

DC entered the serial stakes in 1943 with *Batman*, a fifteen-chapter Columbia adventure starring Lewis Wilson. DC's non-super Hop Harrigan was played by William Bakewell in a 1946 Columbia chapterplay and Ralph Byrd starred as DC's western hero, Vigilante, in a Columbia serial released in 1947. In 1948 the studio released *Superman* in fifteen episodes, with Kirk Alyn as the Man of Steel and Noel Neill as Lois Lane. Columbia struck again in 1949 with *Batman and Robin* (this time with Robert Lowery as the Caped Crusader), and brought back Kirk Alyn in *Atom Man vs. Superman* in 1950.

Superman was the first superhero to have a full-length theatrical film based on his exploits. Well, almost full-length—*Superman and the Mole Men* (1951) clocked in at a breezy fifty-eight minutes, and was the start of actor George Reeves's long asssociation with the Superman role. Fifteen years later, the popularity of the campy *Batman* television show led to an all-new theatrical adventure, *Batman*, starring Adam West, Burt Ward, and several of the other regulars from the TV series.

By 1978 the largest segment of the movie audience was young people—a fact that was not

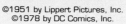

Left: *Superman and the Mole* Men: George Reeves took the lead role in this modest B-picture in 1951, went on to star in the long-running *Superman* TV series, and found lasting fame. Phyllis Coates co-starred in the movie as Lois Lane. Right: New York stage actor Christopher Reeve took the title role in *Superman* in 1978.

lost on producers of big-budget films. That year *Superman*, with Christopher Reeve as the Man of Steel and Margot Kidder as Lois Lane, was released. The movie was given a massive publicity and promotion sendoff—the fact that Marlon Brando was paid three million dollars for a brief appearance as Superman's dad was just one of the attention-getting things about the picture. A clever mix of action, comedy, and impressive special effects, *Superman* went on to become one of the top-grossing films of the year. The next two Superman movies, released in 1981 and 1983, also made it into the box office top twenty.

Finally, in 1989, came *Batman*. With a budget of at least $35,000,000, this grim, gothic adventure film was a considerable departure from the tacky serials of the 1940s and the *Zap! Pow!* silliness of the Batman television show. The movie was promoted with massive public relations and advertising campaigns that exploited the offbeat casting of comic actor Michael Kea-

ton in the title role, and the presence of superstar Jack Nicholson, cast as the villainous Joker.

Batman was a box office smash, grossing over $100,000,000 in its first ten days of release (the take rose to $142,000,000 in another week and by the end of 1989 *Batman* had grossed more than $250,000,000). The magnitude of the movie's success accelerated the sales of a mass of film-related Batman merchandise; the Associated Press estimated that Batman toys, games, costumes, and other products generated retail sales of about $650,000,000.

These eye-popping figures caused Hollywood to look at comic book characters in a new light. Many film projects were rushed into development following the success of *Batman*; not all of them will make it to the big screen, of course, but the preliminary lineup is certainly a strong one: Dr. Strange, the Fantastic Four, Watchmen, American Flagg!, the Rocketeer, Spider-Man, Ghost Rider, Blackhawk, Elektra, Nick Fury, and even Archie.

1950s. Marvel's Epic line offered *Clive Barker's Hellraiser*, an anthology of horror yarns, and DC's Piranha Press put out *Beautiful Stories for Ugly Children*. Independent publishers offered *Taboo*, *Dracula in Hell*, *Living Mummy*, and *Night of the Living Dead*. And just so that younger readers could appreciate the real stuff, original EC horror and science fiction stories became available in full-color reprint comics from Gladstone.

Relaxed climate or not, the heightened levels of sex, violence, and horror in comic books has inspired an inevitable increase of public criticism. To date, the industry has not been able to devise an acceptable system for rating comics—one that will satisfy protesting parents' groups, law officers, and distributors, as well as wary fans, artists, and writers. Some comic books now print the phrase *Suggested for mature readers* on the covers of magazines not intended for children; others put the books in sealed plastic bags. These measures arise as much from a sense of self-protection as anything else; from the middle 1980s onward there have been several instances of comic shop owners across the country being arrested or threatened with arrest for "intent to disseminate obscenity," and similar offenses. Local communities, it seems, are taking up where the Comics Code left off.

Media-watching organizations are also paying attention to comic books again. In the spring of 1989, for example, the National Coalition

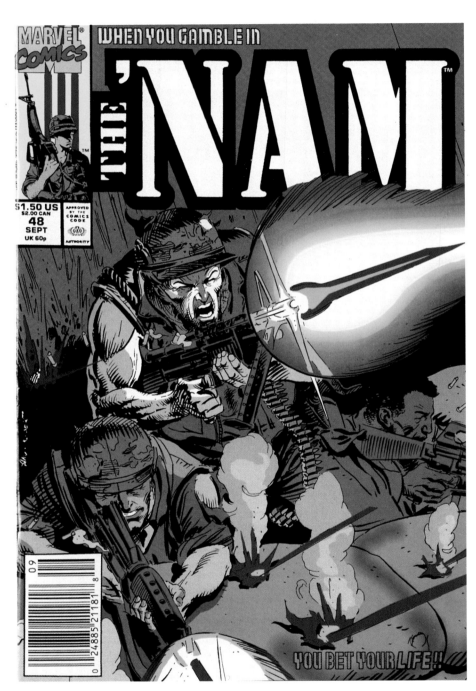

The American experience in Vietnam is chronicled in *The 'Nam*, a believably downbeat war comic published by Marvel. Cover art is by Andy Kubert, son of comic book veteran Joe Kubert.

©1990 by Marvel Entertainment Group, Inc.

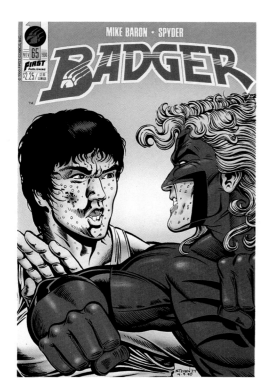

The critical eye: In a press release devoted to comic books, *Badger* was cited by the National Coalition on Television Violence as one of the titles that had unacceptable levels of violence.

©1990 by First Publishing, Inc.

on Television Violence, an Illinois-based watchdog group, sent out a press release devoted to comic book violence. It charged, among other things, that "comics of extreme and hideous violence are quite common and are having a harmful effect on children, teens and young adult readers," and that "87 percent of all comics . . . feature themes of sensationalized violence." Dr. Thomas Radecki, a psychiatrist and the organization's Research Director, was quoted as saying, "The intensity of the violence and degrading sexual material in these magazines is shocking. . . . There is no doubt whatsoever that the large majority of comic books today are having a harmful effect on our young people."

Of the eighty-three comic books surveyed by the NCTV only two, *Alf* and *Slimer*, earned an acceptable rating. Among those judged totally unfit were *Hawkmoon*, *Badger*, *Lone Wolf & Cub*, and *Wonder Woman*. The group spotted sixty-four acts of violence in Wonder Woman's June 1989 issue, including "decapitation, trampling by horses, machine gun fire, bombs, killing with crossbows, and fierce hand-to-hand combat . . . Wonder Woman fights a cheetah woman . . . until she finally kills [her] at the end of the magazine."

It seems safe to predict that attacks on comic books and attempts to regulate their content will increase in the nineties. But, since comics are no longer as pervasive as they were in the fifties—that is, they are no longer spread all over the corner drugstore or neighborhood

grocery—they probably will not get as much critical attention as they did then.

For all of the unsympathetic attention given to comics, times are generally good for comics' publishers, creators, and readers. In an annual report in the *Comics Buyer's Guide* in the spring of 1990, Maggie Thompson presented a predominantly optimistic view of the current state of the comic book business. While DC and Marvel had increased their market share slightly, independents like Kitchen Sink and Eclipse were also expanding. Experts estimated that there were between 3500 to four thousand comic shops across the country and another two thousand or so outlets that included comics among their wares. It was predicted that annual retail sales would reach $400,000,000 in 1990, a rise of well over $100,000,000 over the previous year.

Later in 1990 *CBG* reported that sales figures on many of the top titles had dropped during 1989 and that "while many comic books experienced lower sales figures, so did the nation's mainstream magazines." But since comics, unlike *TV Guide*, *Playboy*, and *Newsweek*, are sold in a growing number of specialty outlets, they may not continue to suffer from what seems to be diminishing sales for magazines of all kinds. The last decade of the century, then, should be an interesting and challenging one for that unique American art form known to fans and detractors alike as the comic book.

Comic books have entertained countless millions of casual readers over the years, and have also inspired the creative energies of dedicated fans, many of whom publish comic book "fanzines" that discuss and dissect comic books. Now nearly 40 years old, comic book fandom is rich with information and ideas, and a source of young artists and writers who will eventually join the ranks of comic book professionals.

While many aspects of popular culture attract fans, comic books seem to have engendered an especially dedicated breed of admirers. Like the equally committed science fiction fans, comics fans write letters, form organizations, issue amateur magazines called fanzines, bestow awards, and hold frequent conventions. They also support several professional publications, such as the *Comics Buyer's Guide, The Comics Journal*, and *Amazing Heroes*, as well as aiding in the rise of the comics shop.

The first fan publication to be devoted to comic books was Ted White's *The Story of Superman*, a twenty-two page, 4- by 6-inch mimeographed booklet that appeared in the summer of 1952. Although the fanzine eventually saw four editions, it was a one-shot publication.

The first comic book fanzine to be regularly issued was *Fantasy Comics*, which lasted from six to twelve issues (accounts differ) beginning in early 1953. Devoted to science fiction comic books and formatted as an 8½- by 11-inch tabloid, *Fantasy Comics* was published by longtime SF fan James Taurasi.

Among the earliest organized comic book fans were those who were enthusiastic about William Gaines's EC titles of the 1950s. Several short-lived fanzines were launched to celebrate these well-drawn and cleverly written comics. These fan publications included *The EC Fan Bulletin, The EC Fan Journal, Concept, EC Scoop, Graham Backers* (devoted to the work of artist Graham Ingels), *The EC World Press, Hoohah,* and *Potrzebie.* The EC 'zines were enthusiastic but, as the *Comic Book Price Guide* points out, "While the fan activity in response to EC comics was certainly noteworthy, it is fair to say that it never developed into a full-fledged, independent, and self-sustaining movement."

Regardless, it seems clear that much of the essence of the later comic book "fandom" movement can be traced back to reader response to EC Comics. The EC magazines themselves encouraged fan involvement and instituted letter columns in their pages. Gaines reinforced reader loyalty (and even made a few dollars) by establishing the EC Fan-Addict Club, which published a fanzine of its own, *The National EC Fan-Addict Club Bulletin.*

By the early sixties, DC and Marvel—by then the giants of the industry—also began paying attention to their readers and soliciting their comments. As the *Price Guide* notes, "The [comic book] letter departments . . . were most influential in bringing comics readers into fandom." The columns, which included the writer's addresses, gave fans

The Facts Behind Superman was Ted White's retitled version of his *The Story of Superman,* which was the first fan publication devoted to comic books.

©1953 by Ted White

Bhob Stewart's *Potrzebie*—a mimeographed fanzine dedicated to EC Comics—was available for just five cents a copy.

©1954 by Bhob Stewart

The second issue of Bhob Stewart's hectographed EC fanzine, *The EC Fan Bulletin*. Bill Spicer drew the cover in the style of EC artist/editor Al Feldstein.

©1953 by Bhob Stewart

across the country a way to contact each other.

In 1960 Dick Lupoff brought forth a fanzine called *Xero,* devoted chiefly to science fiction. It did, however contain the first installment of a series titled "All in Color for a Dime," which discussed comic books of the 1930s and 1940s. The following year Jerry Bails and Roy Thomas began publishing *Alter Ego,* described by the *Price Guide* as "the first true comics fanzine." Nineteen sixty-one also brought Don and Maggie Thompson's *Comic Art,* a fanzine covering both comic books and comic strips. Among its other accomplishments, *Comic Art* was probably the first magazine of any sort to publicly credit artist-writer Carl Barks for his anonymous work on *Donald Duck* and *Uncle Scrooge.*

Throughout the 1960s other fanzines waxed and waned—*Gosh Wow!, The Rocket's Blast Comic Collector, On The Drawing Board*, et al. Sporadically issued, many of them mimeographed, they helped build a national community of enthusiastic comics fans.

By the middle 1960s the comics convention, where comic books and related material are bought, sold, and traded, had come into being. The earliest comic book conventions were held in New York City. According to reliable sources, the very first one took place in 1964 "in an upstairs loft in Greenwich Village." Like many another notion spawned in the Village, the "comicon" idea caught on. At first the conventions were annual affairs, usually held on or around

the 4th of July. Among the earliest people to stage these events were Dave Kaler, Calvin Beck, and John Benson. In 1968, Phil Seuling organized the first Comic Art Convention, held at the New York Statler Hilton. A Brooklyn high school teacher and a longtime comic book collector and dealer, Seuling overflowed with high-energy enthusiasm; his 1968 con went on for four days.

Seuling's early annual conventions, besides offering large quantities of vintage comic books for sale, also featured numerous guests from the professional ranks of comic book and comic strip artists and writers. Among them were Bill Everett, Jack Kirby, Alex Toth, Jim Steranko, Gardner Fox, Walter Gibson, Gil Kane, Joe Kubert, Milton Caniff, and Hal Foster, as well as just about everybody who'd ever worked for the EC line.

In the early 1970s other convention organizers arrived to offer Seuling some competition. Most notable among this group were Adam Malin and Gary Berman, who inaugurated three-day New York City shows called Creation Conventions, which were usually scheduled around Thanksgiving. Seuling, perhaps to stay ahead of the competition, began a monthly series of one-day conventions in 1971. Fred Greenberg got into the convention business in the late 1970s, eventually filling the gap left when Seuling's series faded away after his death in 1984. By that time comicons had long since been established all over America. Today, the country's

EC Comics encouraged communication from readers. This Bill Elder caricature of the EC staff was sent to fans who wrote letters of comment. Clearly, the EC folks didn't take themselves too seriously.

largest cons are annual affairs held each summer in San Diego and Chicago. Additionally, monthly and bimonthly conventions are held in scores of American cities and towns.

Comics collectors and fans got their bible in 1970, when Robert M. Overstreet published the first edition of his *Comic Book Price Guide*. From the start the book had two basic purposes, spelled out by Overstreet in his initial introduction—"Everyone connected with the publication of this book advocates the collecting of comic books for fun and pleasure, as well as nostalgia, art, and cultural values. Second to this is investment, which if wisely placed in the best quality books (condition and contents considered), will lead to dividends over the long term."

To demonstrate that Overstreet was dead right about the investment potential of comic books, one has only to compare the prices in his maiden effort with those in the *Price Guide's* later editions. *Action Comics #1*, for example (the first appearance of Superman), was valued at $250 in fine condition in the *Guide's* first edition; twenty years later, the suggested price for a fine-condition copy was $15,000.

While still in high school in 1971, a young man named Alan Light started *The Buyer's Guide*, a tabloid newspaper for comic book fans and collectors. Although the publication featured articles and interviews, it functioned mainly as an ad

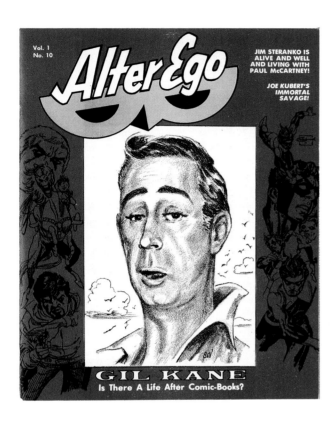

paper, in which dealers and fans could advertise old comics that they had for sale. Light sold *The Buyer's Guide* to Wisconsin-based Krause Publications in 1982, and today the publication is a fat weekly tabloid known as the *Comics Buyer's Guide*.

Another noteworthy fan-oriented publication is Gary Groth's *The Comics Journal*. Originally a tabloid, it developed into a hefty magazine devoted not only to news and interviews but to opinion, evaluation, and sharp criticism.

Although aimed at fans, the *Comics Buyer's Guide*, *The Comics Journal*, and similar publications are professional in execution and distribution. Coexisting with these well-done professional publications are

scores of small-circulation comic book fanzines that carry on the tradition established by the earliest examples of the fanzine phenomenon. These 'zines feature amateur (though not necessarily amateurish) art, fiction, criticism, and full-blown comic book stories. Contributors analyze professional comic book titles and stories, and discuss favorite artists and writers. Most importantly, the fanzines allow their publishers and contributors to be creative. Young artists and scripters who aspire to join comics' professional ranks find that the fanzine experience can be invaluable. In this sense, then, comic books have developed and encouraged a fan following that will ensure the perpetuation of the comic book medium itself.

Above left: *Alter Ego*, originally published by Jerry Bails and Roy Thomas, was one of the best and most influential comic book fanzines of the 1960s. The issue pictured here featured an in-depth interview with the erudite artist Gil Kane. Above right: *The Comics Journal* provides a lively forum for discussion of the aesthetics and business of comic books.

©1969 by Alter Ego Enterprises
©1990 by Fantagraphics, Inc.

INDEX